THE BATTLE OF THE FRONTIERS

Battles & Campaigns

A series of illustrated battlefield accounts covering the classical period through to the end of the twentieth century, drawing on the latest research and integrating the experience of combat with intelligence, logistics and strategy.

Series Editor
Hew Strachan, Chichele Professor of the History of War
at the University of Oxford

Published

Ross Anderson, *The Battle of Tanga 1914*
'An excellent book' *Peter Hart, author of Jutland 1916*

Ross Anderson, *The Forgotten Front: The East African Campaign 1914-1918*
'Excellent... fills a yawning gap in the historical record' *Gary Sheffield, Times Literary Supplement*

William Buckingham, *Arnhem 1944*
'Startling... reveals the real reason why the daring attack failed' *The Daily Express*

Brian Farrell, *The Defence and Fall of Singapore 1940-1942*
'An original and provocative new history of the battle that marked the end of the British Empire' *Professor Hew Strachan*

David M. Glantz, *Before Stalingrad*
'Another fine addition to Hew Strachan's excellent Battles and Campaigns series'
BBC History Magazine

Michael K. Jones, *Bosworth 1485*
'Insightful and rich study of the battle... no longer need Richard play the villain'
Times Literary Supplement

Martin Kitchen, *The German Offensives of 1918*
'Comprehensive and authoritative... first class' *Professor Holger H. Herwig, War in History*

M.K. Lawson, *The Battle of Hastings 1066*
A *BBC History Magazine* Book of the Year 2003

Marc Milner, *Battle of the Atlantic*
'The most comprehensive short survey of the U-boat battles' *Sir John Keegan*

A.J. Smithers, *The Tangier Campaign*
'The fullest account of the British Army's first major expedition abroad'
Professor Hew Strachan

Tim Travers, *Gallipoli 1915*
'A book of the highest importance... masterly' *John Lee, The Journal of Military History*

Matthew C. Ward, *The Battle for Quebec 1759: Britain's Conquest of Canada*

Terence Zuber, *The Battle of the Frontiers: Ardennes 1914*
'The first history of the opening engagement of the First World War'
Professor Hew Strachan

THE BATTLE OF THE FRONTIERS
ARDENNES 1914

TERENCE ZUBER

The History Press

To old friends, who defended Western Europe during the Cold War.

VII (US) Corps Headquarters
3rd (US) Infantry Division
12th (GE) Panzer Division
1st (US) Infantry Division (Forward)
72nd (US) Field Artillery Brigade
9th (US) Engineer Battalion

Cover illustrations: (front) there are no photographs of combat during the Battle of the Frontiers – this picture is from a later period in the war (note the steel helmets); (back, upper) infantry advancing by bounds; (back, lower) infantry advancing in successive waves.

First published 2007
This edition published 2009

The History Press
The Mill, Brimscombe Port
Stroud, Gloucestershire, GL5 2QG
www.thehistorypress.co.uk

© Terence Zuber, 2007, 2009

The right of Terence Zuber to be identified as the Author
of this work has been asserted in accordance with the
Copyrights, Designs and Patents Act 1988.

All rights reserved. No part of this book may be reprinted
or reproduced or utilised in any form or by any electronic,
mechanical or other means, now known or hereafter invented,
including photocopying and recording, or in any information
storage or retrieval system, without the permission in writing
from the Publishers.

British Library Cataloguing in Publication Data.
A catalogue record for this book is available from the British Library.

ISBN 978 0 7524 5255 5

Printed in Great Britain

Contents

Introduction	6
1 German Tactics and Training	12
2 Mobilisation, War Plans, Deployment and Approach March	80
3 Rossignol	108
4 Bellefontaine	128
5 Neufchâteau	133
6 Bertrix	144
7 Maissin-Anloy	152
8 Virton	161
9 Éthe and Bleid	183
10 Longwy	213
11 The Battle South of Longwy	229
12 Conclusions	265
Appendix: Laws of War	285
List of Illustrations and Maps	288
Glossary	290
German Order of Battle	291
French Order of Battle	294
Endnotes	297
Acknowledgments	313

Introduction

Between 1871 and 1914 the armies of France and Germany prepared with unprecedented intensity and determination for the next war, which was sure to be a bloody affair of national survival. For forty-three years both armies trained, developed new weapons and doctrine, and then trained some more. Spurred by crises in the Balkans and Morocco, from 1905 on Europe was swept by an unprecedented arms race, which reached its apogee in 1913. France and Germany were armed and prepared for war as no other countries had ever been before.

Both Germany and France raised mass armies by means of conscription. Upon completion of national service the conscripts returned to civilian life, but also became reservists, liable for the next 20 years to be recalled to the colours in case of war. When these reservists were mobilised and reintegrated into the army, they would multiply the size of the active army by a factor of three or four, producing field forces of some two million men.

Finally, the long-anticipated day of reckoning arrived. Both countries mobilised on 2 August 1914 and then transported their massive armies to the frontiers. From 20 to 24 August 1914 the French and German armies, each some seventy divisions strong, met head-on in Belgium and Lorraine in the Battle of the Frontiers, one of the most hard-fought, most important and most interesting battles in military history.

One would anticipate that the tactical course of these battles would have been of immense and widespread interest to both military professionals and the general public. In addition, one would also assume that military professionals would have been eager to determine how well peacetime doctrine and training stood up to the test of combat.

In fact, quite the opposite is true. Practically everything has been studied concerning the First World War except the pre-war tactical doctrine and training of the German and French armies. Instead, interest in pre-war armies has centred on non-military topics. The relationship between the military and society before the war is a favourite theme for scholarship, in particular the supposed role of the

Introduction

German army in supporting the political and social status quo. A major military history of France concerns itself with social history to the practical exclusion of ground combat itself.[1] The military arms race has been studied purely as a matter of politics, with little reference made as to how these weapons were to be doctrinally employed and none whatsoever as to how they actually performed in combat.[2]

Tactical combat in the first battles from 20 to 24 August has also been of little interest. There has never been a detailed account of the Battle of the Frontiers in English; the accounts of some of the division-sized engagements written in French and German in the 1920s and 1930s are seldom used today.

On the other hand, books on the German and French war plans and the strategic aspects of the Battle of the Marne are legion, fuelled by military, academic and popular fascination with armchair generalship. The armchair general thinks that the campaign can easily be understood in terms of large black arrows, representing the German armies, slashing across a map of France a half page in size.

The focus on strategy is reinforced by the common perception that tactical combat for both the French and German armies in August 1914 consisted of charging with solid masses of infantry, only to have them mown down by machine gun fire. French critics blamed French defeats in the Battle of the Frontiers on such tactics. British accounts of the initial battles describe combat against German infantry in the same terms as those used for fighting Dervishes or 'Fuzzi-Wuzzis', with precise and rapid British rifle fire cutting down rows of German troops. In a study of German military thinkers before the First World War, a professor of strategy at the US Army War College concluded that while the high-level military theorists understood the lethality of modern warfare, the troop leaders just didn't get it. He also said that pre-war German training was poor. In the last paragraph, he concludes that young officers, motivated by a reckless 'spirit of the offensive' launched unprepared attacks.[3] This is a completely orthodox conclusion. The War College professor saw no need to describe how the German regulations prescribed that the infantry attack was to be conducted at company and battalion level or how the troops actually trained. Nor did he give any representative examples of how these unprepared, reckless attacks were conducted. He merely restated what was common knowledge.

This study is predicated on two premises that are diametrically opposed to this common knowledge. The first premise is that tactical combat, not strategy or operations, is the foundation of warfare: as Clausewitz says in Chapter 1 of Book 2 in *On War*, 'Essentially war is fighting, for fighting is the only effective principle in the manifold activities generally designated as war.'[4] The second premise is that soldiers fight the way that they have been trained to fight. Understanding combat means first understanding peacetime tactical training. Armchair generalship relies on common knowledge and vague generalities. Real soldiering is based on attention to detail in tactics and training.

The Battle of the Frontiers

While reference will be made to French tactics and training, the emphasis will be on the German army, for the simple reason that the Germans won almost every initial engagement. The Germans and French had essentially the same goals: the Germans met them, while the French did not.

The Battle of the Frontiers in the Ardennes pitted the German 4th and 5th Armies against the French 3rd and 4th Armies. They met in the sort of manoeuvre battle that both armies had anticipated and been training for. It was the perfect test of the doctrine and training of both armies.

German tactical doctrine and training were cutting edge, and set the standard for the world's armies for the next century. German infantry tactics were based on fire superiority and fire and movement, not massed bayonet charges. German individual and small-unit training was centred on rifle marksmanship and platoon fire tactics, culminating in individual weapons qualification as well as graded tactical live-fire exercises at platoon, company and battalion levels. The German army created Major Training Areas (MTA) that provided room for large-scale manoeuvre and live-fire exercises. The MTA were the heart of the German training effort and not, as the orthodox opinion maintains, the annual *Kaisermanöver*.

The German army was passionate about training and tactics. German officers' careers were determined by their ability as troop trainers and tacticians. Admittance to the *Kriegsakademie*, the General Staff College, and from there to the highest levels of the German army, was based on a competitive examination that tested knowledge of weapons and tactical doctrine.

Both the French and German armies were brave and skilful; the French surely had the second best army in Europe. It was the French misfortune to be opposed by a German army at the height of its powers, one of the very best armies in European history.

Sources

Both the French and German official histories are concerned with strategy and operations, and both state expressly that they do not deal with events below corps level. They are therefore of little help in describing battles at the tactical level.

The *Reichsarchiv* at Potsdam was destroyed in a British firebomb raid on the night of 14 April 1945, and with it practically all of the German army's operational documentation. The only surviving German army documents are those at the archives of the individual German states at Stuttgart, Karlsruhe, Dresden and Munich, which contain a number of pre-war German tactical regulations, training regulations, range firing regulations and after-action reports from tactical exercises. Together they show in detail German doctrine and training at the company/battery, battalion and regimental levels. They also hold the war diaries and combat after-action reports for units from Baden-Württemberg and Bavaria, many of which are quite well written.

Introduction

Three books show what tactical doctrine was actually taught in the German army. On 29 May 1906 the Prussian War Ministry issued a new doctrinal manual for infantry tactics and training, the *Exerzier-Reglement für die Infanterie*.[5] This is our baseline document for studying German tactics and training. The *Leitfaden für den Unterricht in der Taktik auf den Königlichen Kriegsschulen* (Handbook for Tactics Instruction at Royal Military Schools)[6] was used to teach all-arms tactics to young officers. German officers who wished to be considered for acceptance in the *Kriegsakademie*, the General Staff College, were required to take a written examination in which they demonstrated their mastery of tactical doctrine. While there was no official text that they could use to prepare for this examination, Friedrich Immanuel's *Handbuch der Taktik*[7] was the most highly regarded study guide. Lieutenant-colonel Hein's *Kampesformen und Kampfesweise der Infanterie* (Structure and Conduct of Infantry Combat), explained German infantry doctrine and training to the educated public.[8] Training was taken so seriously in the German army that many officers wrote books describing in detail effective training philosophies and methods. Our description of German training will also utilise these.

The German regimental histories published after the war are another major source for the history of German units. Most were written by capable men who were simultaneously four-year combat veterans in wartime and professional men – lawyers, bureaucrats, university professors – in peacetime. The quality of these histories is generally high; some are major military studies of irreplaceable value, a few are quite worthless.

An important source is the battlefield itself. The Ardennes has changed little since 1914, and even most of the towns are not much larger. Walking a battlefield is still very important, and first-hand impressions are much stronger than a map reconnaissance; Neufchâteau in particular was much easier to understand having been there.

There are a few studies of tactical combat that were written by Swiss and French soldiers after the war. The Swiss works are generally excellent. E. Bircher spent considerable effort walking the ground and utilising both French and German sources. R. Allemann, commander of a Swiss infantry company in Zurich, had access to German after-action reports which are now lost. The tactical studies by the French officer and official historian, A. Grasset, a company commander in 1914, as well as Jean Charbonneau's story of his experiences as a small-unit leader in the 7th Colonial Infantry Regiment (3rd Colonial Infantry Division) often provide the only information concerning French actions. But they must be used with caution, for their description of German actions is often completely wrong.

Ostensibly, the French senior headquarters, GQG, did not keep a war diary. The French unit war diaries at all levels, from regiment to army, are poor sources: the entries are short and unenlightening. There are none of the after-action reports that make German war diaries so useful. The French regimental histories published after the war are usually about thirty pages long and worthless. An unusual French-language source is René Bastin's *Un Samedi Sanglant* (A Bloodsoaked Saturday). Bastin is an amateur historian who lives in Tintigny and has written an interesting local history of the battles in the area that is useful for the wealth of detail it contains.

Most of the misinformation concerning tactical combat in the Battle of the Frontiers stems from French sources. In order to explain the terrible pounding it had taken, the French army, from individual soldiers to army commanders to the post-war official history, told tales of running into German machine guns, barbed wire and trenches.[9] Military historians have accepted this at face value. Their willingness to do so was probably influenced by the common perception that the World War in general consisted of trench warfare and mindless slaughter.

No one has considered it necessary to see if the French version of the Battle of the Frontiers was verified by German sources. In fact, the well-written German war diaries and regimental histories show that all the fights in the Ardennes were meeting engagements. The Germans were attacking; there were no German trenches and the only barbed wire was that which the Belgian farmers had put up to fence in their livestock. The French were so disoriented by the violence of the German attack that they literally did not know what had hit them.

Creating a coherent picture from these various sources has not been easy. The memory of what happened in combat is perhaps more subjective than any other. The authors of the source material were subject to impressions of nearly overwhelming power. The units were frequently intermingled. Key leaders were killed before they could put their reports on paper. Times given for events often conflict; soldiers rarely took note of what time it was. While the broad outlines of the battle are clear, the accounts often diverge on questions of detail. It was necessary to compare all accounts and produce the tactically most likely version.

Both the German war diaries and the German regimental histories included first-person accounts, which have been used extensively. They give a vivid description of how German tactics worked in combat, and what it was like to move and fight under enemy small arms, machine gun and artillery fire.

Terrain and Weather

The Ardennes forest in this area of operations consists of rolling terrain, with the lower levels being cropland and the upper levels forested. Long-range visibility was generally poor, blocked by the next hill and forests. Short-range observation was limited by standing crops and the small copses that dotted the countryside. The undergrowth in Belgian forests was very thick, reducing visibility to a few metres and obliging units to move in single file. The small rivers in the area were not obstacles to infantry and cavalry movement, but could present a barrier to artillery. The buildings in the towns are well-built and defensible. The roads were dirt but firm enough to withstand military traffic if dry. This was not good terrain for artillery. The hills both blocked long-range fire and created dead zones, areas of low ground that the guns higher up the hills could not see into. On the other hand, the terrain rewarded well-trained and aggressively led infantry companies and battalions. The weather was very hot during the day, but on the morning of 22 August many areas were covered with a heavy fog.

Time

The German sources used Berlin time; 0500 Berlin time was 0400 French time. All times have been corrected to reflect French time. Sunrise was at about 0400, sunset at about 1815.

Distances

All distances are given in metric units, which is the NATO standard.

Personalities

About a million men were engaged in the Battle of the Frontiers in the Ardennes. In the interests of simplicity, with a few exceptions, all persons will be referred to solely by their position, i.e., commander of the 12 ID, and not by name and grade (Major-General Charles de Beaulieu).

Illustrations and Maps

German small-unit tactics are illustrated by sketches, and each chapter is supported by maps, which are located at the centre of the book

1
German Tactics and Training

After the First World War, German officers stated almost unanimously that the German army of 1914 was the best-trained and best-disciplined in the world, and that peacetime tactical doctrine and training proved themselves unequivocally in combat, leading the German army to 'brilliant successes'.[1] Repeatedly, German soldiers of all grades said that their victorious engagements had been conducted 'just like in training'. Such opinions must be taken seriously, since they were made by some of the most combat-experienced soldiers in modern military history with the benefit of four years of high-intensity warfare to educate and refine their professional judgment.

The foundation for German success in the Battle of the Frontiers was laid in the forty-three years of doctrinal development and training prior to the battle. This chapter will concentrate on the final German tactical doctrine that was implemented in 1906 and used as the basis for subsequent training.

The German army was so serious about training that many German officers regarded combat as merely the final live-fire training test. The regimental historian of the 22nd Infantry Regiment (IR 22) wrote that combat was an opportunity for the regiment to 'show what it had learned and done in decades of hard peacetime work', an opinion also expressed by Otto von Moser, one of the most important German authors on tactics and training.[2]

The Art of War[3]

Combat was characterised by Clausewitz as the realm of friction and the clash of two independent forces. The combat leader must comprehend what is happening on the battlefield in an environment where everything is uncertain and draw conclusions based on limited information. War, in German doctrine, is an art; decision-making and leadership in combat are creative acts.[4] War is not a science, in which decisions can be made by following a set formula. Nor can a war be fought, as some Western armies try to do, according to the principles of business management.

After a long debate, the German Army rejected *Normaltaktik* – applying a standard solution to tactical problems. Every German doctrinal manual emphasised that there was no *Schema*, no biscuit-cutter solution to operational and tactical problems. Each operational and tactical situation had to be evaluated on its own merits. No two situations are alike. Doctrine, the study of military history, and training exercises provide a framework for decision-making, but the soldier uses his intellect and will to solve each tactical problem. Doctrine may emphasise the offensive, but that does not mean that there is a knee-jerk requirement to attack under all circumstances. A German combat leader therefore required clear and sharp judgment and perception, but above all strength of character, determination, energy and equilibrium.

The Nature of Combat in 1914[5]

By 1914 firepower, in the form of magazine-fed small-calibre rifle, machine guns, and quick firing artillery pieces, dominated the battlefield. Whatever could be seen could be hit. Smokeless powder made weapons fire almost invisible and counter-fire much more difficult.

Every army in Europe had noted the consequences of the firepower-dominated battlefield, both in defensive and offensive operations. They recognised that it was necessary for all arms to use the terrain to provide protection against observation and fire. Troops were dispersed in order to reduce casualties. Closed formations could no longer be used if exposed in the open to effective enemy fire. Units could be committed to combat only in broad lines, and had to be further broken down to the point that they could utilise the cover provided by the terrain. On the defensive, even thin lines could present significant resistance, especially if they were in tactically effective positions. The difference between armies lay not in the recognition of the problem, but in the quality of the subsequent training.

German doctrine emphasised that if the proper tactical precautions were not observed, if units attempted to cross open ground under effective fire or failed to adequately disperse, the result would be extraordinarily high casualties in a very short time. On the other hand, adequate use of terrain, proper tactical movement and dispersion would rob small arms, machine gun and artillery fire of much of their effectiveness; the casualties in Manchuria in 1904–05 were lower than those of 1870–71.

Every army but the French adopted combat camouflage uniforms. The German army introduced the field grey combat uniform in 1907, after tactical tests had shown that it offered the best concealment, particularly against long-range or air reconnaissance when troops were marching in column.

The Battle of the Frontiers

The combination of camouflage uniforms, smokeless powder, dispersion and the use of terrain meant that it had become extraordinarily difficult to discern an enemy's location, movement and strength. It was also difficult to tell if one's own fire was effective and if the enemy was taking casualties. For these reasons, it was widely recognised that the battlefield had become 'empty'. Not only had the enemy become invisible, the only members of his own unit that the soldier could see were those in his immediate vicinity. Formal discipline became ineffective. The lethality of weapons fire eliminated the direct influence of the senior leaders over their men. The German army emphasised that combat leadership would be provided by company-grade officers and NCOs. Everything depended on the qualities of the small-unit leader and the individual soldier. Training therefore had to emphasise and reinforce the soldiers' ability to think and act – in particular, to fire and move – in small units or on his own initiative.[6]

Concentration of Mass[7]

The first principle of war for practically any army, at the strategic, operational and tactical level, is to have superior forces at the decisive place and time. German doctrine emphasised that it was also important to conduct the main attack, if possible, against the flank and rear of the enemy. This, the *Handbook for Tactics Instruction* said, was 'the highest accomplishment in the art of war'. No other European army emphasised the flank attack and the envelopment to the degree that the German army did; the French army advocated the frontal attack and breakthrough.

Units under effective fire could not manoeuvre against the enemy flank. Envelopments were generally only feasible if units not in contact marched against the enemy flank. For this reason the German army at the operational level marched on a very broad front, and at the tactical level deployed early from march column to combat formation.

The Offensive[8]

In 1914, all European armies emphasised the offensive. It was thought that the future war could be won quickly in big battles, but only by offensive action. The Handbook said that leaders and troops would never choose of their own free will to stand on the defensive. The attacker has the initiative; he can choose the time and place of the attack and mass his forces there, hopefully against weak points in the enemy defences. However, the attacker had to accept that he was going to take heavy casualties. Nevertheless, the will to win and ruthless determination would secure victory, which was all that counted.

Initially the attacker might well suffer higher casualties than the defender, but once the defender was driven from his position his morale and cohesion would

German Tactics and Training

be degraded and he would be subjected to pursuit by fire. If the attacker continued the pursuit vigorously, the defender might be completely destroyed.

The German army, going back at least as far as Frederick the Great, had a bias in favour of offensive operations, and this bias was reflected in German training and doctrine before the First World War. The Handbook said that troops attack when they feel themselves to be superior to their enemy; the German army clearly thought that this feeling of superiority was most likely to arise not from superior numbers, though this was possible, but rather from high morale: from the soldier's confidence in their leaders, their training, tactics and weapons. Attacking was more difficult than defending, but the act of going on the attack itself gave the troops 'massive moral superiority'.

German doctrine acknowledged that modern firepower had reinforced the effectiveness of defence. As the Boer War had demonstrated, even weak forces on thin, extended fronts could maintain themselves for some considerable time against a frontal attack by superior forces. But firepower could also assist the offensive. If the attacker used the terrain effectively, he could bring his firepower closer and closer to the enemy position. In particular, the attacker could concentrate his fire at a chosen place. If he could do so at vulnerable points, such as a salient in the defensive position, or the flanks, then the firepower advantage would be on the side of the attacker.

It might also be necessary to attack to fix an enemy in place, that is, prevent him from moving his troops, usually to keep the enemy from withdrawing or shifting forces. Fixing an enemy in place would be necessary in order to provide the time for an attack on his flank or rear to be effective. One could attempt to fix an enemy in place by conducting a feint attack, but as a rule the enemy would not be fooled for long and a serious attack would become necessary. In actual practice in August 1914 it was found that at all levels – strategic, operational and tactical – it was nearly impossible to fix an enemy in place. The French were always able to break contact and withdraw.

By adopting the defensive, the defender was acknowledging his inferiority. The defender could chose where he wanted to defend, and prepare his position and the battlefield in order to maximise the effectiveness of his fire, but having done so was forced to wait and react to the enemy's actions. The Russo-Japanese War proved to the satisfaction of practically the entire European military community that even if the defence were reinforced by modern trench works and machine guns the passive (Russian) defence failed and the (Japanese) offensive succeeded.

A successful defensive battle would only be decisive if it facilitated a counter-offensive. The idea that the defender can throw back the enemy attack, and then go over to the offensive in turn (the elder Moltke's defensive-offensive concept) was appealing, but, as military history shows, was also unworkable. A better solution was to go on the defensive on one part of the front, perhaps on terrain not suitable for the offensive, where it was possible to employ fewer forces, which would allow stronger forces to take the offensive on another part of the front.

The Battle of the Frontiers

Tactically and operationally all European armies favoured the offensive, for purely military reasons. It does not therefore necessarily follow that these required the strategic offensive or aggressive political goals: strategy and grand strategy are the function of politics, not of tactics and operations.

The Infantry Regiment[9]

The basic tactical unit was the infantry company. The wartime strength of a German infantry company was five officers (OFF) and 260 enlisted men (EM). The company commander was usually a captain who was responsible for individual, NCO, and squad and platoon training, particularly individual marksmanship and small-unit fire tactics. The company was broken down into a small company command group and three platoons of about eighty men (in practice, between sixty-four and seventy-two men[10]), each platoon consisting of eight squads, each squad led by a sergeant or corporal.

The German non-commissioned officer corps was a particular strength of the German army. Each peacetime German infantry battalion had between seventy-two and seventy-eight career NCOs, while a war-strength battalion had eighty-five NCOs (including four medical NCOs). These were men who had re-enlisted expressly to become non-commissioned officers. They were carefully selected and provided with excellent training by the company commander and army schools. Individual training was in their hands. The company first sergeant, the 'mother of the company', held his position for a considerable period and enjoyed immense prestige and responsibility. The French army was less well provided with NCOs, which was a serious weakness. A French peacetime company usually had only eight NCOs, of which only five were career NCOs.[11] The company also included the combat trains, which consisted of the ammunition wagon and the mobile field kitchen, and the field trains, which included a company supply wagon and a rations wagon.

The German infantry battalion consisted of four infantry companies and the battalion headquarters: twenty-six OFF and 1,054 EM. The battalion commander was usually a major, or perhaps a lieutenant colonel. He was assisted by the battalion adjutant, the most capable lieutenant in the battalion, who was the operations officer, and by a rations officer, in combat usually a reserve lieutenant, as well as a surgeon and a paymaster, who was also the NCO in charge of property. Each battalion had eight bicycle messengers, armed with carbines. The company trains were united under battalion control to form the battalion combat trains (four ammunition wagons, four mobile field kitchens, plus the battalion medical wagon) and the battalion field trains (battalion staff wagon, four company supply wagons, four rations wagons, one sundries – tobacco and similar personal use items – wagon, one battalion supply wagon), together nineteen vehicles, thirty-eight horses and forty-seven men. On the march and in combat, the battalion combat trains stayed close to the battalion, while the field trains could be as far as a day's march behind.

German Tactics and Training

The German infantry regiment was composed of three battalions and a machine gun company: 86 OFF, 3,304 EM, 72 vehicles and 233 horses. The regiment was the most important unit in the German army. The regimental commander was responsible for selecting and training the officer corps. The annual recruit, company and battalion inspections and range firing exercises took place in his presence and largely under his control. Unit pride was directed principally towards the regiment and its history. The regimental commander was a lieutenant colonel or colonel. The regimental staff consisted of three lieutenants: the adjutant (operations officer), an assistant operations officer, and the leader of the field trains (which united all the battalion field trains) as well as the regimental surgeon. The regiment also had a large four-horse wagon with engineering tools: 1,200 small shovels, 275 large shovels, 288 pickaxes, 107 picks, 66 axes, 30 saws and 96 wire cutters. The regimental trains included 72 wagons, 165 EM and 210 horses. In theory the field trains would catch up with the regiment when it billeted or bivouacked, but that rarely happened during mobile operations.

German regiments generally had two designations, first their number within the German army, such as *Infanterie-Regiment 154*, and then their territorial name, in this case *4. Schlesisch* (4th Silesian), or the name of the German state it belonged to, such as *Infanterie-Regiment 100 (1. Sächsisches* – 1st Saxon). The exceptions were the Prussian Guard and the Bavarian army, which were not numbered within the German army and used only their own designations. German regiments were also frequently given an additional name of famous generals or members of the high aristocracy. According to the history of the regiment, infantry units could also be called Fusiliers or Grenadiers. Hence the 6th Infantry Regiment was really *Das Grenadier-Regiment Graf Kleist von Nollendorf (1. Westpreußisches) Nr.6*. In full recognition that this is a cardinal sin against the traditions of the old Imperial German army, for the sake of simplicity we will simply call this regiment IR 6.

Battalions were numbered with Roman numerals I, II, III, and referred to as I/IR 164 (1st Battalion, Infantry Regiment 164). Companies were numbered consecutively within the battalions: the 1st, 2nd, 3rd and 4th companies always belonged to the I Battalion, 5th, 6th, 7th and 8th II Battalion, 9th, 10th, 11th and 12th III battalion. 3rd Company, 1st Battalion, Infantry Regiment 164 was abbreviated 3/I/IR 164 or simply 3/164. The same system applied to cavalry, artillery and engineers.

The tactical organisation of the French infantry was a mirror image of the German. French units were designated first by their number, then arm: for example, *9e Regiment de Infanterie*, which we will abbreviate as 9 RI.

Brigade to Corps

An infantry brigade in both the French and German armies consisted of two infantry regiments and a small brigade staff, and was usually commanded by a brigadier general. In the German army an artillery section of three batteries was often attached to the brigade for tactical control. A German infantry division was a combined-arms force, consisting of two infantry brigades, an artillery brigade, a cavalry regiment, in total, twelve infantry battalions, three or four cavalry squadrons, twelve artillery batteries (seventy-two guns) and one or two engineer companies, plus service and support units. Most division commanders were former General Staff officers. The small divisional staff consisted of a General Staff major and the adjutant (personnel officer), surgeon, intendant, JAG and chaplain. A French infantry division was similar, but had only nine four-gun artillery batteries (thirty-six guns), although it was usually supplemented with corps artillery.

A German infantry corps consisted of two infantry divisions. An active corps included a heavy howitzer battalion and an aviation section: a reserve corps had neither. An active corps usually included twenty-four infantry battalions, six cavalry squadrons, twenty-eight artillery batteries (144 field guns, sixteen heavy howitzers), three engineer companies and an aviation section with six aircraft. The corps staff consisted of a chief of staff who was a General Staff colonel, and four sections: I, the General Staff proper, consisting of the Ia, a General Staff major responsible for tactics and the Ib, a General Staff captain responsible for rations, billeting and intelligence; II (Adjutant); IIIa (Supply); IIIb (Surgeon).

A French corps artillery had twelve four-gun batteries of 75mm guns (forty-eight guns) but no heavy artillery. In total, a French corps had 120 field guns. A French corps also included a brigade of reserve infantry composed of two reserve infantry regiments of two battalions each, four reserve infantry battalions in total.

Development of German Training

The high state of German combat training in 1914 did not happen by accident; it was the result of four decades of increasing emphasis on weapons and tactical training, from a low point after the Wars of Unification to the apogee reached in August 1914.

This process is illustrated by the experience of the Field Artillery Regiment 20 (FAR 20), which had its garrisons in Posen and Silesia.[12] The FAR 20 regimental historian said that training improved in the 1880s. Nevertheless, it concentrated on horsemanship and on gun drill. Tactics and combined-arms training were limited to large-scale exercises and the autumn manoeuvres, and knowledge of the employment of artillery was considered a black art by the infantry and cavalry. In the 1890s range firing was emphasised, and in this decade a battery in the regiment won the corps *Kaiserpreis*, the prize for the best score in the annual live-fire exercise, four times.

In 1899 a fundamental reorganisation took place: the artillery was no longer subordinate to the Artillery Department but was made an organic part of the infantry division. This led to real emphasis on combined arms tactics. The establishment of Major Training Areas (MTA) large enough to allow manoeuvre and live fire training, unhindered by safety and manoeuvre damage constraints, led to an exponential increase in the effectiveness of both gunnery and tactical training.

Realistic gunnery and tactical training, and particularly training for a manoeuvre battle, became the first priority. The regiment fired at MTA Posen for the first time in 1901, and then at MTA Neuhammer in 1906. The regiment would live-fire at the MTA once or twice every winter and had two weeks to train at the MTA in the summer. Combined-arms training at the MTA became commonplace. A similar development took place in infantry training. By the outbreak of war, forty years of continual improvement in training had made the German regiments technically and tactically proficient. The effectiveness of this training would be borne out on 22 August 1914.

The improvement in training was paralleled by progress in FAR 20's living conditions and the quality of life in the garrison towns themselves. In the 1880s the regimental barracks were dispersed in the damp and unhealthy forts at Posen and Glogau. A large proportion of personnel were Poles who spoke no German, so that German instruction was included with training. The Polish and Jewish quarters of Posen were desperately poor. Slowly modern, healthy, barracks were built. Nevertheless, a proper officer's club, which was vital to the regimental officer corps of the day, was not built until 1908. Posen itself became more prosperous and received modern infrastructure and finally a royal palace. By 1914 Posen was a modern city with considerable cultural refinement and FAR 20 lived in good barracks with excellent training facilities.

1906 *Exerzier-Reglement für die Infanterie*[13]

In his study of the effectiveness of German tactical training in 1914, Liebmann said that the German 1888 combat regulations had to be considered 'an extraordinary accomplishment'. It marked the decisive change from shock to fire tactics. It also put an end to parade-ground tactics (*Revuetaktik*) and canned tactical solutions (*Normaltaktik*). The new regulation fostered and required individual initiative and thought. The skirmisher line became standard in combat.[14]

The 1906 *Exerzier-Reglement für die Infanterie* was the base doctrinal tactical document in the pre-war years: there was no combined-arms tactics manual. It is divided into three parts. The first part of the *Exerzier-Reglement* concerns individual and company training. Individual training includes the personal bearing and movements, as well as manual of arms and operating the rifle. Company training includes movement in closed order, in skirmisher line and fire commands. The second part of the *Exerzier-Reglement* covers combat doctrine at the company level. There is also a short third section covering parades and an annex for the drum and trumpet signals.

The first four paragraphs of the *Exerzier-Reglement* state the principles of infantry training and operations in the German army. The infantry was the principal arm on the battlefield, but fought as part of a combined-arms team. Infantrymen must be disciplined and determined, but 'in particular, combat requires leaders and soldiers who are trained to think and use their initiative'. Training must be thorough, but simple. Lastly, each leader must be granted the maximum amount of latitude to carry out his mission.

German Marksmanship Training and Fire Tactics[15]

In mid-October of every year each German infantry company would receive about eighty recruits. Initially, they would be grouped together under a recruit training officer. The training day would start at 0530 when the troops were awakened by the NCO serving as the company CQ (Charge of Quarters). The troops would quickly wash, clean and put on their uniforms, make their beds (straw mattresses and wool blankets) clean their quarters and then go to the mess hall to get a breakfast of coffee and *Komißbrot*, hearty dark bread. Bread is a staple of the German diet and the regimental historian of IR 156 said that the troops liked the *Komißbrot*, and that, between the healthy rations and the *Komißbrot*, the recruits thrived and put on weight, in spite of the heavy and continual physical labour. At 0700 began recruit classroom training, focusing on the soldierly virtues: determination, courage in war and obedience to superiors, including the serious admonition that 'Duty was not an empty word'.

The discovery of smokeless powder in the mid-1880s allowed the development of small-calibre rifles which fired rounds with a muzzle velocity of over 600ms/second, giving the round a much flatter trajectory and ranges over 2,000ms. The first rifle to utilise this technology was the French Lebel 1886/93, an 8mm bolt-action weapon which had an 8-round magazine in a tube below the barrel. The standard German rifle in 1914 was the Gewehr 98, which was issued first to the Chinese Expedition troops in 1900 and the regular army in 1901. It was a magazine-fed, bolt-action rifle, the five-round clip being inserted in front of the open bolt from above. This was a very successful weapon, and remained the standard German infantry rifle throughout both World Wars.[16]

The recruit training emphasis was not on classroom work but on effective use of the rifle and on learning how to use the terrain in combat conditions. After the recruit learned how to stand in formation (facing movements, manual of arms) and march, the recruit instruction quickly moved out of the barracks square and into the local training area and the surrounding countryside, which was especially useful for the men who were from the urban industrial areas. The author of the IR 6 regimental history wrote:

Commensurate with modern requirements, with the passing of time the training was increasingly conducted in the terrain; daily the recruit detachments could be seen in the very suitable terrain near [the barracks] ... running, bounding forward, crawling, aiming at targets and firing blank ammunition ... Training wasn't easy in our hard Posen winters, but given careful supervision by the medical personnel and the hearty

German Tactics and Training

meals our recruits, from the Lausitz and Silesia or from Rhineland-Westphalia, developed brilliantly. As soon as the first Christmas vacation every mother could see in this short time what a strapping fellow her son had become. For our splendid recruits from the coal fields the entire recruit period was easy; they were used to hard daily labour, but they benefited especially from lots of exercise in the fresh air.[17]

The soldier was taught to recognise what targets – human figures – looked like at distances of up to 2,000m and then to estimate the range to those targets. The soldier had to master range estimation if he was to be able to fire his weapon accurately. A rifle bullet travels in a parabola. In order to hit a target at an estimated range of 700m, the rifleman would set his sight at 700m (see Figure 1). This sight setting would cause him to raise the barrel, ensuring that if the weapon were fired accurately the bullet's parabola would pass through the target at that range. He would also adjust the sight picture so that the sight was oriented on the middle of the target. However, if the sight was set at 700m and the target was 400m away, the bullet would pass over its head. If he had estimated the range to be 400m when it was 700M, the bullet would hit the ground well in front of the target.

In three months the recruit period was ended with the 'Recruit Inspection' (*Rekrutenbesichtigung*), which was held by the regimental commander himself in the terrain, usually the garrison's local training area. Frequently companies would be inspected by more senior officers; the regimental historian of IR 156 told of *Rekrutenbesichtigungen* held by the corps commander. This had to be an advantage for all concerned; the senior officers came into immediate contact with the troops and vice versa, in spite of the stress such an event put on the company commander's nerves. Chosen individuals (in some regiments every recruit) were tested on their conduct as a rifleman. The recruit had to show that he could move forward, low-crawling if necessary, and assume a firing position while using the terrain for cover and concealment; that he could identify targets that appeared unexpectedly, estimate the range, set his sights, accurately aim his rifle, and squeeze off his shot; that he could bound forward as part of a squad conducting fire and movement; that he could give an accurate tactical report.

After recruit training was concluded the company would train as a unit. At 0600 the company would fall in under the first sergeant for morning formation. When the company commander approached, mounted on his horse, the first sergeant commanded 'Eyes Right!' The senior officer would report. The company commander would call out 'Good morning, Company!' and the troops would reply 'Good morning, Herr Hauptmann!' Then the company, musicians in the lead, would march through the streets to the local training area (LTA). Training in the LTA would last all morning. The company would march back to the barracks for lunch, which in Germany is always hot and the main meal of the day. It was a particular pleasure to march in behind the regimental band, which always drew the local girls' attention. Sometimes afternoon training included gymnastics using various pieces of equipment, or practice road marches. But once again, the most important training was rifle marksmanship. The rifleman was drilled endlessly on the technique of aiming and firing his weapon: sight picture, placement of the cheek on the butt stock (stock weld), breathing and trigger pull, reloading. Weapons were not locked in the arms room but kept in the hallway outside the squad bay: the soldiers even practiced with their weapons during the evening. Individual dry-firing and live-fire was conducted at the garrison firing range. Each soldier was required to complete a prescribed firing table to at least minimum standards, and repeated it until he did so.[18]

Although individual marksmanship was essential, the goal of German fire tactics was to direct the fire of the entire platoon against a specific enemy target. The platoon was the fire unit in German tactics and the platoon leader, through fire commands, designated the target and the range. The fire of eighty men would not fall at exactly the same range, but some would go over and some fall short (see Figure 2). If the target were at 700m this dispersal would create a beaten zone, called a 'sheaf' (*Garbe*) from 640m range to 760m. The platoon would also spread its fire along the width of the target. The objective of German fire tactics was to place this beaten zone on the enemy unit. The impact of at least some of these rounds would throw up dirt, allowing the platoon leader to judge if his fire was landing properly and adjusting it if it was not. Squad leaders were trained to direct their squad's fire in the same manner. This system was especially important at medium range (800m–1,200m); while individual aimed fire at medium range was difficult, the platoon's beaten zone could be effective.

The rate of fire had to be adjusted to meet the tactical situation. The firefight might well last for hours, so the rifleman could not be allowed to expend his basic load of ammunition in the first twenty minutes. The platoon leader would designate the rate of fire, but the rifleman was also trained to fire only when he thought he could get a hit, and on his own initiative to fire slowly or quickly as the tactical situation required. On the other hand, the troops were also taught that if the enemy was hard to see, fire could be directed at his suspected location (suppressive fire). The platoon leader had two range estimators, who acted as his assistants, watching the effectiveness of the platoon's fire, but also observing the company commander, neighbouring units and the enemy, in order to keep the platoon leader informed; their functions had to be practiced. Platoon combat techniques were mastered as battle drills. Individual soldiers were taught to call out their observations and to pass orders down the firing line. As supports entered the firing line, nearby soldiers told them the target and range. Squad and platoon fire tactics were mastered as dry-fire training at home station and practiced in live-fire exercises, which were conducted at the MTA.

Combat Gunnery[19]

With the introduction of the Model 1871 rifle, which was capable of accurate fire at ranges far exceeding those of the 1848 Dryse needle gun, the German army, with the Combat Gunnery School at Spandau in the forefront, became serious about combat marksmanship. The Spandau school developed squad, platoon and company graded range-firing exercises, which became mandatory in the entire army. In 1877 these were designated combat gunnery courses. Initially, they were held on temporary ranges established in manoeuvre rights areas (civilian land rented or sequestered for training). Beginning in the 1890s the establishment of the MTA (usually about 8x8kms in size) led to the creation of permanent ranges and an exponential increase in the effectiveness of gunnery training. The Spandau school also conducted demonstration all-arms live-fire exercises. All German company commanders attended one of the Gunnery Schools before assuming command, in a program similar to the US Army's Master Gunner Course.

The German army taught that the ability of the individual rifleman to use his weapon, as well as the effectiveness of squad and platoon fire, was crucial to obtaining victory. To train and test this ability, the German army required that infantry, engineer and cavalry units fire annual combat gunnery qualification courses while at the MTA. The modern American army still uses a practically identical procedure. The regulations stressed that combat gunnery ranges were to be conducted in as realistic a manner as possible. The targets were not bulls-eye paper targets, but realistic tactical targets. They could be groups of man-sized silhouettes mounted on sleds pulled by long ropes that would move forward and backwards and would also disappear and then appear for 10–15 seconds, as though the enemy were attacking by bounds. They could also be stationary head-and-shoulders or man-sized pop-up targets (introduced in 1898), which fell over when hit, and were set up depicting firing troops or troops in defensive positions. There were stationary targets that could be turned 90 degrees in order to appear and disappear. Stationary targets could also be set up in rows to depict advancing or withdrawing troops. Targets were also set up in mock villages. The targets were placed irregularly and in large quantity, up to three times as strong as the firing unit, in order to test the unit's fire control. Targets for squads and platoons were not usually at ranges greater than 1,200m. Since ammunition was in short supply, the troops would also conduct extensive dry-fire practices, or practices with blank ammunition, on these ranges.

The squad, platoon and company live-fires were conducted tactically. There were numerous realistic scenarios (attack, defence, etc: the regulation listed forty-three possible scenarios, and that was not exhaustive). The troops were given a situation and mission, the leader issued an order, deploying the troops in the defence or beginning a forward movement; in the latter case, the movement would commence some distance from the firing range. When the targets appeared the troops would assume a firing position, estimate range, pass orders (perhaps disturbed by drummers replicating

The Battle of the Frontiers

combat noise) and open fire. Combat actions might include attaining fire superiority, advancing by bounds and control of fire. A leader could be 'killed' and his subordinate would have to assume control of the unit. The situation would dictate the rate of fire: slow fire (one and a half to three rounds per weapon per minute) against distant targets, in poor light and at targets that were difficult to see; high rate of fire (three to seven rounds per minute) against advancing infantry, artillery, machine guns, march columns, or to attain fire superiority and to cover troops making a bound; highest rate of fire (seven to twelve rounds) just before the assault, to defeat an enemy assault, or in sudden close-range contact. Units had to be able to conduct long periods of accurate rapid fire. The umpire would tell the unit what effects the enemy fire was having on their own unit: none, a few casualties, or demoralising losses. The troops might have to dig in during a long firefight. Pursuit by fire was depicted in several of these scenarios. Experience showed that with 100 rifles firing at 100 head-and-shoulders targets set 1.6ms apart at 1,000m range, twenty rounds per weapon (2,000 rounds overall) had to be fired to hit 25 per cent of the targets. 30–40 per cent of the targets hit denoted the attainment of fire superiority. The company would conduct two combat gunnery firings annually, once under battalion control and the second time as graded qualification firing during the regimental exercises. Live-fires always had the character of an inspection and all members of the unit were observed and rated. The evaluation was based first on whether the range estimation was correct and whether the unit's beaten zone was on target. The percentage of rounds that hit and the number of targets hit were both recorded: the overall evaluation, however, was dependent on the tactical conduct of the troops.

Many units conducted battalion and even regimental live-fire exercises. In 1887 the 1st Foot Guard Regiment held a battalion live-fire exercise against moving targets involving defence, attack, and pursuit. In 1907 the Kaiser established a fund for this regiment to allow it to conduct an annual battalion-sized combat live-fire exercise, including 1,000 rounds per machine gun

The German army was serious about marksmanship and fire tactics. Every soldier had a personal *Schiessbuch* (marksmanship book). The company's marksmanship results were kept in a company *Schiessbuch*. The best individual marksmen were awarded the *Schützenabzeichen*, a coloured cord attached to their epaulette on their Class A uniform. Officers annually qualified competitively with the rifle. Companies – and their commanders – were rated principally on the basis of their gunnery qualification results. The best company in every corps was awarded the prestigious *Kaiserpreis*, (in Bavaria the *Königspreis*) which included a decoration for the company commander, a bust of the Kaiser for the officer's club and a cloth arm insignia for the members of the company.

Machine Guns[20]

Each active-army German regiment included a machine gun (MG) company with six weapons, three ammunition wagons, four OFF and ninety-three EM. The MG Company also had a supply wagon, a pack wagon including engineer tools, and wagon for fodder, plus a mobile field kitchen. The MG were transported on wagons and dismounted to fire. The MG sections assigned to cavalry divisions could fire the weapons from gun carriages, like artillery. A French infantry regiment also had six guns, which they carried on mules or horses.

The standard German machine gun in 1914 was the *Maxim Maschinengewehr 08*, which on its four-legged *Schlitten* (sled) mount, weighed 57kg (126lbs) and had a five-man crew. The MG 08 was difficult to man-carry: two-man stretcher-carry was possible for short distances, but usually a four-man carry was used. In the four-man carry, each man would also carry a box of ammunition. The crew did not have to carry their packs, which were left on the MG vehicles. The gun commander, equipped with binoculars, directed the fire. The mount provided a very stable firing platform, allowing the gunner to precisely adjust fire using an elevation hand wheel and making slight lateral adjustments by tapping the traversing handles. The ballistic characteristics of the MG round – muzzle velocity, trajectory and range – were practically identical to those of the rifle round. The gun was water-cooled, which provided a high rate of fire, but also required a supply of water. Steam rising from the gun could also give its position away. The French used the air-cooled Hotchkiss, which was almost two kg heavier than the MG 08, but was otherwise comparable. The German MG 08 fed ammunition from a 250-round belt; the Hotchkiss fired a 25-round strip, which had to be changed frequently.

European armies are often criticised for failing to recognise the destructive power of machine gun fire. As a consequence, practically all historians maintain that the infantry attempted to attack machine guns in mass formations and were mown down in rows. In fact, German tactical doctrine fully recognised the power of machine guns. The *Exerzier-Reglement* was supplemented in 1909 to provide doctrine for the employment of machine guns: the German army therefore had more than three complete annual training cycles to practice with machine guns. The Handbook said that machine guns had attained an 'extraordinary importance'. They were capable of generating the greatest firepower in the smallest area and in the shortest possible time, quickly producing a decisive effect at the desired place. Immanuel said that 'the machine gun is the weapon of the future, of immense importance'.

The principal concern when MGs were introduced was the same as that after the fielding of rapid-firing rifles in 1848 and magazine-fed rifles in the 1880s – the troops would quickly shoot off all the MG ammunition. But aside from this restriction, the power of MGs was clear. German infantry doctrine recognised that skirmishers advancing without cover in machinegun fire would take heavy casualties at medium range. Given good observation, skirmishers lying prone could be engaged by MGs out to 1,000m range. An assault on machine guns would result in 'enormous casualties'. In an army whose tactics centred on directing rifle fire to the desired place and winning fire superiority, the ability to concentrate a high volume of MG fire (cyclic rate of 500 rounds per minute) in a small area was revolutionary. Six MGs concentrating their fire on one target would 'produce a quick, decisive result'.

Machine guns would best be engaged with artillery or other machine guns. Since MGs could use cover effectively, they would present a difficult target, hard to find and just as hard to hit. Machine guns posed an even more difficult target for infantry fire, requiring a large number of rifles and high expenditure of ammunition, whereas machine guns were able to inflict casualties on the infantry even at long range. Any infantry advance against machine guns required careful use of the terrain and unexpected, quick bounds forward, using the interruptions inherent in MG fire (changing the Hotchkiss 25-round strip, barrel changes). If movement by bounds were no longer possible, the skirmishers should low-crawl until they were within close range, at which point even a squad could take the MG under effective fire.

The German infantry doctrine particularly emphasised that MGs were just as useful in the attack, being able to suppress defensive fire and contribute significantly to winning fire superiority. Because of concern for ammunition re-supply, doctrine called for MGs to be kept in reserve for use at the decisive place and time, and not be committed to long, drawn-out fire fights. Unless MGs could find a good over-watching position, they were to be brought forward into the firing line. Although the water-cooled German MGs, their mounts and ammunition were heavy, doctrine required that the crews man-carry the MGs forward by bounds to keep up with the attack.

In the defence, MGs might be kept in reserve, but the emphasis of the regulation was to employ them from the outset in an over-watching position or on the front line: preparing fields of fire and digging the guns in was important. Choosing flanking positions that allowed fire across the defensive front was considered particularly effective. An important advantage of the machine gun over rifle fire was that the impact of so many rounds in a restricted space made the fire usually easy to observe and adjust. MG fire could be moved quickly and accurately to the exact place that it was wanted, even at long ranges.

The MG 08 was also not an infallible wonder weapon. The history of the 1st Foot Guard Regiment reported that it was too heavy to keep up with the advancing infantry, jammed frequently, and, in spite of the water cooling, required frequent barrel changes (every MG had six spare barrels!).[22]

For all of the machine gun's usefulness, only infantry could take and hold ground. An infantry regiment still consisted principally of infantrymen – 3,000 rifle-armed infantrymen as opposed to six machine guns. Machine guns were most effective on exactly the kind of flat, open terrain that the infantry would try to avoid. In rolling terrain, in built-up areas or in woods, where infantry was most effective, the influence of machine guns would be much reduced. On the manoeuvre battlefields of

1914 the MG 08 and the Hotchkiss could be deadly, but could never become the decisive factor; that function was reserved for the infantry.

Bivouac[23]

Troops that had marched and fought all day needed to rest as comfortably as possible if they were to be able to march and fight the next day. If possible, troops would be billeted in buildings. A large farm could accommodate an infantry company, a large village an entire infantry regiment. The officers might find a bed, but the troops usually slept packed together in a barn on straw. Shelter from inclement weather kept the troops healthy and rested and was an important advantage of billeting, 'A bad billet is always better than a bivouac.' On the other hand, there might be a considerable march to the billet at night and from the billet to the assembly area the next morning. For this reason, or because the unit was in close proximity to the enemy, troops might bivouac in the open, if possible near farms or towns: inhabited areas could supply the troops with water. Each German soldier was equipped with a poncho, which he would attach to other soldier's ponchos to form a tent. Bivouac was practiced in the annual corps manoeuvres.[24]

There were two methods to awaken and assemble a unit that was in billets or bivouac. The first was a normal 'alarm' with bugles and drums, the second, used when close to the enemy, was a 'quiet alarm' using low voice commands.

Rations[25]

Making sure that the troops were well fed was a central concern at all levels of the German army. Troops that were not well fed would simply be unable to conduct the strenuous marches and work required of them in combat. Each command level in the German army had an officer in charge of rations. At corps and division levels this was a career civilian administrator, at regimental and battalion levels the ration officer. The type of rations the troops ate, and whether they had received a hot meal, was a daily entry in the company, battalion and regimental war diaries. The German army was liberally equipped with ration supply vehicles at the corps and army levels, including trucks. Nevertheless, in mobile operations the ration vehicles could not keep up and the German army lived off the land, preferably in the form of ration officers organising the purchase or requisition of bulk foodstuffs from local sources with the cooperation, willing or otherwise, of local government. Payment was in the form of cash or promissory certificates. Frequently the troops requisitioned food on their own, issuing their own promissory notes. They were also not shy about searching abandoned buildings for food. Looting of valuables was a punishable offence.

The German army had only one 'secret weapon' in the First World War: each company had a horse-drawn mobile field kitchen, which consisted of a 200-litre cooking kettle and a coffee maker, providing each soldier with three-quarters of a litre of hot food and a quarter litre of hot coffee. The cooking kettle was an airtight double boiler filled with glycerine. Each meal required 16kg wood or 13kg charcoal as fuel. The mess section also carried bread and breakfast in sacks on the ration wagon. In the morning, the mobile field kitchen dispensed hot coffee to the troops (25kg of coffee for a company). The field kitchen was then filled with water and the mess sergeant prepared a stew from the best of what was available. He was thus able to make use of locally procured meats and vegetables. In particular, German units would requisition and slaughter animals for meat, although freshly slaughtered meat is tough and was best cut into small pieces. One meal for a battalion (1,000 men) required two oxen, six pigs or nineteen calves, 750kg bread (if available), 125kg rice or 1,500kg potatoes (or a like quantity of whatever vegetables were at hand). The mess sergeant loaded this into the kettle, and then lit a fire under it and the mobile field kitchen marched with the company, belching smoke as the meal cooked merrily. When the company stopped for chow, the troops had no more to do than line up and be issued with hot food. In case of emergency, the meal could be cut short and the food issued later. In combat, mess sergeants brought the mobile field kitchen far forward after dark to feed the troops. Units that did not have mobile field kitchens, such as field artillery, were envious of the infantry. The combat effectiveness of the German army, and in particular its ability to march prodigious distances, was due in no small part to the mobile field kitchen. The weakness in this system was the inability to bake bread, and as the German army quickly outran their field bakeries, the troops felt the lack of bread keenly.

Each soldier also carried two iron rations cans that could be consumed only on order. A third iron ration was carried in the company ration wagon. The iron ration consisted of canned meat or vegetables, bouillon cubes and *Zwieback*, salt and sugar, weighing about a pound. The troops liked everything but the *Zwieback*.

In the French army, each squad carried its own cooking equipment and food and was responsible for preparing its own meals and coffee. This was a time-consuming process, and in the morning the French soldier often marched out without having had any coffee; in the afternoon, frequently his meal was cooking on the fire when orders would come down to move out immediately and the food would have to be poured on the ground. At the end of the day, and especially after dark, the troops were often too tired to bother with cooking the meal.

It may come as some surprise that the supply system of the French army was little different that the German, and that the French army preferred to live off the land, even when operating on its own territory or in Belgium.

The Infantryman's Combat Load[26]

The mobility of an army was based on the individual infantryman's ability to road-march as well as to move across country. The soldier's mobility depended on his

German Tactics and Training

physical fitness and the load he carried. Everything possible was done to lighten the German soldier's load, including constructing his canteen and canteen cup from aluminium. The German soldier's pack (in infantryman's slang the '*Affe*', the ape[27]) weighed 11kg in which he carried a change of underwear, a pair of lace-up boots, a field cap, two iron rations, a washing, cleaning, and sewing kit, tent pegs and rope and thirty rounds of ammunition. His coat, wrapped in his poncho, and his mess kit were attached on the outside. His weapon weighed 4kg. On his combat harness he carried ninety rounds in ammo pouches, his bayonet, bread canister, canteen and entrenching tool. The spiked helmet, or *Pickelhaube*, was made of leather, not metal. The soldier also carried two combat wound dressings sewn into both front corners of his battle dress blouse. The total combat load, including clothing, weighed about 24–30kg.[28] To make sure that he carried only that which was absolutely necessary, his combat load was minutely regulated by strict inspections.

The German soldier practiced road marching during his entire period of service and then again when he was called up for reserve duty, and the road-marching ability of the German infantry was extraordinary. The average rate of march for an infantry unit was 10–12 minutes per km (5–6kph). The normal road-march rate for large formations (divisions and corps) was 4kph. Increasing the rate of march for long distances rarely had any benefit: forced marching consisted of increasing the length of time marched and reducing the rest periods. A normal day's march was 22–25km, but the German soldier was capable, if necessary, of moving 40km a day or even more, which is essentially the same distance as a marathon. This demonstrates an exceptional degree of physical training, discipline and morale.

On 22 August in the Ardennes the German VIII and V Reserve Corps made forced marches of over 40km to reach the battlefield, in the August heat, choking on dust, which contributed significantly to the German victory. That about 75,000 men, who three weeks previously had been civilians, could accomplish such a feat is astounding. A solid foundation for this accomplishment had been laid in training, such as that conducted by IR 6, a V Corps unit that surely provided many of the soldiers of the V RK: 'After we had been given the magnificent Wartelager Major Training Area in 1901, roadmarch training increased dramatically. In addition to the yearly marches to and from the training area for regimental and brigade manoeuvres, in practically every major exercise the regiment played the opposing force. That meant daily marches of 50–60km, which benefited training.'[29]

In combat, unit commanders could direct that the soldier to drop his pack. This would reduce his load by the most cumbersome one-third. The commanders thereby ran the risk that his soldiers would be separated from their packs for a longer period or lose them permanently, and with them the coats that kept the soldier warm, the ponchos that kept him dry and formed the bivouac tents, his iron rations and thirty rounds of ammunition. For those reasons, the German soldier almost always carried his pack into combat.

The Battle of the Frontiers

Before engaging in combat, the company ammunition cart would be unloaded and its contents distributed to the troops (about seventy rounds per man), who would carry the extra ammunition in bandoliers and stuff loose clips into pockets or bread canisters. Movement by bounds was therefore conducted by troops who were carrying sixty to seventy pounds of weapons, ammunition and equipment.

No civilian historian who passes judgment on the German soldier can be considered credible until he can attest to the fact that he has, while carrying a combat load, road-marched 25km, conducted 1,000m of advancing by short rushes, and then spent the night in an open bivouac.

March Column and Deployment into Combat Formation[30]

One of the greatest problems concerned with mass armies was moving them. Operational manoeuvre could not be conducted cross-country except for short distances. Each unit had to have a road dedicated for its route of march. The standard German march column had a four-man front. An infantry regiment with its combat trains occupied 1,520m of road, its field trains another 390m. An infantry division marching with an advance guard occupied about 15km of road.

In order to fight the unit had to deploy to the left and right of the road. The length of front a division occupied varied with the terrain, but a rule of thumb said that a division attacked on a 3km front and that to deploy the combat elements of a division would take about three hours. An army corps occupied about 28km of road, the corps would deploy on a 5–6km front and deploying a corps would take five and a half to six hours. Behind the troops and the combat trains marched the field trains, the ammunition columns and ration wagons. The field trains of the division occupied 3km of road, the field trains of the entire corps 7km, the light ammunition columns another 14km of road: together the supply wagons occupied 21km of road, nearly as much road space as the combat units.

Most of the space on the road was taken up by horse-drawn wagons. In an infantry corps, the combat units included 1,608 horse-drawn vehicles, the combat and field trains another 1,288. Each of the 158 artillery pieces with its caisson(s) was horse-drawn. Fodder for the horses, especially oats, had the same importance to an army in 1914 as petroleum products have to an army today. Each horse consumed six kilograms of oats, two and a half of hay and one and a half of straw daily, more for heavy draft horses. In 1914 the German army was fortunate that it could requisition its fodder from local sources and did not have to bring it forward from the depots.

Therefore, it was desirable to dedicate a road exclusively for the march of a single division. A corps was the largest unit that could march on one road. Moving two corps on the same road involved severe tactical and logistic difficulties. The combined combat formations and trains for two corps covered 120km of road. The second corps could deploy only on the day after the first. Elaborate measures had to be taken to ensure that the troops could be fed and re-supplied with ammunition.

German Tactics and Training

Command and Control for Movement and Supply

War consists mostly of marching.[31] But the usual description of the activities of the German General Staff focuses on strategy or politics. In fact, strategic war games occupied little of the time of only a very few General Staff officers. The real operational purpose of the General Staff, and the reason for its creation, was not to produce strategic brilliance, but to move and supply an army corps, which was an immense and complex undertaking. This is the work that most General Staff officers performed, at the division and corps level. They thereby freed the commanders of such concerns, so that they could perform their own command function, which was to direct tactical combat and operations. The famous secret *vade mecum* of the General Staff officer, the *Taschenbuch des Generalstabsoffiziers* (The General Staff Officers Handbook), for which he was personally responsible, said nothing about tactics and operations, and aside from weapons characteristics was concerned solely with the organisational tables of the various units, the length of their march columns and their ration and ammunition requirements. Today, such books are used by the S-4/G-4 (supply officers) and the transportation officer.

In the Ardennes on 21 and 22 August the German General Staff officers usually moved their corps efficiently and without error. The combat power of all the German corps was quickly and effectively deployed and engaged. The French General Staff officers did not perform as well. This is not to say that the French movement was chaotic, but there was excessive friction. Poor organisation of the march of French corps on 21 August meant that many units did not arrive at their bivouacs until long after dark and were unable to put out proper security. On 22 August the French troop-leading procedures were often badly conducted, many times the troops had to march without breakfast and the march columns were not well-organised. Therefore, when contact was made, the French were slower to deploy. Combined with superior German reconnaissance/counter-reconnaissance, the end result was that the Germans were moving their forces at the proper place and time, perhaps fifteen minutes to an hour ahead of the French. This would hardly seem to be a significant advantage, or a reasonable reward for so many years of training and preparation. In fact, this advantage gave the Germans the initiative and laid the foundation for German tactical success in the Ardennes.

Tactical Movement Formations[32]

The most common formations for cross-country movement were the squad column, the platoon column and the company column. In the squad column, the squad moved in two ranks, the squad leader and four men in the first rank and four men in the second rank. In the platoon column, the platoon was formed in a line of squad columns. It therefore had two ranks and had a forty-man front. If the company were moving in platoon column, the platoons would move one behind the other. In the company column, the company moved with platoons abreast. The platoons were formed in squad column, one squad behind the other. Each platoon therefore had a five-man front. This formation was the easiest to use during an approach march. The company could also move on line. The platoons were then formed abreast, in two ranks. Finally the company could move in squad column, one squad behind the next. The road-marching column was a modified squad column, having a four-man front. As a practical matter, on trails in the woods tactical units could march in single file. There were no battalion or regimental movement formations: the battalions deployed individual companies, as the situation required

These were movement, not combat formations. In enemy fire the only combat formation was the skirmisher line or swarm.

The Infantry Company in the Attack[33]

Our baseline for discussing German tactics will be the infantry company in the attack. The purpose of German offensive tactics was to place effective fire on the enemy in order to gain fire superiority, and then close with the enemy by means of fire and movement and destroy him in close combat. This litany can now be repeated by probably any infantry officer in the world.

The German army introduced the concept of fire superiority in the groundbreaking 1888 *Exerzier-Reglement*, and it remained the distinguishing characteristic and cornerstone of German tactics thereafter. Fire included machine gun and artillery fire, but principally it meant rifle fire. Success would be dependant on the training, fire discipline and marksmanship of the individual rifleman. The final assault with the bayonet sealed the enemy's defeat.

Closed formations, such as march columns, were used for approach marches only and could not be employed under effective infantry fire. High and deep targets, such as standing or marching troops in closed formation, could be engaged successfully at long range, which was from 1,200m out to the maximum effective range of the weapon. At medium range (1,200m to 800m), such targets would be destroyed. Low, dense targets could also be engaged successfully at medium range.

When the company anticipated making contact it would deploy from company march column into platoon columns and then, if necessary, into squad columns. Smaller columns were easier to control and able to utilise the terrain and therefore allowed quick movement. Frequently, the company would deploy with two platoons in front with one platoon floowing about 300 metres in support (far enough not to be hit by the small arms fire or artillery shrapnel fire directed at the lead elements), but any other formation that met the requirements imposed by the terrain and situation were permissible. The company would continue to close with the enemy while in platoon or squad column for as long as possible, until it received effective enemy fire. The company would then deploy into skirmishers.

German Tactics and Training

The German army used only one infantry combat 'formation', and that was the skirmisher line or swarm. The 'normal' distance between skirmishers was two paces (1.6m, which sometimes grew to 2m), and was called a 'dense' skirmisher line, but this distance would be greater in more open terrain. One gunnery qualification problem called for a skirmisher line with four pace (3.2m) intervals. Dense skirmish lines were easier to control and provided greater firepower, but were also better targets for defensive fire. Looser skirmisher swarms might theoretically suffer fewer casualties to enemy fire, but the looser they were the more difficult they became to control, while reducing the unit's firepower; too much dispersion compromised the unit's ability to accomplish its mission. It was also very difficult to significantly change the direction of advance of a skirmisher line, which is one reason why the approach march was continued in squad, platoon or company column for as long as possible.

Skirmisher lines moving in the open could be engaged at medium and even long ranges. It was important for skirmishers to move irregularly, by bounds, using all available cover and concealment.[34] The bounds would probably be by platoon, or by squad. If enemy fire was weak or inaccurate, the bounds could be as long as 80m: if it was strong and effective, much less. At the early stage, bounds might be made at a walk. Each platoon might also advance in several waves of skirmishers with 5–6m intervals between skirmishers. The company would advance as close to the enemy as possible and then take a position and return fire. A rule of thumb was that the range for opening fire should be 700m, but in terrain that offered good cover and concealment it might be closer, in open terrain farther away. Behind the firing line the supports (successive waves of skirmishers from the same platoon) and reserve platoons would also advance by bounds, utilizing all available cover and concealment. The reserve platoons could advance in skirmisher lines or as squad or platoon columns (see illustrations).

Effective use of terrain played an essential role in German offensive tactics. If possible, attacking units were to avoid open ground and use the terrain that provided the most cover and concealment. However, it was unlikely that the defender would be so accommodating; rather, he would strive to defend on open terrain that provided him with the best fields of fire. In this case, the attacker would advance in waves of loose, open skirmisher lines with expanded intervals between skirmishers. When the first skirmisher line had bounded forward to a position suitable for beginning the firefight, it would stop and take cover. It would not, however, immediately open fire. Rather, it would wait until the successive skirmisher lines had come forward to form the dense skirmisher line, which alone could generate enough firepower to prosecute the firefight successfully.

The firefight was conducted at the platoon and squad levels.[35] The German infantry would be supported by artillery and machine gun fire. The objective was to place effective fire on the enemy position, cause him casualties, but more important, make him take cover to avoid being hit and thereby spoil his ability

The Battle of the Frontiers

to see his target and aim his weapon. When this occurred, the enemy fire would become weaker and less accurate: the enemy would fire too high. The Germans had gained fire superiority.

The German infantry – individuals, squads, even platoons – would seize this opportunity to bound forward as far as possible, covered by the fire of their comrades. They would then take up a firing position and resume fire. The rearward groups would bound level with or beyond the first group. This is called fire and movement. Determining whether your side had gained fire superiority would not be easy, and making the decision to bound forward would require courage.

At medium and close range (less than 800m), the only manner in which long, dense, skirmisher lines could advance – and survive – was by fire and movement. Fire superiority might be lost: bounding forward reduced German fire and might give the enemy the respite he needed to allow him to expose himself to fire effectively, and it might be necessary to regain fire superiority. Key terrain would be seized that would give especially favourable points to provide fire support, and dug in to serve as offensive strongpoints.[36] As the tactics textbook, the Handbook, said, 'The modern infantry fight has the character of a long, hard struggle for fire superiority. The attacker's skirmisher line, carefully using the terrain and cover, can only advance slowly.'[37] Ammunition re-supply would be difficult, if not impossible, and accurate fire and fire discipline were critical. There would be significant casualties; the strength of the firing line would be maintained by individuals, squads or even entire platoons moving forward into the firing line from the supports or from the reserve platoons. If the attack stalled, the German soldiers were taught to dig in with their entrenching tools and continue the fight in place.

German doctrine was very cautious about individual units pushing forward ahead of their neighbours, for fear that this unit would be defeated in isolation. There was also a tendency at all levels to commit reserves in sectors where the attack had had stalled or failed. The ideal was a uniform advance by all units.

Because formed bodies of troops could not survive in the face of modern fire, and all troops on the battlefield sought cover and concealment, the battlefield became 'empty'. Since the advent of smokeless power and the small-calibre rifle, the firing enemy no longer gave off a cloud of white smoke, but was almost invisible. At the beginning of an engagement, it might not even be possible to tell where the enemy position was. The lethality of modern weapons made the transmission of orders from the rear to the firing line and reports from the firing line to the rear slow and difficult. The noise of weapons firing and artillery exploding was deafening. The company commander was the highest-ranking officer who was able to exercise real tactical control of his troops. Battalion and brigade commanders could commit troops to combat, but lost control of them once they were engaged. Combat leadership was actually the function of the platoon and squad leaders.

German Tactics and Training

It is evident that if the unit was to succeed in these terrifying circumstances, the soldier had to be superbly trained and disciplined, and had to possess courage, high morale, determination, and individual initiative. All were needed if the soldier was to accurately aim, fire and reload his weapon, and then on command – or on his own initiative – jump up in enemy fire, run forward 20ms (carrying pack, equipment, rifle and ammunition), then take up another firing position, fire, and then advance again. Drill occupies an essential role in making this possible.

Barracks-ground training – formal drill – was and is the foundation of military discipline. It involves standing and marching in formation, proper wear of the uniform and military courtesy, such as forms of address and saluting. Formal discipline was always important in the German army, but as of the 1888 *Exerzier-Reglement* less and less time was spent on formal drill in favour of combat training.

The German army used the term 'battle drill' (*Gefechtsdrill*) in its current sense – training and practicing routine combat tasks until they become automatic.[38] Drill allowed the soldier to ignore the terrors of enemy fire, the isolation, the wounds and death of his comrades, sergeants and officers, the thirst, the heat, lack of sleep and fatigue, and carry out his combat tasks. He had been drilled to load, aim and fire his weapon accurately, shift and adjust his fire and clear stoppages in his weapon quickly. He had been drilled to bound forward skilfully.

But drill and discipline alone are not adequate. Ultimately, the infantryman advanced because of personal motivation and morale. The best soldiers are, through drill, courage and dedication, able to apply their judgment and reason to master the tactical task at hand, and to exercise their initiative. These men are the natural battlefield leaders.

Moreover – and this factor has been ignored by the critics of 'Prussian drill' – three-quarters of the mobilised German army would consist of reservists, and in case of necessity even *Landwehr* troops would be committed to combat. These men had not had any military training in years, perhaps not in a decade or more. Yet their training had to have been so effective that they could quickly become soldiers again. German reservists proved decisively that they were able to do so. Only superb training – and drill – could have produced such reservists.

As the German firing line approached the enemy position the enemy would begin to crack and individual enemy soldiers would be seen leaving their positions and heading for the rear. When the firing line had advanced close enough to the enemy position (in peacetime training, 100m), the final step was to take the enemy position by assault. The decision to conduct the assault could be taken by the leaders on the front line or by the battalion or (less likely) brigade commander to the rear. The leader deciding to assault would give the order to 'Fix Bayonets!' that would be taken up by trumpeters and all leaders. At this time, all successive waves moved quickly forward, as did reserve platoons and companies. Riflemen, machine guns and artillery began rapid fire. The company or battalion commander would then give the command 'Charge!' (*Rasch Vorwärts!*). This signal was repeated by all drummers and buglers. The battalion standards were unfurled and the troops assaulted the enemy position shouting 'Hurrah!'

When the enemy position had been taken, the troops advanced far enough to take a firing position and pursue the retreating enemy by fire. Since French doctrine emphasised the immediate counterattack to retake a lost position, the assaulting unit would organise the conquered position for the defence. The actual pursuit would only begin after the unit had reconstituted itself, that is, brought the squads, platoons and companies back together, re-established the chain of command by replacing leaders that had been killed or wounded and re-supplying ammunition.

This offensive combat drill has become the standard for all armies. This is the same combat drill – including the assault – that I was taught as a recruit in basic training in 1968 and that I used as an infantry platoon leader in 1973 and as a mechanised infantry company commander in 1980.

Artillery was to do its best to suppress the enemy artillery, but its primary mission was to support the infantry by bombarding the enemy position. There was generally no 'artillery preparation' prior to the infantry attack. This was felt to be ineffective. The defender would hide or hunker down in his fighting position and the bombardment would waste ammunition and advertise the area of attack, while accomplishing nothing more than tearing up the shrubbery. Rather, the infantry advance would force the defenders to open fire, thus revealing their positions and establishing the targets for the artillery bombardment.

Victory would not come cheap and casualties, particularly in officers, would be heavy. The German army continually emphasised that victory had to be obtained '*koste, was es wolle*' (cost what it may).

Tactical Communication[39]

The most important technical means of communication was the field telephone. A German army headquarters included a field telephone section that was responsible for communications with the army rear area HQ and with the national telephone system. The section included three wire platoons, which were capable of laying 6–7km of telephone line on overhead supports a day. Wire could be laid more quickly directly on the ground, but was likely to be broken. The corps telephone section was responsible for communications with army headquarters. It would only establish telephone communication to division headquarters when the divisions were in contact with the enemy. The corps did not establish direct telephone communication with each other. The corps had five wire platoons, with 27km of wire, each platoon consisting of four squads. The squads would lay or take up wire simultaneously. Brigades and regiments also had telephone sections, but in combat communications were likely to be by courier or personal contact. Artillery batteries used telephones to connect the battery commander to the guns.

'Heavy' radio telegraphy equipment was used between army headquarters and the *Oberste Heeresleitung* (OHL), and between cavalry divisions/corps and army headquarters. These 'heavy' sets had a range of 150km. 'Light' sets were used to communicate between the cavalry reconnaissance squadrons and the cavalry division and cavalry corps headquarters. 'Light' sets had a range of 40km when communicating with each other and 80km with the 'heavy' sets. Radio telegraphy was to be used only when other means of communication had failed or would be too time-consuming. Radio telegraphy was known to be susceptible to atmospheric interference and users of radio telegraphy were warned to anticipate significant delays.

Couriers in automobiles could cover 25–50kph, bicycle couriers 15–20kph. By 1914 mounted couriers were suitable principally for short distances and rough terrain.

Command and Control in Combat[40]

The friction involved in war itself and the power of modern weapons created an environment in which command and control in combat was difficult at best. Especially within the zone of effective enemy infantry fire, and to some degree also of artillery fire, sending reports from the front to the rear and transmitting orders from rear to front was dangerous, time-consuming and very unreliable. Orders from superior commanders would be transmitted slowly and could easily be overtaken by events.

The German solution to this problem was *Auftragstaktik*, or mission-type orders. The commander not only gave his subordinates a mission but also explained his intent – his concept of the operation. At each level, subordinate leaders were given a mission, but the manner in which that mission was executed was left up to that leader, with the caveat that the leader was responsible for acting within the parameters of the intent of his commander. It was also possible that situations unforeseen by the superior commander would arise. The subordinate leader was then authorised to act on his own initiative and report to his superior as soon as possible.

The system of *Auftragstaktik* was emblematic of the German philosophy of leadership, training and war-fighting. To be effective, it required that leaders at all levels be thoroughly familiar with German tactical and operational doctrine. Producing the necessary level of tactical skills necessitated intensive tactical training, not just at schools but at the unit level. Commanders at all echelons had to be personally responsible for the tactical competency of their subordinates. Such a system gave wide scope in combat for company commanders, platoon leaders and NCOs, while requiring that regimental and battalion commanders pay close attention to their training.

The Battle of the Frontiers

Cadre Training[41]

Winter was used for the tactical training of NCOs and officers. NCO training was principally a company matter, in which patrolling and tactical reporting played a large role. In the winter of their second year of duty, conscripts were given specialised training, such as first aid, use of field telephone and bicycle, or training to become an NCO candidate.

For the officers, in the winter battalion and regimental commanders conducted tactical exercises without troops (TEWT) and assigned graded written tactical problems (*Winterarbeit*). In the 1880s war games (*Kriegsspiele*) became obligatory. The 1st Foot Guard Regiment held a war game almost every week, as well as a TEWT once a year.[42] The goal of these exercises was simple: training officers in the rapid analysis of the military situation and in writing short, clear, effective orders. This involved an analysis of the friendly and enemy situation, understanding the commander's concept of the operation and his specific orders to each unit, and analysing the terrain and weather and using the available time wisely. The factors the officer had to consider varied with each mission: defence, attack, movement to contact, etc. The officer had to arrive at his own decision and a concept of the operation for his unit and issue his order.

In the preceding century, no army mastered these troop-leading procedures as well as the German army. On the battlefield on 22 August 1914 the advantages this gave the German army were small and sometimes intangible, but vital. The German officers almost always had a quick and sure grasp of the situation; the French officers were usually caught playing wait-and-see.

The General Staff Examination

In the years immediately preceding the First World War, about 700 young officers annually took the examination for admission to the General Staff College (*Kriegsakademie*). This examination principally tested the officer's knowledge of tactical operations and is further evidence of the German army's commitment to tactical excellence. Commercially available study guides, such as that written by Major Krafft[43] and Immanuel, provide a detailed description of the test and the high level of tactical expertise demanded of the officers. In addition, Krafft's bibliography is indispensable for the study of the pre-First World War German Army.

There were eleven principal test categories: tactical doctrine (formal tactics); a tactics problem (applied tactics); weapons; fortifications; terrain analysis; drawing a tactical terrain sketch; military history; geography; language (translating a text from French, English or Russian) and mathematics (algebra and geometry). The candidate was warned that proper preparation would take an entire year. Two or three hours were allowed to answer each question: the test would have taken several days. The questions from these tests are indicative of the priorities set by the German Army. One question on doctrine asked, 'Describe the characteristics

of freedom of action for subordinate leaders in the three combat arms in combat.'
In weapons, one question asked, 'What role will the machine gun play in combat in the open field and fortress warfare?' – fortress warfare being very similar to trench warfare. In fortress warfare itself, one question asked about the use of obstacles in permanent and field fortifications. In part, the recommended answer described the sophisticated use of barbed wire in field fortifications. The questions in military history frequently dealt with the lessons to be derived from the Russo-Japanese war.

Every year about two or three young officers per regiment committed themselves to an intensive study of modern warfare. Over the course of several years a high proportion of the regimental officer corps would have made such a study. No officer corps in modern history has been so well prepared for combat as was the German Army in 1914.

Cavalry[44]

A cavalry squadron comprised 6 OFF and 163 EM. A cavalry regiment was normally made up of a command group (8 OFF, 30 EM) and four squadrons: 36 OFF, 688 EM. Every cavalryman was armed with a lance, which was considered the primary weapon, being thought particularly effective in mounted combat against enemy cavalry. He was also armed with a carbine, a shortened version of the standard infantry rifle. The regimental combat trains included two wagons with bridging material, a telegraph wagon, two packhorses with medical equipment and a cavalry medical wagon. The field trains included three wagons.

German cavalry was divided into strategic cavalry (*Heereskavallerie*), which comprised the greater part of the German cavalry, and tactical cavalry, which was organic to wartime infantry divisions. The divisional cavalry, one regiment (three squadrons) per infantry division, conducted tactical reconnaissance, usually in conjunction with the division advance guard. Cavalry regiments assigned to reserve divisions were called half-regiments, but in fact had three squadrons, about 26 OFF and 510 EM. Divisional cavalry also provided messengers and carried orders.

The strategic cavalry was organised in wartime into eleven cavalry divisions. A cavalry division had three brigades, each cavalry brigade being made up of two cavalry regiments. Compared to previous German cavalry formations, such as those used in the Franco-Prussian War, which were composed overwhelmingly of cavalry armed with sabres and lances, not rifles, and were therefore tied to the infantry corps for protection, the Handbook said that modern strategic cavalry had become an all-arms, flexible force, with greatly increased firepower and the capability for independent operations. In particular, each cavalry division included an organic machine gun company. The cavalry division possessed a significant communications capability, with a communications section of six horse-drawn wagons for communications equipment (telegraph, telephone, signal lamps and heliograph) and a communication equipment truck. Four passenger vehicles were available to carry messages. Wireless telegraphy equipment would be also be assigned as needed. *Heereskavallerie* was further organised into four cavalry corps, each with two or three cavalry divisions, several battalions of light infantry, wireless telegraphy, a bridge train and engineers.

The Handbook stated that the horse defined the parameters of cavalry operations. The horse allowed cavalry to move quickly; the mass and the tendency of the herd to charge forward gave it force in close combat. On the other hand, horses were hard to control when being fired upon, especially by artillery, or when their rider was attempting to fire. Cavalry was expensive, and training the horse and rider required time. Cavalry operations were therefore characterised by speed of movement, and cavalry preferred to fight by attacking with the lance while mounted. Cavalry would, however, often be placed in the position where it needed to use its carbine on foot. Frequently, cavalry would use both mounted and dismounted combat in conjunction with each other. Cavalry was not suited to attrition battles. The Handbook did not mention an important drawback concerning cavalry's maintenance-intensive qualities. The horses had to be unsaddled, watered, fed, curry-combed and rested frequently if they were to remain healthy. This not only required time, but during this period the cavalry unit was immobile and practically defenceless. Standard operating procedures therefore usually prescribed that the cavalry withdraw behind the infantry to bivouac. This often involved exhausting and time-consuming marches each night and the next morning.

The usual description of German cavalry before the war emphasises Kaiser Wilhelm's penchant for conducting divisional or corps-sized cavalry charges at the annual *Kaisermanöver*. From this, it is inferred that German cavalry trained principally for its supposed role as *Schlachtenkavallerie* – to attack infantry on the battlefield with mass cavalry charges. This is completely erroneous.

All German doctrinal manuals agreed with the Handbook of Tactics Instruction, which says that 'The most important role for cavalry lies in reconnaissance.'

At the beginning of the war, when the two armies were moving to contact against each other, the cavalry corps, usually moving in division columns, had the mission of gathering operational-level information concerning the movements of the enemy infantry corps. The most effective means for cavalry to conduct reconnaissance was to first drive away the enemy cavalry. Cavalry combat would usually take the form of meeting engagements. German cavalry would attack enemy cavalry wherever they found it. The enemy cavalry could be fought either with the lance while mounted, or dismounted with the cavalry carbine, according to the situation. The cavalry carbine would principally be used not against enemy infantry but against enemy reconnaissance elements: mounted cavalry, dismounted cavalry, or light infantry and bicycle infantry.

Reconnaissance was conducted principally by patrols, usually of about 20 men led by an officer. If possible, cavalry patrols would attack enemy cavalry patrols. Of course, there was the caveat that such attacks could not compromise the reconnaissance mission, nor be tactically reckless, but the offensive tenor of the regulation was unmistakable. A reconnaissance squadron would back up the officer patrols. Each reconnaissance squadron was responsible for a 15–20km sector. If the patrols ran into resistance that prevented them from carrying out their mission, the reconnaissance squadron's task was to clear away the enemy force, if necessary in dismounted combat. A reconnaissance squadron was to be able to advance 30–35km daily. It would pass the reports of the officer patrols to higher headquarters by means of field telephone, signal lamps or messenger. A specialty of the strategic cavalry was the long-range patrol to conduct operational reconnaissance or destroy sensitive targets deep in the enemy rear with explosives.

The *Heereskavallerie* was also to push back the enemy's advanced combined-arms units or bypass them and penetrate as far as his corps and divisional columns, and into his rear areas. As the two infantries closed in on each other, the cavalry corps lost their room to manoeuvre and were moved sideways to the army's flanks. From there, they would attempt to attack the enemy's flanks and rear, which was the best employment for cavalry in combat. There it was also well positioned to begin the parallel pursuit of the defeated enemy. The most important combat role for the cavalry was in conducting the pursuit or covering the withdrawal.

When the opposing infantry corps closed on each other, the divisional cavalry's tactical reconnaissance role became vital. The cavalry patrols would be supported by the advance guard infantry. It was necessary to determine the enemy's strength and direction of march in order to decide where and when to deploy the corps and divisions. When contact was made, the divisional cavalry continued to conduct reconnaissance, now in the form of combat patrols, principally against the enemy flanks and rear. This might well require dismounted combat or even foot patrols.

All cavalry also performed a counter-reconnaissance function, attacking enemy cavalry patrols to prevent the enemy cavalry from obtaining information concerning the locations and movements of the German infantry.

The historian of the 20th *Uhlan* Regiment (27 ID, XIII Corps) says that the regiment's peacetime training in all sorts of patrolling and security missions (including cavalry night patrols) was outstanding, and that the regiment was liberally supplied with officer and NCO patrol leaders who wanted nothing better than to demonstrate their skills in combat.[45]

In German cavalry doctrine, therefore, mounted action would take place primarily against other cavalry, not infantry. Large-scale mounted attacks, said the Handbook, were a thing of the past, if only because it was no longer possible to find extensive stretches of open terrain to conduct them on. In the last century, buildings had sprung up everywhere, as had the barbed wire that was used to enclose livestock. Against cavalry masses, the infantry could use individual terrain features (such as small copses) as strongpoints. Immanuel said that it was clear

The Battle of the Frontiers

that attacks over open ground against combat-capable infantry 'could result in the complete destruction of the attacking cavalry'. Mounted attacks could still be conducted against targets of opportunity: in this case, a concealed approach and surprise were a precondition for success. Against infantry, machine guns and artillery the chances for the success of a mounted attack were greatest if the cavalry was able to attack a flank. Given the range and effectiveness of modern weapons, this would be difficult to achieve. It was still possible to charge weak infantry units: units whose morale had already been broken in combat or second-rate reserve and third-rate territorial units. If a charge had to be made frontally against infantry, very wide intervals had to be used at high speed (beginning gallop at a greater than usual distance) that 'provides a means to avoid casualties'. Infantry would usually be attacked in several waves, from two or more sides if possible. Against artillery, it was best to attack when the guns were limbering up, or unlimbering, or against the front of artillery that was in a covered, defilade position. The *Kaisermanöver* cavalry charges were pure theatre, and the German army knew it.

For dismounted combat, a cavalry squadron with 160 men had two tactical options. Half the riders could dismount, forming two rifle platoons. Each remaining mounted man led one riderless horse, which allowed the horses to be moved at the trot or gallop. The horse holders would then move or remain out of the line of fire, probably at least 300ms to the rear. This option optimised mobility (the ability to quickly bring the horses forward) at the expense of firepower. Or, three-quarters of the riders could dismount, forming four rifle platoons. The horseholders, again 300m or so to the rear, were then responsible for three horses in addition to their own, and they generally dismounted, too. The horses could then move only at a walk. This option optimised firepower at the expense of mobility.

Dismounted cavalry used the same tactics as did the infantry, with the caveat that the cavalry did not have the depth or staying power that the infantry possessed, was unsuited to long drawn-out combat and was much more sensitive to casualties. Cavalry would most likely attack dismounted to remove obstacles to its reconnaissance or to seize key points, such as bridges or rail stations. The cavalry was to avoid frontal attacks and demonstrate with one element against the enemy front, while other elements use cavalry speed and mobility to manoeuvre and attack the enemy flanks and rear. Cavalry then resumed mounted operations as quickly as possible. Cavalry would conduct a dismounted defence to delay the enemy, to hold key terrain or towns until the infantry could arrive, to block enemy reconnaissance forces, or to defend their bivouacs.

Whatever some cavalrymen might have said concerning the possibility that cavalry still could successfully charge infantry, the infantry itself was unimpressed. The infantry was sure that it had no reason to fear cavalry, so long as it could use its weapons, even if the cavalry was much stronger in numbers. Weaker infantry could successfully conduct a firefight with dismounted cavalry; the cavalry horses presented a special weakness.[46]

German Tactics and Training

The French strategic cavalry was composed of ten cavalry divisions. This strategic cavalry would be reinforced by infantry battalions and artillery. Each French corps had a light cavalry regiment assigned (six squadrons). There was no divisional cavalry. French reconnaissance patrols were to avoid combat. In reconnaissance and security the French relied on combined-arms teams to confuse the enemy concerning the location of the main body and force him to deploy. The French thereby separated reconnaissance, which was conducted far forward by the strategic cavalry, from security, which was the responsibility of the corps cavalry and at the infantry division, by local foot patrols.

In August 1914 the French cavalry failed to perform both the reconnaissance and security roles. The French cavalry divisions manoeuvred almost aimlessly. The French corps cavalry remained so close to the infantry that tactical security was non-existent. As a result, the French higher commanders were poorly informed concerning German operational movements and the French infantry was repeatedly surprised.

Reconnaissance and Counter-reconnaissance[47]

A distinctive characteristic of German tactics was the use of patrols at all tactical levels and by all arms. Immanuel said that great care must be committed to training this difficult operation. At the army, corps and divisional levels, the principal mission of the cavalry was reconnaissance/counter-reconnaissance. Infantry regiments, battalions and companies made extensive use of tactical patrols both prior to making contact and during combat itself. Artillery batteries sent officer patrols far forward to acquire targets. Infantry patrols were seen as a method of discovering the location of enemy artillery so as to direct counter-battery fire. Engineer companies patrolled to prepare for their mobility/counter-mobility missions: in particular prior to river crossings, and clearing or constructing obstacles. Infantry, artillery and engineer company commanders were all mounted and routinely rode forward of their units in reconnaissance. If the enemy had constructed a prepared defence, all four arms patrolled extensively to determine as much as possible about the enemy position. Patrolling did not stop once contact was made: combat patrols were continually used to clarify both the enemy and friendly situation.

On 22 August 1914 superior German patrolling continually gave the German commanders an operational and tactical intelligence advantage over the French and was one of the reasons that the German leaders stayed one step ahead of the French decision-making cycle.

Aircraft[48]

By 1914, strategic and operational reconnaissance was largely the function of reconnaissance aircraft. Each German active army corps and army headquarters had an aviation section, usually of six aircraft; reserve corps had none. Aircraft were capable of detecting strategic rail movements and troop movements from the railhead until they were about a day's march from making contact. Some consideration was already being given to conducting movements at night to avoid air observation, and to camouflaging bivouacs. Aircraft were less useful for tactical reconnaissance because they had to land, generally at the corps or army airfield, to report by telephone and the time required to do this and then send the report forward usually meant that the information was overtaken by events. Tactical air recon was therefore limited to movements in the enemy rear area, such as reserves coming forward. Aircraft could also be used to carry orders and reports quickly between higher staffs. Thought was also being given to using aircraft as bombers, but their low payload limited them to a harassment role. Both the French and the Germans maintained that the other side used aircraft to direct artillery fire, while their side had not. In fact, it appears that little was done by either side before the war to develop techniques for directing artillery fire from aircraft, and that methods to do so were taken ad hoc during the campaign.

Field Artillery[49]

The mission of the field artillery was to support the infantry. The objective was also to bring a superior number of guns into action at the decisive place and time. In German doctrine the priority of fire was directed against the targets that were most dangerous to the infantry. At the beginning of an engagement, priority of fire was normally given to counter-battery fire, to cover the infantry approach march. The intent was to gain fire superiority over the enemy artillery. During the infantry firefight, priority of fire was generally given to fire on the enemy infantry, but counter-battery fire would continue to be conducted. Given the increased use of the terrain for cover and concealment by all arms, targets for the artillery would often be fleeting and there would not be enough time to eliminate the target entirely.

The French Model 97 75mm gun was the first to incorporate a recoil brake. Since the gun was now stable, the gun aimer and loader could remain seated on the gun, which allowed an armoured shield to be added protect the gun crew. The new French gun could fire up to twenty rounds a minute, against eight or nine for the German *Feldkanone* 96, which had just been introduced. Given this increased firepower, the size of the battery could be reduced from six guns to four. The French also introduced the armoured caisson. The 75mm caused a sensation and the French imagined it to be practically a war-winning weapon. French tactics prescribed that the 75mm would provide the firepower necessary to support the infantry attack with *rafales*, intense bursts of fire, to shake the enemy infantry. This was area fire, which made up in volume what it lacked in accuracy.

German Tactics and Training

German divisional field artillery consisted of two weapons: a 7.7cm flat-trajectory gun (*Feldkanone* 96 n/A) and a 10.5cm high-trajectory light howitzer (*leichte Feldhaubitze* 98/09). The maximum effective range of the 7.7cm gun is a subject of some controversy; there were frequent complaints that the French 75mm considerably outranged the German gun. In fact, the theoretical maximum range was rarely relevant. In practice, the maximum effective range was variable, depending on the ability of the battery commander to acquire targets, see the fall of shot and adjust his shells onto the target. The author of the FAR 25 regimental history said that 4,400m was long range, and targets at 5,000ms were out of range,[50] even though the maximum range of the shrapnel fuse for 7.7cm gun was 5,300m, and for the contact fuse 8,100m.

The light howitzer was provided with a recoil brake and the tube could be elevated to a high angle, which allowed it to fire easily from covered positions. The parabolic arc taken by the shell made it very effective against targets behind cover and in field fortifications. The howitzer was a German specialty: the French army did not possess any. Instead, the French developed a shell for the 75mm had fins that gave it a curved line of flight supposed to mimic that of the howitzer shell. This expedient was unsuccessful in combat and the French were to regret the lack of a howitzer.

A wartime-strength German battery included six guns or howitzers, 5 OFF, 188 EM and 139 horses, the battery commander's observation wagon, two supply wagons, a ration wagon and a wagon for fodder. Each regiment had six batteries divided into two three-battery sections, which were commanded by majors. A field artillery regiment included 36 guns, 58 OFF, 1,334 EM and 1,304 horses, including two light ammunition columns, each with 24 caissons. There were 4 OFF, 188 EM and 196 horses to each ammunition column. Ammunition columns were formed only at wartime and for a few training exercises. The field artillery did not have mobile field kitchens, which was found to be a severe problem in mobile operations. In each active army corps there were three gun and one howitzer regiments: one division had two gun regiments, the second a gun and a howitzer regiment. Reserve divisions had only one gun regiment.[51]

A German field artillery piece was drawn by six horses and consisted of the gun, its limber and a six-man gun crew, and an ammunition caisson, with its own five-man crew. The gun and caisson were provided with armoured shields that protected the crews against small arms fire and shrapnel. The gun could be operated even if 50 per cent of the crew were casualties. Artillery batteries could immediately replace losses in personnel and horses by drawing on the regimental ammunition columns, which took replacements from the divisional ammunition columns and so on.

The gun commander rode on a horse, 'drivers' rode on the gun team horses, the gunners rode on the limber or the gun itself. The German field artillery battery of six guns would generally deploy in firing position with 20 paces (about 13m)

The Battle of the Frontiers

between guns. The caisson and two of the caisson crew would deploy to the right side of the gun. The gun and caisson limbers with the horses, 'drivers' and the two remaining caisson crew would pull back 300m to the rear so that they would not be engaged by counter-battery fire directed at the guns. In practice, this proved to be too close and the horses and limbers were often hit by fire aimed at the guns. When the battery needed to move, the horses and limbers would be brought forward. The light ammunition columns would deploy 600m behind the gun line and move forward based on flag signals.

The horses were the vulnerable point in an artillery battery. The guns could not unlimber and go into position, or limber up to withdraw, without significant horse casualties if they were in infantry fire at medium range (800m to 1,200m). Under close-range infantry fire (under 800m) the vulnerability of the horses immobilised the battery.

There were two types of battery positions. In the open firing position the guns were not covered or concealed. The gunners could see to their front and directly aim the guns over open sights. The guns were also visible to the enemy. A battery could occupy an open position easily and could fire quickly and effectively, especially against moving targets. It could rely on the gun shields for protection against small arms fire, but in an open position it was visible to enemy artillery and vulnerable to counter-battery fire. Open positions would be used in a mobile battle.

In a covered (or defilade) firing position, the guns went into battery position behind cover or concealment (frequently on the reverse slope of a hill). The guns were aimed by the battery commander, who set up his command wagon in a position where he could observe the enemy; the guns were then laid in for direction from the battery command wagon using an aiming circle (similar to a theodolite) and firing commands (deflection and elevation, type and number of rounds, fuse setting) were usually transmitted by field telephone from command wagon to the guns. Covered battery positions were nearly invulnerable to counter-battery fire, unless the dust thrown up by the muzzle blast betrayed the gun's position. Frequently the enemy would be reduced to attempting to suppress guns in a covered position by using area fire based on a map reconnaissance of likely covered positions, a procedure that demanded large quantities of time and ammunition. The disadvantage of covered positions was that occupying them was time-consuming, because of the extensive reconnaissance needed to find a suitable position in the first place, followed by the time necessary to lay the battery using the aiming circle. Adjusting fire would take more time than in an open position. Covered positions would be used at the beginning of an engagement, in artillery duels, and against stationary targets and dug-in positions.

There was also a half-covered position, in which the guns were defilade, but could be aimed by the gunners standing on the gun. Such positions were preferable to open positions while at the same time allowing a more rapid support of the infantry that completely covered positions.

German Tactics and Training

Guns could also occupy an overwatch position. The battery was then deployed in a covered position, laid on an azimuth in the general direction of the expected target. When the target was observed, the battery was manhandled into firing position.

If the time and suitable positions were available, the artillery would initially occupy covered positions, but in the course of the battle, the artillery would almost always be forced to displace and fire from half-covered or open battery positions. If necessary the artillery, like the infantry, was to advance by bounds. Some batteries might be moved forward to provide close-range direct-fire support. When the infantry began the assault, the artillery would fire on the enemy defensive position for as long as possible, until the danger of friendly fire became too great (usually 300m) and then shift its fire to the rear of the enemy position. When the enemy withdrew, he would be pursued by fire, with the artillery moving forward at a gallop and on their own initiative, if necessary, to keep the enemy in range.

Prior to the introduction of long-range quick-firing artillery around the turn of the century it was common to employ artillery in long continuous lines. In order to use the terrain effectively and avoid counter-battery fire, artillery was now to be employed in groups. Enemy counter-battery fire was rarely able to destroy a gun or caisson; its usual effect was to suppress the guns by forcing the crews to take cover. For that reason, the crews were to dig revetments around the gun positions as soon as possible, even in the attack.

If the guns came under effective fire, the artillery commanders had to decide, on the basis of the overall situation, whether the gunners could cease fire and take cover, which involved the crews' retreating several hundred metres, leaving the guns and caissons in place, or if the artillery had to continue to fire, even if it meant that the crews were destroyed or the guns were overrun. Under overwhelming fire the artillery commanders down to battery level were authorised to order the crews to take cover.

It was the responsibility of the artillery to maintain liaison with the infantry through the use of forward observers (FO). The FO would communicate with his battery through field telephones or signal flags. His most important mission was to keep the guns informed as to the relative locations of the friendly and enemy troops, so that as this distance was steadily reduced, the guns could place fire on the enemy for the longest possible time. The artillery also regularly sent forward officer patrols, frequently in conjunction with cavalry patrols, in order to develop targets for their batteries.

The standard shell for gun artillery was shrapnel with a time fuse. The shrapnel shell exploded above and in front of the target, covering the target area with metal balls. In practice, setting the time fuse was difficult and shrapnel often burst too high. There was also a high-explosive round with contact fuse, which was used by howitzers and also by guns.

Beginning in the 1890s the German artillery underwent a profound transformation.[52] In 1890 the cannons were not provided with recoil brakes and gunnery practice took place from open positions at ranges of less than 3,000m. Firing from covered positions was inaccurate and slow. Then the improvements came fast and furious. FAR 69 recorded receiving the light howitzer in 1899, with aiming circle and field telephones to facilitate firing from covered positions. In the spring of 1906 FAR 69 received the cannon with recoil mechanism and gun shield. In 1907 a new artillery regulation introduced a doctrine commensurate with the new equipment and made combat effectiveness the sole standard for training. Firing with time fuses became normal, the field guns received stereoscopic battery telescopes, field telephones (1908) and aiming circles, and armoured observation wagons. Reservists were recalled to active duty to receive training in the new equipment. The German field artillery in 1914 had good equipment and had plenty of time to train with it.

Heavy Artillery[53]

For over twenty years prior to the First World War, the German army worked to perfect its heavy artillery, which involved constructing a mobile 15cm *schwere Feldhaubitze* 02 (sFH 02 – heavy field howitzer 1902) for the corps artillery and a 21cm mortar for the army-level artillery, and then creating the techniques and doctrine to use them. Originally, the impulse for this development was the need to be able to quickly break the French fortress line, and in particular the *Sperrforts* located between the major French fortresses. This mission shifted to one which emphasised destroying French field fortifications and finally to counter-battery fire. Particular emphasis was also laid on integrating the sFH into combined arms training, including live-fire exercises.[54] By the beginning of the war, the German heavy artillery was fully proficient in all three missions. No other country in Europe possessed such combat-effective heavy field artillery. French heavy artillery was not so numerous, nor so mobile, nor as technically and tactically effective as the German.

Every German active-army corps included a battalion of four batteries of *schwere Feldhaubitze*, each battery having four guns, sixteen guns and thirty-two caissons in total. The battalion also had an organic light ammunition column. The reserve corps did not have this battalion, which significantly reduced its combat power.

The 15 cm gun was characterised by the destructiveness of its high-explosive shell (bursting radius 40m to the sides, 20m front and rear), combined with its long range (most effective range 5500m, max effective range 7,450m) and high rate of fire. It was particularly effective against enemy artillery, which was otherwise protected by its gun shield, and against infantry in field fortifications (the shell came down nearly vertically and was capable of penetrating 2m of overhead

German Tactics and Training

cover) or in defilade behind masking terrain. It was less effective against moving targets than the field artillery. The heavy field howitzer was less mobile than the field gun, but nevertheless was able to move long distances at a trot. The sFH battalion normally fought as a unit, firing from covered positions.

The 7.7cm gun fired a 6.85kg shell at a rate of up to 20 per minute. The 10.5cm howitzer fired a 15.8kg shell at a rate of four per minute; the heavy howitzer fired a 39.5kg shell at a rate of three to six per minute.

The German army also possessed a mobile 21cm mortar, which was principally intended for assignment at the army level, to be used against permanent fortifications. A mortar battery had four mortars; each battalion consisted of two batteries. The mortar could move only at a walk, the gun being separated for movement into three sections: gun carriage, barrel and firing platform.

The German field army began the war with 808 15cm sFH, 112 21cm mortars, 196 10cm canons and 32 13cm canons; 1,148 mobile heavy guns in total. It had a store of 1,194,252 shells, that is, about 1040 shells per gun.

The French field army, in contrast, had only 308 heavy guns, which were older and technically inferior to the German guns, mostly 155cm 'Rimailho' canons that had to be broken down in two sections for movement, with a maximum range of 6,300m. The Germans therefore had 4–1 superiority in heavy artillery. The French also had 380 'de Bange' heavy guns in siege artillery units.[55]

Each French division had nine four-gun batteries; the corps artillery consisted of twelve more batteries. Heavy howitzers were an army weapon; a French corps could not expect to receive more than four guns. The Germans thought that the French would augment each corps with another six reserve batteries, which was not the case. A French corps therefore at best had 120 guns versus 158 (including 16 heavy howitzers) for the German corps. The French began the war with about 1,300 shells for each 75mm.[56]

General Heer, one of the leading authorities on French artillery, wrote a perceptive comparison of French and German doctrines. Heer began by saying that both armies expected the war to consist of manoeuvre battles, and both armies emphasised the offensive. However, the French laid particular emphasis on movement, especially the decisive advantages that accrued to forward movement. The Germans, on the other hand, recognised the importance of firepower and understood how to use it better than the French. The German leadership was convinced that infantry could not advance in the face of modern firepower, and especially not against artillery fire. They considered it essential that the battle begin with systematic counter-battery fire. Live-fire exercises taught the Germans the value of heavy artillery in mobile battles in general, but especially in counter-battery fire. Finally, the Germans decentralised the control of artillery down to division level. There were no corps and army artillery commanders.[57] Thomasson said that the German optical fire control was outstanding, and unknown to the French. It permitted the Germans to be able to adjust artillery fire 'magnificently'.[58]

The Battle of the Frontiers
Artillery and Infantry[59]

By 1906, combined arms tactics meant infantry-artillery cooperation. Infantry and artillery were to complement and support each other. Infantry protected the artillery; the principal mission of the artillery was to support the infantry. Artillery was to be deployed at least 600m behind the infantry so that the one would not suffer from fire directed at the other arm.

The writers of German doctrine did not fully recognise that in a mobile battle it was nearly impossible to maintain communications between attacking infantry and supporting artillery, which would become apparent only during the Battle of the Frontiers. This would lead to delays in the artillery supporting the infantry as well as numerous incidents of friendly fire.

Infantry could minimise the effect of enemy artillery fire by careful use of the terrain, continual rapid movement and dispersion. The history of *Infanterie-Regiment* 127 said that this was commonly practiced in peacetime.[60] In particular, platoons could be broken down into successive waves of open skirmisher lines with 300m intervals between lines to reduce vulnerability to artillery fire.

Nevertheless, the *Handbuch* said that infantry could not advance in the face of strong, effective artillery fire. This presented a quandary. The preparatory bombardment by the friendly artillery had little chance of completely suppressing the enemy artillery, which was provided with armoured gun shields and deployed in covered positions. The infantry advance could not wait for the artillery to gain fire superiority, which might never occur. The infantry attack and the counter-battery battle would necessarily proceed in parallel to each other, and the infantry would almost surely have to advance under at least some enemy artillery fire.

Deliberate Attack

If the enemy had decided to stay on the defensive, it might have been necessary to conduct a deliberate attack. The attack was deliberate because the attacker had the time to make careful preparations. This is not to say that the attacker could be dilatory: in war, it is always dangerous to waste time. But the lethality of modern weapons made a careful, systematic approach towards a combat-ready opponent on the defensive absolutely imperative. German doctrine recognised two types of deliberate attack: against a deployed enemy and against a dug-in enemy

Attack on a Deployed Enemy[61]

The infantry attack on a deployed enemy was the baseline tactic for all German attacks. The attack on a dug-in enemy followed the same principles, but was conducted even more slowly, with more preparation and heavier artillery support, and the infantry advance itself was probably conducted by night. A meeting engagement followed the same principles, but was conducted more quickly, with

German Tactics and Training

less reconnaissance and preparation time, and it was more likely to begin at short ranges, leading to a violent close-range firefight and quick assault.

The doctrine for an attack on a deployed enemy as well as against a dug-in enemy were directly derived from the older procedures for an attack on permanent fortifications, that is, from siege warfare, which shows that the German army recognised the strength of firepower and the protection afforded by field fortifications in the modern defensive.

In an attack on a deployed enemy, the attacker had the time to conduct careful reconnaissance with patrols led by infantry, cavalry, artillery and engineer officers, while the main body was still advancing. After adequate reconnaissance had been made, the first decision to be taken was whether the attack should proceed immediately, or if the approach march would be delayed to deploy under the cover of darkness. In either case, the first step was for the forward infantry elements to establish a protective screen behind which the artillery would deploy, usually about 3,000m to 4,000m from the enemy.

The artillery then would begin the artillery preparation fire, primarily counter-battery fire, in an attempt to gain artillery fire superiority. However, it was unlikely that the enemy artillery could be suppressed. An hours-long preparatory bombardment by the artillery against the (suspected) enemy infantry positions before the infantry attacked was felt to be of little value. Only when the infantry attack began would the enemy occupy his defensive positions and open fire, thereby giving the friendly artillery targets to fire at. Initially, priority of artillery support would be given to counter-battery fire; as the enemy infantry began to fire, priority of artillery support would be shifted to the enemy infantry.

The infantry would then deploy, if possible on a covered and concealed position, protected as much as possible from enemy artillery by the terrain and friendly artillery fire. In open terrain this infantry line of departure could be as far as 3,000m to 5,000m from the enemy front line. The attack order specified each unit's mission and attack sector. The concept of an attack sector was an innovation of the 1906 *Exerzier-Reglement*. A war-strength company (250 men) would generally deploy on a 150m front, a battalion on a 300m front (with two companies forward) or 450m front (with three companies forward), a brigade with six infantry battalions on a 1500m front. The attack sectors were kept intentionally narrow to allow a deployment in depth, in order to have supports and reserves available to replace casualties on the firing line. In sectors where success could be expected, the forces were stronger, in sectors where success was unlikely, weaker. The infantry would advance systematically, from phase line to phase line designated on recognisable terrain features. Units would remain in march column for as long as possible, utilizing the cover and concealment provided by the terrain, and preceded by a skirmisher screen and patrols. Units that could exploit favourable terrain were permitted to advance quickly, while those forced to use open terrain would advance more slowly.

The Battle of the Frontiers

When the infantry began to receive effective enemy infantry fire the infantry attack proper would begin with the deployment of the forward platoons into a skirmisher line, which would advance first by using the cover and concealment in the terrain, then by bounds. The objective was to advance until enemy fire became so effective that it became necessary to occupy a firing position in order to suppress it. The manner in which the skirmishers were deployed and moved was dependant on the mission and situation. On terrain that provided cover and concealment, strong, dense skirmisher lines, moving forward in unison as far as possible, were employed. Open terrain called for an initial deployment that was weaker and farther away from the enemy and the advance would be slower and more careful. In open terrain the platoon could deploy in waves of loose skirmisher lines. If a significant distance had to be crossed under effective enemy fire to reach the firing position, or if the situation was not clear or the engagement was to begin slowly, then the open skirmisher lines were to be committed carefully. However, the overall situation might require that strong forces be committed on open terrain.

A company would normally begin its advance by deploying one and a half or two of its three platoons as skirmishers, with the remainder following in platoon or squad column. When the skirmishers had reached a point where they could engage the enemy by fire a dense skirmish line would be formed and the firefight would begin, with the aim of winning fire superiority.

Once fire superiority had been attained the advance by fire and movement would begin. One element would give covering fire while the other element bounded forward to a favourable firing position. The size of the advancing unit depended on the effectiveness of the enemy fire. If that fire was weak, not much covering fire would be needed and large groups – platoons or half platoons – could bound forward. If the fire were strong perhaps the only a squad or even an individual soldier could advance.

German doctrine emphasised that the infantry firefight could easily be hours long and drawn out, and could not be rushed. The difficulty, given the lethality of modern weapons, inherent in attacking a deployed enemy was fully recognised.

Time and again, both the regulation and tactics experts emphasised that every tactical situation was unique and that uncertainty would be the norm. They therefore warned repeatedly against any attempt to apply biscuit cutter solutions to tactical problems. The best corrective against such a tendency was training outside the *Kaserne*, on the ground.

Testing Infantry Doctrine

Since the work in the 1850s and 1860s of the modern Prussian army's first great tactical trainer, Prince Friedrich Karl, German tactical doctrine was developed and tested in the field through troop exercises at the major training areas (MTA).

German Tactics and Training

The 1906 infantry attack doctrine, based on the lesson learned from the wars in South Africa and Manchuria, was also tested by the Combat Gunnery School in Spandau and in major exercises. One such test was a brigade attack over open ground described by Lieutenant Colonel Breitkopf of the Bavarian Combat Gunnery School.[62] The exercise was conducted at the Lechfeld MTA, a level plain made up of gravel covered by tufts of grass (it is now a Luftwaffe airfield). The description of this attack was presented as a lecture and was published as a FOUO (For Official Use Only) document within the Bavarian Army.

The attack over flat, open terrain was the most difficult mission in pre-war infantry tactics.[63] There was some doubt that, in the face of modern firepower, it was even possible at all. Breitkopf warned that this exercise was to present only one example of how such an attack might be conducted. The inevitable changes caused by the situation, enemy, terrain, weather and so forth would lead to other tactical decisions, methods and procedures being employed. He opposed any application of a standard tactical procedure (*Normaltaktik*) as well as pretty but unrealistic 'parade ground' tactics. On the contrary, the most important factor on the modern battlefield was the initiative of the subordinate leaders.

In this exercise the brigade was assumed to be in the centre of a corps attack, that is, there were brigades attacking to its right and left. The Exerzier-Reglement said that a brigade would have taken about thirty minutes to deploy from a march column.[64] At the beginning of the exercise the brigade was in a covered assembly area 2,100m from the enemy front. The exercise began with the attacker sending out reconnaissance patrols, which had to penetrate the defender's security elements.

For the sake of simplicity, and so as to be able to isolate and test the infantry battle, the effect of artillery fire was not considered in this exercise. It was assumed that the defending artillery was in large part suppressed by the attacking artillery, and that the attacking artillery caused as many casualties among the defender's infantry as the defending artillery caused among the attacking infantry. The German army was, however, not doctrinally optimistic about the ability of the attacking artillery to suppress the defending artillery.[65]

Breitkopf also pointed out that in actual combat everything would happen much more slowly: one hour of movement and firing in the exercise might require ten hours in actual combat.

The brigade plan was to deploy its two regiments abreast, ten companies on a 1,500m front. Each of the four front-line battalions committed two or three companies in the first line, leaving a second line made up of the battalion reserves, six companies. In the third line were the four companies of the regimental reserves and in the fourth line four companies of the brigade reserve.

The first task was for the attacking infantry to close within medium rifle range in order to begin the fight for fire superiority, which in this exercise meant crossing the 900m of open ground between 2,100m and 1,200m from the enemy position.

The Battle of the Frontiers

The Handbook said that the concern at this stage, given the highly lethal combination of the defender's small arms, MG and artillery fire, was to avoid casualties; this meant dispersion.[66] Breitkopf said that live-fire tests against moving targets (rows of targets on multiple target sleds) representing a dense skirmisher line had resulted in casualties of 28 per cent. A more open skirmisher line would also take 28 per cent casualties, but because there were far fewer targets in it, it would take much longer and require a far greater expenditure of ammunition to attain the same absolute number of hits. Based on the characteristics of defensive rifle fire at long range[67], the optimal attacking skirmisher line would have intervals of five to six metres between soldiers. The lead companies, on a front of 150m, should therefore advance in successive waves of skirmisher lines of twenty-five men each. The waves followed 300m apart. Such dispersion would slow movement, but the tactical situation did not demand a rapid advance. At about 1,200m from the enemy position, the first wave was to stop and begin to establish a firing position. However, it would not open fire until at least three more waves had arrived, giving one-metre intervals on the firing line, or the strength of one platoon. Reserves would follow dispersed and moving by bounds.

At 0900 the lead ten companies formed up in the attack position behind a low rise with a dense skirmisher line (about one and a half platoons) in front. The troops were given their instructions concerning the conduct of the attack. At 0930 the first wave of skirmishers with five to six metre intervals began the forward movement at a run. The enemy opened (simulated) fire. Umpires designated where this fire was ineffective and caused no casualties; the advance was continued at a walk. Otherwise, it was conducted by bounds. The advance became irregular, as some units made rapid progress and others did not. If troops took casualties while lying down, then they were in the beaten zone of the enemy fire and advanced quickly to move out of it. At every halt the NCO and officer leaders attempted to re-establish order and encourage the troops.

At 1000 the lead elements approached to within 1,200m from the enemy position and began to establish a firing line by digging in with entrenching tools and by utilizing all available cover, and were joined by the following waves. The attackers did not open fire until 1130, when a dense skirmish line had been formed. The supports and reserves remained covered and concealed in the attack position, 900m to the rear. With the beginning of the firefight the first support waves moved out at a walk to within 300m of the firing line and then took cover. When it was necessary to replace casualties to maintain the strength of the firing line, supports moved forward in open skirmisher lines by bounds. The reserves also moved out at 300m to 400m intervals, in a single line and at a walk so long as they did not take effective fire. If they received effective fire and began to take casualties, they were to move forward by bounds.

The enemy fire on the brigade left flank was less effective, and the brigade concentrated its reserves there as the most likely place to penetrate the enemy

German Tactics and Training

position. The right-hand regiment, which was taking more effective enemy fire, was informed that the brigade reserve would not be committed in its sector.

At 1300 the situation was as follows. Of the twenty-four infantry companies in the brigade, nine and a half had been committed to the firing line. The battalion on the left had experienced the least resistance and had committed only four platoons of twelve platoons (one and a third of its four companies), its neighbour on the right had committed seven platoons (two and a third companies), and the two battalions of the right regiment nine platoons (two and two thirds companies) each. Most of the regimental and the brigade reserves were not receiving enemy fire. The brigade commander was told that the overall situation now required that he press the attack. At 1310 he issued the order to the battalion commanders to begin forward movement; at 1320 this order reached the front line company commanders, at 1330 the firing line increased it rate of fire. The front line now began to advance using fire and movement.

Breitkopf noted that the most effective bound was that conducted by an entire platoon at once, but enemy fire might make it possible for only half platoons, squads or individuals to bound forward. The smaller the bounding group was, the more rifles were available to cover it by fire. On the other hand, the smaller the group, the shorter the bound, in order to avoid masking the supporting fire. Breitkopf noted that the Gunnery School had conducted live-fire exercises in 1906 to test the effectiveness of defensive fire against small groups of moving targets bounding forward at irregular intervals. The ability of the defending squad and platoon leaders to direct fire against small attacking targets was degraded. Individual fire was less effective against poor and irregular targets than unit fire and the effectiveness of the defensive fire in general against such targets was reduced by 50 per cent. On the other hand, a 1903 live-fire test, using large quantities of ammunition, showed that if the attacker tried to low-crawl 80m he was exposed to enemy fire for a 105 seconds, more than three times longer than a thirty-second bound, and that low-crawling was very fatiguing. Low-crawling was, however four times more effective for short distances than bounding forward. Breitkopf said that recent combat and numerous tests had shown that attempting to move across open terrain, without fire support, in order to begin the firefight at close range, was hopeless.

The most important task in an attack over open ground was the firefight at medium range (approximately 800m to 1,200m). Using his rule that actual combat took ten times longer than live-fire training, Breitkopf said that crossing the ground from 1,200m to 800m from the defensive position would take three to four hours. It was therefore important to move as quickly as possible in the area from 1,200m to 1,000m from the defender and bring plenty of ammunition.

The attacker's fire could be effective, particularly since the defending line was stationary. A live-fire test in 1903 (using the older Type 88 munitions) in which an attacking group, moving in short bounds, crossed the area from 1200m to 1000m from the defenders in twenty-two minutes, while in the process their fire hit one third to one quarter of the defenders (head-sized targets). In 1905 and 1906, tests using the modern Type S munitions showed that the attacker's fire was 40 to 50 per cent more effective.

Breitkopf then cited Japanese experiences with this form of attack in Manchuria. A brigade of the Japanese 5th Division began to advance 1,800m from the Russian position; at 800m it began to use fire and movement, bounding with platoons, half-platoons, squads and individuals until it got to within 300m to 500m of the Russian position, where it dug in. The advance took three hours and the unit suffered seventeen per cent casualties. Another Japanese battalion at Mukden needed three and a half hours to move by individual and squad bounds to within 400m of the Russian position. Failure to conduct movement by short bounds could be catastrophic: the Japanese 3rd Guard Regiment attempted to attack with six to seven companies in the first line, moving in long (80m) bounds. The regiment was stopped 600m from the Russian front with 43 per cent casualties.

In our exercise the left and right elements of the left-flank battalion took little effective fire and were able to bound by platoons, even though the middle of the battalion hung back. These forward elements took up firing positions and under their covering fire the battalion centre advanced by squad and individual twenty-five metre bounds. The next battalion on the right committed two reserve platoons to the firing line and held the last two platoons ready to do the same.

The important thing, Breitkopf said, was to carry the attack forward. There were no attack formations or pre-determined sequences of movement. It was irrelevant as to who sprang or crawled forward first. Even the smallest unit used moments of fire superiority to go forward. Rearward units then strove to get forward, too. Support and reserve leaders watched the situation on the firing line and pushed their troops forward whenever they found it necessary or advantageous.

The regimental reserve companies advanced to replace the battalion reserve companies that were now committed on the firing line. As the reserve companies of the left-hand regiment were committed, the brigade reserve companies replaced them. By 1630 the entire brigade firing line had fought to within 400m of the enemy front line. Enemy fire was inaccurate and individual enemy soldiers could be seen moving to the rear.

Doctrinally, the assault should begin as soon as the enemy has been weakened enough to permit it. Breitkopf noted that determining when this has occurred is frequently not easy. The effectiveness of infantry fire at short range, Breitkopf said, is fully recognised and requires no further comment. In Manchuria the Japanese had often enough begun the assault only to be met by effective Russian defensive fire, which forced them to halt at close range in front of the Russian position. At Colenso, in South Africa, instead of assaulting General Buller ordered the with-

German Tactics and Training

drawal, at the same moment that the Boers were considering abandoning their position. If the assault was stopped, it was absolutely necessary for the troops to hold the terrain that they have won.

The regulation, Breitkopf noted, did not mandate a particular method for conducting the assault. The important thing was to finish the enemy off with the bayonet. If the leaders on the firing line decided to assault, they made this known to the battalion or brigade commanders through a pre-arranged signal. If the brigade or battalion commanders in the rear made the decision, the signal 'fix bayonets' was sounded. The firing line began rapid fire and all supports and reserves moved forward quickly. The assault would probably not be conducted by the entire line at once, but by each element as soon as the opportunity presented itself. Once an element began its forward rush, it continued its movement until it had broken into the enemy position. Sections of the firing line that occupied favourable positions remained in place to continue to give assaulting elements covering fire.

In Manchuria, Japanese assaults differed according to their estimate of the enemy resistance. They began 350m, 300m or 250m from the Russian position and attempted to break into the position in one rush. If the Russian position had not been sufficiently weakened (was not *Sturmreif*) the Japanese would stop and resume rapid fire. Frequently the battle would then go on for hours. Sometimes the Japanese attack would stall 400m or 500m from the Russian position. The Japanese did not lack courage or energy, but the moral and physical force of the soldiers on the firing line had been exhausted, and because the Japanese often deployed operationally on too broad a front, they lacked the supports and reserves necessary to give new impetus to the attack. In these circumstances, the Japanese had no other choice but to wait for darkness in order to bring up additional forces. The Russians often withdrew from their positions during the night, without waiting for the Japanese to renew their assault.

In the exercise, the decision to conduct the assault was first made on the left flank of the front line at 1645. The signal "s s s" [*Sturm, Sturm, Sturm* – assault, assault, assault] was given to the rear and was picked up all along the firing line. The assault was made at 1700 and was successful: the enemy abandoned his position. The retreating enemy was pursued by fire. The assaulting forces prepared the position for the defence; troops not necessary in the defence were pulled back and reorganised to serve as reserves.

Introduction of the magazine-fed rifle had led to widespread concern that the troops would quickly fire off all of their ammunition. Breitkopf said that combat experience had shown that this was true only for poorly trained troops, such as the Turks in 1877–78; troops in the Chilean War (1891) managed to fire off their basic load of ammunition (180–200 rounds) in thirty-five to forty minutes. On the other hand, well-trained Japanese troops with an assault load of 160 rounds (120 rounds basic load, 40 additional rounds for the assault) never ran out of ammunition. The Japanese also employed well-trained carriers to bring ammunition forward in combat.

In the German army the regimental combat load of ammunition was 340 rounds per man. This was divided into an individual basic load of 150 rounds (120 rounds in ammo pouches, 30 in packs) 70 rounds in the company ammunition wagon (this ammunition was distributed in bandoliers as the assault load before the attack); and 120 rounds in the unit trains.

In Manchuria, Breitkopf said, much to everyone's surprise, 86 per cent of the casualties were caused by rifle fire, 11 per cent by artillery fire and 3 per cent by the bayonet (such casualty figures led pre-war theory to underrate the effectiveness of artillery fire), Breitkopf's conclusion was that Manchuria confirmed the rule that improvements in weapons and increases in the size of armies lead to a lower percentage of casualties overall, but casualties in individual units would reach the highest levels of those in previous wars. This, he maintained, supported the German emphasis on rifle marksmanship and tactics based on rifle fire.

The German army began the First World War with a tactical doctrine that emphasised the dominance of firepower on the battlefield. Artillery support was essential, but the battle could only be won if the German infantry drove off the enemy infantry and took the enemy position. This could only be accomplished if the German infantry, through fire and movement, could close with and destroy the enemy.

These infantry tactics have been adopted by practically every combat-effective infantry force today. The sole difference is that today the volume of infantry firepower has been vastly augmented, with magazine-fed bolt-action rifles being replaced by automatic assault rifles, light and medium machine guns, grenade launchers, light and medium anti-tank missiles and hand grenades. In spite of all this firepower, it is still recognised that if the enemy is determined, it will be necessary to destroy him with 'close combat', if necessary, with the bayonet. That German tactics have triumphed is due to the fact that they succeeded on the battlefield. There were competing tactical systems that failed, such as the British artillery-dominant tactics used on the first day of the Somme, Pershing's US Army human-wave assaults in 1918 and French defensive tactics used in 1940.

Trench Warfare[68]

In 1911 the new regulation *Feld-Pionierdienst aller Waffen* (Combat Engineer Tasks for all Arms) integrated engineer training, principally digging in, river crossing and clearing obstacles, into the training of all combat arms. In 1914 every soldier had an entrenching tool.[69] The German infantry regiment was remarkably well supplied with engineer tools. Complaints that the German army in 1914 did not like to dig in must be seen from the perspective of the four subsequent years of trench warfare. During the Battle of the Frontiers the German infantry and artillery dug in as much as possible in mobile warfare.

German Tactics and Training

Given time, the defender would dig in his defensive position. Given enough time, he would provide it with a complete suite of field fortifications, including defensive and communications trenches, overhead cover, dug-in guns, observation posts and obstacles.

German doctrine emphasised that the disadvantage of the dug-in position was that the defender had to commit troops to hold it, regardless of whether the enemy attacked it or not, and the defender thereby lost both his freedom of movement and the initiative.

The attacker had the ability to choose the time and direction of attack and would use it to attack weak areas in the defence, such as a flank. He could also mass his fires against one section of the defensive line. He might well decline to attack the dug-in position at all, in favour of manoeuvring the enemy out of it. Manchuria had shown the unfavourable situation the Russian army fell into when it defended a dug-in position.

The principles for the attack on field fortifications were the same as those for an attack on a deployed enemy, but more stringently applied, and differed little from those used in attacking permanent fortifications – that is to say, attacking field fortifications was the same as siege warfare. The more time that a defender had to work on his field fortifications, the stronger they would become. The strength of the field fortifications would determine the methods used to attack them. Large-scale attacks on strong field fortifications could last several days, perhaps longer.

Prior to deploying the main attacking force, infantry, cavalry, artillery and engineer patrols would reconnoitre the defensive position by day. For his part, the defender would seek to slow the attacker's progress towards the entrenchments as much as possible, using advanced positions, artillery fire, and counter-reconnaissance patrols. When the sector to be assaulted had been identified, the infantry would move forward by night and establish a defensive position for the artillery, which would then, also by night, occupy previously reconnoitred battery positions. The attacking artillery would probably open fire at dawn the next morning.

The infantry attack on field fortifications could not begin until the defending artillery had been suppressed to the degree that the infantry could begin the forward movement without excessive casualties. Determining whether this had been achieved or not would be difficult, for if the defender saw he was losing the artillery duel, he could order his batteries to cease fire, saving them so that they could engage the attacking infantry. Artillery bombardment of unoccupied infantry defensive positions was a waste of ammunition: the attacking artillery could only fire on entrenchments after the infantry attack forced the defender to man them in strength.

An infantry attack against a dug-in enemy would usually be possible only at night. A daylight attack could only be made if the attacking artillery were demonstrably superior, or the enemy forces significantly inferior or composed of poor-quality troops. The night attack had to be prepared by extensive infantry, artillery, and engineer reconnaissance. Before beginning the attack the troops would drop their packs and load up with several days of food and ammunition. The routes for the approach march and the lines of deployment were to be clearly marked and recognisable at night. The troops would advance quietly in dense skirmisher lines (less than two-metre intervals). Firefights were to be avoided. The objective was to approach as near as possible to the enemy position and then quietly dig in. The machine guns would also be brought forward and dug in. It would be best if the troops could approach to assaulting distance at night and then conduct the assault at dawn, but the manifold frictions associated with a night attack would make this unlikely. At dawn the firefight would begin. It was quite likely that initially any advance in daylight would be impossible and that the night attack must be repeated in the same manner the next night: reconnaissance, preparation, clearing obstacles, advance and dig in, as often as it was necessary to bring the infantry close enough to conduct the assault. Night attacks might also be made to take individual defensive positions.

The infantry attack would force the defending infantry to come out of cover and man the trenches, providing the attacking artillery with targets. The defending artillery would unmask and open fire, and the German heavy howitzers would engage them. The attacker would choose a main point of effort and those entrenchments would be given priority of fire, including heavy howitzer fire. The artillery would fire around the clock. Positions with overhead cover presented a particular problem. They could only be engaged with high-angle fire (howitzers or mortars) using delayed-action fuses. It would hardly be possible to conduct an effective artillery preparation of an extended position provided with overhead cover.

The assault would be conducted as carefully planned and coordinated daylight attack. Extensive patrolling allowed a picture of the enemy defence to be formed. Weak points in the enemy position would be identified. Infantry-engineer night patrols would cut lanes through obstacles; it would hardly be possible to manually destroy all the obstacles and very difficult to destroy obstacles with artillery fire. Artillery would be brought forward for use in the direct-fire role. Supporting infantry, machine gun and artillery fire on the entrenchments would seek to prevent the defender from exposing his head above the parapet. His overhead cover would be destroyed with high-angle fire. Skirmisher lines would advance to provide close fire support, followed by combat engineers with assault tools. Finally, infantry *Sturmabteilungen* – assault groups – would break into the enemy position. These *Sturmabteilungen* would be task-organised and carefully briefed to assault specific objectives.

In 1895 FAR 69 participated in a week-long field-fortification exercise which included a live-fire shoot against trench systems.[70] Such exercises became a regular part of the regiment's summer training program. The regimental historian for IR 109 says that, as a result of the Russo-Japanese War, attacks on field fortifications at

German Tactics and Training

night and with the use of entrenching tools were practiced extensively.[71] The 1st Foot Guard regimental history reported practicing attacks on field fortifications in September 1912 and 1913 (with a four-hour exercise critique!) and that such attacks became commonplace in the last peacetime manoeuvres.[72]

Immanuel warned that future warfare would frequently take on the characteristics of the war in Manchuria: a long, tough fight over field fortifications. An attack on a French defensive position would not be easy. Immanuel said that the French were the masters in constructing field fortifications and in fortifying towns.

German pre-war doctrine held no illusions about the prospects for an attack in trench warfare. Field fortifications might put a halt to offensive operations. Attacks on field fortifications would be long and hard and there would be no breakthroughs. The attacker might himself be forced to occupy a fortified defensive position as well. When the fronts solidified into trench warfare, the German army was intellectually and materially far better prepared for it than the French.

Meeting Engagement[73]

All of the battles fought in the Ardennes were meeting engagements. Meeting engagements result when both sides are in motion, usually in more or less converging directions of march, and they make contact. Given that reconnaissance, reporting and the transmission of orders at the tactical level in 1914 were horse-powered, if two forces were marching towards each other, they were, under contemporary conditions, closing at high speed. Commanders had little information to act upon and little time to act. Almost always, in such situations, the first indication that the enemy was in the immediate vicinity was when the advance guards of the opposing march columns ran into each other.

In a division march column, the advance guard might consist of a cavalry patrol followed at a considerable distance by an advance guard infantry regiment, reinforced with artillery batteries. The advance guard regiment would lead with a point company, followed at a distance of several hundred metres by the advance guard battalion, then the first battalion of the regiment's main body, then an artillery section (three batteries), and then the rest of the regiment. The advance guard would occupy about 4km of road. Behind the advance guard regiment would follow, intermixed, the remaining infantry regiments and artillery sections of the main body. The regimental, brigade and division commanders would initially be located with the advanced guard regiment. The mission of the advance guard was (and is) to push aside smaller enemy forces and prevent them from delaying the main body; if larger enemy forces are encountered, the advance guard must give the main body time to deploy into combat formation, gain information concerning the enemy's strength and movements, and seize and hold key terrain.

The *Exerzier-Reglement* noted that the distinguishing characteristic of the meeting engagement is the lack of knowledge concerning the enemy. Usually the divisional commander would have to make fundamental decisions – to attack, defend or withdraw, and how to deploy his division – in a state of uncertainty. He could be sure that the side that deployed first, and most correctly, would secure the initiative. If, as usually will be the case, he had little knowledge of the enemy, then he must base any decision to attack on the overall situation. It is clear that in a meeting engagement the *Exerzier-Reglement* and Handbook were encouraging leaders at all levels to attack. This was preaching to the choir.

The *Exerzier-Reglement* and Handbook had surprisingly little to say about meeting engagements. This is because underneath the official regulations lay, unstated, the culture of an army, which expresses itself in the army's history, biases for action and training methods, and the decisions that the army instinctively feels are right. There is even a frequently used German military word for this culture – *Truppenpraxis*. In the German army, the *Truppenpraxis* displayed a pronounced preference for the mobile warfare and the meeting engagement. This preference was established by Yorck von Wartenberg's development of advance guard procedures in 1813. It celebrated a great success in the 1st Guard Infantry Division's attack as the advance guard of the 2nd Army at Königgrätz. The Guard's operations were a thing of military beauty, as leaders at all levels aggressively used their tactical skill and initiative to push to the top of the decisive terrain at Chlum. The Prussian III Corps at Vionville-Mars la Tour in 1870 fought an equally brilliant advance guard battle. In the 1880s the principles of meeting engagements were formalised and integrated into German doctrine by Schlichting.[74]

As Lieutenant Colonel Hein noted, 'the characteristics of meeting engagements are particularly agreeable to the German way of war'.[75] He said that 'the independence of subordinate leaders can celebrate its greatest triumph here' and 'some bold stroke is quite appropriate'. Meeting engagements call for 'independent bold action, tempered by well-considered conformity with the intent of the superior commanders' – in other words, that German specialty, *Auftragstaktik*. No other army, Hein said, considered the meeting engagement in the manner that the German army did.

Of the doctrinal works, only Immanuel gave a detailed discussion of the meeting engagement. Immanuel emphasised that there was no set formula for a meeting engagement; even with good reconnaissance, enemy strength and location would be difficult to determine and it might not even be clear that a meeting engagement was taking place. Waiting for better intelligence would be fatal. The situation needed to be developed by aggressive action, forcing the enemy onto the defensive

The tone of the *Exerzier-Reglement* as well as German *Truppenpraxis* was fundamentally different than that of French doctrine, derived from Bonnal, which held that the advance guard was capable of developing a clear picture of the enemy and that the mass of manoeuvre should not be committed until it had completely deployed behind the advance guard. The French, following their ideas of Napoleonic generalship, thought that the contours of the battle could be seen and the battle could be centrally controlled. The Germans were equally sure that neither was possible. The Battle of the Frontiers in the Ardennes would show who was right.

Envelopment[76]

The surest way to success, the *Exerzier-Reglement* said, was to combine a frontal attack with an attack on the enemy flank. The goal was not merely to push the enemy back, as was the case with a frontal attack, but to cut off the enemy's line of retreat and destroy him. An enveloping attack would not enjoy surprise: the enemy would detect its approach. Therefore an attack on the enemy front was necessary to fix the enemy forces in place, preventing the enemy from shifting his troops to meet the attack on the flank, or from withdrawing. Co-ordinating the two actions would be difficult. It was important that the frontal attack not be defeated before the flanking attack could be effective. On the other hand, troops in contact could not be shifted to attack an enemy flank. At a minimum, the flank attack had to be made by unengaged reserves. The most effective flank attack was made by operational manoeuvre, by troops whose approach march led them to the enemy flank.

Defence[77]

The *Exerzier-Reglement* said that infantry firepower in the defence was very strong and therefore required fewer troops. In a well-prepared position a division might hold a nine-kilometre front, three times the frontage it would occupy in the attack. An infantry company would usually defend a trench 150m long. The defender was rarely able to choose a defensive position on its merits alone; usually the overall situation determined the line on which he must defend. The defence was capable only of holding a position. The offensive alone could bring victory. The Handbook emphasised that only enough forces should be committed to the defence as were absolutely necessary to hold the position, in order to create the largest possible reserve for the counterattack, in particular, the best response to an enemy envelopment was a counterattack.

The principal requirements for a defensive position were an open and long-range field of fire and freedom of movement in and behind the position. The artillery position would be at least 600m behind the infantry line of defence. Artillery would like to be able to conduct observed fires out to 4,000m or 5,000m range; infantry needed a field of fire out to medium range (700–1,200m). Good fields of fire immediately in front of the position were also important. The weakness of a defensive position lay in its flanks, so long as these were not covered by terrain obstacles or other troops: a good defensive position had to

The Battle of the Frontiers

possess at least one secure flank. It was seldom going to be possible to find a defensive position that was strong everywhere, particularly if the position were a long one. Favourable terrain could be weakly held, unfavourable terrain must be more strongly held. In organising the position, the defender observed priorities of work. First priority was to clear fields of fire and determine ranges. Then fighting positions were dug and communications cable laid down.

The Handbook noted that, given the lethality of modern weapons, field fortifications were particularly useful, but required considerable time to construct. The defence was to consist of battalion battle positions built around company strongpoints, with the intervals between the strongpoints being covered by fire, and not a continuous line of trenches. Immanuel provided an exhaustive discussion of a formidable position fortified according to German doctrine, including wire obstacles. Field fortifications lost much of their effectiveness if they were observed by the enemy, so they had to be well-sited in the terrain and camouflaged: 'what can be seen, can be hit', applied to the defender, too. Security patrols must prevent enemy reconnaissance patrols from approaching the position. German doctrine called for the organisation of one defensive line: strong forces in the security zone in front of the main line of resistance, such the French habitually used, might confuse the enemy as to the real location of the main line of resistance, but could also lead to defeat in detail and would obstruct the fire from the main position. In allocating forces in the defence, it was important to maintain a strong reserve (*Hauptreserve* – the same term used in fortress defence). In pre-war doctrine, troops did not occupy the entrenchments until an infantry attack was anticipated, but rather were held in a covered and concealed position to the rear. It was felt that keeping the entrenchments strongly manned merely gave away their position and led to needless casualties due to the resulting enemy artillery fire. An important advantage of the defensive position was that it allowed the stockpiling of rifle ammunition; if remunerative targets presented themselves at long range, they could be engaged. Machine guns, which occupied little space but produced high volumes of fire, were seen as powerful weapons in the defensive. They needed to be dug in, concealed and protected by obstacles and supporting infantry positions. Night defence required aiming posts and aiming bars to direct fire at predetermined directions, as well as night security patrols and listening posts.

Initially, the defending artillery would engage the attacking artillery. If it appeared that the defending artillery would lose the artillery duel, it would cease fire and the gun crews would take cover to resume firing when the attacking infantry advanced. When the attacking infantry began to advance, the priority of fires would be changed to engage the attacking infantry. Artillery fire would mass on an enemy penetration.

The defeated force would find withdrawal during daylight to be very costly. If the infantry were engaged in a close-range firefight, withdrawal might be impossible. Generally the withdrawal would have to be conducted under cover of darkness.

Pursuit and Delay[78]

Defeating the enemy on the battlefield would result in only half a victory. The defeated force would generally be disorganised and practically helpless. But without an energetic pursuit, the enemy would quickly recover. The pursuit should crown this victory with the complete annihilation of the enemy. The admonition to conduct a ruthless pursuit probably appears in every doctrinal manual ever written. German doctrine added a more realistic appraisal of the prospects for conducting a pursuit. It noted that military history offers few examples of ruthless pursuit and as a consequence, few battles of annihilation. The defeated enemy was, in spite of his exhaustion, able to make truly remarkable marches in retreat. The attacker had just survived a tremendous ordeal and was exhausted; the natural tendency was for him to relax. The attackers would also be disorganised, low on ammunition and hungry. Key leaders would have been killed or wounded. The Handbook made the prescient observation that, given the immense size of the modern battlefield and the nature of combat, it was also going to be difficult both to recognise the extent of the victory and the condition of one's own troops: the victor could not begin the pursuit until he knew that he had won the battle. The Handbook obviously felt that forewarned was forearmed, because, having said this, it reiterated the need for ruthless pursuit.

Initially, the pursuit was conducted by fire. The victorious force would overrun the enemy position and advance far enough to put fire on the retreating enemy. If the combat had taken place in a town or woods, this meant advancing to the opposite edge of town or the far side tree line. Machine gun and artillery fire were particularly effective in pursuit. If the enemy moved out of range, a general pursuit along the entire line followed in order to prevent the enemy from reorganising or establishing a new defensive position. The artillery would advance by bounds.

The infantry was the arm least suited for conducting a pursuit, which was primarily a matter for cavalry and artillery. The truly effective pursuit would be a 'parallel pursuit' developing out of an envelopment, in which the pursuer moves on roads parallel to those of the retreating forces. This allows the pursuing forces to occupy blocking positions at critical choke points (such as bridges) in the enemy rear. The most important and most profitable cavalry mission was the conduct of the pursuit.

The victorious troops and leaders would be tired. Motivating them to conduct an immediate pursuit was very difficult. The leaders were instructed, if necessary, to act with severity towards their own troops in order to press the pursuit: 'whatever collapses [men or horses], lays where it falls'; the remainder presses on.

The Handbook noted that by this time it was probably dark. The defeated force would conduct a night march in order to break contact. It was therefore necessary that the pursuit also be continued during the night. The entire force would not be able to continue the pursuit. The infantry would finally be exhausted. Cavalry would continue the pursuit until it encountered occupied towns or defensive positions. It would then maintain contact. Cavalry units conducting parallel pursuit would continue to advance in order to be able to block enemy lines of retreat on the following day, when the pursuit would be resumed in order to place fire on the enemy and, if possible, block his routes of withdrawal.

Retreating forces would use rear-guards to delay the pursuit. The objective of delaying operations is to slow the pursuer down and to allow the retreating force to break contact, either in order to withdraw or to re-deploy elsewhere. The *Exerzier-Reglement* emphasised providing rear-guards with strong artillery, which would fire at long ranges, forcing the enemy to stop, take cover and deploy. Rear-guard infantry would also fight at long ranges in broad formations. The infantry would withdraw before becoming decisively engaged.

Combat in Woods and Towns[79]

Woods and well-built towns could become focal points for combat. Woods and towns should not be defended on the forward edge, which merely attracted artillery fire. The defenders should deploy either in front of the woods and towns or inside them. If the attacker pushed into the woods or towns, the defender had to drive him out again by counterattacks. Towns in particular needed to be integrated into the overall line of defence. The interior of the town should be defended house by house, in close combat if necessary.

In attacking a town, it was necessary to conduct a thorough artillery preparation, particularly with howitzers. The attacker must also seek to envelop the town. The attacker should penetrate to the far end of the town, bypassing centres of resistance within the town itself. This would cut off the defenders inside the town, who could be mopped up later, and prevent reinforcements from reaching the defenders.

The attacker should focus on breaking into the woods by first taking projecting salient in the tree line. Once in the interior of the woods, maintaining unit cohesion was essential. The advance was conducted in dense skirmish lines on narrow fronts, with supports and reserves following close behind.

German doctrine held that combat in towns and woods would never be decisive; only open ground allowed the full development of firepower. Rather, combat in towns and woods would become fragmented and push back and forth for hours, with the methods of the attacker and the defender becoming indistinguishable.

Defence of a River Line[80]

German doctrine held that it was harder to defend a river line than it was to attack it, and that military history showed that the defence of a river line almost always failed. Given the German emphasis on reconnaissance, this was to be expected: the river severely restricted the defender's reconnaissance, leaving the defender in the dark as to the attacker's dispositions. This made the defender particularly vulnerable to feint attacks. The defender could rarely defend the riverbank, because it was often dominated by high ground on the other side. Rather, he had to defend strong points on high ground some distance from the river, and hold a large reserve. The river magnified the advantage the attacker enjoys in choosing the place and manner of the attack: the defender would be surprised by the enemy attack and his main body will almost always arrive at the decisive point too late.

Operations at Night and During Limited Visibility[81]

Night operations included night road marches, approach marches to an attack position, reconnaissance and security and limited-objective attacks. The procedures for night operations would change little for the next 70 years.

A night attack posed any number of difficulties. The first was land navigation: during night movement it is difficult for leaders to maintain the direction of march, to be sure of their location, or to estimate how far they have moved. It was difficult to send orders or receive reports. There was an increased possibility of friendly fire incidents, while on the other hand it was not possible to gain fire superiority or receive artillery support.

The German army therefore concluded that large-scale night attacks were nearly impossible, but that night attacks could be conducted against limited objectives. Such attacks had to be well reconnoitred and prepared. The requirement was to gain surprise, which favoured dark nights. The plan of attack was to be kept as simple as possible. Battalions would advance with two companies in the first line, preceded by a weak skirmisher screen, followed by the other two companies, with the companies themselves in company or platoon column. The intent was to avoid a firefight and close in to immediately attack with the bayonet.

For defence at night, patrols and listening posts would provide security. Rifles and machine guns would be oriented on their night defensive fires by placing stakes in the ground connected by a stick to keep from firing too high, and the artillery would lay their guns for elevation and deflection on their night targets.

It was often advantageous to conduct night approach marches, particularly in order to cross open ground, to close in on a strong position, or to cross an obstacle, so that the firefight could begin at close range at dawn. In fact, given strong enemy field fortifications, the night approach march followed by a dawn attack might be the only possible offensive option. The Handbook said that such attacks might play a significant role in the next war.

The Battle of the Frontiers

Careful preparation was the essential precondition for night movements and operations. Routes of march and deployment lines had to be carefully reconnoitred by officer patrols. March routes also had to be easy to recognise and then marked. Troops had to wear a recognition badge, such as a white armband, and know the password and countersign. Movement was by compass and conducted from phase line to phase line, stopping at each in order to insure co-ordination.

Attacks in dense fog shared many of the problems of night attacks. The danger of friendly-fire incidents was acute and it was easy for the leaders to become disoriented. Movement was by compass and by easily recognisable terrain features. The troops remained in tight formations and care was taken to preserve co-ordination between units. Fog was a significant factor in several of the engagements in the Ardennes on 22 August.

The Major Training Area

An army fights the way it has been trained; the quality of that training is decisive.[82] The German army did not defeat the French in the Battle of the Frontiers because of its formal barracks square discipline, nor its tactical doctrine, nor *Auftragstaktik*, but because of the superiority of the training that was conducted at the German Major Training Areas (MTA). The number of German regimental histories that mention training, especially at the MTA, and affirm how effective that training was, is quite remarkable. The history of IR 20 expressly connects MTA training with the development of German doctrine.[83] Otto von Moser, a senior serving officer and prominent military writer, said that in 1914 the XIII AK in which he served was a crack unit, one of the reasons for this excellence being the MTA at Münsingen, which was an 'outstanding training area for realistic combat training of troops of all arms, probably the best in all of Germany'.[84]

This is not to say that German training was perfect. There was plenty of criticism that the training areas were too small and that there was not enough time and ammunition, among other things. To some degree, such criticism is inevitable: I can attest from personal experience that aggressive officers and NCOs in combat-arms units can never get enough time, space and ammunition to train with. But whatever its faults, the German army prior to the First World War was one of the best-trained in military history.[85]

In 1911 the German army possessed 28 MTA: 22 large ones and 6 smaller, comprising 102,328 hectares of land. Each active army corps had its own MTA. In addition, there were three MTA for the artillery, including the new extra-large artillery range at Grafenwöhr. The German MTA were big enough to allow infantry and artillery live-fire training without endangering the surrounding countryside.[86] They could accommodate manoeuvres by units up to brigade and division size without concern about manoeuvre damage. The German MTA had good barracks and were superbly equipped. For example, at the Lechfeld MTA

German Tactics and Training

in 1901 a target range for light howitzers to practice against field fortifications was built. In 1903 Lechfeld was authorised to buy *Müller'schen Schlitten* – target sleds allowed more effective depiction of enemy units advancing by fire and movement. In 1908 the MTA at Lechfeld built rifle-fire simulators to realistically depict enemy troops firing. Döberitz, outside Potsdam, had a permanent suite of field fortifications to allow practice in their attack and defence.[87] In 1914 electrically-activated pop-up targets were installed at MTA Grafenwöhr.[88] Every German infantry unit spent at least one three-week time block in the summer conducting highly realistic range firing and tactical exercises. Artillery, cavalry and engineer units also spent a similar period of time at the MTA. Many units were able to squeeze in additional weeks at the MTA for company training during the spring.

Since 1893 the German heavy artillery had dedicated firing ranges at the MTA at Thorn and Wahn.[89] These permitted exceptionally realistic training from a broad palate of tactical situations and terrain, including firing from covered positions and adjusting fire using only the map. These MTA were large enough to allow artillery battalions and regiments to conduct live fire as tactical units. The targets were realistic. The heavy artillery emphasised quickly but methodically adjusting fire onto the target, followed by a devastating fire for effect: 'dumping a crushing mass of ordnance on the target'. The heavy artillery also held a *Kaiserpreis* live-fire competition, which for every battery might end in firing '100 rounds from the 15cm guns at 4,000m in twenty minutes, with effective fire distribution and accuracy, against a half-covered enemy battery'. For twenty years preceding the war the German heavy artillery had conducted outstanding live-fire and tactical training. The German army began the war with heavy artillery that was not only materially superior to the French, but was integrated into the combined-arms team in a manner that the French heavy artillery was not. The momentum this training generated would allow the German artillery throughout the war to offset Allied numbers of guns and masses of munitions with its tactical and doctrinal superiority, which culminated in the 'hurricane bombardments' of 1918.

The French had twenty-six MTA, but only eight of these were large and the total area comprised 56,142 hectares. Small MTA were disproportionately less useful because of range safety firing restrictions and the inability to exercise with larger units. Moreover, many of these French MTA had been in operation for only a short period. The facilities at French MTA were not up to the German standards; lack of barracks made them unusable for large portions of the year. Only one third of French active units could exercise annually at a MTA; some isolated units could not do so at all. The deficiencies of French MTA were compounded by the poor quality of the French local training areas and garrison firing ranges.

German doctrine and training worked synergistically. German doctrine was effective because it was developed and tested at the MTA. In turn, the doctrine did not remain a dead letter but was intensively practiced by the troops at the MTA. French doctrine was based on historical example and wishful thinking; there was little opportunity to obtain the corrective of practical experience. But much worse, doctrine notwithstanding, the French lacked the facilities to teach individual marksmanship, fire tactics or unit tactics.

In combat at the company level, the well-practiced German battle drills resulted in greater German combat power: more effective fire, better and faster movement. At the leadership levels from battalion to division, German commanders arrived at a more accurate estimate of the situation and acted decisively; the French leadership performed far worse on both accounts.

German Field Training[90]

Tactical training with troops (as opposed to training without troops, such as terrain rides and war games) was conducted from the individual to the army level at the local training areas, major training areas and manoeuvre rights areas. Aside from training for the attack and defence, tactical training principally included road-marching, first aid, outpost duty and patrolling, field fortification and living in the field. Most field training was individual and almost all individual and squad training was at home station. In the last years before the war, such training in IR 109 emphasised tactical movement by squads, the use of the entrenching tool, the loss of company commanders, platoon and squad leaders and monthly night exercises. Some platoon and company training could usually be accomplished at the local training areas. In the winter, it might be possible to train on frozen fields near the garrison.

Training from company to brigade levels was conducted during an annual three to four-week period at the Major Training Area in the summer. At the MTA the mornings would be occupied with field training, the afternoons with combat gunnery range firing. Live fire exercises were conducted at squad, platoon and company levels. MTA training would include the *Bataillonsbesichtigung*, the battalion tactical test and the *Regimentsbesictigung*, the regimental tactical test, both conducted by the corps commander. Five to six days annually were devoted to the regimental manoeuvres at the MTA, four to five days for the brigade manoeuvres. Division and corps training took place during the two-week corps manoeuvre period in a manoeuvre rights area at the end of the training year in September.

An excellent appreciation for the scope of German tactical training can be gained from a book of exercise scenarios by a *Generalleutnant* Liebach.[91] For eight days of battalion training at the MTA Liebach proposed: two attacks on a deployed enemy (including combat in woods); advance guard; two meeting engagements; counterattack in the defence; night attack on a fortified position. Other missions were intermixed. For six days of regimental training he proposed: an attack on a deployed enemy; two meeting engagements; delay and breaking contact; envelopment and parallel pursuit; night attack on field fortifications.

German Tactics and Training

Brigade training, covering a four-day period, was similar. Liebach's program is most heavily weighted in favour of meeting engagements; the defence is hardly mentioned. The scenarios for the tactical training tests at battalion, regimental and brigade levels would be similar to the training scenarios.

An idea of the high quality of German field training (*Felddienstübungen*) can be gained from reading training after-action reports (*Gefechtsberichte*) for these exercises. The exercise could be opposing force, against a notional enemy designated by flags, or a tactical exercise without troops. The exercises might last only half a day, but were carefully prepared and conducted. As in all German training, the exercise director determined the general situation (*Allgemeine Kriegslage*) and the situations for Blue and Red. After the exercise, the Blue and Red commanders submitted after-action reports. These reports described the situation, information on the enemy, orders received, troop-leading procedures and commander's decisions, movements and 'combat', including a well-drawn sketch. The exercise was then reviewed and carefully commented on by the two higher echelons: for a company-level exercise, by the battalion and regimental commanders. The conduct of the exercises themselves was of a tactically high standard. These field-training exercises demonstrate the importance that the German army attached to tactical training.[92]

Subsequent to actual combat actions the German army would require after-action reports, in order to understand what factors influenced the fight and develop lessons learned. An unintended consequence is that the modern historians can use these excellent analysis of combat actions which were included in German war diaries, written by officers who had been trained in peacetime to write after-action reports.

IR 127's regimental history gives an impressive list of the regiment's tactical training.[93] In the LTA the regiment conducted night training exercises against IR 180 and road marches for the regimental trains. At the MTA the regiment conducted combined-arms live-fire exercises and, in 1910, a firepower demonstration put on by the field and heavy artillery. The regiment had a penchant for fortified positions. Its parent unit, the 51st Brigade, built a position reinforced by field fortifications in the Black Forest and then spent three days attacking and defending it. The regiment conducted attacks on a permanent fortress, 'Fortress Hugo', built at the Münsingen MTA, and also practiced attacking permanent fortifications during in the fortress exercises at Ulm in 1907 and 1913. When trench warfare came, the German army was far better prepared for it than any other European army.

Many peacetime corps commanders enjoyed immense reputations as tacticians and troop trainers: Prince Friedrich Karl first of all as commander of III Corps before 1866, then Schlichting as commander of XIV Corps[94] and later Bülow as commander of III Corps[95] but none more that Count Haeseler, a student of Friedrich Karl and commander of XVI Corps in Metz. Such men, working at the MTA, initiated innovations in German tactical doctrine that were later integrated into the regulations as well as German *Truppenpraxis*. In this manner, Schlichting was instrumental in the changes that were written into the 1888 regulation, including the emphasis on *Auftragstaktik* and the meeting engagement.

Haeseler led XVI AK from its creation in 1890 until 1903.[96] He had no interest in anything (such as the parade ground) that did not promote combat effectiveness. The regimental history for FAR 70 said that the spirit of Count Haeseler was: 'Training in the field as often and as long as possible, both day and night, and in conjunction with other arms!' Haeseler's particular interest was mobility: all three arms marched long distances cross-country and conducted long night marches. Haeseler's artillery went places that field guns had never gone before. The Mance valley in the old 1870 battlefield was considered impassable for individual guns; at the end of Haeseler's command large artillery units were traversing it. Artillery manoeuvred with fully loaded ammunition caissons. Haeseler had a field ploughed to accustom the artillery to movement across the furrows and his infantry marched unheard-of distances. He threw out outmoded concepts and revolutionised training. For example, he required that both infantry and artillery train for 'danger close' artillery support (shells falling 300m and less from the infantry). Every battery live fire test included support of an infantry attack or defence down to the closest ranges. Pop-up targets that appeared suddenly multiplied the artillery fire-control problems. In August 1898 Haeseler conducted a six-day siege exercise at Metz that the historian of IR 135 said was 'famous'. By the turn of the century men like Haeseler insured that German training was the most realistic and effective in the world.

Corps Field Training Exercises[97]

At the end of the training year, after the crops had been brought in and there was less concern over manoeuvre damage, each corps conducted a one or two-week field training exercise (FTX) on farmland in the corps area that had been designated a manoeuvre rights area. These were generally opposing-force exercises, with one division manoeuvring against the other, or a corps manoeuvre against a notional enemy (marked with flags) with the corps commander being the exercise director in both cases. These exercises had considerable advantages: the troops manoeuvred in unknown terrain; combined-arms tactics could be practiced; in an opposing force exercise there was a real 'enemy'; in a manoeuvre against a notional enemy the entire corps operated together.

In the 1870s and 1880s these exercises were leisurely affairs that each day were over by noon, and followed by a comfortable bivouac or billets with the local population. The regimental bands would play and the troops could relax. In the 1890s exercises became more realistic, and a manoeuvre 'day' might last 48 or 72 hours. The *Kaisermanöver* became especially tough, particularly because of the long forced marches.

German Tactics and Training

The division, brigade and regimental after-action reports for the XII Corps manoeuvre from 18 to 22 September 1913 survive.[98] The after-action reports were structured in a manner similar to that used for a war diary, including the attachment of orders and situation reports. These after-action reports give considerable insight into the German tactics just before the war. The XII Corps exercise deployed the entire corps against a notional enemy marked by flags. On 18 September a meeting engagement was played. The initial contact was between the corps cavalry brigade and an enemy cavalry brigade. The advance guard infantry battalion went over to the defensive and dug in, to give the following brigade time to deploy. IR 103's infantry and machine gun fire and supporting artillery fire defeated an enemy attack and the effectiveness of the artillery fire, in particular, allowed the division to go over to the offensive. On one occasion the infantry could not advance, on another occasion it could not withdraw, because of enemy artillery fire. On the morning of 19 September the corps pursued. IR 102 attacked enemy forces on high ground while IR 103 attacked the town of Eiserode, which had been prepared for defence. The field artillery and corps heavy howitzers, advancing by bounds, supported the attack. IR 103's attack stalled and the brigade reserve was committed in its sector. By 1230 the enemy was wavering and the 63rd Infantry Brigade, which had gained fire superiority, conducted the assault, which succeeded, but at the cost of very heavy casualties: IR 102 was practically destroyed and the remnants of IR 103 had to be withdrawn. II/102 IR's after-action report portrays a doctrinal infantry firefight. The two leading companies, 5th and 7th, took fire from Eiserode and returned that fire at 1000m to 1100m range. They then began to advance by bounds. 6/IR 102 was committed to reinforce the two leading companies, followed by the 8/102 and the attached engineer company. The battalion then conducted the assault, whereupon the umpire declared that both II/102 and the defending battalion were no longer combat-effective. The enemy conducted a counterattack against the 64th Brigade, which went over to the defensive. The attack was stopped in good part by concentrated artillery fire. The cavalry brigade defeated an enemy cavalry charge by a mixture of dismounted fire and mounted counterattacks. On 22 September two enemy cavalry charges against the advance guard were unsuccessful. Dismounted cavalry and bicycle troops also fired upon the advance guard. At another point, the corps commander halted the advance in the woods, fearing that if the main body left the cover of the trees it would be exposed to enemy artillery fire. All in all, this appears to have been an excellent FTX.

The Battle of the Frontiers

French Training

The chief of staff of the elite border-security French VI CA admitted after the war that the cardinal French sin was a mediocre program of tactical training.[99] One of the most important French post-war official historians, Lieutenant Colonel A. Grasset, was sharply critical of French training prior to the war.[100] He said that the peacetime strength of the units was too low to conduct effective training, and that the firing ranges and training areas were inadequate. In short, training had a lower priority than saving money or sparing public inconvenience. The NCOs were good, but there were too few of them: when mobilised, many companies had a warrant officer, a first sergeant and only one other professional NCO. There was an equal shortage of active-army officers, and the reserve officers did not have the tactical proficiency necessary to solve even a moderately difficult tactical problem. Thomasson, another important French military author, said that in the ten years before the war that the French infantry had used the 1904 regulation, many units had modified doctrine to create their own local tactics, and there was no tactical homogeneity.[101] The state of training in French units was very uneven: some units were quite good, others 'less than mediocre'.

The commanders of the French 4th and 5th Armies seconded this poor opinion of French training. In 1912 Lanrezac, the future commander of the 5th Army, wrote an evaluation of the state of French tactical training.[102] He said that many senior officers were poor tacticians due to a lack of practice. Officer training had to be culminated with opposing-force exercises, with units at war strength, held in large areas with which the troops were unfamiliar. It would appear that none of these criteria were being met. Lanrezac said that as it currently stood, the time at Major Training Areas was largely consumed by range firing, while the major field training exercises were not large-scale enough to be effective. In 1914 Lanrezac said that the French officers were not tactically capable of conducting offensive operations. Long after the war the commander of the French 4th Army, Langle de Cary, said that French training for both the troops and the cadres did not pay sufficient attention to detail. But the wooded terrain in the Ardennes put a premium on precision and care in tactics at all levels; leaders had to anticipate problems, be prudent, yet vigorous. 'This was not always the case in the marches through the woods north of the Semois, nor in several attacks.'[103]

The pre-war French army was convinced this lack of training was outweighed by the fact that Frenchmen were not only excellent natural soldiers, but superior to the Germans. General Percin, one of the most important French writers on military affairs, said that the French race was naturally warlike, and that the effectiveness of the French soldier was due more to these natural qualities that to drill, which he found to be actually harmful.[104] The chief of staff of VI CA presented the usual French point of view.[105] He said that in 1914 the Germans had laid out an entire plan of operations in advance. The French, in contrast, had only established a plan of deployment that served as a basis for manoeuvre. The Germans would attempt to methodically execute their plan, but woe betide them if unforeseen events occurred, for they were too rigid to adapt successfully. The French, on the other hand, were ready to improvise and make rapid decisions, and thus able to respond more quickly to changing situations than the Germans. At the unit level, the French believed that there was an unbridgeable gap between the German officers and men, and that German obedience was based solely on discipline. The German soldier therefore lacked initiative. The cordial relationship between officer and man in the French army fostered independent thought and action. The Germans were motivated not by patriotism, but by a desire for conquest and pillage. The French, exasperated by German aggression and brutality, fought because it was necessary to finish with German bullying. Such attitudes provided the fundamental assumptions for French operational and tactical decision making. They were not based on rational observation of the German doctrine and training, but national and racial stereotypes.

French Operations and Tactics[106]

In contrast with German doctrine, which was the product of the MTA, French doctrine largely drew on historical example, such as Bonnal's defensive-offensive doctrine based on the Napoleonic *bataillon carée*, or on pure reason, such as Ardant du Picq's Battle Studies[107] or Grandmaison's theory of the offensive.[108]

The German evaluation of French operational doctrine emphasised the French intent to manoeuvre; Bonnal's doctrine. The lead element in a French army would be an advanced guard corps, which would follow the cavalry. A day's march behind the advanced guard corps the remaining corps would be spread out, each on a separate road. The French wanted the enemy to concentrate against the advance guard, whereupon the remaining corps would manoeuvre and attack.

In contrast to the Germans, who emphasised envelopments, the French emphasised the breakthrough. At both the operational and tactical levels the French intended to mass forces in up to divisional strength on a narrow front and in great depth in order to rupture the German line.

There is little doubt that the Germans described French operational doctrine accurately. However, in August 1914 there is practically no evidence that the French employed this doctrine. In particular, the French armies did not employ an advance guard corps. As Immanuel noted in 1910, the French *Règlement sur le service des armées en campagne* contained only a short description of combined-arms combat. On the other hand, several influential generals presented varying ideas concerning operations. Immanuel said that the lack of clarity in French tactical principles was unmistakable. The French operated in a doctrine-free environment, which did not promise well for the success of French arms.

One of the few common threads in French tactics was 'security'. Particularly at the division level, 'security' against enemy attack and ambush was thought to be ensured by company or battalion-sized detachments which moved tactically on dominating terrain on the flanks. Such detachments were thought to be strong enough to force the enemy to fight and reveal himself. However, these detachments moved slowly. They were also isolated and there was a danger that they would be overwhelmed. Worse, they did not provide security; they operated too closely to the main body and the Germans moved too quickly to provide a warning to the main body.

Tactically the French army emphasised the offensive. The French concept of infantry fire and movement was significantly different than the German. There was no mention of fire superiority. Fire supported movement; there is no indication that the French recognised that fire could prevent movement. Quite the contrary, only movement was 'decisive and irresistible'; 'moral force is the most powerful component of success'; 'the attack corresponded to French national character'.[109] Immanuel's *Tactics*, from which these quotes are chosen, appeared in 1910, a year before Grandmaison's famous lectures inaugurating the offensive *à outrance*. The French tactical commitment to the offensive was derived from the 1904 tactical regulation and predated Grandmaison.

The French tactical offensive favoured elaborate, baroque manoeuvre. Battles would unfold relatively slowly and could be controlled at the divisional, corps and army levels, and manoeuvre – the employment of reserves at these levels of command – would be decisive. There was no distinction, such as that in German doctrine, between a meeting engagement and the attack on a deployed enemy. French attacking units were divided into four elements. First, there were the troops that opened the engagement (*qui vont s'engager*), then their supports and reinforcements (*renforts*), and finally the *troupes de manoeuvre* that conducted the decisive breakthrough or *envelopement*. In addition, the commander might withhold a reserve for unforeseen circumstances. The battle was divided into three phases: preparatory, decisive attack and completion. During the preparation the smallest possible French force would seek to engage and fix in place the largest possible enemy force. This battle could last hours or days. It would provide the commander with the opportunity to mass his main force for the attack at the decisive place (probably a breakthrough) followed by the pursuit. French artillery doctrine advocated the gradual commitment of the artillery, beginning with a small group of guns, retaining a reserve and adding artillery at suitable places. This complex procedure practically ensured that French troops would be committed in driblets and defeated in detail.

French doctrine for the defence prescribed a layered defence in depth and the defensive-offensive. Detachments would be employed in strongpoints forward of the main line of resistance to confuse the enemy and force him deploy prematurely. The defensive position proper would be held with the minimum forces possible, also occupying strongpoints. The emphasis was on the use of local reserves to conduct counterattacks and the resumption of the offensive (*retour offensif*) through a counterattack by the main reserve.

German Tactics and Training

Comparison of French and German Training and Tactics[110]

Thomasson described the differences between French and German training methods by a – perhaps apocryphal – statement from a German officer. The German officer said that the German Army admired the French Army, but the Germans felt themselves to be superior due to their training methods. The Germans had been using the same system for 70 years and it had been tested in 1866 and again in 1870–71. It was not a brilliant system, but a solid and simple one that suited the German temperament. The Germans had a 'cult of discipline'. Their training was uniform, due to the importance of reservists in modern warfare. The German regimental commander followed prescribed training methods and doctrine. The company commanders carefully trained the cadres. The actual training was the domain of the subordinate leaders. The French complained that this resulted in equally mediocre units. The Germans replied that the French allowed their regiments to experiment; in the German army, the Lehr Battalion conducted experimentation centrally. The German goal was not (as in the French army) to develop individualism, but rather NCOs who were good trainers and soldiers who were vigorous and attentive. The French thought the German soldiers to be slow and terrified. The German officer said that the French were wrong.

Comparison of French and German Command and Control[111]

Thomasson said German orders contained no more detail than was absolutely necessary. The recipient of a German order had to study the situation and the order so as to determine what his own instructions should be. He could not merely transmit the order unchanged to his subordinates. Not so with French orders. In order to ensure that he was obeyed exactly, the French senior officer, believing that he could anticipate every contingency, prescribed actions in the minutest detail. Such orders were time-consuming to write and therefore often arrived late. The task of the subordinate leaders was much simpler in the French than the German army: in three-quarters of the cases, the French order was so detailed that everything was already prescribed and the French officer could pass the order to his subordinates virtually unchanged.

The French system, Thomasson said, had most unhappy consequences. Frequently the lower echelons found that these detailed orders simply could not be executed. The highest headquarters were too remote both organisationally and physically to appreciate the consequences of their orders. Such detailed orders also prevented the lower units from exploiting opportunities that might present themselves. Subordinate units had to request changes in the orders, causing further delay and uncertainty.

The Battle of the Frontiers
Grandmaison and the Offensive *à outrance*

French defeats during the Battle of the Frontiers have been explained by the pernicious effects of the offensive tactics of Colonel de Grandmaison which, it is generally contended, involved mindless massed bayonet charges that were usually massacred by dug-in German machine guns. Critics of Grandmaison's offensive tactics contend that the French should have remained on the defensive.

The French army adopted offensive tactics long before Grandmaison. The French had concluded that their defeat in 1870 was due to the fact that they had been strategically, operationally and tactically defensive. The French preference for impregnable '*positions magnifiques*' surrendered the initiative to the Germans, who harried the French from pillar to post. The French therefore developed a 'passionate cult of the offensive in all its forms'. They were reinforced in this conclusion by reading German doctrine, which mandated the offensive, and German histories of 1870–71, which attributed German success to this offensive doctrine.[112] The distinctive characteristic of French operations was the emphasis on 'manoeuvre' and the successive commitment of reserves instituted by Bonnal in the 1890s.

In fact, Grandmaison's offensive *à outrance* dealt with a problem that modern military historians rarely acknowledge: Bonnal's emphasis on 'security'. Grandmaison argued that not only was this time-consuming itself, but the commander was encouraged to wait and be sure rather than act decisively. While the French commander was dallying, the German commander would be acting, thus securing the initiative. In addition, the use of all these detachments frittered away strength and weakened the main body. French attack procedures would commit forces in successive driblets. The German forces attacking decisively and in strength would crush the French. Grandmaison's critique was prescient.

Grandmaison's solution was to dispense with both the detachments and the successive attack and attack the enemy in full strength wherever he was found. The force of this attack would secure the initiative for the French, which itself would provide security. Of course, any infantry attack was to be tactically sound, use the terrain intelligently and be adequately supported by artillery.

French tactics in the two decades prior to the First World War always emphasised the offensive. Grandmaison wanted only to ensure that French attacks were made in a timely fashion and in maximum strength. However, after the catastrophe in the Battle of the Frontiers, the French army needed a scapegoat. Grandmaison, who had died leading his regiment, was selected as the 'fall guy'.

In any case, Grandmaison's tactics were practically irrelevant in 1914. Although Grandmaison first presented his ideas on tactics in 1906,[113] he did not receive a wide hearing until 1911.[114] The doctrinal manuals which supposedly reflected his offensive tactics were published so late that they could have had no influence on French unit or officer training. The operational manual, *Instruction sur la conduite des grandes unites* appeared on 28 October 1913, the tactical manual *Service en cam-*

pagne on 2 December 1913 and the infantry training manual, which was supposed to have been the real source of the French *malheur*, on 20 April 1914! Percin expressly stated that these new manuals had no effect on the French infantry, which went into combat using the 1904 regulation, which Percin said was excellent.[115] If anything, the introduction of a new set of manuals at this late date did nothing but add to the uncertainty already present in French doctrine. It comes as no surprise that there is little trace of an offensive *à outrance* on 22 August 1914 in the Ardennes.

Tactics, Doctrine, Training and the Battle of the Frontiers

In war, Napoleon said, everything is simple, but even the simple things are difficult. The German army took heed of this warning. It developed a simple and sober tactical doctrine based on the destructive effect of modern firepower. It then spared no pains to ensure that the troops were trained to perform their simple combat tasks in the exceptionally difficult environment of the modern high-intensity battlefield.

French doctrine was neither so rational nor so simple. The French nation failed to provide the army with the resources for training, particularly land for large training areas, that the German did. In compensation, French doctrine relied on historical precedent that was no longer applicable and racial stereotypes that were irrelevant. The premise of this history is that an army will fight the way it has trained. The Battle of the Frontiers shows how superior doctrine and training led to German tactical victory.

2

Mobilisation, War Plans, Deployment and Approach March

Mobilisation

The peacetime German army consisted of 29,000 OFF and 725,000 EM. On mobilisation, the field army included 2,292,679 troops: 1,538,000 reservists, Landwehr and Landsturm men were called back from civilian life to rejoin the army. Some sixty-seven per cent of the German field force was made of up non active-duty personnel. In the 50 active army divisions, at the conclusion of mobilisation two thirds of the combat arms personnel and almost all of the service and service support personnel were not active-duty. Tweny-nine additional reserve divisions were raised using non-active duty personnel and small active-duty cadres.[1] The German heavy artillery was overwhelmingly composed of reservists. During the war its peacetime strength of 1,420 OFF, 33,250 EM and 3,400 horses rose to 11,000 OFF, 270,000 EM and 136,000 horses. The number of heavy artillery personnel increased by a factor of eight, the number of horses by a factor of 40.[2] The French army was similar: it mobilised 1,710,000 reservists and 1,100,000 territorial troops.[3]

The first day of mobilisation for both armies was 2 August 1914. Once mobilisation was declared, time was measured in days of mobilisation. Between the 1st and the 20th day of mobilisation, the German rail system moved 2,070,000 men, 118,000 horses and 400,000 metric tons of material on 16,700 trains to their mobilisation stations.[4] A particular problem for the German mobilisation was that most of the horses were in the agricultural east, while most of the population was in the industrial north. Marrying these two groups to their units, which were stationed throughout the country, required considerable dexterity.

Mobilisation, War Plans, Deployment and Approach March

Mobilisation proper consisted of three tasks. The first was that of issuing uniforms and individual equipment. The active army soldiers turned in their blue peacetime uniforms and were given field grey. Reservists had to be issued everything. Next, the active army units had to be brought up to war strength: IR 63 had a 'present for duty strength' on 1 August 1914 of 31 OFF, 1,267 EM; its mobilised strength was 61 OFF and 3,071 EM.[5] Finally, the reserve units and almost all the combat support and service support had to be created from incoming reserve personnel and the piles of equipment stored in the depots.

Mobilisation was the responsibility of the combat-arms regiments. In peacetime the regiments were required to maintain the uniforms and equipment and establish a plan for billeting the recalled personnel and then dividing up the active-duty cadres and reservists among the units. There was a mass of work to be accomplished in this period, strictly controlled by the mobilisation schedule, the *Mobilmachungskalendar*. Ammunition had to be uploaded, horse furniture adjusted. Guard duty occupied a considerable quantity of manpower, a situation that was not improved by the rumour that the French were trying to sneak vehicles loaded with gold across Germany to Russia. The search for the 'gold autos' and French spies frequently paralysed movement.

Nevertheless, most units had enough time to fit in a road march and gunnery training before beginning the rail deployment. It is a certainty that every regimental commander did so while holding his breath. On the one hand, half of his personnel or more were reservists or *Landwehr* men. On the other hand, he was now dealing with 'war strength' units two or three times larger than those he had trained in peacetime. Most units, like II/FAR 41, were 'pleasantly surprised'. The farm horses pulled almost better than the 'active army' horses. The reservists drove their vehicles as though they had never done anything else. The gunners quickly got back into form. Only the use of the aiming circle required additional training.[6] For infantry units the first priority was getting the reservists marching fit, and no opportunity was lost to conduct route marches. Some units had more stragglers than others, but by the time operations commenced, all were ready.

IR 47 was representative of the state of training of the German army in August 1914: it was as well trained as any unit that had ever gone to war. It had spent much of the month of July at the Wartelager MTA. The entire garrison of Posen, IR 47's home station, had just conducted a full FTX, including all of the supply trains. The regiment used the available time during mobilisation to conduct field exercises, live fire and first aid training. In the assembly area there was more combat training, and more instruction in the articles of war, including admonitions that looting was forbidden.[7] Every minute of training time counted: two battalions of IR 46 conducted a night training exercise on the night of 30–31 July and only then returned to garrison.[8]

The active army units created a staggering number of reserve and supply units. Field Artillery Regiment (FAR) 42 established the II. *Abteilung* (section – bat-

81

talion equivalent) staff, 3 batteries and a light munitions column of Reserve Field Artillery Regiment (RFAR) 11, plus the 2nd, 3rd and 4th artillery munitions columns for VI Corps, Reserve Artillery Munitions Column 22, the staff of the *Landwehr* artillery ammunition section, and the replacement detachment for FAR 42 itself, including a headquarters element and 2 batteries. All of these vehicles were horse-drawn: FAR 42 received about 2,500 requisitioned horses, which had to be distributed among the units and fitted for harnesses.

On 1 August 1914 the 5th Battery of FAR 42 (5/FAR 42) at peacetime strength included 19 NCOs, 4 trumpeters, a medic, 94 EM, (118 EM total) 2 officer candidates and 80 horses. It gave up to the other units that it helped form 11 NCOs, two trumpeters, 26 men (39 EM) and 19 horses. To bring the battery up to war strength (148 EM and 139 horses) it received 67 reservists and *Landwehr* men and 78 requisitioned horses.[9] The mobilised battery consisted of just as many reservists and Landwehr men as it did active-duty personnel and more requisitioned horses than 'active-duty'.

German units were recruited locally. Many of the reservists were allowed to return to the unit in which they had performed their active duty. Old comrades met one another again. Most German company commanders held their positions for eight years, so reservists often served under their old CO. In the 1st Foot Guard Regiment, the commander of the MG company from 1909–1913 became the commander of the MG Company of the 1st Guard Reserve Regiment.[10]

A reserve field artillery regiment, such as RFAR 9, received a small cadre from the parent regiment.[11] The battalion, section and battery commanders and adjutants were all active-army officers. Half of the lieutenants were active, half reserve. The battery first sergeants and a few NCOs and gunners were transferred from the parent unit, but the mass of the enlisted personnel were older reservists and *Landwehr* men who did not know each other and were frequently unfamiliar with new equipment and doctrine. The worst problem, however, was the fact that all of the horses had been requisitioned. Few had been ridden and some had never even been shod. Nevertheless, it was absolutely essential that the reserve artillery regiment be combat-ready by the time the division made contact, for this regiment provided the only fire support the division would receive.

The pre-war 'enlightened' German press, such as the satirical magazine *Simplicissimus*, routinely characterised German reserve officers as social-climbing 'boobies'. Modern studies of German reserve officers treat them solely as a manifestation of German militarism. The question of the military efficiency of German reserve officers never arises. In fact, the reserve officers were essential to the functioning of the German army. There were simply not nearly enough active-duty officers to lead the mobilised German army. In IR 19, which was representative of the German army as a whole, only one of the three platoon leaders in each company was active-army, two were reservists and the fourth officer was a senior NCO or officer candidate. All three battalion ration officers were reservists.[12] IR 11, like most German regiments, had twice as many reserve officers as active duty. Twenty-six reserve officers joined the regiment, while twenty-eight active-duty officers and seventy reserve officers went elsewhere, mostly to form new units.[13] The reserve officers generally performed their combat leadership duties in an exemplary fashion. Due to the high officer casualty rates, in a few weeks reserve officers frequently became company commanders.

The commander of 2/FAR 69 wrote to his mother that the weeks after mobilisation were 'the happiest of his life', because he was able to experience 'the magnificent spirit of the German people at that time'.[14] He commanded a battery that 'did not cost him a minute's worry'. There was a general feeling that everything that had happened to that point would be insignificant compared to the events that awaited them: all this in combination with days of unbroken sunshine.

During mobilisation, every German regiment without exception was deluged with a mass of volunteers. The German army conscripted only 55 per cent of every year group, so there were thousands of young men who had never performed military service and therefore had never become reservists. To these were added students, who were exempt from conscription. They now streamed to the regimental *Kasernen*. In Württemberg, which had a peacetime army of 1,331 OFF and 29,591 EM, 8,619 volunteers were accepted; many others had to be deferred[15] By the 6th day of mobilisation FAR 42 in Upper Silesia, which was heavily Polish, had 600 volunteers; nearly equal to the peacetime strength of the regiment.[16] FAR 25 in Frankfurt am Main had 800 volunteers by 5 August. Only 450 could be accepted. They immediately began pulling guard duty and performing details.[17] A Württemberg unit, IR 119, enlisted 1,192 volunteers in August and September.[18] All wanted to deploy with their local units; many were afraid that they would not get to fight. Practically all were assigned to the unit replacement (*ersatz*) detachment for training and would deploy in October.

Reserve Units[19]

The question of the use of reserve units in combat was also one of the most hotly-debated military questions in Europe before the war. Could reserve units be committed to front line combat, or were they capable only of performing secondary duties, such as blockading fortresses?

After the war, apologists for the French defeat in the Battle of the Frontiers contended that the Germans had won only because they had used reserve units on the front line, while the French had not; the French lost solely because superior German numbers overwhelmed them. General Percin said that the Germans sent 34 corps against France, 21 active and 13 reserve, which meant that the Germans were half again as strong as the French. The German and French active armies were both 700,000 men strong. But the Germans employed 1,300,000 reservists to fill out the active army units and create reserve units. He accused the French

General staff of having confidence only in active-duty units. For that reason the general staff refused to organise them. The French used only 600,000 reservists to complete the active army units, while 1,200,000 French reservists were left in the depots because there were no cadres, uniforms or weapons for them (the French official history said there were 680,000 men in depots).[20] In Percin's calculation, the French reserve divisions did not count at all.

Percin contended that in France the pre-war question of the use of reserve units had a political dimension. It would probably more accurate to say that in France the question of reserve units was political first and military second. The defenders of the Three Years Law said that active-duty soldiers were superior to reservists, and supported their case by maintaining that even the Germans did not intend to use reserve units in the same manner as active army units. In parliamentary debates on 3 and 19 June 1913, three important politicians, including Messimy, the Minister of War, stated that the Germans had no intention of using reserve units on the front line. On the other hand the most important politician on the French left, Juares, said that the Germans would use their reservists on the front lines, and for that reason the French must, too.[21]

Percin, whose sympathies were clearly with the French left, asserted that the real reason for the Three Years Law was to professionalise the French army so that it would be an instrument in the hands of the upper classes in maintaining internal order or staging a *coup d'etat*. The irony of this argument is that it is the same one made by leftist German historians concerning the real function of the German army – the maintenance of domestic order.

In August 1914 the Germans, according to Percin, had 1,300,000 reservists and *Landwehr* men in Belgium. In fact, the Germans had 10 reserve corps and seven *Landwehr* brigades in Belgium, with about 380,000 men. The Germans, said Percin, had employed a genuine *levée en masse*. This would have been a considerable surprise to the German Chief of the General Staff, Moltke, who argued for the three years prior to the war that the Germans had not employed all their available manpower, as the French had done. Percin was also one of the first post-war military commentators to make the erroneous assertion that every German corps raised a reserve corps, which would have given the Germans 25 reserve corps instead of the actual 13.

The assertion that the French did not expect the Germans to use reserve corps on the front lines is expressly contradicted by Plan XVII itself, which states 'In conclusion, the [German] reserve corps, which is to be employed in the same manner as the active corps, has become, according to the new mobilisation plan, more homogeneous and with better cadres than previously, although it continues to have less combat power than an active corps'. The French believed that such a use of reserve corps was a recent development, occasioned by the 1913 German Army Bill. The enemy estimate in Plan XVII said that the total force that the Germans would initially employ against the French was 20 active corps, 10 reserve corps plus 8 reserve divisions, 68 divisions in total, which was correct.[22] The French force included 43 active-army and 25 reserve divisions, for 69 divisions (plus eight territorial divisions). While the two sides were practically even, the addition of the British Expeditionary Force would give the *Entente* numerical superiority.[23] This was precisely the argument that the chief of the British General Staff made in favour of sending the BEF to the continent.

In fact, both doctrinally and in actual operations, there is little to distinguish the French and German use of reserve divisions, which both war plans treated as normal manoeuvre units. The Germans organised reserve corps, the French created groups consisting generally of four reserve divisions. Indeed, every French corps included a reserve brigade with four reserve infantry battalions. Plan XVII said that the law on infantry cadres of 23 December 1912 allowed the French to reinforce the cadres of their reserve divisions, and that it was permissible to anticipate their utilization along with active-army units in the front line, where they could fulfil some of the missions assigned in the current plan to active army units.[24] Amazingly, even Percin admitted that Joffre used reserve units in the front line from the very beginning. Percin says that the failure of some reserve units to perform adequately was due to a lack of equipment and poor training.[25] In the French plan, the limited-duty units were the third-line territorial divisions.

Thomasson said that French reserve units were poor.[26] There were too few company-grade officers and NCOs. The French reservist was required to conduct only 17 days of refresher training during his entire reserve obligation. Exceptions were generously granted, so that only 25 per cent of those called back for training actually appeared. Grasset said that reservists could choose the times at which they conducted their refresher training, and naturally chose times in which little training was being conducted.[27] Thomasson judged that French reservists therefore became 'demilitarised.' German reserve units were polar opposites, having high-quality cadres and excellent discipline. The chief of staff of the French VI CA candidly admitted that 'Both sides committed reserve units to the front line ... those of the enemy were more solid, therefore better.'[28]

Nevertheless, both sides were making a virtue of a necessity. Reserve units were weaker than active army units, and both armies explicitly recognised this. The soldiers were older, out of shape and had not conducted training in years. Reserve units were less well equipped: a German reserve division had one regiment of 7.7cm guns instead of the two in the active division. The reserve corps had no light howitzers, no heavy howitzer battalion and no aviation detachment. Twenty-two German reserve infantry regiments did not have machine guns. This meant far less firepower. Any professional soldier in 1914 would have had to assume that an active army unit should have been able to defeat its reserve counterpart.

The surprise in August and September 1914 was not that the Germans used reserve units in the front lines, but that German reserve units were the tactical equals of French active units. The Battle of the Ardennes pitted eight French active corps against five German active and three reserve corps. The German reserve corps frequently performed better than the French active corps. The German VI RK had to fight with an open left flank all morning and into the afternoon against elements of the French V CA and VI CA. The German reservists died hard; there was no collapse and they held on long enough for the V RK to conduct a prodigious forced march and shore up the open flank. The elite French 5th Colonial Brigade was destroyed in good part by German reserve units. This tactical prowess of the German reserve units was due to solely to superior German individual training.

War Plans

On 2 August, the *Oberste Heeresleitung* (OHL), the German headquarters, issued the *Aufmarschanweisungen*, the deployment instructions, to the seven west front army headquarters. In general terms, the 6th Army in Lorraine and the 7th Army in Alsace would hold the German left flank, while the 5th, 4th and 3rd Armies in the Ardennes advanced to the Meuse and the 2nd and 1st Armies advanced through the Belgian plain north of the Meuse to secure the area between Namur and Brussels. The principal mission of the 1st Army was to guard the right flank.

The Germans were painfully aware that they had no idea how the French were going to deploy or what the French intentions were. The Germans suspected that the French might conduct their main attack in Lorraine. In that case, the 6th Army, supported by the 7th, would fall back to defend the Saar river line between Metz and Strasbourg. The 5th Army, which was deployed east of Metz precisely to meet this contingency, would advance through the belt of fortresses at Metz to attack the French left flank. The 4th Army would then move southwest to protect the flank and rear of the 5th Army. If the French did not attack into Lorraine, then the 5th and 4th Armies would advance to the northwest, so that the 5th Army could take up position to the north of Metz-Diedenhofen, with the 4th on its right; 5th, 4th and 3rd Armies would then advance to the Meuse, with the 3rd Army to the north of Givet, the 4th between Givet and Neufchâteau, the 5th between Neufchâteau and Metz-Diedenhofen. The rate of advance would be determined by the progress of the right-flank 2nd and 1st Armies, all five armies conducting a giant wheel to the left. The 5th Army was instructed to maintain contact with the Metz-Diedenhofen fortress complex. The 4th Army was to guard the flanks of both the 5th and 3rd Armies. It was possible that the French would cross the Meuse to conduct their main attack in the Ardennes. It was also possible that the French would defend on the Meuse. Whether the French did one or the other, they might also launch a counterattack from Verdun against the left flank of the German 5th Army.

The French war plan, Plan XVII, estimated that 'the bulk of the German forces will probably be deployed on the Franco-German border'. There was a strong possibility that the Germans might launch their main attack through Metz against the Meuse between Verdun and Toul. Whatever the Germans did, the concept of the French plan was clearly stated: 'In all cases, the intention of the commander in chief is to attack the German armies as soon as all French forces have been deployed'.[29] The initial objective was to surround Metz. Plan XVII had two variants: in the first, the French army would not enter Belgium; in the second, it would. On 2 August General Joffre, the French commander, implemented the second variant. The French 1st Army would deploy in the south, centre of mass on the border northeast of Epinal. On its left was the 2nd Army, centre of mass Nancy. Their mission was to attack into Alsace and Lorraine.

In the Ardennes, the German 4th and 5th Armies would be opposed by the French 3rd Army, (initially composed of the IV *corps d'armée* (CA), V CA and VI CA, 7th Cavalry Division) deployed on the Côtes Lorraines between Verdun and Nancy, and commanded by Ruffey. To the left of the 3rd Army was 4th Army (XX CA, XVII CA, Colonial Corps, 9th Cavalry Division) to the northwest with the centre of mass at St. Ménehould, commanded by Langle de Cary, a veteran of the Franco-Prussian War who had reached mandatory retirement age on 4 July 1914. The 3rd Group of Reserve Divisions (54 *division de réserve* (DR), 55 DR and 56 DR) was arriving to take over the defence of the Côtes Lorraines. The initial mission of the 3rd Army was to invest Metz on the west and northwest sides, while the 2nd Army invested Metz from the south. The attack could begin as early as the 12th day of mobilisation. The mission of the 4th Army was to attack on the 3rd Army left in the direction of Arlon. By 13 August the 3rd Army would move to the north of Verdun, with the 4th Army on its left, centre of mass on the border opposite Longuyon-Montmédy. The 5th Army would be on the left flank, centre of mass Mézières. The 4th Group of Reserve Divisions was concentrated on the far left flank south of Hirson. Sordet's Cavalry Corps was to assemble at Montmédy and be prepared to conduct reconnaissance towards Luxembourg, Arlon, and Bastogne. The French intelligence collection plan made it clear that the French thought that the Germans might defend in the Ardennes with reserve units.

Deployment

The first units to deploy on both sides were the covering force units. The French covering force was ordered to take up its positions on 30 July, even before the declaration of mobilisation. It consisted primarily of the five corps stationed on the border. These corps were kept at such high peacetime manning levels that they needed few reservists to reach war strength. The German covering force was ordered to deploy late on 1 August. It consisted of XVI Corps at Metz and brigades moved from the interior at peacetime strength.

The German rail deployment began on the 5th day of mobilisation (6 August). Moving an active army corps required about 140 trains; a reserve corps 85, a cavalry division 31. Daily, up to 660 trains moved on the 13 German deployment rail lines, which meant a train every 10 minutes.[30]

The Battle of the Frontiers

The battle of the Ardennes involved the German 5th Army (V AK, XIII AK, XVI AK, V RK, VI RK), which deployed to the area east of Metz-Diedenhofen, and the 4th Army, (VI AK, VIII AK, XVIII AK, VIII RK, XVIII RK) which deployed north of the 5th with the centre of mass of the three active corps on a line Echternach–Saarburg–Sierck. The last unit, VI RK, completed its deployment on 15 August. *Heereskavalleriekorps* (HKK) 4 was deployed with the 6th Cavalry Division (KD) at Diedenhofen and the 3rd KD to the immediate north of Diedenhofen, HKK 1 with the 5th KD facing Arlon and the Guard KD at Wiltz. The presence of nearly half of the west-front cavalry in the Ardennes is an indicator of OHL's uncertainty concerning the mission of the French forces opposite the Ardennes.

The rail deployment had a profound effect on German troop morale. The German soldier's willingness to press the attack on 22 August '*koste, was es wolle*' (cost what it may) was reinforced the minute that his battalion left the gate of the *Kaserne*. The march to the *Bahnhof*, the rail station, was an immense patriotic festival; even in the most communist districts of German industrial towns, the entire route was lined with cheering crowds. As IR 19 began its march to the rail station in Görlitz:

> '...it was already dark, but thick masses of people had been standing along the streets for hours, waiting, in order not to miss the opportunity to wave one last time to their loved ones and friends ... The musicians in front, the unfurled colours directly behind them, the battalions marched with firm step down the street, singing. It rained flowers, soon everyone had a bouquet in the barrel of his rifle, and from all sides gifts were thrust in the hands of the marching soldiers ... The city fathers waited at the rail station ...'[31]

The historian of IR 22 said:

> 'None who were present will forget the march out of the garrison. The shouts of "Hurrah!" were never-ending, The battalions were accompanied by a sea of waving flags, a rain of flowers, but also by those taking leave of their friends and loved ones, ...it was a mood of festive seriousness, for all, the officers, men and the thousands that shouted their goodbyes or accompanied the troops, were aware what immense fate had taken its course.'[32]

But perhaps the greatest impression was made by the rail march itself.[33] This was the first time that most of the troops had seen so much of their Fatherland, and the effect was profound. For units from eastern Germany the trip took three days and three nights. The weather was spectacular, sunny and clear, the countryside heartbreakingly beautiful, especially along the Main River and in Franconia, which was the route followed by many of the 5th Army troop trains. The units assigned air guards on the flatcars to watch for enemy aircraft.[34] It was soon discovered that this was the best place to enjoy the wonderful scenery and weather, and the officers began to move to the flatcars too. The regimental history of FAR 20 recorded:

'Now the journey continued, along the Main River, past proud Lichtenfels castle and [the pilgrimage church] of Vierzehnheiligen, past verdant meadows and fields, villages and towns. It was as though Mother Germany once again wanted to show her sons in the most vivid and stirring manner possible that which they had to protect against the claws of their greedy enemies'.[35]

RIR 37:

'I realised on this journey, for the first time, how beautiful our Fatherland is… For three days we rode straight across Germany, and everyone present will remember it forever. At the rest halts there was an excess of food and drink, offered by beautiful hands with an enchanting laugh and an entrancing glance that struck the hearts of many a warrior, both young and old. As the train left the station the cries of 'Hurrah!' did not cease – fluttering handkerchiefs, waving hands, moist eyes –shouts of '*Auf Wiedersehen!*' everywhere.'[36]

A soldier from IR 38 wrote:

'You cannot imagine what a triumphal march through Germany we experienced… At every stop, crowds of women and girls greeted and mothered us. Flowers in profusion at every new rail station and coffee, tea, lemonade, cake, rolls, fruit in such quantities that we almost exploded. All of this during a wonderful rail trip in glorious weather through a rich, blessed countryside… One thing became clearer and clearer to us as we departed to defend our German fatherland: we wanted victory, we had to be victorious, and we would be victorious… the confidence in us that was conveyed by the shouts of joy of the people and by the verdant beauty of the German countryside, spurred us on and set itself so deeply and firmly in us and would rise again glowing in difficult hours – until we had performed our complete duty'.[37]

Then came the *piece de résistance*: crossing the Rhine. The experience of IR 88 was typical.[38] The regiment made a 75-minute rest stop at Bingerbrück. In 20 minutes the troops had been served a hearty soup of beef with barley. The troops then lay down in the sun to admire the scenery. On the opposite side of the Rhine stood the Germania statue, erected to commemorate the establishment of the German Empire in 1871. To its left was the romantic castle of Ehrenfels, and on an island in the Rhine the *Mauseturm* (Mouse Tower). Upstream lay the beautiful town of Rüdesheim. A few soldiers began singing '*Die Wacht am Rhein*', a powerful patriotic song, with the refrain: 'Dear Fatherland, you can be sure, the Watch on the Rhine stands firm and true'. Soon the entire regiment, 3,000 men, was singing, the Rhine valley echoing in reply. The regimental historian wrote that this song, at this place and in this hour, was an oath.

Approach March

Terrain

The triangle of the Ardennes forest extends like an arrowhead with its base in Germany into southern Belgium and France. It is bordered on the north along the line Givet–Meuse–Liège, on the west by the Meuse River, and to the south by the line Sedan–Montmédy. The Ardennes is thinly populated; it is hardly possible for troops to live off the land. The Ardennes does not favour operational manoeuvre. The road net is not well developed and the forests and underbrush are thick and practically impenetrable. Much of the farmland is poorly drained pasture, which is almost marshy.

There were two obsolete French fortresses on the border, at Longwy and Montmédy. In order to enter the Ardennes from the southwest, as the French armies would be doing, it was necessary to cross the tributaries of the Meuse: the Chiers, Othain and Semois. The valleys consist of open farmland; the hills in between are forested. Within the Ardennes forest there are two large open areas. The first is the cleared land along Semois valley from Florenville to Arlon. The second is a band of open ground extending from Neufchâteau towards Arlon. This area is dotted with small woods and marshy pastures. Most of the fields are enclosed by thick hedges, barbed wire, or both.

The nature of the terrain made the operational problem for both armies extremely complex. From a military point of view, the area of operations consists of a series of east-west obstacles: river valleys alternating with lesser or greater bands of forest. On the other hand, only the open river valleys are suited to military operations.

The French were advancing in echelon, with their left wing leading. There would therefore be battles in the open ground of each of these river valleys: near Longwy on the Chiers, at Virton-Ethe on the Crusnes, at Tintigny on the Semois and around Neufchâteau.

The terrain strongly favoured the German army. It rewarded good reconnaissance, march discipline, effective staff work and initiative, particularly at the tactical level. The terrain mercilessly punished deficiencies in all of these areas.

French Enemy Estimate

Observing the density of the German rail net behind Metz, the *Deuxième Bureau*, the French General staff intelligence section, concluded that the Germans would concentrate up to 11 corps behind the Metz-Diedenhofen fortress complex and in Luxembourg as a mass of manoeuvre and then shift those forces into Lorraine or Belgium. The French did not obtain any solid intelligence on the location of the German assembly areas during the German rail deployment, and therefore retained the pre-war assumption that the Germans would mass behind Metz. On 9 August the French thought that 17 German acive-army corps opposed them, while four corps opposed the Russians. Since the French had 21 active army corps, the French thought they had numerical superiority. They estimated that there were five or six German corps in Belgium, five to eight corps located at Metz-Diedenhofen-Luxembourg, with more on the way, one to three corps in Lorraine, a corps plus in Alsace. Five corps were unaccounted for.[39]

In fact, the German armies were evenly deployed from Alsace to the north of Aachen. The German 4th and 5th Armies were behind Metz and in Luxembourg, but did not have the decisive role that the French ascribed to them. The French intelligence analysts had been trained according to the theories of Bonnal, who doctrinally employed a large mass of manoeuvre, and were mirror imaging – writing the German plan as a French officer would have written it.

The pre-war calculation of the *Deuxième Bureau* was that the Germans could attack as of the 13th day of mobilisation.[40] Expecting to find the Germans in the northern Ardennes, Sordet's Cavalry Corps of three divisions was sent into Belgium on 6 August and reached the area west of Liège on 8 August. On 9 August he found nothing at Marche. Neither he nor French aerial reconnaissance could find any German forces as far east as the Ourthe River because there were no German forces there, nor would there be any there until around 18 August. Sordet's cavalry had moved ten days too soon. Nor did the Belgians provide much useful information.[41] By 12 August Sordet had moved to Neufchâteau but still made no contact; he then pulled back to the west bank of the Meuse on 15 August and was attached to 5th Army. Sordet reported that it was impossible to supply the cavalry in the Ardennes and that air recon was unreliable in the dense woods. His cavalry corps had conducted an eight-day march without obtaining any information concerning the German forces. In order to find the German 3rd, 4th and 5th Armies, the French cavalry would have had to advance across the Belgian Ardennes to the border with Germany and Luxembourg; it was unable to do so.[42] The German deployment was not completed until 17 August and the German 5th and 4th Armies did not begin their advance until 18 August. The French had great difficulty understanding why the Germans were not as far to the west as they expected them to be.

By 10 August, the French saw indications that the Germans were digging in on the Ourthe between Liège and Houffalize. The French intelligence summary on 13 August reported that in the Ardennes there were only two German corps (VIII AK at Luxembourg and XVIII at Aumetz – the latter was actually XVI AK) and two cavalry divisions.[43] The French were beginning to get the impression that there were no German troops in the Ardennes. This was not an illogical conclusion. It is more than 100km from the sparse German railheads in the Eifel, in the German Ardennes, to the Franco-Belgian border. The Ardennes is thinly populated and heavily forested, with few and poor roads. Crossing it would pose significant problems in supply and traffic control. At the end of the approach march lay the Meuse River, a formidable obstacle. It would seem unlikely that the Germans would commit significant forces from the very start of the campaign into such an out-of-the-way and difficult theatre of war.

In the skirmishes between cavalry and foot patrols during the first week of the war, the French thought that their troops were generally victorious, returning with prisoners, horses and weapons. The chief of staff of VI CA said that 'this filled them with great joy.'[44] French pre-war predictions of the natural superiority of the French soldier seemed to be justified.

Between 7 and 10 August the French VII CA had advanced towards Mühlhausen in the upper Alsace and been thrown back into France by the German XIV AK and XV AK. On 14 August the French 1st Army and 2nd Armies attacked into Lorraine. Joffre was fully aware that the German forces to the east of Metz could attack through the fortress to the south into Lorraine: he gave the 3rd Army the mission of attacking any such German sortie in the flank with two corps, while on 15 August he told the 3rd Army to be prepared to invest Metz from the west.

By 15 August the French recognised the strength of the German forces in the general vicinity of Liège. Joffre told the commanders of the 4th and 5th Armies that the Germans were going to make their principal effort 'to the north of Givet' with a second group marching on Sedan and Montmédy. The 4th Army estimate of the situation on 16 August said that these forces represented the German mass of manoeuvre, and that aerial reconnaissance showed that there were no significant German forces at Arlon or Luxembourg in the southern Ardennes. Joffre based on his plan of attack on the idea that the Germans had left their centre weak in order to strengthen the force north of the Meuse. He therefore decided to break the German centre in the Ardennes. On 15 August GQG ordered 5th Army on the left flank to march north to an area west of Givet. 4th Army was to be prepared to attack towards Neufchâteau. On 16 August the 3rd Army was told to hand over the area between Verdun and Toul to a group of reserve divisions in order to be able attack north of Metz towards Longwy.[45]

German Enemy Estimate

As soon as The German 4th Cavalry Corps (*Heeres Kavalleriekorps* 4 – HKK 4) had completed rail deployment, OHL wanted it to conduct deep reconnaissance from the area north of Diedenhofen as far west as the Meuse. On 10 August HKK 4 was able to cross the Othain, but 6 KD ran into serious resistance at Mangiennes and Billy on the high ground to the west and was forced to recross the Othain.[46]

HKK 3 had the same experience in Lorraine that HKK 4 had on the Othain: the cavalry corps were unable to penetrate the French security forces and could not obtain any operationally useful intelligence. It became rapidly apparent that cavalry was unable to conduct the strategic reconnaissance mission that peacetime doctrine had anticipated.[47]

The first significant German intelligence estimate was made on 13 August. The Germans had detected the French preparations for the attack into Lorraine and decided that the French were going to commit their main body there: 16 corps and two groups of reserve divisions, 38 to 40 divisions in total, about 60 per cent of the French army.[48] The German 5th Army was alerted to be prepared to attack through Metz against the left flank of the French offensive, and the German 4th Army to be prepared to guard the right flank of the 5th Army. However, by 16 August the German forces in Lorraine had made contact with the French, and it was clear that the French forces were not nearly so strong. On 17 August the 5th Army stood fast. The German cavalry did obtain some success. On 14 August the German 3 KD pushed the French 4 DC out of Etalle and was able to send reconnaissance squadrons to Carignan and Montmédy, where it established that the French were digging in on the Chiers. The German 6 KD ran into French security forces at Mercy-le-Haut on 17 August and was also able to see that the French were across the Chiers.

The German estimate of the French strength north of Verdun at this time was vague. It was thought that there were two French corps at Dinant and a group of three corps north of Sedan, but OHL knew nothing concerning the French forces in front of the 5th Army.[49] Nevertheless, on 17 August OHL issued the order for the right wing to begin the advance on 18 August. On 18 August German aerial reconnaissance detected French units marching north from Montmédy, Stenay and Dun.

The German left wheeling movement through the Ardennes was far from being as easy as it sounds. While the 5th Army left flank was in the immediate proximity of the enemy, the right flank had to move three days' march to the northwest to come on line. At the same time, the 4th Army, also moving northwest, had to march about 100km through the Ardennes to reach the French border. In addition, the 4th Army sector was narrow, so that the three active corps had to march in the first wave and the two reserve corps in the second. Given the thin road net in the Ardennes, moving and supplying the army required masterful staff work.

Civilians

In German Lorraine the German troops found that the inhabitants were restrained, probably fearful that the war was about to come to them.[50] The Germans were pleasantly surprised by the reception they received in Luxembourg. The Luxembourger used German in the schools, but the language of the government was French and the dialect in the countryside was difficult for the German troops to understand.[51] Nevertheless, almost without exception, the German regiments commented on Luxembourger hospitality. IR 62, for example, found that the Luxembourger willingly provided quarters for its troops.[52] A NCO in IR 88 reported that the German troops received a friendly reception from soldiers in the Luxembourg fortress. The weather was very hot, and the citizens set out buckets with water: one man even gave the troops water from his garden hose.[53] The German units were able to purchase food and supplies without difficulty, and German troops were forbidden to requisition anything; everything had to be paid in cash. The history of IR 6 added, as did several others, that the march was just like the annual peacetime *Kaisermanöver*.[54] IR 81 found that the Frankfurt beer wagons it was using to haul supplies couldn't ascend the hills in the Ardennes. It bought wagons in Luxembourg to replace them.[55]

When the German troops crossed the border into Belgium, the attitude of the local population changed dramatically for the worse. The conduct of the population of Belgium made it clear that the Germans were in an enemy country. Some of the inhabitants had fled; the rest regarded the German troops with sour faces.[56]

French troops entering Belgium received a warm reception, with Belgian civilians offering them food, coffee and water, as well as volunteering information concerning the enemy, most of which was inaccurate.

French Advance and Enemy Estimate after 16 August[57]

The French intelligence estimate for 16 August said that there were two German armies with a total of seven corps on the Meuse, an army with three corps in The Belgian Ardennes, and another army in Luxembourg with three corps. There was an army with four corps in Lorraine and another with three corps in Alsace, which had 'disappeared' three days ago. There were also five German corps in East Prussia. Only the Guard Reserve Corps could not be accounted for.[58]

In fact, the Germans had eight active corps along the Meuse (1st and 2nd Armies), three in the Belgian Ardennes (3rd Army), three in Luxembourg (4th Army) three behind Metz (5th Army) and six in Lorraine (6th and 7th Armies). There were only three active-army corps in East Prussia.

By 16 August the French 4th Army had reached the Meuse at Sedan and Montmédy, where it remained to the 19th. The 4th Army had been heavily reinforced, receiving the XI CA, 52 DR and 60 DR. The IX CA was being transferred to it from the 2nd Army and the Moroccan Division, newly created in Bordeaux, was also earmarked for the 4th Army. Joffre was building his decisive attack force. On 18 August the 3rd Army moved up to the Othain and remained there on the 19th.[59]

By 16 August, according to pre-war calculations, the French had assumed that the Germans would have already begun their advance. Indeed, following the skirmish at Mangiennes, the French had expected an attack to the northeast of Longuyon 15 or 16 August. In fact, by 14 August the German 1st Army had already begun crossing the Meuse, but the general advance of the German right wing did not begin until 18 August, with the German 3rd and 4th Armies advancing north westward into the Ardennes.

A German aviator captured on 17 August gave the French the complete order of battle and locations for the German 2nd Army, including the fact that it contained three reserve corps. The French therefore suspected that the German 1st Army was located near Liège. A French intelligence estimate said at 1800 on 18 August that the Germans had thirteen to fifteen corps in Belgium, with seven to eight of those north of Bastogne, six or seven of them south of Bastogne in the Ardennes. (In fact, there were 17 German corps in Belgium or entering it, 11 north of Bastogne and six south of it.) It appeared that that the German 2nd Army was crossing from the south to the north side of the Meuse. French air observation detected large bodies of German troops (probably the German 4th Army) moving northwest, but there were no German forces west of the line Houffalize–Bastogne–Libramont. The VIII AK, which had its home station in Trier, had been identified when it entered Luxembourg on 2 August. The French identified XVIII AK in the area of Bastogne and Neufchâteau. The only German unit that the French 3rd Army could identify in its sector was XVI AK, which had its home station at Metz. General Abonneau, with the 4th and 9th divisions of cavalry, was sent forward on 17 August to the area of Virton and Neufchâteau and on 18 August pushed back the German 3 KD.[60] No attempt at deep reconnaissance was made by either 4 DC or 9 DC, which stationed themselves a safe 10km in front of the French infantry corps.

The French assumed that VIII AK and XVIII AK were covering the movement of the German mass of manoeuvre from the area of Luxembourg and the rear of Metz to the northwest. The German 4th and 5th Armies were moving northwest; they would, however, turn west in two to three days.

On 19 August the French identified German units crossing to the north side of the Meuse between Liège and Huy. The French 4th Army thought that the '*masse centrale*' of the German forces was moving north-northwest, parallel to the 4th Army front. 3rd Army detected movement in estimated division strength across the Moselle to the north but did not attach any special significance to this. French cavalry and aerial reconnaissance could find no German units in the area of Longuyon–Virton–Tintigny–Arlon: there was nothing in front of the French security elements for a distance of 40–50km, which was essentially correct.[61] On 20 August, British intelligence indicated that the German 2nd Army was crossing to the left bank of the Meuse and had identified five German corps as far west as Louvain.[62]

The French 1st and 2nd Armies continued the attack in Lorraine. On 20 August they were met by a counterattack launched by the German 6th and 7th Armies.

The Battle of the Frontiers

By evening French 2nd Army had been badly beaten and was in full retreat, pulling the 1st Army with it.

At 1500 on 20 August GQG transmitted to the 4th Army its concept for the forthcoming main French offensive through the Ardennes. Joffre believed that the German army was divided into two masses, one in Lorraine, the second moving on both sides of the Meuse. The latter was the main German attack. In order to make it strong enough for a deep envelopment of the French left, the Germans had left few forces in the Ardennes. It would appear that Joffre thought that the German mass of manoeuvre, which he had originally supposed to be located east of Metz, was marching through Belgium towards the Meuse to join the German main attack. Joffre told 4th Army on 20 August that it was not yet time to attack, for the Germans were moving off to the northwest and 'the more troops that move out of the area of Arlon… and Luxembourg, the better it is for us'.[63]

The French 3rd and 4th Armies would attack towards Arlon–Neufchâteau in an echelon right formation, with the left flank of 4th Army leading. Each corps would form a lower stair-step to the right, with the lowest step being the French VI CA on the right flank of the 3rd Army. A newly formed group of reserve divisions, the Army of Lorraine, held the ground between Verdun and Toul and prepared to invest Metz. At 2030 on 20 August the GQG attack order was issued to 3rd Army. The 3rd Army's mission was to guard the right flank against advance from Metz while at the same time attacking towards Arlon. The attack order for 4th Army was issued in fragments on 20 and 21 August. The 4th Army was to conduct the main French attack to push the opposing German forces into the angle formed by the Meuse at Dinant-Namur and the Ourthe. The attack by the 4th Army would catch the left flank of the German main attack as it was moving northwest and roll it up, pushing the German forces south of the river into the Meuse and cutting the lines of communication of the German right wing.[64] Joffre's plan was similar to that of Napoleon at Austerlitz. It was not a spur-of-the-moment inspiration. Prior to the war the French had decided that an offensive in the Ardennes would cut off the lines of communication of a German offensive into Belgium.[65]

On 20 August 4 DC and 9 DC were deployed on the far left flank of the French 4th Army, where they made contact with German forces and were thrown back 15km, without being able to advance beyond Neufchâteau. They correctly identified the German 21 ID, but also the 24 ID, which was incorrect. GQG thought that the Germans were preparing to defend on the Lesse between Rochefort and Dinat, and that there were no German forces in the area of Longwy, Arlon and Virton, and probably none near the western Ardennes at all: GQG expected that the 4th and 3rd Armies would conduct a two to three-day approach march before making contact. 4th Army was instructed to avoid fatiguing the troops during the march on the 22nd.[66] 4th Army took elaborate precautions to avoid detection by the Germans, crossing the Chiers on the night of 20-21 August to avoid German aerial reconnaissance. The lead

Mobilisation, War Plans, Deployment and Approach March

elements and infantry reconnaissance forces were cautioned against becoming involved in combat prematurely.

On 20 August the French 4th Army identified the German VIII AK, apparently moving northwest towards a Meuse crossing, as well as XVIII corps, also apparently moving northwest, but not VI AK south of it. The French 3rd Army may have detected the German XVI AK north of Metz, but had failed to detect the right wing of the German 5th Army. On that day, V AK had reached Etalle, 12km west of Arlon, with XIII AK 10km southwest of Arlon, unobserved. These two corps would remain stationary on 21 August, again avoiding detection. None of the three reserve corps in the sector – V RK and VI RK southeast of Longwy, or XVIII RK behind XVIII AK – had been detected, with a total of six German active and reserve corps invisible to the French. The German left flank was not at Neufchâteau, and there was no gap in the German centre.

The French 4th Army, with six corps, was advancing on an 80km front. On 21 August the advance guard of II CA was to reach Bellefontaine, the Colonial Corps Saint-Vincent and Jamoigne, the other three corps held in place. The 4th Army intelligence summary of 1345 on 21 August did not mention any significant German forces in the area of operations. The II CA advance guard did not reach its objective, Bellefontaine, which was held only by the corps cavalry. The lead element of the corps was about 6km to the south at Meix devant Virton. The 3rd Colonial Division (DIC) did not reach Saint Vincent until after dark. XII CA had a serious engagement when the advance guard regiment of 23 DI made contact with enemy forces at Pin. On the left, the two cavalry divisions were unable to cross the Our due to enemy security detachments. The German 4th Army HQ, which had been located at Trier, was now known to be at Bastogne, further reinforcing the idea that the German mass of manoeuvre had moved northwest.

The 3rd Army order for 21 August was only issued at 0200 that morning, which did not speak well of the effectiveness of French staff work. The VI CA chief of staff had to write his own order in great haste and even so the divisions received it the same hour they were supposed to begin movement.[67] 3rd Army crossed the Chiers on 21 August, with V CA marching on Signeulx, IV CA on Virton, with VI echeloned right behind IV. 7 DC was on the far right flank, where it could contribute nothing to the 3rd Army reconnaissance effort.

The French 3rd Army intelligence estimate issued at 1500 on 21 August showed no serious German forces in sector, which was the same conclusion reached by the 4th Army intelligence estimate issued at 1345.[68] The 4th Army commander, de Langle de Cary, tried to explain the failure of his army to conduct effective reconnaissance by blaming Joffre. In order to prevent contact between infantry reconnaissance forces from developing into a premature battle, Joffre had ordered that these should remain hidden and avoid contact, an order 4th Army passed on to the corps on 20 August.[69] Reconnaissance would be conducted by the two cavalry divisions in the 4th Army sector. Langle said that had he been allowed

The Battle of the Frontiers

to conduct infantry reconnaissance, he would have detected both the German forces and the field fortifications that they had constructed.[70] This is absurd. On 20 August the French and German forces in the 4th Army sector were so far apart that they were not in the range of infantry patrols. More to the point, the French advance began on 21 August and the admonition against making contact had become moot.[71] 4th (and 3rd) Army reconnaissance had failed on 21 and 22 August, but this failure cannot be blamed on Joffre.

On 16 August GQG had placed the 3rd Group of Reserve Divisions under 3rd Army control with instructions that the reserve divisions were to defend the front between Toul and Verdun and prepare to invest Metz from the southwest.[72] These instructions were also sent directly by GQG to the Commmander of the Reserve Division Group, General Durand. Ruffey, the 3rd Army Commander, decided that the defensive mission could be accomplished with the 55 DR and 56 DR and the forces in Toul and Verdun, and instructed Durand to make 54 DR and 67 DR available to move behind the flank of VI CA during the attack. Ruffey's instructions to Durand contradicted the instructions given to Durand by GQG. The confused command situation had created an environment ripe for error.

GQG then formed the Army of Lorraine consisting of Durand's 54 DR, 55 DR, 56 DR, with 67 DR arriving and 65 DR and 71 DR en route, under General Maunoury. Its mission was the same as that of the 3rd Group of Reserve Divisions, to hold the heights of the Meuse south of Verdun and mask Metz. The GQG staff work surrounding this action was particularly poor. Confusion abounded. Maunoury did not arrive at his new headquarters until 1730 on 21 August. 3rd Army was probably not informed of the change until 22 August. Ruffey and Maunoury did not meet until 22 August. On the evening of 21 August 3rd Army headquarters thought these reserve divisions were still under its control and ordered them to guard the army right flank. The reserve divisions were actually under Maunoury's control, who was still assuming command. The reserve divisions therefore lagged far behind the 3rd Army right flank, which was now in the air.

GQG's orders for 22 August directed the 3rd and 4th Armies to continue the advance to the north an attack the enemy wherever he was found.[73] GQG reiterated that the intent was to push the Germans into the Meuse between Namur, Dinant and the Ourthe. The German left flank was identified at Neufchâteau; 4th Army was admonished not to tire out the troops with long marches before the battle, 3rd Army was ordered to march in echelon right to protect the flank of 4th Army, and to conduct careful reconnaissance as far out as possible

Later commentators, especially Grasset, would criticise this emphasis on the offensive, implying that these two armies should have operated cautiously when contact was made, *à lá* Bonnal, developing the situation slowly and conducting extensive reconnaissance before committing the main body. Aside from the fact that the Germans were fully capable of simply overrunning such a timid procedure, this critique fails to recognise that these two armies were conducting the French main attack. If the 4th and 3rd Armies were hesitant, the German right wing would either escape the French trap or defeat the Allied left wing before the careful advance of the 3rd and 4th Armies would have made themselves felt.

In the 4th Army sector on 22 August, one division of IX CA was arriving by rail movement behind the army left flank; XI CA, on the army's left, was to march to Maissin; XVII CA on Ochamps-Jehonville; XII CA Libramont-Recogne; the Colonial Corps, minus the 2nd Division, which was army reserve, on Neufchâteau; II CA on Leglise. It was evident that neither GQG nor the 4th Army headquarters thought that significant German forces were in the vicinity. On 22 August 3rd Army was to continue the advance on Arlon, with IV CA marching on St. Leger-Chatillon and Etalle, V CA Rachecourt-Meix le Tigne, and VI CA following echeloned right.[74]

German Enemy Estimate and Advance, 20 August[75]

On 20 August the OHL intelligence had identified only four French corps between Mézières and Verdun. However, there were thought to be strong French forces on the lower Chiers south to Montmédy and from there behind the Othain, especially near Spincourt. The French had only begun unloading their reserve divisions on 19 August. There was not enough information available to allow any sort of conclusion concerning French intentions nor were there indications of a French offensive.

On 20 August the lead elements of the German 4th Army had reached the Ourthe. The German 5th Army had reached Arlon on 20 August, with the VI AK to the northeast of the town, V AK at Arlon and XIII to the south. VI RK was south of XIII, XVI AK was on the army left flank just to the north of Diedenhofen and V RK was in reserve to the east of Arlon. Crown Prince Wilhelm, the commander of the 5th Army, issued orders for the 5th Army to stand fast on the 21st. The 52nd Brigade of the 26 ID, reinforced with heavy artillery (two battalions of heavy howitzers and two of 21cm mortars), was sent ahead to begin the bombardment of Longwy, which could be a hindrance to any advance to the Meuse. The artillery began firing on the afternoon of 21 August. This was a strong indicator that at this time neither OHL nor 5th Army expected a French attack across the Meuse. Rather, they anticipated that the French would defend on the Meuse and the Germans would have to make an opposed crossing.

During the course of the day on 20 August German reconnaissance brought in valuable information, especially on the 4th Army front. The French had begun to advance from the area of Hirson-Mézières, and French forces had approached to within 15km to 20km from the boundary between 4th and 5th armies. Contact with the enemy in the 4th Army sector was possible on 21 August.

The Battle of the Frontiers

IR88 at Longlier, 20 August[76]

On 20 August IR88, of the 21 ID, XVIII AK, 4th Army, had completed its day's march just before 1100 and was occupying quarters: I/88, III/88 and the MG Company in Massul, 6/88 and 7/88 in Molinfaing. As 5/88 and 8/88 were marching on Laharie, rifle fire was heard from the direction of Longlier; evidently, German patrols were making contact. Both companies deployed to attack towards the west. As they moved out, they took small arms and artillery fire. At the entrance to Longlier they rescued a German cavalry patrol that had been defending a farm against French bicycle infantry. The two companies conducted a short firefight and then assaulted the town, clearing it of the bicycle troops and Belgian *franc-tireurs*. Elements of 6/88 then began a firefight with French troops advancing from the south. At 1100 III/88 began moving to the south of Longlier and by 1200 had joined the firefight, supported by the MG company, while I/88 reinforced II/88 directly. By 1430 the French were falling back all along the line. IR88 policed the battlefield, burying 200 French KIA and carrying back 68 WIA as POWs. The regiment also took 150 unwounded POWs, all from the French 87RI, which took at least 418 total casualties (many walking wounded could have evaded capture). IR88 lost 9 OFF and 154 EM KIA and WIA, about 40 per cent of the losses of the French 87 RI.

The commander of 12/88 submitted a detailed after-action report. The other three companies of III/88 had passed through the Hochut Forest and taken up firing positions just beyond the tree line. 12/88 was responsible for left flank security. At 1300, when the company had passed through the forest, it was instructed to swing to the left of the battalion to take the enemy, who was defending about 800m to the front on the hill west of the rail line, in the flank. This required that the company move further to the south. It avoided casualties by moving in platoon bounds until it reached terrain that provided cover against French fire, which permitted it to move forward to a firing position 700m from the suspected enemy position. The French troops were still invisible, but the company began taking heavy fire and sustained casualties. Suddenly, French troops could be seen moving across a mowed field, from one hayrick to another, towards a rail line which ran halfway up the hill. 12/88 adjusted its fire onto these troops; the impacts of the German bullets, throwing up dry puffs of dirt, were clearly visible. The beaten zone of 12/88's fire was on target. But 12/88 lay in open ground also, exposed and taking casualties; the company commander ordered it to advance to the next covered position, which was the same rail line the French were heading for. 12/88 conducted squad and platoon fire and movement until it reached a ditch next to the rail line, which provided excellent cover – unless the French crossed the rail line, at which point the entire company would be enfiladed. The company commander therefore ordered his troops to assault to the other side of the rail line. The '10 or 20' surviving French troops on the other side surrendered; the hillside and ditch were filled with dead and wounded French troops, testi-

Mobilisation, War Plans, Deployment and Approach March

mony to the accuracy of 12/88 rifle fire. 12/88 had been engaged with 1/87RI and 2/87RI, which were attached to the French 9th Cavalry Division. The assistant surgeon of III/88 found 40 or 50 French shot in the open field behind the rail line.

By a fortunate circumstance, we have a report of the same battle from Corporal Albert Courouble of 2/87 RI, written on 25 August 1914. Courouble began by saying that he had not believed that their 'wonderful battalion' could have been destroyed in two hours. 2/87 RI had stopped at Hamipré, 4km from Longlier, where the firefight began. The French troops advanced singing, almost running. At 1,400m distance the officers pointed out the German line. The French ran up the last slope dividing them from the Germans, reached the top, threw themselves to the ground and sought cover at the end of a potato field. They were met by heavy and accurate fire, though the company did not take any casualties. Courouble was convinced that the Germans had dug in and were expecting them. The battalion commander said that they would wait until the Germans had fired off all their ammunition, then advance. When the German fire did stop, the battalion commander ordered the troops to move out. The entire line ran forward and was met by heavy German fire that immediately caused casualties. The French troops became confused and many panicked. After 50m they encountered a wire fence, which had only one passageway. The entire group ran through it, single file. The casualties were already serious. Exhausted, the troops threw themselves down behind whatever cover they could find. Twenty men were hit while hiding behind a single hayrick. MG fire hit twenty more men lying in the bed of a shallow stream. The German fire seemed to slacken, and the surviving French troops ran for the only available cover, the rail line. Fifteen or twenty made it. Finally, he could see the Germans. The company commander appeared, white as a shroud, shouting to the battalion commander 'Look, my company is lying out there; the poor children. What folly! What have you done? You take over; I'm going to report!' and he ran away, at which point someone yelled 'The captain is bugging out!' Now there was a complete panic; everyone wanted to flee, but there was nowhere to go. 'The instinct for self-preservation forced us forwards. Without thinking, we ran with a sergeant up the rail embankment. He and I were hit by the same bullet; he was killed, I was wounded. The enemy was 20m in front of us. I closed my eyes. When I opened them, I was surrounded by Germans who, by the way, treated me well. The battle began at 1330. By 1500 it was over.'

Corporal Muthig of 8/88 reported that his company conducted fire and movement for three hours. Then suddenly something popped out of the hay field to his front. He was not sure what it was at first, until his lieutenant, looking through field glasses, saw that the French were breaking for the rear and called out 'Rapid fire!' 'The French were wearing the same uniforms as in 1870!' Muthig said, and added cryptically 'Oh, what a life!' The French tumbled to the ground. Many of the fleeing French had no pack, no weapon, no coat and sometimes not even a hat. 'It was laughable. Suddenly the signal for the assault was blown, and everyone ran forward yelling 'Hurrah!' When they reached the first bushes, the effects of their fire were clearly visible. 'The French lay in heaps, many were groaning. It was a heartbreaking picture.' Captain Zimmer, Commander of 4/88, gave a different perspective:

> 'Now the 3rd Battalion rolled rapidly like a wave out of the shadows of the woods down to the rail embankment, a human wave full of force and will. Then I saw the leaders jump onto the embankment and the human wave followed … the rifle fire resumed, aimed at the high ground. Soon, however, they jumped down from the embankment and ran forward. The German artillery adjusted their fire onto the pine trees, and their shrapnel shells began to land in quick succession. All at once there was movement in the pines. Here and there the Red-trousers appeared and ran back towards the heights. The artillery placed its fire in front of the retreating French and our men open up rapid fire. Our major called: 'Trumpeter, sound Fix Bayonets! Assault by companies!' The trumpets sounded and the drums rattled and we ran down the hill, came to the hedge and saw before us the same embankment. The French lay behind the hedge, one man next to the other, most dead or wounded due to the flanking fire of III/88.'

This same scenario would be repeated throughout the Battle of the Frontiers. The German infantry was more mobile than the French by virtue of the simple fact that the Germans carried wire cutters and pick-axes to cut down the farmers' heavy barbed-wire fences and the French didn't. The German battalion and company commanders used the terrain far better than the French. The German commanders understood how direct fire tactically and the French didn't. The Germans moved by bounds, using fire and movement and the French didn't. The Germans fixed the French in front and turned the French right flank, gained fire superiority, pushed the French out of their position and delivered a punishing pursuit by fire. Longlier was a scenario straight out of a German regimental tactical test. IR 88 passed their test; the French 87 RI failed.

The inability of the French cavalry divisions to obtain an accurate picture of the advance of the German 4th and 5th Armies led to serious mistakes in French operational and tactical planning. Due in great part to IR 88's success at Longlier, the French 4th and 9th Cavalry Divisions were pushed out of the way of XVIII AK and were not able to determine what the Germans were doing, nor hinder their movements. The anonymous author of the FAR 25 regimental history said that the French cavalry simply would not fight. From the smallest patrol up to the level of cavalry corps, the French cavalry avoided combat and when it unexpectedly did meet German forces, such as at Longlier, the French cavalry withdrew.[77] The German cavalry was able to screen the movements of its own forces, while on 21 and 22 August it provided accurate information concerning the French advance.

Throughout the Ardennes campaign, Belgian civilians reported to the French that large bodies of German troops were in the immediate vicinity. The French commanders gave these reports little credence. Some French historians have maintained that these reports were reliable and should have been acted upon. In fact, the Belgian civilians generally exaggerated both the size of the German force and the length of time it had been in the area, and were unable to distinguish between reconnaissance units and the German main force. For example, prior to the engagement of the French 8DI with the German 9 ID at Virton, Belgian civilians told the French on 21 August that there were 1,500 Germans in the town of Ruette, when in fact there was a patrol, and that there had been that morning 1,500 Germans at Virton, when in fact it had been a platoon of seventy men.[78] It is quite likely that, living in isolated Virton, the Belgian civilians had never in their lives seen 1,500 people in the same place. Their reports were more a distraction than an asset.

5th Army Decides to Attack, 21 August[79]

August haze and thunderstorms made German aerial reconnaissance almost impossible for most of 21 August. 4th Army thought it had detected two French corps at Montmédy. The 4th Army continued its march to the northwest on 21 August. The 4th Army orders for 22 August focused on concentrating the army, in anticipation of making contact. VIII AK was to march to a point halfway between Bastogne and Givet to support the left flank corps of the 3rd Army (XIX AK). VIII RK, which was following, was to march to Bastogne. XVIII AK would move northwest, 25ID to Libin and 21ID to Libramont, in order to make room for XVIII RK, which was to join the first line of corps to the east of Neufchâteau. VI AK was to concentrate at Leglise-Mellier, prepared to march west southwest.

The problems associated with marching through the Ardennes had a negative influence on the 4th Army's situation on the day of the battle. The three front-line corps were spread out, with little mutual support. XVIII RK was able to catch up but VIII RK was a day's march to the rear.

On 21 August 5th Army cavalry did signal service, identifying strong French forces moving northeast across the entire length of the Chiers, with additional forces to the north and the probability of forces at Verdun. The 3 KD, on the army right flank, ran into the French 100RI and 126RI (XII CA) at Izel. On the army left flank, 6KD made contact with French infantry; the attached II/RIR 98 took heavy casualties. Strong French columns of all arms had been seen advancing towards Longuyon and Landres.[80] This was a critical juncture in the battle. The Germans were aware of the French advance, while the French had no idea that two German armies were a day's march to their front.

The Battle of the Frontiers

The German 5th Army HQ had also received word on 21 August that the German 6th Army had beaten the French 2nd Army in Lorraine. The 5th Army need not have any further concern for the situation for its left flank from Lorraine, and there was no possibility that it would have to attack through Metz to aid the 6th Army.

The 5th Army chief of staff, Major-General Schmidt von Knobelsdorf, thought that the French were advancing in the 5th Army sector in order to protect Longwy and Montmédy and split the German 4th and 5th Armies. In his estimate the extensive forested areas would hinder any 5th Army defence and the assault on Longwy needed to be protected. It was therefore better to attack the French in sector on 22 August than to defend. Such an attack would catch the French marching up from the valleys of the Chiers and the Othain. Schmidt communicated his intention telephonically to Lieutenant Colonel Tappen, the operations officer at OHL, at 1530.

Moltke sent a telegram that reached 5th Army HQ at 1845, denying 5th Army permission to attack. He said that it was necessary to conduct a coordinated right-wing attack which meant giving the 4th Army time come up on 5th Army's right and waiting until 2nd and 3rd Armies were ready to attack the Meuse at Namur-Givet. The enemy needed to be allowed to run into the right-wing envelopment. The best course of action was for 5th Army to defend. An advance by 5th Army would also push the right flank of the 5th Army forward, exposing it and the left flank of the 4th Army to French attack, which had to be prevented. Moltke did not need to state the other obvious objections to a 5th Army attack: if the 5th Army advanced the fortresses of Longwy and Montmédy restricted German movement; that the 5th Army attack would be frontal; that it had that it had no hope of being decisive and operationally nowhere to go – the French would surely be able to defend or delay on the multiple river lines to their rear. Any 5th Army advance would expose the Army's left flank to a counterattack from Verdun – the bugbear of German strategy for the last 15 years. Moltke's logic was impeccable.

Knobelsdorf called OHL back and said that 5th Army was already in close contact with the enemy (which was not true) and that 5th Army merely intended to defend with V AK on the right flank while attacking no further than Virton-Longuyon-Audun le Roman. Illogically, Moltke now gave his assent. The Reichsarchiv argues, unconvincingly, that Moltke thought 5th Army would only be conducting a limited offensive to gain a favourable defensive position. But regardless of the depth of the attack, it involved a full-scale battle far in front of the rest of the right wing and well before the 2nd and 3rd Armies could make contact. A battle now was so premature that even 5th Army's own reserve, V RK, was not properly positioned to fight. Moltke's concerns for the right wing of the 5th Army, as well as for 4th Army's inability to bring all of its forces into battle, proved to be amply justified.

Mobilisation, War Plans, Deployment and Approach March

On 20, 21 and 22 August, at the same time that OHL had to make momentous decisions concerning the pursuit in Lorraine and the conduct of the attack in the Ardennes, it was faced with a crisis in East Prussia. The commander of the 8th Army there, Prittwitz, and his chief of staff were relieved and on 22 August replaced by Hindenburg and Ludendorff. OHL was trying to direct and coordinate the actions of eight armies. According to the normal calculation of the maximum 'span of control' this was three or four armies too many. The attempt to subordinate 1st Army to the 2nd Army commander, and 7th Army to the 6th Army commander, were counter-productive, since the 1st and 7th Armies continually appealed the orders they received to OHL. Moltke has been criticised for weak leadership. In fact, his character was not the problem; OHL was trying to do too much, was overwhelmed, and lost control of the armies altogether.

Knobelsdorf had issued his attack order to the assembled corps chiefs of staff at 1600, but kept them at 5th Army HQ until OHL granted permission to attack. The 5th Army intent was to attack on the morning of 22 August with nearly 400,000 men on a front of over 60km in order to destroy the French forces east of the Crusnes-Chiers line, which was also the limit of advance. V AK would defend the Army right flank at Virton, with 3 KD securing its right rear. XIII AK would attack to the north of Longwy and VI RK to the south, both aiming towards Longuyon. V RK would conduct a forced march to cover VI RK's exposed left flank. XVI AK would attack towards Joppecourt.[81]

On the other hand, 5th Army reported to OHL that the V AK would extend its right as far as Tintigny in order to cover the 5th Army right flank. This was completely inaccurate; V AK would not come within 20km of Tintigny. 5th Army's behaviour had become reckless.

Knobelsdorf, the 5th Army Chief of Staff, appears to have decided that the army of the Crown Prince of Prussia was not going to defend or withdraw in the face of a French attack, but would attack under all circumstances, regardless of the intent of OHL or the posture of his own or the other right-wing armies.

When the chief of staff of V AK, Lieutenant Colonel Kessel, returned to his corps late on the night of 21 August, he pointed out to the corps commander the danger to the corps' exposed right flank and recommended that a general staff officer, Captain Wachenfeld, be sent the 25 RD (XVIII RK) headquarters to ask for support. XVIII RK denied 25 RD permission to move to cover V AK's flank, citing 4th Army orders to move to the west of Neufchâteau. This was the correct decision; had XVIII RK turned south, it would have left a gaping hole in the centre of the 4th Army. On his own initiative, Captain Wachenfeld then went to VI AK HQ, where he arrived at 0200. The corps commander, General Pritzelwitz, agreed that it was necessary for VI AK to cover the V AK right and asked 4th Army HQ for authorization to swing VI AK 90 degrees to the south. This was the first that the 4th Army commander, Duke Albrecht of Württemberg, had heard of 5th Army's intention to attack; neither OHL nor 5th Army had

The Battle of the Frontiers

notified him. In fact, OHL had last told Albrecht that V AK was marching on Tintigny, and for that reason VI AK had intended to stay at Leglise-Millier. 4th Army was poorly positioned for this unexpected fight. VIII RK was a day's march to the rear. VIII AK was far to the north, covering 3rd Army's left flank, and would not reach the battlefield until 23 August. Pulling VI AK to the south would leave the centre of the army covered only by two very strung-out corps, XVIII AK and XVIII RK. Nevertheless, with admirable military *coup d'oeuil*, at 0300, 22 August Duke Albrecht ordered VI AK to march to Tintigny.[82]

At 1100 22 August 4th Army received one last surprise. Air recon reported that as of 1015 five French divisions had reached the line St. Medard-Suxy and must soon strike the middle of the 4th Army, XVIII AK and XVIII RK, with superior force.[83]

In the Battle of the Frontiers the argument that the German General Staff had a 'genius for war' falls flat on its face. German operational planning in the Ardennes came far closer to military malpractice than to genius. Moltke demonstrated his inability to reach a decision and impose it on his subordinates. The 5th Army attack had no possible operational justification; in fact, the attack was premature and an operational liability. Even the 5th Army was not ready to fight. Until V RK arrived in the middle of the afternoon there was a corps-sized hole in 5th Army centre. VI RK's left flank was in the air and the corps was in danger of being defeated; 9ID on the 5th Army right flank was also exposed to attack by forces twice its strength. Had VI AK not plugged the hole, the Colonial Corps and II CA would have penetrated the gap between 4th and 5th Armies. 4th Army had to fight with only three of its five corps on line. Knobelsdorf was relying solely on the superiority of the German units at division level and below to bring a tactical victory. It is easy to suspect that Knobelsdorf's primary interest was in enhancing his reputation and career by winning a battle as soon as possible. Knobelsdorf had what German soldiers called *Halsweh* – a sore throat – that is, he was seeking a *Pour la mérite* to wear around his neck.

Joffre's plan had succeeded. Thanks to the 5th Army's ill-considered offensive, and in spite of the miserable performance of French reconnaissance, he had concentrated five active corps, II CA, XII CA, XVII CA and XI CA and the single best corps in his army, the Colonial Corps, against three corps of the left and centre of the 4th Army (VI AK, XVIII RK and XVIII AK), one of which was a reserve corps.

Of the thirteen armies engaged on both sides in the Battle of the Frontiers, only one would really shine, and that was Duke Albrecht's German 4th Army. Beginning at about 0300 on 22 August, the chain of command in the 4th Army was presented with completely unexpected situations that demanded faultless troop-leading procedures. At every level, from army HQ to individual companies and batteries, the 4th Army leadership rose to the occasion. As fate would have it, the German 4th Army was opposed by the French main attack. The offensive by the French 4th Army represented the sole chance that the Entente would have to win the war before American intervention in 1917. The German 4th Army was precisely the unit to ensure that this did not happen

3
Rossignol

The Destruction of the 3rd Colonial Division[1]

The Colonial Corps (CAC – *Corps d'Armée Coloniale*) was the elite unit of the French army. By law, conscripts could not be employed outside metropolitan France. To fight France's colonial wars and police its overseas empire, a volunteer force was needed in addition to the Foreign Legion and the marines. The Colonial Corps, composed entirely of long-service volunteers, was that unit. Most men enlisted for three to five years, and almost all had been under fire overseas. The Corps' reservists were mostly former Colonial Corps soldiers. The Colonial Corps was thus similar in composition and quality to the British regular army.

The Colonial Corps consisted of three divisions, home-based in Paris and the French port cities. The 3rd Colonial Division (3 DIC) had its HQ in Brest. The 1st *Regiment d'Infanterie Coloniale* (1 RIC) was stationed in Cherbourg, the 2nd (2 RIC) in Brest, making up the 1st Colonial Brigade. The 3rd Brigade was composed of the 3rd Regiment (Rochefort) and the 7th (Bordeaux). The division artillery, the 2nd *Regiment d'Artillerie Coloniale* (2 RAC) and the corps cavalry, the 3rd Regiment of *Chasseurs d'Afrique*, were stationed at Constantine in Tunisia. The division commander, General Raffenel, was 58 years old and had enjoyed a brilliant career in combat overseas, as well as commanding the 86th Infantry Brigade at St. Dié from 1911 to 1914. He had assumed command of the division on 20 June 1914.

3 DIC, 21 August

By 0500 21 August the 3 DIC had completed its night march across the Chiers to avoid German air observation and had occupied billets in towns on the north side of the river, including Miex devant Virton. Due to poor staff work, which would plague the French forces on 21 August, 3 DIC then had to move so that II CA could occupy the area. Marches and counter-marches ensued. Traffic control collapsed. Two-thirds of the 3 DIC moved in daylight and was observed by German aerial reconnaissance. The division got little sleep and no hot food. At 1600 on 21 August it began to rain. By the evening of 21 August the mass of the division was billeted near Limes, with regiments in security 5km further forward at Saint Vincent, and with the 5th Colonial Brigade on its immediate left; II CA was far to the rear on the right.

On 21 August the French 4 DC and 9 DC had been pushed back by the German XVIII AK. By that evening 9 DC had billeted in Straimont, 5km south west of the German 12ID at Neufchâteau. The Colonial Corps cavalry regiment, the 3rd Chassueurs d'Afrique, sent two patrols out the night of 21–22 August. The area was found to be 'infested with *Uhlans*'. One patrol did not return and the second turned back after taking fire at Rossignol. Neither patrol gathered any useful information.

German patrols were very active. Around midnight, a squad from the *Chasseurs d'Afrique* ran into a group of *Uhlans*, which withdrew. German patrols were seen watching the Semois crossing points. The lead element of the *Chasseurs d'Afrique*, marching to join the 3 DIC column on the morning of 22 August, had a firefight in Rossignol with a German infantry patrol and took casualties.

3 DIC, Morning, 22 August

The Colonial Corps order, issued at 1800 21 August, directed the corps to march to Neufchâteau on 22 August, with 3 DIC on the right, marching through Rossignol, and 5th Colonial Brigade on the left, marching over Suxy. Because the Corps would transit the Forest of Neufchâteau–Chiny, the Corps cavalry regiment, the 3rd *Chasseurs d'Afrique*, would follow the advance guard. 2 DIC was held back west of Montmédy as the army reserve. XII CA was on the corps left, marching on Recogne and Libramont, II CA on the right, marching on Leglise. The corps order said that the only enemy forces in the area were those of the German 3 KD and 8 KD, which had been defeated by the French cavalry on 17–18 August.

The 3 DIC order of movement was 1 RIC, 2 RIC, Division Artillery (2 RAC), 3 RIC. 7 RIC followed, guarding the corps artillery (3 RAC); the column was 15km long. The movement order for 2 RIC conveys the prevailing attitude in the division: 'Today a 33km march. Arrive at Neufchâteau at 1100 and billet. No contact expected.'

The advance guard battalion (I/1 RIC) missed its movement time at 0630 because it was in contact with German cavalry patrols. Then the rest of the regiment, which was to lead the main body, missed its movement time because the staffs did not know where the units were located and orders consequently arrived late. At 0800 the Colonial Corps was informed that II CA on the right was three hours behind 3 DIC, exposing the 3 DIC right flank.[2] This was not an auspicious beginning. Heavy fog hindered movement until it lifted at 0700, revealing a clear, sunny sky.

German VI AK, 21 August – Morning, 22 August[3]

On 21 August the VI AK marched only a short distance, but in pouring rain. French reconnaissance therefore had little opportunity to observe the corps. The majority of the troops had to bivouac in the open. The night was cool and the morning clammy with fog. The ration columns did not reach the troops, and it was not possible to obtain enough food from requisitions in the poor and sparsely populated Ardennes. The only solace for the tired, wet and hungry soldiers was that the mail came forward for the first time in the campaign.

The corps issued a warning order at 2300 on 21 August for both divisions to be ready to move on short notice. The corps movement orders reached the divisions at around 0420. Both divisions were to begin movement at 0600, 12ID on Rossignol, 11ID on Tintigny. The corps had already been informed of the presence of the French cavalry divisions about 5km to the west. Strong enemy forces were known to be approaching from Montmédy–Longuyon–Landres and contact was expected. Nevertheless, the exact location of large French units was not clear. French forces were to be attacked wherever encountered.

Meeting Engagement, 3 DIC

A reserve cavalry squadron (6/6th Dragoons) provided security immediately in front of the 3 DIC advance guard. The choice of this reserve squadron, when a regiment of professional cavalry was available (the *Chasseurs d'Afrique*), can only be explained by the fact that the division did not expect contact. As usual, French cavalry stayed close to the infantry for protection. The Dragoons were engaged about 600m south of Rossignol by dismounted German cavalry, which withdrew. The Dragoons advanced through Rossignol and then 500m into the forest of Neufchâteau where they were again engaged by cavalry. At 0740, the Dragoons were engaged for a third time 1,500m into the woods, this time by infantry, and stopped cold. The commander of 1 RIC was told that this could not be a large German force because Germans were 35km to the east of Neufchâteau, and that it was important to move quickly through the woods. He therefore committed the advanced guard battalion, II/1 RIC. The forest was deciduous, mixed with pines. The undergrowth was very thick, and only the occasional clearing offered visibility up to 50m. A wall of fire met II/1 RIC. Immediately there were heavy casualties; the commanders of the 5th, 6th and 8th companies were killed, the CO of the 7th Company wounded. A violent standing firefight developed at point-blank range. The fight became hand-to-hand at several points. The rest of 1 RIC was committed; all three 1 RIC battalion commanders were killed while standing on the road, as if on manoeuvre.

The remainder of 3 DIC was strung out on the road. 2 RIC was entering Rossignol; the divisional artillery, 2 RAC, was crossing the bridge at Breuvanne; 3 RIC was entering St. Vincent. Two battalions of 7 RIC had taken a wrong turn and were marching cross-country to regain the correct route. At the rear of the column was the corps artillery, 3 RAC.

At about 0930 it was difficult for the commander of 3 DIC, General Raffenel, to judge the seriousness of the fight; all that he could see were the wounded coming to the rear. Although all of 1 RIC was engaged in the woods, he still refused to believe that he was in contact with a major enemy force. His concern was to bring forward 3 RIC and clear the woods.

By 0800 the lead element of the 3 DIC divisional artillery, I/2 RAC, had advanced until it was at the southern entrance to Rossignol, followed by II/2 RAC, whose last vehicles were at the Breuvanne bridge and III/2 RAC, which was south of the bridge. The firefight in the woods ahead prevented 2 RAC from advancing. As would soon become clear, the ground was too soft to move the guns off the road.

At 1015 I/2 RIC was sent into the thick woods to the right of 1/1 RIC, but became completely disoriented and strayed to the right. II/2 RIC was committed on the left. It took heavy fire from an invisible enemy, probably II/IR 63 on its left flank, lost most of its officers, including the battalion commander, and by 1100 the battalion broke for the rear.

Meeting Engagement, 12 ID

At 0740 4/2nd *Uhlan*, patrolling ahead of the 12 ID advance guard down the road in the Forest of Neufchâteau/Chiny, took fire, deployed left of the of the road and returned the fire, and was quickly supported by the point company, 3/IR 157, and then all of I/157, whose commander was soon killed. In the thick woods and heavy undergrowth command and control at company and platoon levels ceased, and it became a close-range firefight conducted by squads, buddy teams and individual soldiers. In 20 minutes, II/157 and then the engineer company were committed. The troops fired off their basic load of ammunition, but the leader of the ammo section brought his wagons nearly to the front line with resupply.[4]

In the early morning of 22 August the German 3 KD had sent a reconnaissance squadron through Rossignol to Izel, where it observed the advance of 3 DIC and reported it to 12 ID. Nevertheless, 12 ID was not prepared to make contact in the Forest of Neufchâteau/Chiny. The division should have and held the artillery to the north of the woods until it secured the southern tree line and could deploy the guns south of the woods. Instead, the division conducted a standard route march. When the divisional cavalry made contact inside the woods, I/FAR 57 was stuck in the forest in march column, unable to back out of the woods and defenceless. This was not a shining hour for the 12ID's General Staff officer.

By 0900, an hour and twenty minutes after contact had been made, 12 ID engaged III/157. Casualties mounted quickly, especially among the officers; the staff officers of the 78th Infantry Brigade took the place of fallen and wounded leaders, a testimony to both their professionalism as well as the willingness of the German soldier to follow unknown officers in combat. Against practically all doctrine, the machine gun company of IR157 took part in the fight in dense woods and the suppressive MG fire was particularly effective. The 2nd *Uhlans* were deployed on foot, in the woods, to cover IR157's left flank against I/2 RIC

At 0900 the 78th Brigade Commander informed the commander of 12 ID of the intensity of the fight in front. The division commander ordered the second regiment in the march column, IR63, to swing down the road to the right towards Termes and outflank the French left. II/FAR 57 was attached to provide support. Combat patrols from the 2nd *Uhlan* scouted ahead. The 12 ID commander was not deterred from making this bold manoeuvre by his lack of information concerning the enemy to his front or by a report from an *Uhlan* patrol that a strong French force was on the road to Suxy (5th Colonial Brigade). Grasset was full of admiration for his rapid, firm decision and clear orders, which he said was the result of training received in *Kriegspiele*: 'A simple, immediate and thorough application of doctrine, nothing more'.[5]

IR 63 reached the tree line north of Termes at 1100. Patrols reported French forces on the high ground southeast of Termes and south of Rossignol. III/IR 63 deployed east of Termes, with I/63 on its left and the MG Company in support. These units drew very heavy enemy small arms fire from I/3 RIC moving north from St. Vincent. II/63 guarded the regimental rear in the direction of Rossignol and saw off a strong enemy attack (probably by II/2 RIC) 'with heavy casualties', then established contact with IR 157 and began to attack on the French left flank.[6]

Slowly but surely the German infantry increased the pressure on the French infantry and then began to gain ground, pushing 1 RIC out of the forest. By 1115 the commander of 1 RIC ordered a withdrawal to a hill some 250–400m south of the treeline. IR 157 had defeated 1 RIC, the elite regiment of the French army, a feat of arms of the first order.

Analysis of the Meeting Engagement

Grasset's explanation for the defeat of 1 RIC, I/2 RIC and II/2 RIC in the woods owes more to national stereotypes than it does to serious military analysis: according to Grasset the French, fired by the *Furia Française*, threw good sense to the winds and attempted to close *à la baïonette*, while the phlegmatic Germans stood on the defensive and did not attack until the French had exhausted themselves.[7]

It is difficult to envisage an offensive *à outrance* in the thick undergrowth of this forest: 'bayonet charges' would have been physically impossible. Nor does Grasset's analysis find support in German accounts of the battle, which clearly describe a close-range and very costly firefight in which the Germans themselves continually tried to move forward.

Charbonneau, who was a machine gun section leader in 7 RIC, went Grasset one better. He said that the 1 RIC and 2 RIC were defeated because they 'neglected security'; 'security' being a codeword in the French army for sending out numerous patrols and detachments and doing nothing until their reports were available. The Germans would never have allowed the French the luxury of such a methodical and time-consuming procedure.[8]

For both Grasset and Charbonneau, and many other French soldiers and historians, the French did not lose because – heaven forbid – the Germans had better doctrine and training. Disdain *tout court* for what the Germans did is evident in Grasset's book, which, so far as German units are concerned, is riddled with errors and is completely unreliable. This is the weakness in the French analysis; the Germans do not receive adequate consideration. In French eyes, the sole German contribution to the French defeats was that the Germans were in far greater numbers. Grasset was convinced that the Germans outnumbered the French by better than 2–1. In fact, the French were not outnumbered: the odds were generally even.

Charbonneau's initial reaction, written on 23 August, was that was that that the Germans had defeated 1 RIC and 2 RIC because the Germans had defended in trenches. These two explanations – an offensive *à outrance* against German field fortifications – neatly reinforced each other. The foolish offensive *à outrance* and the German use of field fortifications passed immediately into French newspaper accounts of the battle and from there into French military literature. The commander of the French 4th Army, Langle de Cary, cited German trenches, complete with barbed wire obstacles in 1935 in an attempt to excuse his defeat in the Battle of the Frontiers. He even repeated the old excuse that the Germans had more machine guns than the French, which was also untrue.[9] Anglophone accounts of the Battle of the Frontiers accepted the French excuses uncritically, so that modern accounts of the French defeat cite the offensive *à outrance* and the German use of field fortifications as the reason for French defeat.

Blaming the offensive *à outrance* and inferior numbers for French defeats allowed the French army, and later, its apologists, to assert that there was nothing fundamentally wrong with French army, and by no means were the Germans better soldiers. All that was necessary was to remove the pernicious influence of Grandmaison who, fittingly, had been killed in action, and the French would reassert their military superiority.[10]

After the war Charbonneau recognised that the existence of German fortifications was a 'legend' created by French front-line officers who were so stunned by the violence of the German attack and their own 'enormous losses' that they attributed the destruction of their units to the only causes that seemed plausible: trenches, machine guns and barbed wire. But by 1928, when Charbonneau's book appeared, exposing myths was futile; the belief in the existence of German trenches was invulnerable.

The Germans won this meeting engagement because IR 157's rifle fire was far superior to that of 1 RIC, because the machine gun company IR 157 engaged itself in a fight in the woods at point-blank range and that of 1 RIC followed doctrine and did not, and because the left flank of II/2 RIC was turned by two companies of II/IR 63. These factors all point to a superiority of German training, leadership and infantry tactics as the true causes of French defeat.

IR 63 and FAR 57 at Termes

III/IR 63 and I/IR 63 would conduct a day-long firefight east of Termes, first against elements of the 3 RIC coming from the south, then at 1500 against the 22 RIC coming from the southeast. IR 63's fire was consistently effective. The opposing units were pinned to the ground and took heavy casualties; I/IR 63 and III/IR 63 were able to maintain their positions in spite of being outnumbered by more than 2–1 for at least three hours.

II/FAR 57 went into action behind IR 63, oriented to the south, unaware that the French artillery was on the Rossignol road. At 1,300m range 2/2 RAC detected the German artillery and destroyed the three left flank guns of 6/FAR 57, with their crews, and mortally wounded the battery commander. This engagement forms a prominent part of every French account of the battle. It is the only success the French artillery would enjoy this day. 4/FAR 57 and 5/57 occupied superb firing positions and were able to effectively engage targets for the entire day. Initially, both batteries fired on 1 RIC and 2 RIC as they were withdrawing from the woods. 4/FAR 57 continued to fire on the French as they attempted to defend north of Rossignol, while 5/FAR 57 suppressed a French battery near St. Vincent.[11]

11 ID

The mission of German 11 ID was to march from Thibessart through Tintigny towards Bellefontaine. Delayed by the fog, 11 ID crossed the start point at 0645. At 0700 the division commander received a report from the cavalry that strong columns of infantry were marching from Jamoigne to Rossignol. At about 0900 a patrol reported to the 11 ID advanced guard commander that there was a stationary artillery column on the Rossignol–Mesnil road and that infantry could be seen south of Mesnil.

At 0915 I/FAR 6 set up 500m southwest of Harinsart and opened fire on this column. Initially the German artillery fire caused confusion but few casualties and III/2 RAC was able to join the rest of the regiment south of Rossignol. 6/FAR 6, on the other hand, took casualties from counter-battery fire. But FAR 6 moved at 1300 to an open firing position west of Ansart from which it could place direct fire on 3 RIC, the Mesnil bridge, and the French artillery; it could clearly observe its fire landing in the French battery positions. Amazingly, the regiment drew no French counter-battery fire for the rest of the day. FAR 6 batteries continually bounded forward to engage targets more effectively. Infantry-artillery coordination was good. Infantry patrols reported the excellent effect the fire of I/FAR 6 was having near the Semois bridge, and at the request of the infantry FAR 6 conducted an effective artillery preparation against Mesnil. A French battery in a hide position at Mesnil was flushed out by the German infantry attack and attempted to flee; it was destroyed by rapid fire from 1/FAR 6 and 2/FAR 6. FAR 6 continued to engage profitable targets for the entire day, even though this meant that it supported 12 ID instead of its parent unit, 11 ID: the German army prized combat effectiveness higher than form.[12]

The 3rd Colonial Brigade commander ordered 3 RIC forward to protect the divisional artillery. III/ 3 RIC was able to cross the Semois under artillery and small arms fire and, with great difficulty and taking heavy casualties, insert its troops into the artillery column. By now the bridge was practically blocked by wagons of the artillery and the divisional trains and the bodies of men and horses. Everyone in 3 DIC thought the bridge had been destroyed. The Semois was 15m wide, deep and had marshy banks; it could not be forded by vehicles and was difficult even for infantry to cross. Half of II/3 RIC was also able to cross and take up a position north of Breuvanne. When it was I/3 RIC's turn to cross, the battalion was pinned down west of Mesnil by fire from Termes. The two battalions of IR 63 had adjusted their beaten zone well: in a short time, intense German small arms fire killed three company commanders and four lieutenants and wounded the battalion commander. The 3 DIC commander was told that the Mesnil bridge was under artillery fire, but was not impressed; he did not understand that his division was cut off, and his artillery was stuck on the road and could not withdraw.

The divisional cavalry for 11 ID, 11th *Jäger zu Pferde* Regiment, had found Tintigny was free of enemy troops but reported that Bellefontaine was occupied. It dismounted to hold the Semois crossing until the advance guard arrived. At 1000 the commander of the 11 ID made the last in VI AK's series of brilliant tactical decisions. He sent the 21st Infantry Brigade through Tintigny to attack Bellefontaine. Thus, one German brigade would bottle up the French II CA for the rest of the day. The 22nd Infantry Brigade was ordered to attack St. Vincent, cutting off all but one regiment of the 3 DIC.

The Battle of the Frontiers

While IR 38 was marching out of Tintigny and the staff of the 22nd Infantry Brigade and 1/FAR 6 were entering it, these units took fire from the houses. II/FAR 42 reported that the inhabitants had barricaded a street with tipped-over wagons and a garden seat, tied together with wire. II/FAR 42 moved through the town at speed, taking inaccurate fire that managed only to wound several horses. A long street battle ensued with armed civilians, during which the German troops set fire to houses to flush out the defenders, and several civilians were killed. 1/FAR 6 fired on buildings at 500m range, including the church tower.[13]

Colonial Corps

At 0900 the commander of the French 4 DI, the lead unit of II CA, sent a situation report to his neighbour on the left, the Colonial Corps, which reached CAC at 0930. The report said that the lead brigade of the 4 DI had secured Tintigny and halted there, and that a brigade was marching on St. Marie. The rest of the corps was at Montmédy, Sommethonne, Villers-la-Loue and Miex-devant-Virton. The II CA would march on Marbehan and Léglise.[14]

One of the first things a combat-arms officer learns is that his reports must be accurate; if you say that you are at town A, you had best be at town A. Failure to scrupulously observe this rule can have horrifying consequences. Case in point: the commander of the French 4 DI assumed that his lead brigade was at Tintigny and reported that assumption to the Colonial Corps (and presumably, II CA, which would have passed this report on to 4 Army). The Colonial Corps had every reason to believe that its rear was secure and that 4 DI had a bridgehead on the north bank of the Semois, enabling it to cover the 3 DIC right. In fact, at 0900 the German IR 10 was in Tintigny, soon to be headed for Bellefontaine.

Only at 1130, when the Colonial Corps (CAC) HQ itself took fire while it was moving from St.Vincent to Tintigny, did it learn that two regiments of the 3 DIC were engaged near Rossignol. The CAC commander could make no sense of the situation at all. At 1135 he reported to 4th Army that enemy artillery firing from positions east of Mesnil (FAR 6) had been silenced (untrue), that the advance guard of 3 DIC had encountered resistance at the treeline north of Rossignol and that the Colonial Corps was continuing the attack. Illogically, he therefore requested the release of the army reserve, 2 DIC, back to the Colonial Corps. The Colonial Corps commander also took it upon himself to personally deploy a battalion – II/7 RIC – east of St.Vincent to protect the town.

By 1215 the CAC commander recognised that 3 DIC had been stopped in front while a second German column had taken the division in the right flank. His concept was for the corps to face to the east and attack. 3 DIC was to hold Orsainfaing and the woods west of Harinsart. 7 RIC was to hold St.Vincent. It is not clear whether 3 DIC ever got this order, but the question is moot; 3 DIC was dying. At this point even an attempt to break out to the south would probably have led only to a slaughter.

The 2 DIC commander, on his own initiative, at 1330 sent 22 RIC to attack towards Thermes to take some of the pressure off 3 DIC. The attack was not provided with artillery support and could advance only slowly against the fire of I/IR 63, III/63 and 4/FAR 57. By 1800 III/22 RIC and two companies of I/22 RAC had taken half the town of Termes against elements of both German battalions, when the French regimental commander ordered them to withdraw. The regiment had lost 2 OFF and 54 EM KIA and 14 OFF and 182 EM WIA.

At 1400 the Colonial Corps sent another situation report to 4th Army, which still failed to explain that 3 DIC was surrounded, and asked again for the release of the 2 DIC. 2 DIC had reached Jamoigne, its limit of advance, at 1200. The Colonial Corps would not be given control of the 2 DIC until 1700, at which time it was instructed to defend in place.

Command and Control

The superiority of German doctrine and command-and-control – embodied in *Auftragstaktik* – over the conventional French top-down system now becomes evident. 3 DIC was being destroyed: the Germans knew it, and the French divisional and corps commanders did not. French doctrine emphasised that the senior commanders could read the battlefield and fine-tune the battle. German doctrine emphasised the fog of war and the need for senior commanders to deploy their units and leave the execution to their subordinates. At brigade, divisional and corps levels the German commanders took responsibility for their level of operations. The French commanders were passive and waited for orders from higher headquarters.

Apologists for the French army contend that had the 2 DIC moved immediately, the 3 DIC might have been saved. Indeed, Grasset sees the 2 DIC pushing into Rossignol, defeating the German 12 ID and turning the day into a victory for the Colonial Corps.[15] This is unlikely. At 1230 no one in the French chain of command above the commander of the 1 RIC knew how serious the situation in the woods was, nor did the divisional or corps commander understand that 3 DIC was cut off. The Colonial Corps commander had hardly made a plausible case that he needed to be given the army reserve. Even had the French 4th Army HQ returned 2 DIC to the Colonial Corps, orders had to be issued down the chain of command, and the 2 DIC still had to move to the battlefield and defeat VI AK, all in a half a day. Moreover, by the time 2 DIC, the army reserve, would have been moving to rescue 3 DIC, the 5th Colonial Brigade on its left was in serious trouble and the 33 DI (XVII CA) was in worse condition, with no support to be had. On what basis should all of the 2 DIC have been sent to help 3 DIC?

The Battle of the Frontiers

Grasset would have us believe that the destruction of the 3 DIC was an accident; with a bit more luck the Colonial Corps would have enjoyed '*un beau success*'. Indeed, there is a school of apologists for the French army who have consistently explained French defeats at the hands of the Germans in the twentieth century in precisely this manner: this is the current explanation for the French collapse in 1940.[16] But the destruction of the 3 DIC, and the French disaster in 1940, were not accidents. These victories were the result of German doctrine and training that were far superior to those of the French.

Rossignol

The new position or 1 RIC and 2 RIC on the ground north of Rossignol suffered from the standing grain, which limited the fields of fire. Of the original 5,000 men only 900 EM and and 15 OFF remained. The real strength of the position was provided by the machine gun companies of 1 RIC and 2 RIC – twelve machine guns in all. By 1200 the German IR 157 had reached the treeline north of Rossignol opposite the two colonial regiments.

The commander of 3 DIC still did not recognise the gravity of the situation; comforted by the report that half of 3 RIC had arrived. Nevertheless, he ordered the engineer company to prepare Rossignol for defence. 3 DIC sent a report to corps at 1215. The artillery fire falling in Rossignol was ascribed on friendly fire from II CA. The report said that the position of the division was exposed, and therefore dangerous, but not desperate; the division was capable of holding out for as long as necessary.

At 1300 the commander of the division artillery said that his guns were taking small arms and MG fire and asked for permission to withdraw some 6,000m to the rear. The division commander refused. He told the artillery commander that 3 RIC, 7 RIC, the corps artillery and the 2 DIC were coming and that 3 DIC had to stand fast.

Any further German attack across the open ground north of Rossignol required artillery support. Two cannons from 1/FAR 57 were unlimbered and manhandled down the road, the crews protected by the armored gun shields. They set up just south of the treeline and at 1310 began to methodically blast the French machine guns at close range with pinpoint accuracy. Under this covering fire the first two guns were joined by the remaining 16 of I/FAR 57.[17]

The commander of 12 ID had kept 24th Infantry Brigade in reserve, in part as insurance against an attack by the 5th Colonial Brigade against his right flank and rear. Now he began piling forces onto the reeling 3 DIC. At 1200 he sent IR 62 forward to reinforce IR 157. I/IR 62 advanced on both sides of the road, with II/62 to its east and III/62 to the west. I/62 and II/62 reached the firing line by 1330, III/62 by 1430. At 1300 the commander of 12 ID sent I/IR 23 down the road to reinforce the attack; it was engaged by 1400.

Three German regiments were now intermixed on the treeline facing Rossignol, but the German army had trained for just such an eventuality, and leaders took control of the troops nearest them. Corporal Tinzmann of the 2nd *Uhlan* Regiment had advanced with the infantry to the treeline. The next task was to take Rossignol. Tinzmann wrote: 'An officer yelled 'Bound forward!' but the newly-arrived men hesitated. So I yelled 'Comrades, you're from the 62nd Regiment! Don't let the men of the 157th show you how it's done!' That helped; everyone bounded forward after the French. An NCO fell down, wounded. He said 'Take charge of my squad!' I took his sidearm and yelled: 'Squad, listen up! I'm taking charge!' The advance continued by bounds'.[18]

At 1400 the defence north of Rossignol began to crack: the close-range battle between German armored artillery pieces and French machine guns in the open could have only one outcome. Most of the French MGs were destroyed or suppressed, the Germans won fire superiority, and fragments of the French line began to move to the rear. French artillery fired in support of its infantry. I/FAR 57 switched to counter-battery fire, suppressing the French artillery. By 1500 the defence north of Rossignol had been reduced to 500 men. The German infantry advanced by bounds, in small groups and using the grain for concealment, II/IR 62 against the French right, II/23, I/62, I/157 against the centre, I/23, II/157 and III/157 against the left, supported by the machine guns of all three regiments. When the Germans were within assault distance, the French attempted a desperate counter-charge, which was cut down by German fire. The French left flank collapsed. At 1600 the French remnants streamed back to Rossignol, the German infantry in pursuit. Only six French companies remained to defend Rossignol: III/2 RIC and two companies from III/3 RIC.

This was a textbook doctrinal German infantry attack, modified to fit the terrain: the woods offered a covered and concealed approach that brought the German infantry almost to assault distance. The German artillery and machine guns provided the apogee of 'close and continuous fire support'. There were no German bayonet charges: the advance was methodical, by fire and movement, using the advantages of the terrain. Grasset even described the German advance as 'infiltration', prying the French line apart piece by piece.[19] The only thing that separated this exercise from dozens, probably hundreds of similar exercises conducted on German MTA, was that this was truly 'live-fire'.

Around 1230 the French divisional artillery on the Rossignol road began to take small arms and MG fire from the west (IR63) and then artillery fire from III/FAR 6, the heavy howitzer section. The French artillery regiment attempted to set up its guns but drew fire from 11/III/ IR 10 and the machine gun company IR 10 that had taken a position near Orsainfaing. German fire mowed down the men and horses in the ammunition columns. At 1400 the German infantry (5/IR63, 6/63, I/IR 23) began to close in on the French guns from the west, which returned fire at 1,300m range. Contrary to pre-war expectations, the fire from the vaunted 75mm did not sweep all before it. At 1500 the guns began to take fire from the east, too (IR 62, which had moved past Rossignol) at 1,000m to 1,200m range. For the German infantry this was literally a target from qualification range firing at the MTA, while Grasset said that the German infantry 'used the terrain to perfection'.[20] French artillery casualties mounted.

Command and control of the 3 DIC collapsed around 1400. The divisional staff had dispersed and the commanding general could not be found. At 1500 the CG turned up alone and carrying a rifle at the HQ of the 3 RIC south of the Semois. He was covered with mud from crossing the river. The CG told the commander of 3 RIC that the battle up front was lost. He then disappeared from the 3 RIC HQ and was not seen again alive.

12 ID continued the advance by bounds, which even Grasset says was executed 'just like in training', the troops acting on their own initiative, enveloping knots of French resistance.[21] Just as doctrine stipulated, 12 ID did not conduct a direct assault on Rossignol, but ordered a double envelopment, 78th Brigade to the west, 24th Brigade to the east; the units were so thoroughly intermixed that each brigade took charge, as far as possible, of whatever German troops that were in its sector.

FAR 21 deployed south of the treeline and gave supporting fire against Rossignol and the French artillery at 600m to 800m range, quickly expending 428 rounds. Seventy-eight French troops surrendered to 1/FAR 21, with a French captain formally handing his sword to the battery commander.[22]

Two platoons of 4/IR 23 swung wide to the west of Rossignol and were joined by 1/IR 23. This ad hoc group then assaulted a farm on the southern end of Rossignol, taking prisoners the 3 DIC staff (and with them, all the records and orders), 250 men and capturing 2 MGs. The commander of 1/23 then conducted a leader's recon to the south to see if he could find the French artillery, which he knew to be in the area. Cresting a small rise, he saw before him 2 RAC. He sent back for his company and scooped up a stray platoon from another company, deployed them just below the crest and designated zones of fire. At his whistle signal, 200 riflemen rose up and fired a salvo, followed by a deafening rapid fire. The defenceless French artillerymen quickly surrendered. As the German infantry swept though the French battery positions, the effects of German counter-battery fire were plain to see.

The battle to the north of Rossignol had stalled from mutual exhaustion. II/IR 23, the 12 ID reserve, was therefore committed straight down the road to Rossignol. It passed over the practically inert German line, which was 400m to 500m from the town. French fire was also weak. The battalion reached the edge of the village and a line of dead French soldiers, each hit in the head, testimony to German rifle marksmanship. II/23 then had to wait for the German artillery fire to lift. In the interval, II/23 was joined by an engineer company, a company from IR 62 and four more companies. An officer reported that a group of French in the centre of the town appeared ready to surrender. The commander of II/23 ordered his men to fall into formation and marched them in step into Rossignol with drums beating. When he reached the town square, in front of the church, a French general, 10 officers and about 200 men came out of a house with arms raised. The prisoners were moved into the church. Rossignol was in German hands. The French general at first refused to believe that his unit had been beaten by one division, and added, 'This bounding forward under fire is something we cannot do!' French troops, whose retreat had been cut off, streamed in from all sides and surrendered. 7/IR 23 swung around the eastern edge of the village to its southern end and captured the 3 DIC's staff baggage, including the division map store, which contained maps of Germany as far as the Rhineland and the Ruhr.[23]

About 800 or 900 French soldiers attempted to break out to the east, but were stopped by the farmer's barbed-wire fences and 11/IR 10, the flank-guard near Orsainfaing, and which took 4 OFF and 197 EM from 1 RIC and 3 RIC prisoners.[24] The 3rd Chassueurs d'Afrique, which had fruitlessly moved back and forth behind the front, unsuccessfully trying to find something useful to do, now attempted to break out to the southwest. Only one squadron escaped; the rest of the regiment was destroyed. On the other hand, 2nd *Uhlan* made no attempt to pursue or even to conduct reconnaissance, but bivouacked at the treeline north of Rossignol.[25]

St. Vincent

At 1200, 7 RIC reached St. Vincent, where the Colonial Corps commander deployed II/7 RIC east of the town personally. The Colonial Corps artillery, 3 RAC, went into position at St. Vincent, taking such effective German artillery fire in the process (probably 5/FAR 57) that its deployment was disrupted.[26]

Around 1200 the German IR 51 advanced from Tintigny through the woods east of St.Vincent with all three battalions on line, I/IR 51 in the centre, II/51 on the left and III/51 on the right. The woods concealed the regiment's approach until it was stopped at the treeline by fire from II/7 RIC, located in another woods immediately east of the town. The two units became locked in a standing firefight at ranges of 500m to 800m.

The IR 51 regimental commander had kept three companies in reserve. 7/51 was committed on the left to close a gap with IR 38. 5/51 and 9/51 were soon committed on the right to stop what was thought to be a French attack from Mesnil (it was probably elements of 3 RIC trying to withdraw). Both company commanders attacked aggressively, closely supported by 1/FAR 6, whose battery commander had led his guns forward on his own initiative. The French were surprised by the appearance of these two companies in their rear. Two squadrons of the French 6th Reserve Dragoons attempted to retreat through Mesnil and were cut down by rifle fire at 700m to 800m range: another target straight from MTA gunnery qualification. One IR 51 platoon took 80 dismounted cavalry prisoners near Mesnil, then engaged mounted French cavalry at 100m range.[27]

The Battle of the Frontiers

II/7 RIC suffered severely. The battalion commander wrote in 1915 that at the beginning of the engagement he immediately lost almost all of his officers and NCOs.[28] The commander of 5/7 RIC and two lieutenants were killed and the company reduced to 30 men; 6/7 RIC took 100 casualties, including two lieutenants KIA. The machine gun companies of both IR 51 and IR 11 were held in reserve and not committed until 1600, four hours into the engagement, so most of the 7 RIC casualties were due to German rifle fire.

IR 11 deployed at about 1400 on the right of IR 51 in order to attack the centre of French resistance, the Ferme du Chenois.[29] Together, the two regiments approached under heavy small arms and artillery fire to within 300m of the farm. Since the French MG fired 25-round strips, the IR 11 troops used the periods when the MG gunners reloaded to bound forward. II/FAR 42 supported the German advance, which nevertheless was not making much progress. Using the terrain, 5/FAR 42 approached under cover to within 200m of the Ferme du Chenois and unlimbered. The battery was manhandled into position and began point-blank rapid fire on 10/7 RIC and the remnants of 5/7 RIC and 6/7 RIC. The French fire slackened and both German regiments, with Colonel Rassow, the commander of IR 51 in front, immediately began the assault. 5/FAR 42 followed in order to provide supporting fire at 100m range against the town of St. Vincent.[30] 7 RIC left its positions and ran. I/IR 11 had swung around the French left and was able to push into the French rear unopposed. When FAR 42 lifted its fire on St. Vincent, I/IR 11 entered the town and closed off the line of retreat for II/7 RIC; the two German regiments took 400 POWs at St. Vincent. IR 51 captured two MGs as well as four automobiles containing the Colonial Corps HQ maps and records; the German 4th Army was thus informed of the complete French 4th Army deployment in detail. I/IR 11 could not continue the pursuit because the way was blocked by fire from FAR 42. 1/7 RIC and 2/7 RIC, on the 7 RIC right flank, had to fall back across a large open field. The Germans followed their doctrine and training: they pushed through to the far side of the French position, where they opened effective pursuit fire on the two luckless French companies, which were held up by the barbed wire bordering the farmer's fields. Their losses, Grasset said, were 'dreadful'.[31] The Colonial Corps artillery, 3 RAC, had begun pulling back at 1530, leaving behind 100 dead horses and 14 immobile caissons. Its fire did, however, cover the further withdrawal of 7 RIC.

The position of 5/3 RIC and 6/3 RIC on the north side of the Semois had become untenable due to German fire. The companies attempted to withdraw to the south side of the river in very dispersed formations – 5/3 RIC in an open single file – but both companies were shot to pieces; 5/3 RIC lost 1/3 of its strength. I/3 RIC, 7/3 RIC and 8/3 RIC north of the Breuvanne also suffered from the well-adjusted fire of IR 63. Elements of the German 5/IR 51, 9/51 and 7/IR 11 attacked Mesnil from the south and took 300 men from 3 RIC prisoners.

11th *Jäger zu Pferde* Regiment, which had guarded the 11 ID left flank during the battle, attempted to pursue 3 RIC and 7 RIC, but there was still fighting in St.Vincent which blocked that route, and the regiment could not find a crossing over the Semois, so it swung towards Rossignol, but got no further before dark because the roads were clogged with guns, wagons and prisoners.[32]

As darkness fell, the remnants of 3 RIC and 7 RIC were able to break contact and fall back on 2 DIC. En route, they found the body of the 3 DIC commander, General Raffenel. At St.Vincent 7 RIC was outnumbered 2–1 in infantry, but had a 3–1 advantage in artillery (48 guns against 18 German). Nevertheless, the German infantry was able to close with 7 RIC and push it out of its position. 3 RIC was practically destroyed in a standing firefight with IR 63, a further testimony to the effectiveness of German small arms fire.

The Colonial Corps situation report of 2200 said that the debris of 3 DIC had fallen back into the woods in the west. 2 DIC with the remainder of the artillery, which had already been 'sorely tried', was organising a position behind the Semois from Pin to Jamoigne and Valansart.[33]

Casualties

IR 157, the most heavily engaged German unit, lost 18 officers and 163 EM KIA, 21 OFF and 379 EM WIA. Five of the officers later died of wounds (DOW).[34] IR 51, which was also heavily engaged, lost 10 OFF and 257 EM KIA, 10 OFF and 356 EM WIA.[35] FAR 57 had provided superb artillery support, firing 5,353 rounds, losing 3 OFF and 37 EM KIA, 4 OFF and 60 EM WIA. It had 80 horses killed, most of which were replaced with captured French artillery horses.[36] The Germans took 3,843 prisoners, including two general officers, and captured 39 artillery pieces, 103 ammunition caissons and 6 MGs.

According to Grasset, 3 DIC probably lost 10,500 men KIA, WIA and POW.[37] 1 RIC, 2 RIC, 2 RAC and 3rd *Chasseurs d'Afrique* were completely destroyed. 3 RIC lost 2025 men KIA, WIA and POW. 7 RIC took 1380 casualties (including 41 OFF); most 7 RIC companies had taken 70 per cent casualties (two companies were guarding the corps airfield and had not been engaged). Both 3 RIC and 7 RIC were no longer combat-effective. 7 RIC was reformed; II/7 RIC and III/7 RIC were consolidated to form three companies, I/7 RIC formed two more.[38] The two engaged regiments of 2 DIC took 777 casualties.

An unusual characteristic of the battles in Belgium is that most fallen of both sides were buried near the battlefields. There are 1,700 French and 700 German dead buried near Rossignol. The Germans owned the battlefield and were scrupulous about honoring their dead. German military cemetreies from both world wars are in beautiful condition, cared for by the *Kriegsgräberfürsorge*, which collects donations and sponsors trips by youth groups to tend the cemetreies. Most French soldiers rest in unmarked graves.

The Battle of the Frontiers

The Colonial Corps monument, erected in 1927, is located north of Rossignol where the road enters the woods, and says that on 22 August at Rossignol-St. Vincent 4,083 soldiers from the principal units of 3 DIC 'died on the field of honour'. There were also 2,379 unknowns, perhaps 75 per cent of which were from the 3 DIC. The total number of 3 DIC dead was probably 6,000. The monument lists 877 dead from 1 RIC. Adding another 45 per cent unknowns (395) would give 1 RIC a total of 1,272 KIA. 2 RIC had a known loss of 795 dead and, including unknowns, a probable total loss of 1,145 KIA; more than 33 per cent of each regiment. Using the same procedure, 2 RAC lost 474 known KIA, 683 in total and 3rd *Chasseurs d'Afrique* 365 known, 525 total KIA, half of both units. 3 RIC lost 696 known KIA, 1002 total; 7 RIC 669 known, 963 KIA total.

Such high numbers of KIA are astounding. Moreover, there are normally upwards of three or four WIA for each KIA. Most of the soldiers in 3 DIC were killed or wounded. It is almost unbelievable, but the 7 RIC really did take 70 per cent casualties. These high casualty rates show three things. First and most important, that the 3 DIC was a superb unit. The Colonial Corps soldiers fought where they stood. Most of the Colonial Corps soldiers who were taken prisoner were surely wounded. When Grasset says that only 500 men from 1 and 2 RIC fell back into Rossignol, he was probably correct: the other 4,500 were dead or wounded in the woods or on the defensive line north of the town. Such heroism makes the Foreign Legion's famous last stand at Cameroons pale in comparison. The loss rates for 3 RIC and 7 RIC were little less. Second, almost all of these casualties were inflicted by German rifle fire. The battle in the woods north of Rossignol took place without artillery support at all, and the machine guns had a very limited field of fire. At St. Vincent, there was little German artillery support and the machine guns were held in reserve until late in the battle. Third, and a corollary to the effectiveness of German rifle fire, is that German losses were far fewer than the French. For all of the Colonial Corps' heroism and discipline, the Germans were more effective soldiers. They generated more accurate firepower and they were able to combine fire and movement. On the surface these are simple tasks, but tasks few modern armies have been able to accomplish, and none so well as the German army in 1914.

23 August

On the morning 23 August the 7 RIC was ordered by a corps general staff officer to withdraw to Limes. French command and control had broken down completely; the regiment marched without any contact with the units on the left or right, or with higher headquarters. Fortunately for 7 RIC, the only enemy contact was against German cavalry patrols.[39] The local population, which had greeted the advancing French troops with joy, gave the retreating 7 RIC a reception that was 'not very warm'.[40]

The extent of VI AK's victory was not evident on 22 August. The first orders on 23 August were for the German regiments to dig in, and work began at 0600. Patrols quickly established that the French were nowhere in the area. At 0800 IR 63 attacked towards Frenois. At 1000 I/IR 63 began to receive strong French small arms fire and was pinned down until 1500, when German artillery support finally made further advance possible. The regiment then began to take fire from French artillery. The regimental commander was killed at the head of his regiment. The regiment reached Les Bulles at dark. It was surely not evident to the regiment at the time, but it had been fighting a French rear-guard. In two days of fighting the regiment lost 26 OFF and 700 EM.[41]

IR 157 found that French prisoners carried civilian clothes in their packs, which in the strictly disciplined German army was impossible. The German troops immediately drew the conclusion that the French carried civilian clothing in order to escape captivity or to become guerrillas (*franc-tireurs*). On 23 August the regiment made contact only with *franc-tireurs*, first taking fire in Rossignol then in Les Bulles. Two armed civilians were captured in Les Bulles and executed.[42]

IR 51 spent the morning policing up the battlefield. At 1200 it moved out in pursuit, but was immediately slowed by heavy French rear-guard artillery fire, which lasted all afternoon and caused serious casualties; the regiment advanced no farther than Frenois. But French morale was crumbling: a three-man patrol on bicycles surprised 62 French in a house and took them prisoners.[43]

IR 23 moved to the area near Mesnil, where it was subjected for hours to harassment and interdiction fire by French artillery, which was generally ineffective but tested the nerve of the troops and caused the units to change position. The distinguishing characteristic of the German pursuit across France was to be the French use of rear-guard artillery. The French had a seemingly unlimited quantity of artillery ammunition, which they expended liberally against both the German advance guards and suspected German infantry assembly areas and artillery positions. The ability of such extravagant use of artillery shells to prevent pursuing forces from overtaking the defeated enemy had not been foreseen in pre-war doctrine.

Lessons Not Learned

Upon mature reflection, Charbonneau said that the defeat of the Colonial Corps was due to three factors; the superiority of German training and doctrine not being one of them.[44]

The first was the failure of French reconnaissance. On 20 August the French cavalry reported the Germans moving north of Neufchâteau–Bastogne. On 22 August the Colonial Corps cavalry, ostensibly due to fog and wooded terrain, did not detect the German advance. For these reasons, the Colonial Corps was surprised. Why German operational and tactical cavalry had detected the French advance was not explained.

Second was the failure of the French theory of the advance guard, that is, the idea that the advance guard could significantly delay the enemy, giving the main body time to manoeuvre. This theory had nothing to do with Grandmaison, but was the essential element of Bonnal's doctrine, which had been implemented in the French army in the late 1890s. Charbonneau said that the advance guard concept failed if the enemy attacked at once 'appearing like a jack-in-the-box', not only against the front but also against the flanks. Again, French defeat was not a result of superior German doctrine, but deficiencies in French tactics.

Third, Charbonneau said the offensive *à outrance* failed because it did not incorporate the concept of fire superiority. He did not acknowledge that fire superiority was the foundation of German offensive tactics. He did say that disregard of the effects of fire increased in the French army as the lessons of 1870 slipped further into the past. Indeed, to Charbonneau the offensive *à outrance* had been taught as French doctrine for most of the period before the First World War, thereby absolving Grandmaison of instituting a radical change in French tactics.

Charbonneau steadfastly maintained that pre-war French tactical doctrine and training recognised only the offensive and that his division was defeated because it attacked recklessly. But neither 3 RIC nor 7 RIC made any attempt to conduct an attack of any kind, much less a reckless offensive *à outrance*. 3 RIC was pinned down by German fire, which eventually destroyed the regiment. There was no attempt by 3 RIC to ignore the effects of enemy fire charge with the bayonet. As Charbonneau well knew, his own regiment, 7 RIC, was overrun while attempting to hold a defensive position.

Given the choice between drawing conclusions from what he had seen with his own eyes and parroting the party line, Charbonneau came down foursquare on the side of conventional wisdom. Charbonneau's cognitive dissonance is symptomatic of the subsequent problems in the discussion of the Battle of the Frontiers.

Conclusions

Six regiments of German infantry had crushed five regiments of long-service French professional infantry. Two of the French regiments had been destroyed, two others destroyed to all intents and purposes.

French operational and tactical doctrine and procedures had proven to be inferior to the German in every category. French reconnaissance had failed; German reconnaissance was effective. The German command and control functioned superbly; reports came in on a timely basis, the correct tactical decisions were made and orders issued promptly. In particular, German units supported one another across corps and division boundaries. French command and control collapsed almost immediately upon contact, beginning with a failure at all levels to report on an accurate and timely basis. German decentralization of execution led to smooth movement and prompt engagement of all combat power. The French were caught trying to fight while in march column and never succeeded in establishing a coherent front. The German artillery provided close and continual fire support; the French artillery served only as target practice for German riflemen and gunners. Repeatedly, German infantry fire inflicted crippling casualties on French units of all arms.

The Battle of Rossignol was nothing less than a complete vindication of German tactical doctrine and training. The entire system worked synergistically, producing a combination of speed of movement and firepower that overwhelmed one of the best divisions in the French army in the course of a day's combat.

4
Bellefontaine[1]

The German 22nd Brigade Blocks the French II Corps

On the evening of 21 August the French II CA was in an unenviable position. It had been assigned a very narrow front that gave it the use of only one road. To further complicate matters, its march route crossed with units from both the Colonial Corps on its left and IV CA on its right. The corps' advance was also slowed due to excessive caution while conducting local reconnaissance, the legacy of the French fascination with 'security', as well as the reluctance of the corps commander to bivouac in the woods above Meix devant Virton. The corps was supposed to have reached Bellefontaine, but that evening only the 19th *Chasseur* (cavalry) regiment was at Bellefontaine. The *Chasseurs* reported that there were 1,500 Germans digging in at Tintigny (it was in fact a weak detachment from the 4 KD). The 4 DI was 6km to the rear, west of Virton, and the 3 DI was north of Montmédy, almost at the same level as 2 DIC, the Army reserve. II CA bivouacked strung out along 25km of road.

On the morning of 22 August the II CA advance guard regiment, 120 RI, entered Bellefontaine at 0715 and began establishing a defence with II/120 in the town. III/120 was moving into the field to the right, marching in echelon right, all four companies on line. Each company was preceded by combat patrols and had two platoons forward, two in the second line 300m to the rear. The platoons marched in half platoon columns with large intervals. I/120 was echeloned behind the right flank of III/120, waiting for the rest of 4 DI to catch up.

Meanwhile, IR 10, the advance guard of the German 11 ID, had been moving since 0535, preceded by the division cavalry regiment, 11th *Jäger zu Pferde*.[2] At 0705 IR 10 received a report that strong enemy forces were marching from Jamoigne to Rossignol and left 11/IR 10 at Orsainfaing as flank guard. At 0805 the lead element entered Tintigny. 11th *Jäger zu Pferde* had seen French forces moving from

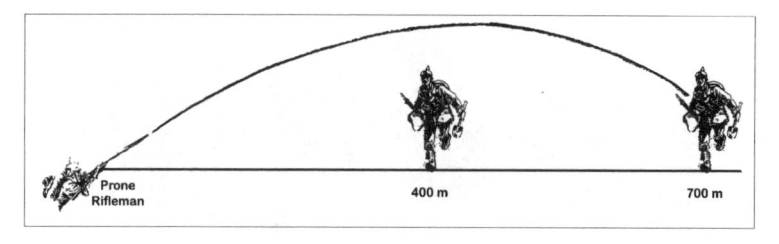

1 The trajectory of a rifle bullet at 700m range. The parabolic arc taken by the bullet causes it to pass over a target at 400m away.

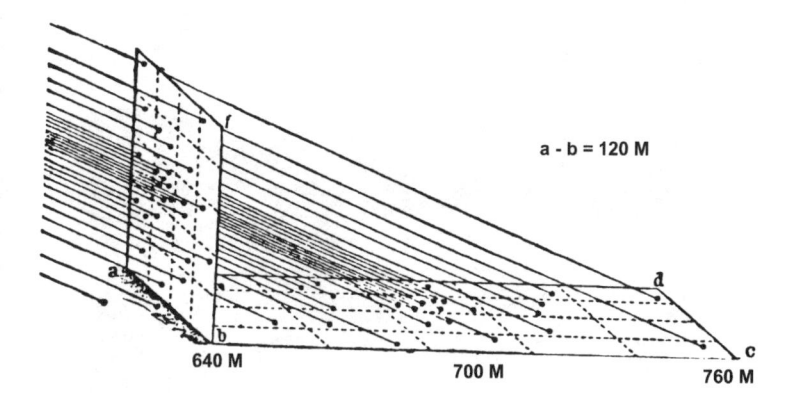

2 Beaten zone at 700m. Dispersion of a platoon's fire: with point of aim at 700m, beaten zone extends from 640m to 760m.

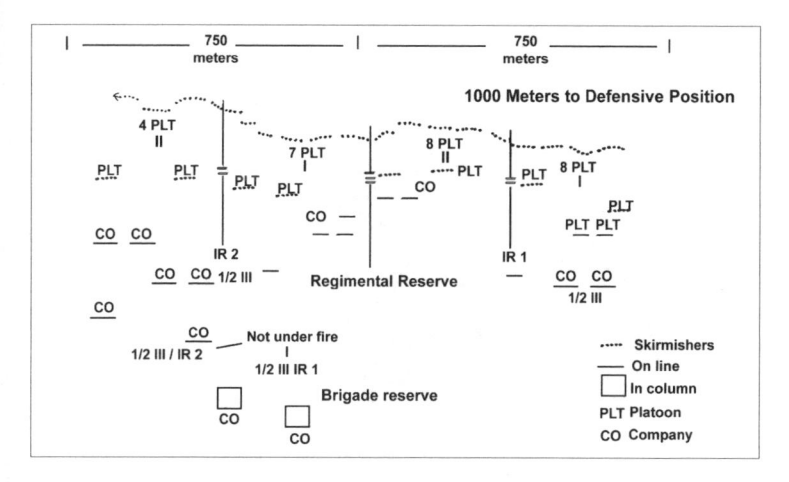

3 Breitkopf's attack: the situation at 1300. The attacker's front is 1,000m from the defensive position. The attack is making the most progress on the left.

Top: 4 Infantry in march column.

Above: 5 The infantry is advancing in successive waves with large intervals between each wave. Supporting artillery fire is landing on the objective.

Left: 6 Infantry advancing by bounds.

7 Infantry advancing by bounds. The soldier on the right has his entrenching tool ready. The two soldiers on the left provide covering fire.

8 Infantry advancing by bounds. The squad leader observes the enemy.

9 Troops on the firing line provide covering fire while other troops bound forward. In the centre of the picture is the platoon leader (with binoculars). One of the range estimators observes the company commander to the rear, while a second observes forward. Supporting artillery fire lands in front.

Top: 10 Machine-gun team advancing. In the background a second MG provides covering fire.

Above: 11 Infantry in the assault.

Left: 12 A cavalry patrol. The troopers are dispersed and alert, and armed with lance and carbine.

13 Artillery advancing under fire at a gallop.

14 Marksmanship training before the First World War.

15 A typical obstacle course before the First World War.

16 The German sFH 02 15cm heavy howitzer.

17 Marching German infantry.

18 Departure from Schwabisch Hall, 14 August 1914.

Top: 19 Baranzy from the south (French perspective).

Above: 20 Longwy. Baranzy-Signeulx Road from the south (French perspective).

Left: 21 Battery command post 5/FAR 49.

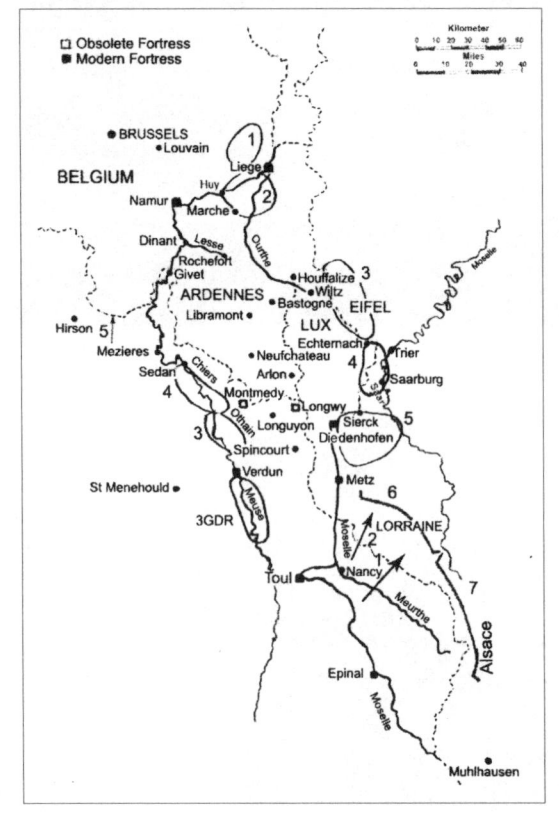

Above: 22 Longwy, Baranzy. The German XIII Corps took the town form the French 9th Division.

Left: 23 The position of the French and German Army on 17 August.

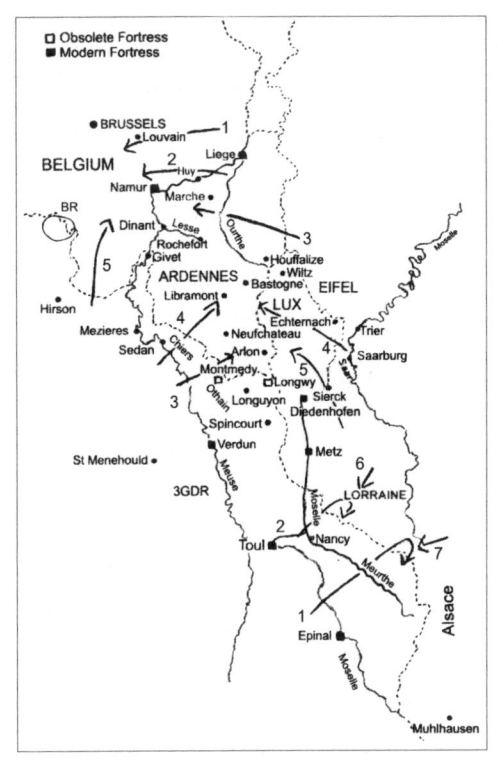

24 The movement of the French and German Army between 18–20 August.

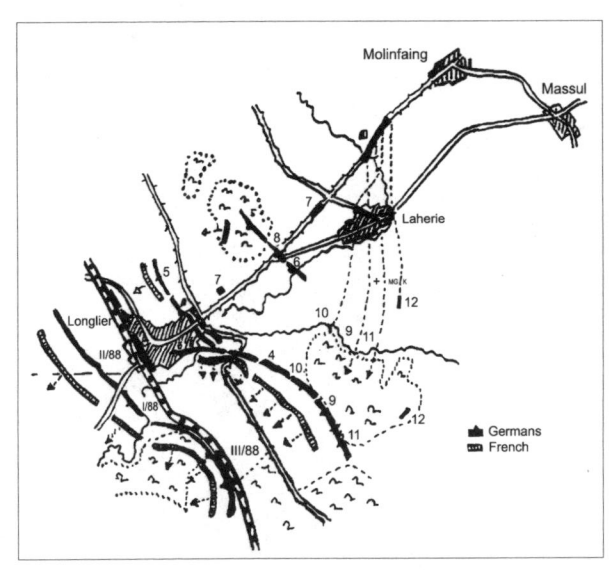

25 Longlier, 20 August 1914. Meeting engagement between the German 88th Regiment and French 87th Regiment.

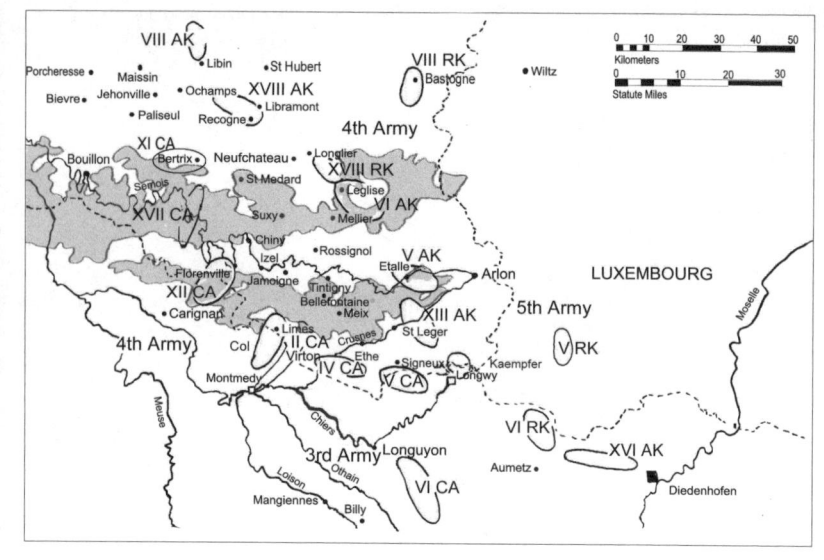

26 The position of the French and German Army on the evening 21 August.

Below: 27 The position of German VI and V Corps, French XII, Colonial and IV Corps in Rossignol, Virton.

Right: 28 German VI Corps destroys the French 3rd Colonial Division at Rossignol.

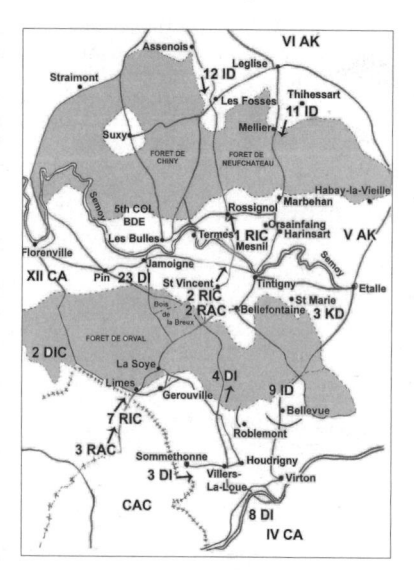

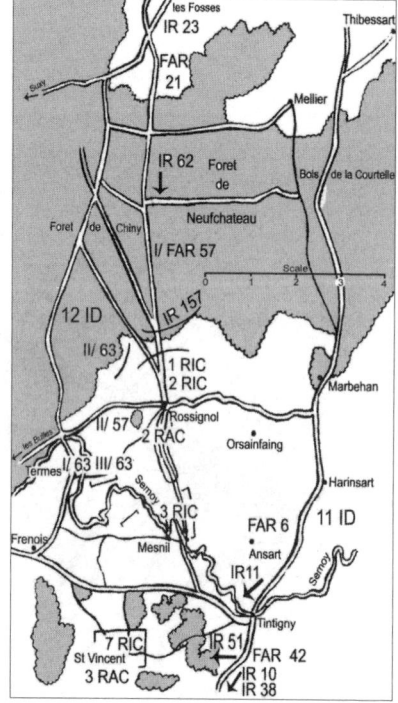

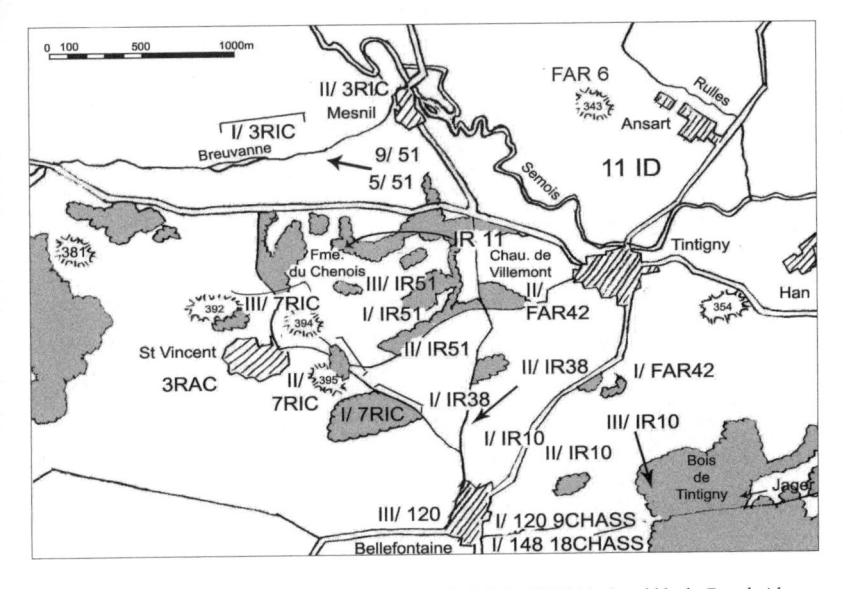

29 11th Division defeats 7th Colonial Regiment (3rd Colonial Division) and blocks French 4th Division at St Vincent, Bellefontaine.

30 German XVIII Reserve Corps destroys French 5th Colonial Brigade at Neufchateau.

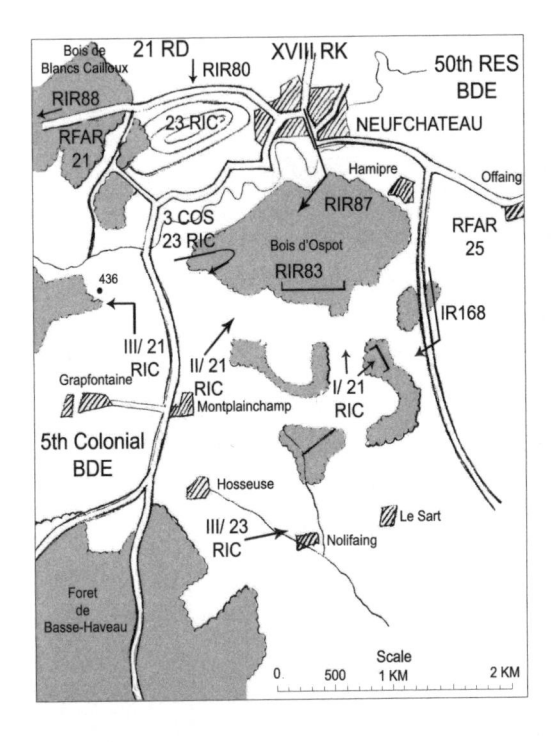

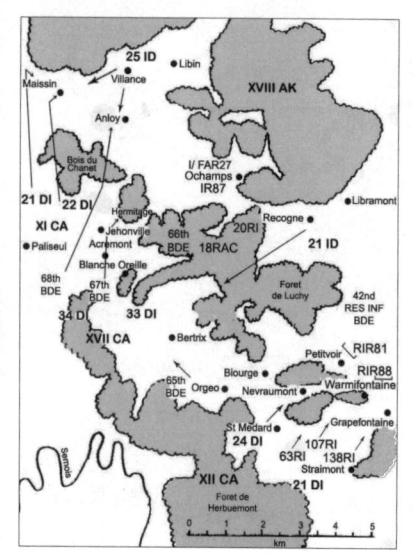

31 The German right flanks holds. The German 25th Division stops the French 21st, 22nd and 34th Divisions. The German 21st Divisions destroys the French 33rd Division. The German 81st and 88th Reserve Regiments stop the French XII Corps.

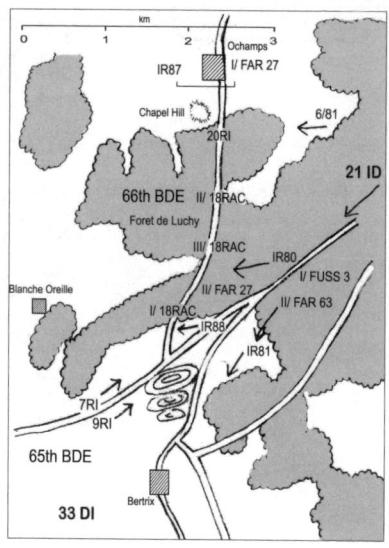

32 The German 21st Division destroys the French 33rd Division at Bertrix.

33 The German 25th Division holds off the French 21st, 22nd and 33rd Divisions at Maissin, Anloy.

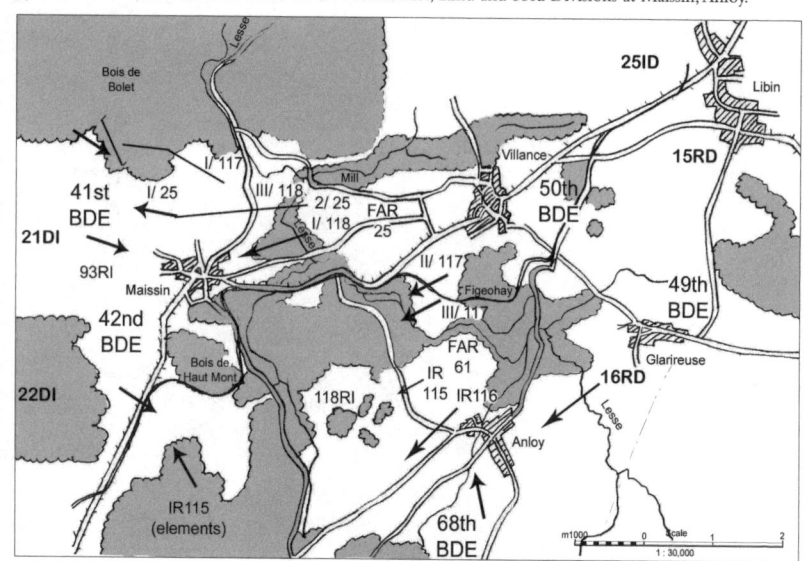

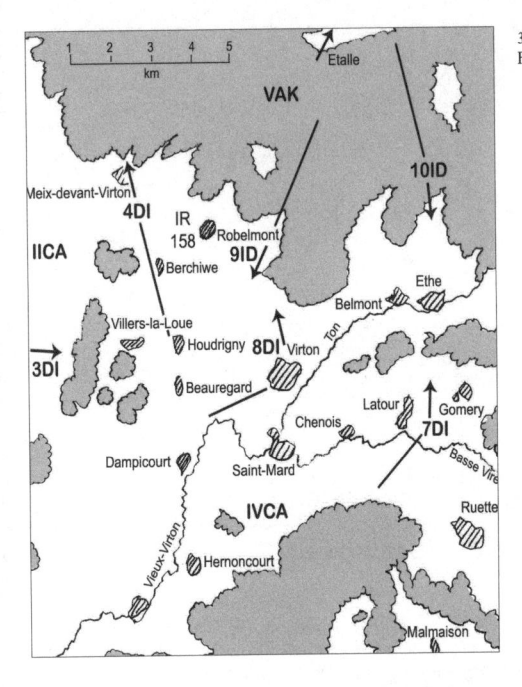

34 The German V Corps defeats the French II and IV Corps at Virton, Ethe.

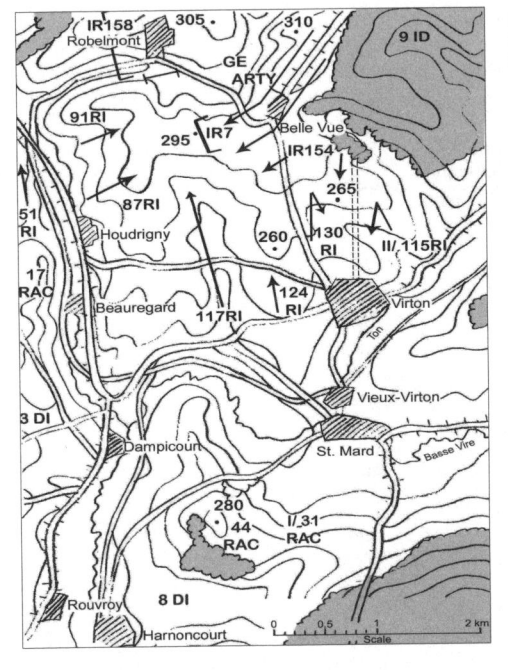

35 The German 9th Division destroys the French 8th Division and stops the French II Corps at Virton.

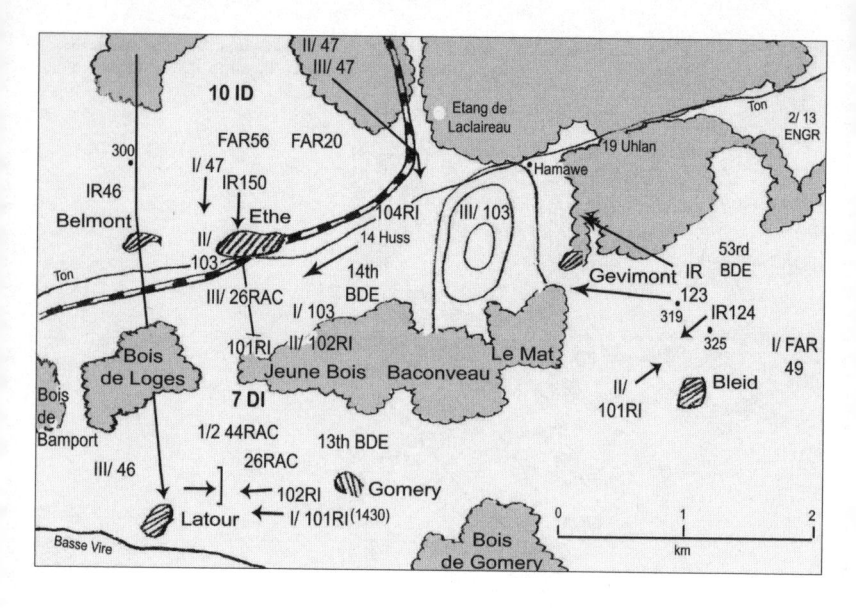

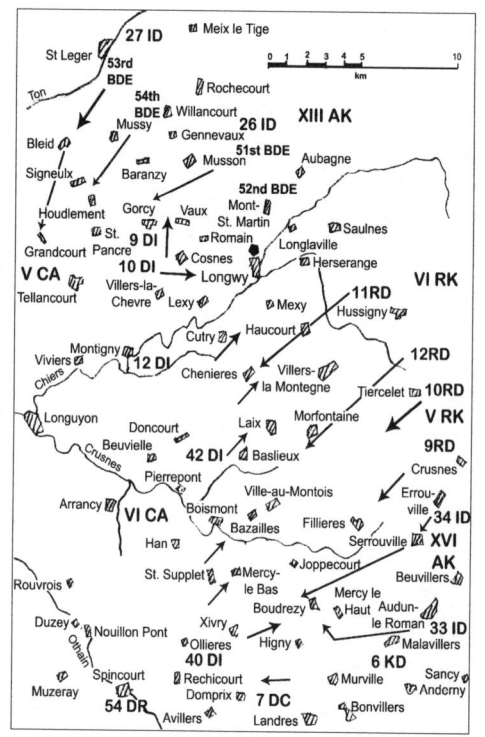

Above: 36 The German 10th Division and 53rd Brigade destroy the French 7th Division at Ethe.

Left: 37 The Battle of Longwy. The German left flank (XIII, VI Reserve, V Reserve, XVI Corps) defeats the French right flank (V Corps, VI Corps).

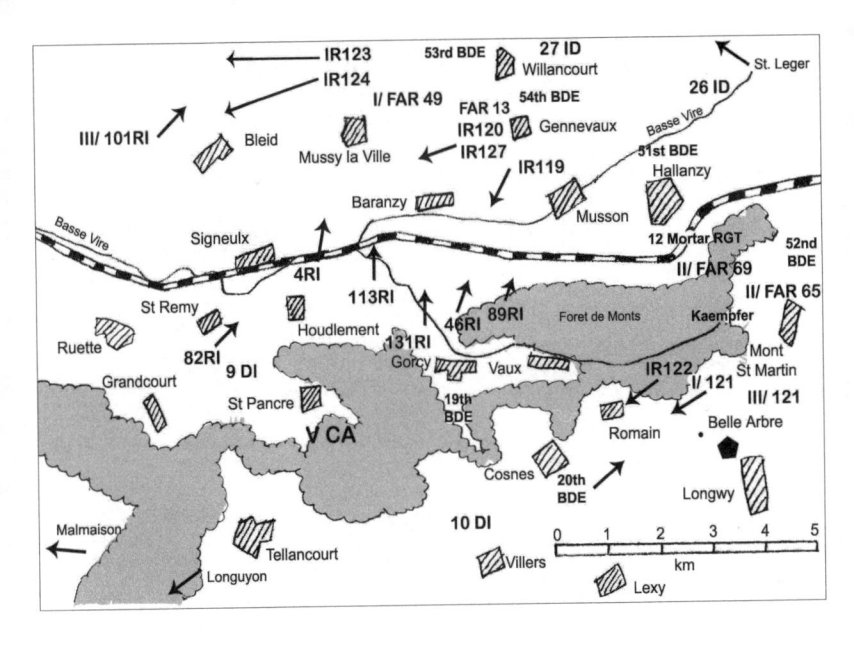

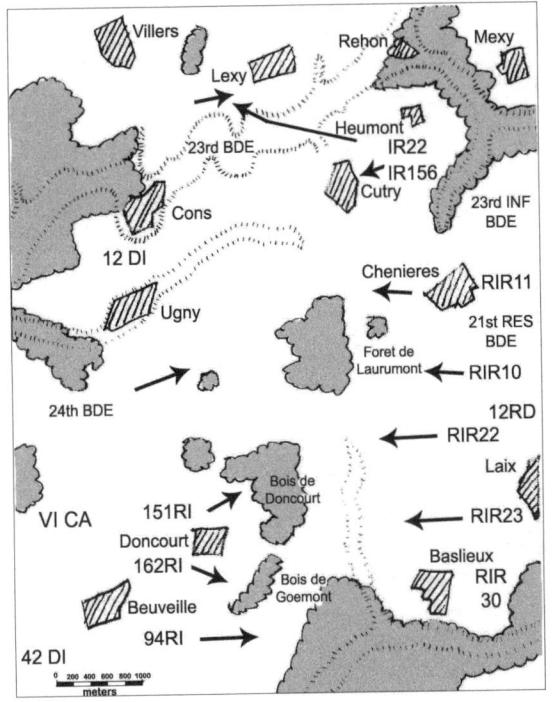

Above: 38 The Battle of Longwy. The German XIII Corps defeats the French V Corps.

Left: 39 The Battle of Longwy. The German VI Reserve Corps stops the French 12th and 42nd Divisions.

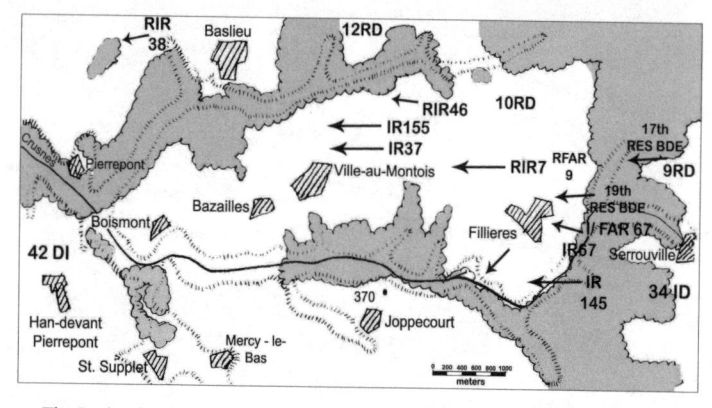

40 The Battle of Longwy. The German 34th Division and V Reserve Corps defeat the French 42nd Division.

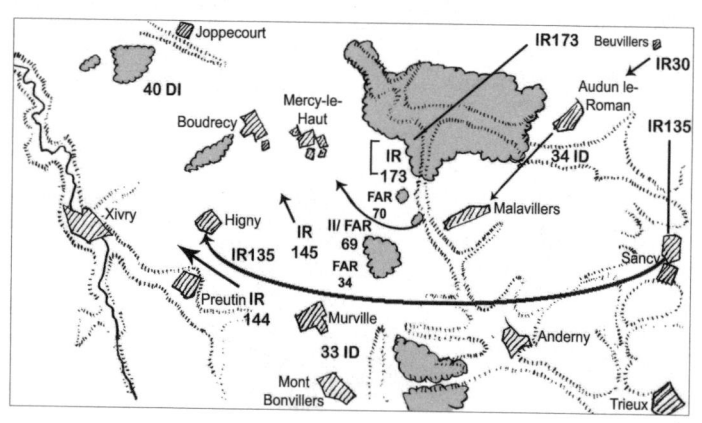

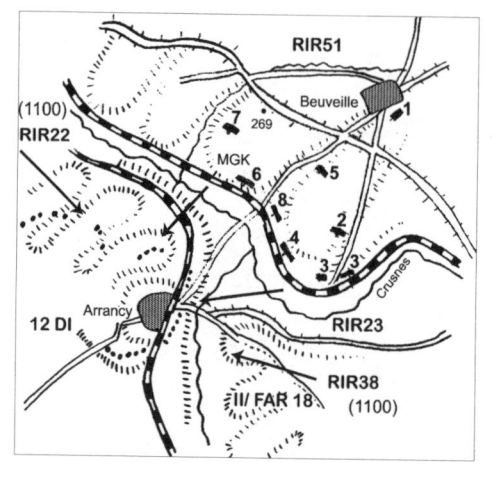

Above: 41 The Battle of Longwy. The German XVI Corps destroys the French 40th Division.

Left: 42 The German 12th Reserve Division defeats the French 12th Division at Arrancy, 24 August.

Bellefontaine

Bellefontaine north towards Tintigny; the lead battalion, III/10, therefore occupied the south edge of the town.

At 0900 the commander of 4 DI sent his report to the Colonial Corps, saying that his lead elements were at Tintigny. However, it was the German IR 10 that was assembled at Tintigny, not the French 4 DI, and shortly after 0900 IR 10 attacked, with I/10 to the west of the road to Bellefontaine (two companies forward, one in battalion reserve, one guarding 2/ FAR 6), II/10 to the east (three companies in first line, one in battalion reserve), III/10 and the MG Company in regimental reserve. By 0920 the lead skirmisher line was 700ms south of Tintigny, where it took fire from Bellefontaine and the woods to the northeast and northwest. The lead companies worked forward to within 700m of the enemy. I/10 committed its reserve company when a gap appeared in the battalion centre. 12/10 came under fire and joined II/10. 9/10 and 10/10, reinforced by a MG platoon, attacked into the Bois de Tintigny to the east. IR 10's attack in the blazing summer sun soon became more and more difficult.

The situation for French 120 RI was not rosy either. At 0945 German fire began to be effective, allowing the German infantry to advance. French casualties were heavy: II/120 lost all its company commanders, the commander of III/120 was killed by an artillery shell while mounted on his horse. Two companies of 148 RI reinforced the defence of Bellefontaine. Arriving reinforcements – elements of 18th *Chasseur* battalion at 1100, 9th *Chasseurs* at 1115, (both light infantry) then I/147 RI) were drawn to the right to protect that flank from the German advance through the Bois de Tintigny. Here six German companies from both infantry regiments and two *Jäger* battalions from the 3 KD had pushed through as far as the Bellefontaine-St. Marie road.

I/FAR 42 was brought forward shortly after 0915 to a covered position 400m south of Tintigny.[3] The limbers were sent back to Tintigny, where they took fire from the inhabitants of the town. Initially, I/FAR 42 engaged in a duel with French artillery. Observation was poor, blocked by small copses and the fact that the German positions were lower than the French, so after 30 minutes I/FAR 42 bounded forward to within 1000m of Bellefontaine. Shortly after 1100 II/FAR 42 took up positions south of the Semois and joined the fight for St. Vincent. Suddenly, firing broke out in Tintigny, and 5/42 took fire from a house 15m behind the battery. One of the members of the limber crew complained of being shot at over a considerable period from that house. The fire was answered by a round of shrapnel with a contact fuze 'to quiet down the residents'.

IR 38 was following I/FAR 42 in the march column. The lead battalions, I/38 and II/38, passed through Tintigny and deployed to the south of the town, on the west side of the road, on the right of IR 10, at 1030.[4] III/38 took fire from civilians in the houses that was heavy enough to force the battalion to clear the buildings individually. The battalion was then retained as brigade reserve. I/38 and II/38 moved forward but could gain ground only slowly. As was the case practically everywhere on 22 August 1914, the enemy was invisible. The advance was by short individual bounds or by crawling. The regimental commander committed the MG company. One platoon tried to set up with II/38 and was immediately destroyed; both officers and the entire crews killed or wounded and one gun wrecked by a direct hit from an artillery shell. The other two platoons set up successfully with I/38, though artillery fire forced frequent changes of position.

About this time, a column from the German 9 ID had placed effective fire on the road near Meix devant Virton, which was the II CA route of march. II CA was now cut in two and the last regiment of 4 DI, 91 RI, was engaged against the German 9 ID. Only eight battalions and nine batteries would be available to 4 DI for the fight at Bellefontaine.

At 1130, the French 4 DI sent another fanciful situation report to II CA: 'The advance guard has halted between Bellefontaine and Tintigny with a battalion which has pushed in the direction of march as far as Ansart'. This was wildly inaccurate: there was no mention of 120 RI being in contact; a report that French forces were at Ansart was criminally negligent. But worse was to follow. II CA reported to 4th Army that 'General Rabier [the 4 DI commander] reported that he had halted with the 1st *Chasseurs* and three-quarters of his division at Bellefontaine, Tintigny and Ansart'.[5] French reporting was now pure fiction.

By 1200 German artillery had interdicted the area between Bellefontaine and the tree line to the south, preventing any French movement in that area. The German light howitzers had also taken the north side of the village under fire.

At 1400 elements of 120 RI and 147 RI abandoned the firing line on the edge of the village and pulled back to the barricades in the centre. A resident of Bellefontaine remembered a battery of German field guns being set up at the entrance to the town and firing at the French at point-blank range.[6] After a five-hour firefight, IR 38 had begun to gain fire superiority, and at 1530 II/38 assaulted into Bellefontaine from the north while I/38 attacked from the northwest and 10/38 and 12/38 from the northeast, mixed with elements of IR 10. IR 38 found that the French had in some places abandoned the position, while in others they defended it in hand-to-hand fighting. Further advance was blocked by 'unwelcome artillery fire from both sides'. The French II/120 RI, reinforced by III/147 RI still held the centre of the village.

In Bellefontaine both sides were exhausted and the fighting died away. At 1700 the German 21st Brigade ordered a general withdrawal to St. Vincent. The French artillery observed the German movement and began an intensive barrage, although the French infantry was completely inert. The intermixed German units withdrew with great difficulty under the control of the nearest officer. The French withdrew from Bellefontaine during the night. The French 4 DI thought that it had been fighting 'the larger part of a German corps' rather than a brigade.

Bastin provides us with one of the few French histories that includes the kind of first-person accounts so common in German sources. It is noteworthy because the French soldiers complained bitterly of taking friendly artillery fire. The episcopal archives contain a statement from a Belgian *abbé* to the effect that the French 9th *Chasseurs* had fired into the French infantry in front of them, and that the French artillery had often shelled French infantry.

Bircher, relying on French sources, says the 120 RI lost 27 OFF and 901 EM KIA and WIA; 147 RI lost 8 OFF and 137 EM, 9th *Chasseurs* 9 OFF and 86 EM. In total, the French lost 527 KIA at Bellefontaine.[7] Bastin said that there were 86 French bodies lying behind a hedge along the road to Saint Marie. None were wounded: 'they had probably been killed twice rather than once.'

The German regimental histories say that IR 10 lost 12 OFF and 98 EM KIA, 12 OFF and 800 EM WIA; IR 38 lost 13 OFF and 222 EM KIA, 28 OFF and 735 EM WIA.

23 August

The 21st Infantry Brigade reoccupied the tree line north of Bellefontaine at 0700 on 23 August. The field kitchens, which had not been seen for 24 hours, arrived. Patrols discovered that the French had withdrawn. At 1100 the brigade, 'mentally exhausted from the combat of the previous day', began a slow march over St. Vincent; the dead were still lying on the battlefield, and the intensity of the fighting only now became apparent.

At 1200 FAR 42 fought an hour-long artillery duel with the French rear-guard at 3,600– 3,800m range that cost seven KIA and twenty MIA. As was often the case in the first battle, the limbers had been set up, according to regulation, 300m behind the gun line and were hit by fire intended for the guns themselves. Another tactical lesson was learned, and in the future the limbers would be deployed further to the rear.

The 21st Brigade continued the march against harassment and interdiction fire from French rear-guard artillery for the rest of the day and bivouacked at dark to the west of Jamoigne. II/FAR 42 fired another 2,000 rounds. Given the intensity of the previous days' fighting, this advance was no mean accomplishment, but, largely because of French rear-guard artillery fire, fell far short of giving the French the *coup de grace*.

Conclusions

The mission of the French II CA was to protect the right flank of the Colonial Corps. By attacking at Bellefontaine the German 21st Infantry Brigade prevented the French II CA from accomplishing that mission and thereby sealed the fate of 3 DIC. 21st Brigade could have attempted to defend south of Tintigny, which would have surrendered the initiative to the French, who might then have had the time to gather their wits. A German defence would also have surrendered

The Battle of the Frontiers

the manoeuvre space the French needed to deploy and attack. Instead, the 21st Brigade attacked. This rocked the French back on their heels and bottled them up with at Bellefontaine. The violence of the 21st Brigade attack convinced the French that they were dealing with a much larger force and left them happy that they were able to hold a part of the village, with no thought for attacking to assist 3 DIC. Once again, the German doctrinal emphasis on the offensive showed itself to be correct.

Bellefontaine also answered the question of the feasibility of an attack over open ground in the face of modern firepower: such an attack could succeed. The French occupied a good hasty defensive position. The terrain afforded the attacker only one advantage, which is that it allowed a concealed approach to about 700m from the enemy. According to German doctrine, this was an optimal distance to begin the firefight. Otherwise, there is little to choose between the flat, open terrain at the Lechfeld MTA, where Breitkopf's attack exercise was held, and the terrain north of Bellefontaine.[8] Doctrinally, for the attack to succeed, the attacker should have been significantly stronger than the defender. It is therefore remarkable that the German attack progressed even though the forces engaged were equal: a testimony to the superior combat power generated by German training, discipline, rifle marksmanship, and offensive spirit. Since the enemy was invisible, German fire created a beaten zone in the area of the French defensive position. The Germans also effectively used the advantages that the initiative accorded the attacker. The German advance on the covered and concealed avenue of approach in the Bois de Tintigny threatened the French right and fixed their attention in that direction, allowing a concentration of superior force against Bellefontaine itself.

Since the Germans had no idea of French strength and actions, the German tactics were not the result of express calculation, but of the correct application of a superior tactical doctrine. As German doctrine anticipated, the firefight was protracted and the attack across the open north of Bellefontaine proceeded only slowly, with individuals using every opportunity to move forward short distances and thus gain more effective firing positions. The firefight lasted four hours before the French defence in Bellefontaine began to crumble, and five hours into the firefight the Germans were able to assault and throw the French out of their defensive position entirely. German artillery fired on the French infantry from open positions at 1,000m range and suffered little from French counter-battery fire. Helpful as German artillery support was, the decisive factor was German rifle fire, supported by the machine guns. As German doctrine anticipated, the assaulting troops were exhausted and further advance would have required fresh forces, which were not available.

5
Neufchâteau[1]

The Destruction of the 5th Colonial Brigade

The 5th Colonial Brigade had its home station in Paris and was the elite of the elite Colonial Corps. The mission of the 5th Colonial Brigade on 22 August was to cross the Semois at 0600, on the left of the 3 DIC, and march through Suxy to Neufchâteau, arriving at about 1000 or 1100. The 5th Colonial Brigade battle group included the 21 RIC and 23 RIC, an artillery section with three batteries, two platoons of engineers and a platoon of the 6th Reserve Dragoons: 6,000 infantry, 12 75mm guns, 100 engineers and 25 cavalrymen. The order of march put the dragoons in the lead. The advanced guard consisted of two battalions of 23 RIC, followed by the main body – the remaining battalion of 23 RIC, two battalions of 21 RIC, the artillery and then the last battalion of 21 RIC, followed by support units. The column was 6km long.

A kilometre north of the brigade start point at Les Bulles the dragoons took fire from the tree line of the Fôret de Chiny. Grasset said that twenty 'very bold' dismounted German cavalrymen allowed the French cavalry skirmishers to approach, emptied their magazines at them, jumped back on their horses and fell back 300m or 400m to repeat the procedure.[2] The French became cautious and adopted painstaking counter-ambush tactics. Company-sized infantry patrols checked out the tree line around the Suxy clearing, a time-consuming process: it was already 1000. At the north end of Suxy the German cavalry again fired on the dragoons, who fell back behind the infantry. The German cavalry disappeared, the advance resumed. Upon reaching the bridge over the stream southwest of Neufchâteau, the dragoons were fired on from two isolated houses, losing three WIA and several horses. They fell back behind the infantry one last time.

The German cavalry had completely dominated the small French cavalry detachment, first forcing it to stay close to the infantry, and then pushing it behind the advanced guard. 5th Colonial Brigade reconnaissance was reduced to close foot patrols. By now the most important thing on the minds of the 5th Colonial Brigade soldiers was to get to Neufchâteau as quickly as possible, bivouac and get the cooking fires burning. When the French point element reached the isolated houses where the dragoons had taken fire, the German cavalry had disappeared. However, the sound of heavy wagons moving to the north was quite audible. The advance guard company climbed the hill to the west of Neufchâteau in time to see a German column on the road to Bertrix disappear into the woods. At 1130 they opened fire at a range of 800m on dismounted German cavalry there, spooking the horses. The Colonial advanced guard battalion had now crossed to the north of the bridge. A platoon was ordered to reconnoitre through Neufchâteau. At 1200 this element took intense fire from the Bois d'Ospont and the town itself.

French XII CA, Morning, 22 August[3]

On the morning of 22 August the XII CA was to the left and ahead of the Colonial Corps. The day's objectives were Libramont and Recogne. The advance guard began the march from the line Bertrix–Straimnont–Suxy at 0900. The 23 DI on the right marched from Izel through the Forêt de Chiny towards Straimont, the 24 DI on the left, with the corps artillery and engineers, through Florenville, Forêt de d'Herbeumont, Saint Medard and Neuvramont. Four and a half hours later, at 1330, 23 DI made contact with enemy forces southwest of Grapefontaine and Warmifontaine, which are about 4km north of the advance guard's start point at Straimont.

This slow rate of advance can perhaps be explained by the fact that XII CA had received a report on 21 August of 'large enemy columns moving from east to west in the direction of Neufchâteau … towards Arlon'. Where this report originated, and why it is not reflected in the French official history or in the Colonial Corp's intelligence estimate, is a mystery.[4] The corps war diary said that the intelligence estimate for 22 August was unchanged from the previous day. It seems as though XII CA was expecting contact and moving with extreme caution.

Since XII CA would face only weak German forces on 22 August the corps was under no pressure and was free to conduct a Bonnal-style battle, with the corps gradually collecting reports and then carefully committing forces. Initially 23 DI engaged 107 RI on the left towards Warmifontaine, 138 RI on the right towards Grapfontaine, supported by the division artillery. Then 63 RI was committed left of 107 RI. At 1430, the French artillery gained fire superiority and the French infantry was able to advance.

The German XVIII RK, Morning, 22 August

The German XVIII Reservekorps (RK) consisted of the 21 Reservedivision (RD) and the 25 RD. The 25 RD was composed of IR 168, an active-army unit, and three reserve regiments, Reserve-infanterie Regiment (RIR) 83, RIR 116 and RIR 118. The divisional artillery was provided by Reserve-feldartillerie Regiment (RFAR) 25. 21 RD was composed of RIR 80, RIR 81, RIR 87, RIR 88 and RFA 21.

At 0300 22 August the commander of the 4th Army, Duke Albrecht of Württemberg, authorised VI AK to move south to cover the right flank of V AK, and at the same time he sent orders to XVIII RK to assemble at Neufchâteau and to be prepared to move south as well.[5] On the morning of 22 August XVIII RK was marching to the southwest to its assembly area, 21 RD in the lead.

At 1000 21 RD reported to XVIII RK that a patrol from its 7th Reserve Dragoons had located enemy infantry northwest of St. Médard; the cavalry could not determine the enemy strength because it continually ran into enemy forces, and that the division was moving to the heights west of Petitvoir to support the cavalry. At 1030 the cavalry reported to 21 RD that strong enemy forces were on the heights between Ordeo and Biourge. The lead elements of 21 RD halted 2.5km west of Neufchâteau, on the heights west of Petitvoir. The wagon noises that the advance guard of the 5th Colonial Brigade heard were the last elements of the 42nd Reserve Brigade entering the Forêt de Blancs Cailloux.

At 1100 the Chief of Staff of XVIII RK sent a cavalry patrol to Straimont to determine if it was occupied. This patrol was returning when at 1140 it made contact with the French 6th Reserve Dragoons leading the 5th Colonial Brigade. The German cavalry occupied the two houses near the Neufchâteau bridge, engaged the French cavalry and then reported this contact to the commander of 21 RD, who was surprised to find French forces on his left flank. At practically the same time, the fire of the 5th Colonial Brigade against the rear of the 42nd Reserve Brigade was heard, and the commander of XVIII RK was informed by cavalry reconnaissance of the approach of a strong enemy column from Suxy to Neufchâteau.

Only at noon did Duke Albrecht, the commander of the 4th Army, receive reconnaissance reports that showed that five French divisions were marching against XVIII AK and XVIII RK.[6] A strong French attack was directed against the centre of the 4th Army. At about noon 21 RD was ordered to defend from the heights east of Petitvoir–Warmifontaine to Grapfontaine.

As the battle developed, XVIII RK gained the impression that it was engaged with a corps-sized force. Conscious of French strength, the corps acted cautiously. The 49th Reserve Brigade was kept in reserve and not committed that day. While the corps estimate overrated the strenth of the 5th Colonial Brigade, this caution was nevertheless justified, for the French XII CA was not engaged by any other German units and in a position to roll up the XVIII RK right flank.

21 RD was in a perilous position. RIR 81, the lead element of 21 RD, was massively outgunned by the French 23 DI, while RIR 88 following it was in march column in the Forêt de Blancs Cailloux. The division's situation was, however, significantly improved when RIR 80, on the west side of Neufchâteau, moved to

engage the head of the 5th Colonial Brigade and RIR87 was ordered to occupy the Bois d'Ospot, which was the decisive terrain in the corps sector. This was the sort of outstanding tactical appreciation for the terrain that wins battles.

Petitvoir: RIR81 and RIR88 Against French 23 DI

At 1100 the advance guard of the 21 RD, RIR81, made contact with French forces near Petitvoir. RIR81 was instructed to attack through Petitvoir, occupy the high ground and woods on the western side of the town and dig in.[7] I/RIR81 was to attack north of the road, II/R 81 to the south, III/ R 81 was regimental reserve. RIR81 was one of the reserve regiments that did not have a machine gun company. The brigade then designated III/R 81 as its own reserve, but RIR81 was not immediately notified.

The lead battalions soon took fire. By 1230 they had approached to within 400–500m of the enemy, at which point an intense firefight developed; enemy small arms and artillery fire became very heavy and losses mounted quickly. The regimental commander was now informed that III/R 81 had become the brigade reserve and no longer under his control. Nevertheless, the battalions continued the attack and approached to within 200m of the enemy. At 1400, due to the order of the 21 RD, the brigade instructed RIR81 to withdraw to the high ground east of Petitvoir. The RIR81 commander sent his adjutant to brigade HQ to object that the regiment was decisively engaged, could not withdraw, and to ask for the return of III/R 81. Brigade refused to release III/R 81 and renewed the order to withdraw. The regimental commander reported that this would result in the destruction of the regiment and once again asked for III/R 81. At 1500 I/R 81 began to retreat, taking 'enormous losses'. 5/ R 81, on the left, was outflanked and destroyed. The commander of 5/R 81 said that the wounding of the II/R 81 battalion commander early in the battle contributed significantly to the battalion's failure to withdraw in time. The remnants of I/R 81 and II/R 81 took heavy casualties from French artillery as they withdrew. The two battalions lost 14 OFF KIA and 466 EM KIA, MIA or POW, about 25 per cent of their strength. III/R 81 had occupied a position east of Petitvoir and helped the other two battalions break contact.

Two battalions of RIR81, with no artillery support and no machine guns, had stood up to most of the French 23 DI for four hours. Largely for this reason the French XII CA was unable to advance on 22 August. Nevertheless, this success was due entirely to the heroism of the two battalions of RIR81 and was made unnecessarily costly by a number of German command errors. The regimental commander was not kept well informed about the overall situation and therefore resisted the order to withdraw. His regiment had made good initial gains and withdrawal seemed unnecessary and costly. He apparently didn't know that the rest of the division was engaged against forces approaching from the south could not support him.

RIR 88, following RIR 81, could not reinforce RIR 81 because French forces were approaching from the south. Led by II/ R 88, the regiment turned left towards the heights north of Warmifontaine, which were taken with the assistance of III/R 88 and four batteries of artillery, but there the attack stalled. Through the afternoon the regiment held its position against 23 DI with I/R 88 and II/R 88 facing west and III/ R 88 facing south, taking casualties from well-aimed French artillery fire. At about 1700 III/R 88 was able to advance, taking 100 POWs and capturing two MGs.

23 RIC against RIR80 and RIR87

RIR 87 moved through Neufchâteau and entered the Bois d'Ospot, from which the lead elements engaged the point section of RIC 23. Captain Triol's company from 23 RIC reinforced the point and pushed the lead elements of RIR 87 back into the woods, but Tirol in turn was stopped as more troops from RIR 87 arrived. Subsequent units from RIR 87 began taking heavy and effective artillery fire that slowed their advance considerably.

The commander of I/23 RIC sent most of 4/23 RIC to occupy the hill west of Neufchâteau. These troops adopted very open formations but still took casualties from German fire originating at Neufchâteau.

The second battalion of the 5th Colonial Brigade advanced guard regiment, II/23 RIC, had stopped to rest at Grapfontaine. The commander of the advanced guard regiment brought the battalion forward to support I/23 RIC. 5/23 RIC and 7/23 moved by bounds up the hill to the north, while 6/23 and 8/23 moved and towards the Bois d'Ospot. By 1300 the rifle and MG fire from RIR 87 cut the three Colonial companies in the Bois d'Ospot to ribbons and the remnants were pushed out of the woods to the southwest.

At 1300 the lead two companies of III/ RIR 80 and a MG platoon, moving south towards the Neufchâteau–Petitvoir road, made contact with the elements of I/23 RIC and II/23 RIC on the heights west of the town. A standing firefight erupted. RIR 80 began to attack even before the order to do so arrived from brigade. I/R 80 deployed on the left of III/R 80, II/R 80 was held in reserve.

RFAR 21 fired on I/23 RIC as it advanced on the hill west of Neufchâteau at ranges of 900m down to 400m, as well as II/23 RIC as it moved north from Grapfontaine.[9]

The Germans had engaged five infantry battalions in the same amount of time that the French needed to deploy two. I/23 RIC and II/23 were now dispersed in small groups on a 2km front on the hill west of Neufchâteau, completely cut off and taking fire from three directions. Only at 1215 did the 5th Colonial Brigade commander learn that his advance guard, which he thought was engaged with cavalry, was opposed by superior forces and was in serious difficulty.

The Battle of the Frontiers

21 RIC Against RIR 83 and IR 168

At 1230 the 5th Colonial Brigade commander issued an operations order. He said that the first two battalions of 23 RIC, the advance guard, had made contact and were completely deployed. They were instructed to defend in place if they could not attack. The brigade commander's intent was to manoeuvre to the right to 'disengage' the advanced guard and allow 3 DIC to intervene on the right. He therefore committed two battalions of 21 RIC on his right flank, to take first the Bois d'Ospot and then to take the high ground east of Neufchâteau. One battalion of 21 RIC was retained as brigade reserve. III/23, which had been detached on a flank-guard mission, reducing the infantry strength of the brigade by 1/6, was marching to rejoin the brigade. Immediately after issuing his order, the 5th Colonial Brigade commander learned from a liaison officer that the 3 DIC was engaged in a violent combat at Rossignol. This did not change his estimate of the situation.

If one ever needed an example of the intellectual challenge inherent in evaluating a tactical situation in Clausewitz's fog of war, this is it. Faced with a completely unforeseen tactical situation, the 5th Colonial Brigade commander needed to immediately and accurately make his estimate of the situation and utilise his combat power in the most effective manner. The commanders of the German XVIII RK, 21 RD, 41st Reserve Infantry Brigade and so on had practiced tactical leadership on map exercises, TEWTs, staff rides and war games throughout their entire careers. In general, they made a quick, accurate estimate of the situation and issued effective tactical orders. The commander of the 5th Colonial Brigade failed his most important tactics test. He did not recognise that the enemy was far stronger than his brigade. He did not see that his advance guard was surrounded and had, for all intents and purposes, been destroyed. Retaining a battalion in reserve only ensured that the brigade's combat power would be committed in driblets. Only at 1500 did a report reach the 5th Colonial Brigade commander that convinced him of the full gravity of the situation which faced the two advance guard battalions. At that time, it was impossible for him to change anything.

At 1400 the German 25 RD was in an assembly area with the lead elements at Marbay, southeast of Neufchâteau, when it received the XVIII RK order to attack through Hamipré and Hosseuse and then turn left towards Suxy. When the lead elements reached the rail crossing east of Hamipré, a report arrived saying that the French column from Suxy had occupied Hosseuse. RIR 83[10] was committed into the Bois d'Ospot and RFAR 25[11] took up firing positions near Offaing, direction of fire Le Sart. Grasset said that RFAR 25 'covered the right flank of I/21 RIC, Montplainchamp and the Hosseuse farm with shells.'[12] IR 168 turned down the road towards Rossignol, I/IR 168 to the right of the road II/168 to the left.[13] At about 1430 German and French patrols made contact south of the Bois d'Ospot.

French artillery west of Hosseuse fired effectively at the German infantry at the Bois d'Ospot and prevented IR 168 from advancing. IR 168 also took heavy small arms and MG fire in its right flank, committing all three of its own MG

Neufchâteau

platoons here to the firefight. Three times IR 168 tried to advance; three times artillery fire prevented it from doing so.

The attack plan of commander of the 21 RIC was to advance his battalions by bounds. I/21 RIC would move on the reverse slope of the hill at Nolifaing and Le Sart. It would emplace its MG to cover the infantry as they crossed over the crest of the hill. I/21 RIC would then occupy a position where it could fire on the tree line of the Bois d'Ospot, covering the advance of II/21 RIC on its left. When both battalions were on line, they would assault the woods. There is no trace in this plan of offensive *à outrance*.

On crossing the crest of the hill at 1330, I/21 RIC observed IR 168 moving south from Offaing. The two right hand companies and a section of machine guns occupied a copse 500m north of Le Sart, facing northeast, while the two left hand companies continued the advance on the Bois d'Ospot until they reached a crest 800m from the treeline, when the Germans opened fire, which did not stop the French advance; RIR 83 was probably just arriving and had few rifles on line. When the two companies closed to within 300m from the treeline the German fire forced them to take cover and take up the firefight with German troops on the tree line.[14] At the same time (1430) the two right-flank companies were also engaged.

The 5th Brigade after-action report maintained that the Germans had been dug in. Grasset embellished this in 1923, saying that the Germans occupied several lines of trenches in the Bois d'Ospot, prepared in advance and reinforced with barbed wire.[15] The regimental history of the German RIR 83 shows that there never were any German entrenchments deeper than the skirmisher pits that the Germans – and French – dug during the firefight. The Germans began the fight just as the French had, after deploying out of march formation into skirmisher lines. Any barbed wire had been installed not by the Germans but by the landowner to fence in his livestock.

To the left of I/21 RIC the commander of II/21 RIC sent 7/21 forward to set up a base of fire near the stream to cover the advance of the rest of the battalion. 500m from the Bois d'Ospot it was met by terrific fire and lost the company commander and 60 men. About 1,000m from the tree line the other three companies deployed in a wedge formation and began to advance, but immediately met a wall of small arms fire. The battalion was able to advance 200–300m due to its high morale and effective artillery support, but in 20 minutes it was stopped cold, losing 25 per cent of its effectives. II/21 RIC then halted and attempted to return the German fire. The 5th Colonial Brigade commander then committed 12/23 between the two battalions. It met the same fate as II/23. In the middle of the firefight the artillery battery supporting 21 RIC ran out of ammunition and had to withdraw to resupply.

When III/23 RIC returned from its flank guard mission, the 5th Colonial Brigade sent the brigade reserve, III/21 RIC, towards the Neufchâteau stream to reinforce 23 RIC on the hill west of Neufchâteau. III/21 took such heavy fire from I/ RFAR 21, located only 1,000m away near the Blancs Cailloux, as well as infantry and MG fire, that it never even reached the stream. It found cover on Hill 436, about 700m north of Grapfontaine.

When RIR 83 tried to advance south of the Bois d'Ospot it was initially stopped by French MG fire. However, in spite of the French MG and artillery fire, the concentric attack of the German regiments IR 168 and RIR 83 began to gain ground against I/21 RIC. The Germans also continued to pile on forces; at 1500 RIR 116 moved down the road to Rossignol and then swung right, with the 4th Dragoon regiment on its left flank, to attack the 5th Colonial Brigade right flank.[16] At the same time, IR 168 took Hamipre and advanced on Hosseuse farm. The 5th Colonial Brigade commander committed his last reserve, 10/23 RIC and 11/ 23, to shore up his right flank. Both companies were engaged by rifle, MG and artillery fire while advancing and then were destroyed in close combat. At around 1600, bands of Colonial soldiers, becoming ever more numerous, began to head from the north to the rear. The 5th Colonial Brigade was beginning to collapse. Repeated assaults drove the French infantry back slowly; a French counterattack from Nolifaing was broken up by the massed machine guns of IR 168 and RIR 83. The Germans advanced as far as Nolifaing and Le Sart and dug in there. The commander of the 21 RIC was wounded and captured.

The Destruction of 23 RIC

The two battalions of 23 RIC on the high ground west of Neufchâteau were pounded all afternoon by fire from RIR 80, RIR 87 and I/RFAR 21. German troops pushed into the French rear and reached the bridge over the creek, cutting off French retreat. That they could do so in spite of the fact that III/21 RIC was supposedly in the immediate vicinity at Hill 436 would indicate that III/21 was no longer in the fight. The commander of 23 RIC was killed while trying to move his CP out of the front line. At around 1600 the Germans began to assault the French position. The remaining soldiers of the two Colonial battalions are killed or captured: with the Germans in their rear in strength, few succeeded in escaping. By 1700 the two battalions had been destroyed and the Germans occupied the high ground.

Withdrawal of 5th Colonial Brigade

None of the battalions of the 5th Colonial Brigade were combat-effective any longer, and two had been destroyed entirely. Only the French artillery allowed the remnants of the Colonial infantry to assemble in the Forêt de Basse-Heveau. III/21 withdrew mostly intact to Grapfontaine and then to the forest, as did the remnants of 12/23. German artillery shelled 9/23 RIC in Montplainchamp, causing 30 KIA. I/21 and II/21 pulled back in squad-sized groups. At 2000, still without orders, but having heard that XII CA was withdrawing, the 5th Colonial Brigade commander ordered the remnants the brigade to withdraw to Suzy. At 2400, 2 DIC informed 5th Colonial Brigade of the defeat of 3 DIC. On the morning of 23 August the brigade continued the withdrawal to Les Bulles. This put the Brigade well out of the range of German pursuit.

The Colonial Corps situation report of 2200 said that the 5th Colonial Brigade had taken Neufchâteau, then was 'crushed' by strong enemy forces and the brigade's debris had fallen back to Jamoigne.[17]

XII CA

The corps' left-hand division, 24 DI, took Nevraumont, a minor village south of Rossart, without serious opposition and advanced to the north when the advance guard regiment, 108 RI, was attacked. It was reinforced by three more battalions and an artillery group and 'was able to maintain its position'. 50 RI and a battalion of 126 RI were committed successively and by 1400 the enemy had been pushed back into the woods north of Nevraumont. There was no German artillery fire. The division bivouacked 1km north of Nevraumont at 1900, about 6km south of its objective. 24 DI was almost certainly engaged only with elements of I/RIR 81. Only seven of the division's 12 battalions had been committed. 23 DI stopped at Warmifontaine; apparently only the division advance guard and the artillery had been in contact. At 1800 the French 4th Army reported that XII CA had 'collided' with German troops and that the fight had been particularly serious at Nevraumont, which had been taken.[18]

When the 5th Colonial Brigade commander realised that his brigade was in serious trouble, probably after 1500, he asked 23 DI on his left for assistance. The war diary of XII CA says that the commander of the 23 DI sent three battalions to assist the 5th Colonial Brigade and the 23 DI commander asked that he be given control of the corps artillery. This was granted 'immediately' at 1640. None of these units reached the 5th Colonial Brigade area of operations. The XII CA war diary says that the withdrawal of the 5th Colonial Brigade forced 23 DI to fall back 1000m.[19]

The day's objectives for XII CA were Libramont and Recogne. In spite of the fact that the corps was at most opposed by two German reserve regiments, one of which had no machine guns or artillery support, the corps stopped 5km short of its objectives. Sixteen of the corps' twenty-four battalions had been engaged. One of the principal reasons for the French defeat in the Ardennes was the inertia of the XII CA, while the 5th Colonial Brigade was being destroyed on its right and 33 DI being destroyed on its left. Once again, the French problem was not the offensive *à outrance*; in this case the problem was a lack of interest in advancing at all.

The Battle of the Frontiers

Franc-tireurs in Neufchâteau

During the afternoon the XVIII RK rear echelon passed through Neufchâteau and drew fire from the houses. A regular street fight developed; the liaison officer of RFAR 25 had to take part in the battle with his pistol.[20] The ammunition columns of RFAR 21 also took fire from the houses.[21] Several armed civilians were caught in the act and executed. The firing continued into the night, requiring the commitment of a battalion of RIR 118, which conducted a house-to-house search and burned down several of those from which it received fire. The civilian population was finally put under guard in two farms.[22]

Casualties

The Colonial Corps monument says that 21 RIC lost 780 KIA and 23 RIC 760 KIA: 23 RIC, which had been surrounded, lost fewer KIA than 21 RIC, which had engaged the Germans frontally. Twenty-five per cent of the Colonial Corps unknowns probably belonged to 5th Brigade (600 men), for a total of 2,140 KIA. The killer on this battlefield was German firepower *tout court*, but especially German rifle. The Germans took six OFF and 463 EM POW. The 5th Colonial Brigade therefore lost 2,600 men killed or captured out of 5,000 infantry engaged (the engineers and artillery did not take any casualties).[23] There is no record of the number of wounded, but if there had been as many WIA as KIA, then barely 1,000 infantrymen of the original force were still fit for duty.

XVIII RK, in combat against both XII CA and the 5th Colonial Brigade, lost approximately 2,400 men KIA, WIA and MIA.[24] Some 480 of these belonged to RIR 81 in its fight against XII CA. XVIII RK took about 1,800 casualties fighting the 5th Colonial Brigade, which suffered about 3,600 casualties.

Conclusions

The 5th Colonial Brigade put up a magnificent fight. Elements of 21 RIC held out for five hours while surrounded by forces more than twice as strong in infantry and which were supported by artillery firing at point-blank range. The 5th Colonial Brigade's 12 artillery pieces were opposed by 48 guns of the XVIII RK, but still provided excellent supporting fire. Nevertheless, it cannot be gainsaid that two brigades of German reserve infantry destroyed the elite brigade of the French army. Even more impressive was the performance of the RIR 81 and RIR 88, which, assisted by the failure of the XII CA corps and division commanders to act aggressively, stopped the French XII CA.

Grasset said that the clearest advantage that the Germans possessed was German tactical doctrine: 'the brutal and immediate engagement of the totality of available forces'. 'Brutal' was a widely used French code word to emphasise the absence of German military sophistication.[25] Brutal or not, German doctrine and troop

Neufchâteau

leading were superior to the French in practically every regard: in reconnaissance, in reporting and in tactical leadership at the corps, divisions and brigade levels.

The asymmetrical nature of these battles threw some factors into stark relief. The French XII CA could employ its entire corps artillery against two German reserve regiments supported by three batteries of artillery: the French artillery was assured of fire superiority from the start. Nevertheless, it took four hours to defeat two battalions of RIR 81, and RIR 88 was able to hold its positions. Similarly, I/RFAR 21 was unable to destroy two battalions of the 5th Colonial Brigade, although it could engage them almost unhindered at point-black range. Infantry in a hasty defensive position clearly posed a difficult target for artillery. Infantry trying to move in the open was another matter. I/RFAR 21 hammered III/21 RIC so badly when it tried to advance north from Grapfontaine that the battalion was rendered combat-ineffective in minutes.

Once again, there were no bayonet charges, nor were French tactics characterised by the offensive *à outrance*. Whether it was the 23 DI attacking RIR 81, RIR 80 and RIR 87 attacking 23 RIC or the IR 168 and RIR 83 in a meeting engagement with 21 RIC, there was first an hours-long firefight, and only after one side had gained fire superiority was it able to advance. Once secured, fire superiority did allow the attacker to advance without prohibitive casualties, push back the defender and seize the objective.

In these battles, fire superiority was a function of numerical superiority. But if the defender occupied terrain that offered cover and concealment it could conduct an effective firefight against superior forces. Even though 23 DI probably deployed seven or eight times the firepower as the two battalions of RIR 81, RIR 81 held brushy and wooded terrain on high ground and it took the French three hours to gain fire superiority. The German units attacking 23 RIC probably had five times the firepower of 23 RIC, but the experienced colonial soldiers were able to find cover on the rocky and brushy high ground west of Neufchâteau and the firefight went on for four hours. Together IR 168 and RIR 83 had three to four times the firepower of 21 RIC, but were able to advance only slowly. However, II/21 RIC was caught in the open and smashed by German small arms fire at once. In terms of discipline, morale and combat effectiveness, the reservists of the XVIII RK stood in no way behind the elite professional soldiers of the 5th Colonial Brigade.

6
Bertrix

The Destruction of the 33rd Division D'Infanterie[1]

On 21 August the German 25 ID (XVIII AK) had marched northwest from Recogne to Libin, the 21 ID, which was following it, marched from Longlier to Libramont. On 21 August the German 4th Army's orders for the following day called for XVIII AK to essentially hold in place, with 25 ID moving a short distance to Anloy. 21 ID was to remain at Libramont, while occupying Ochamps with IR 87 and I/FAR 27. This would leave the corps in an isolated position, separated from VIII AK on its right by 15km of woodland. The gap with the VI AK on the left would be filled by XVIII RK. When, at 0400 22 August, 4th Army issued its order for VI AK to move south to assist V AK, there was no change in the orders for XVIII AK At 0930, however, AOK 4 grew concerned for the 10km gap from Neufchâteau and Recogne between XVIII AK and XVIIII RK, and ordered XVIII AK to march south to Bertrix–Orgeo. But at 1130 XVIII AK received reports of strong French forces advancing on a broad front, from Offange to Bertrix. Sending the corps south would expose its right flank. XVIII AK therefore ordered the corps to march on a wide front, 25 ID to Anloy and Jehonville, 21 ID to Bertrix. Duke Albrecht was unhappy with this deviation from his orders, and arrived personally at XVIII AK HQ at 1300 to try to divert XVIII AK troops towards XVIII RK. The XVIII AK commander stood by his decision, which in the event was correct. Nevertheless the German 4th Army was very fortunate that the French XII CA did not advance into the gap between XVIII AK and XVIII RK and rupture the entire army front.[2]

The French XVII CA consisted of the 33 DI (65th and 66th Brigades) and the 34 DI (67th and 68th Brigades) and was marching north in three brigade columns. On the right, the 66th Brigade moved on Ochamps. In the middle, 67th Brigade marched to Blanche Oreille. On the left, the 68th Brigade marched towards

Offange. The advanced guards were to cross the line Paliseul–Bertrix–Straimont at 0900. 65th Brigade, on the far right, was to march to and hold St. Médard until relieved by the advanced guard of XII CA, which was a half a day's march to the rear. The advance guard of XII CA arrived at 1130 and the 65th Brigade marched to Blanche Oreille as the corps reserve.

Throughout the morning of 22 August the German 21 ID received reports from the 6th *Uhlan* Regiment of contact with French cavalry at Bertrix, Acremeont and Jéhonville. At 1200 a report arrived of a strong French column of all arms marching from Bertrix to the north in the direction of Ochamps. At 1245 an order arrived from XVIII AK instructing 21 ID to advance towards Bertrix. In spite of continual and accurate reporting by 6th *Uhlan*, XVIII AK was not aware that the French were in the Fôret de Luchy in strength, and the corps commander expected to make contact on the west side of the Fôret de Luchy.

On the other hand, the war diary for the French XVII CA said that reconnaissance discovered only German cavalry at Sart, Jehonville and Herbuemont. As 33 DI was entering the Fôret de Luchy the attached cavalry squadron reported that the woods were free of enemy troops. The French tactical cavalry reconnaissance was once again operating much too close to the infantry, in this case barely one terrain feature to the front. It had failed to detect a regiment of German infantry and three batteries of artillery entering Ochamps less than 1km from the northern tree line of the Fôret de Luchy.

Ochamps

The French 66th Brigade column was led through the Fôret de Luchy by 20 RI, followed by II/18 *régiment d'artillerie de campagne* (RAC) and then III/18 RAC and I/18. Two platoons of 11 RI were inserted between each of the artillery batteries; a standard precaution to guard artillery when transiting wooded areas. At 1335, as the lead element of 12/20 RI left the Fôret de Luchy in the direction of Ochamps it was met by light small arms and then artillery fire. 12/20 took Chapel Hill 600ms north of the treeline from the German security forces stationed there. 20 RI immediately deployed but was prevented from moving past the tree line by German artillery fire.

Detachment von der Esch (IR 87 and I/FAR 27) was occupying an assembly area 1km east of Ochamps, that is, the detachment had not dug defensive positions, when at about 1400 the detachment commander received a report from his security elements that French forces were advancing from the Fôret de Luchy and had taken the Chapel Hill. I/FAR 27 immediately opened fire to great effect. II/IR 87 advanced through Ochamps and took up a position on the southwest side of the town, with I/IR 87 to its rear. Then III/IR 87 was ordered to take the Chapel Hill. In spite of the fact that the French had no artillery support, the attack made little progress and took significant casualties. Only when the French began

The Battle of the Frontiers

to feel the pressure of German forces in their rear did IR87 take the Chapel Hill, where the attack was stopped on order.

6/IR81 had been providing security for the corps howitzer batallion. The howitzers found a firing position west of Recogne, releasing 6/81. The company commander encountered the brigade commander, who ordered him to take his company down the Ochamps road to assist IR87. After moving some ways through the thick undergrowth of the Fôret de Luchy, 6/81 began taking fire; the enemy was invisible. The company commander ordered the troops to fix bayonets and charge. They soon came to a large opening in the forest and saw, 150m to their front, what the company commander estimated was one intact and deployed French company and scattered squads in company strength. The French had been caught completely by surprise. 6/81 immediately opened rapid fire which killed or wounded a great many French troops; the rest surrendered. The French troops belonged to 2/11 RI and elements of 10 RI and 25 RI. The German company captured a major, two captains, three lieutenants as well as 56–58 men. In order to prevent the troops from being fired upon by wounded or 'dead' French troops, the commander of 6/81 ordered his company to sweep the battlefield, breaking the French rifles and 'waking up' French soldiers feigning death. The company then continued the attack through the woods. After a short firefight the remaining French to its front fled and at 2030 6/81 reached Ochamps. The company had lost 4 EM KIA and 2 OFF and 12 EM WIA.

Fôret de Luchy

French 33 DI Artillery

On hearing that 20 RI had made serious contact, the 33 DI artillery commander tried to turn his batteries around to get them out of the woods. However, the last artillery section, I/18 RA, had just entered the woods north of Bertrix when it came under attack by German infantry. Dead horses and immobile vehicles quickly blocked the forest road. The 33 DI artillery was now trapped on the road in the woods. The artillery commander therefore ordered the guns to unlimber and fight it out where they stood.

German IR88

At 1120 the lead regiment of the German 21 ID, IR88, was ordered to move towards Bertrix. The regimental order of march was I/88, II/88, MG Company, III/88.[3] II/FAR 27 marched intermixed with the second regiment, IR81, the next unit was FAR 63 (light howitzer), followed by the corps heavy howitzer battalion, I/Foot Artillery 3, and last IR80.

On I/88's left the woods had given way to fields covered with high gorse when the point element drew fire from that direction. The point company deployed to the left of the road. At the same time, the last company of I/88 drew small arms fire from the right and deployed in that direction. The battalion adjutant detected French artillery to the right, and the centre two companies of I/88 moved to attack them. Their advance was delayed by the gorse, which gave the French artillery enough time to unlimber and cover these two companies with fire.

The rest of the regiment went down on one knee to the right side of the road. The II/88 commander reacted immediately, ordering his battalion to attack to the right of I/88, 7/88 on the left, 5/88 in the middle, 8/88 on the right, 7/88 in reserve. The left two companies, moving through gorse, took small arms, MG and then artillery fire. The 21 ID commander personally ordered III/88 to attack to the right of II/88, which was soon joined by the MG company, whose commander engaged his unit on his own initiative.

The attack of II/88 was quickly halted by fire from an invisible enemy. 5/88 lost all its officers. I/88 suffered severely from French artillery fire. At 1430 II/FAR 27 raced pell-mell down the road and deployed behind IR 88. The guns advanced over ditches in the gorse field, unlimbered immediately behind the infantry and engaged targets, mostly French infantry, initially at 1,000–1,200m, then at close and finally at point-blank range, often directed onto targets by the infantry. 6/ FAR 27 fired off its basic load of ammunition in 30 minutes, which was immediately resupplied. As II/FAR 27 began to run out of ammunition, I/FAR 63 pulled up, greeted by cheers from the infantry.[4] All organisation was lost, the artillery units were intermixed, and each gun acted on its own initiative. The German artillery began to suppress the French artillery and gain fire superiority. The commander of 4/FAR 27, who had climbed up on his observation ladder, saw French limbers suddenly appear at a fast trot directly in front of his battery in order to move the French guns there. He ordered rapid fire at 400m range and smashed the guns, limbers and teams. In a similar manner, 6/FAR 27 destroyed a second French battery.

The commander of 21 ID ordered IR 81 to swing to the south of IR 88 in order to attack to IR 88's left. The following regiment, IR 80, was to attack to IR 88's right. With the artillery fire support, II/88 and III/88 were able to advance and both battalion commanders committed their reserve companies. At the same time, IR 80 came on line to the right of IR 88. The German attack began to gather steam. The Germans reached the French artillery, stuck on the road, which led to a bitter fight as the French gunners and infantry desperately defended the guns. Corporal Muthig of 8/88 reported:

'After a three-hour firefight the French finally fled, just as 'Fix bayonets!' was sounded. This was followed immediately by 'Charge!'... We had hardly advanced 200m when, in the right-hand corner of the woods, on the middle of a path, we found enemy guns that were in the process of moving off; they had already brought forward the limbers and horses. Now we made a wild assault towards the guns, which could no longer move because some of the horses had been hit. The guns were undamaged. But the pursuit was not over. The signal 'Charge!' sounded continually.'

III/88 destroyed I/18 RA and took 12 French guns. The French began to retreat; the Germans pursued the French as far as the rail line, stopping only when darkness fell.

German IR80[5]

IR80 was initially designated the corps reserve, but soon after IR88 made contact, IR80 was committed to the right of IR88. The regiment moved forward at double-time, in the heat, fully loaded; soon 'their tongues were hanging out to their necks'. The battalions were committed as they arrived, first I/80, then II/80, and finally III/80. In the Fôret de Luchy 1/80 and 4/80 ran into French artillery that had already been engaged by II/FAR 27 at close range. Only a few French guns had succeeded in unlimbering by the time that the rifle fire of both companies killed the gun teams and rendered the French guns immobile. Most of the crews were killed or wounded and the remnants tried to escape as the two companies stormed the battery positions. Elements of I/80 and II/80 continued the attack to the west end of the Fôret de Luchy and then bivouacked near Bertrix. About half of IR80 (2/80, 6/80, 7/80, 10/80, 11/80, 12/80) swung to the right in the Fôret de Luchy and came up behind the French troops engaged with IR87, forcing them to surrender or withdraw. This group bivouacked near Ochamps.

French II/ 18 RA

A French officer patrol found a withdrawal route to Jéhonville. II/18 RA (4/18, 5/18, 6/18) was ordered to take this route, which was to be secured by infantry. 7/18 RA and 8/18, which were still intact, were also ordered down this route. II/18 made it out of the Fôret de Luchy but took a wrong turn at the crossroads east of Jéhonville, and headed towards Blanche Oreille. This led II/18 over Hill 471 and straight into the field of fire of the German artillery. II/18 was completely destroyed. 7/18 saw the fate of II/18 and turned off the road but was caught in the barbed wire that lined the fields and meadows in profusion. It was then engaged by German artillery fire and the battery commander, with great difficulty, was able to save only two guns. 8/18, which followed 7/18, managed to avoid the wire but in so doing moved into a marshy area. The entire battery became stuck and only one gun and six caissons could be saved.

Bertrix

French 65th Infantry Brigade

By 1630 the 65th Brigade had reached Bertrix and both its regiments, 7 RI and 9 RI, were committed towards the Fôret de Luchy to try to redeem the situation. They ran straight into IR81, effectively supported by artillery. The 7 RI war diary said that the regiment took heavy small arms fire when it reached the crossroads leading to Ochamps and Recogne.[6] III/7, leading the column, deployed to the left of the road, I/7, following, to the right. II/7 was delayed by artillery 'fleeing in disorder' as well as troops from other units which blocked the roads. Troops from 9 RI and 12 RI, also 'fleeing in disorder' were rounded up by 7RI and put into the line. German artillery fire immediately began falling on the position, as well as rifle fire from the woods to the front. The regiment held on for 25 minutes and then broke for the rear (*cede completement*). When darkness fell the regiment conducted a 'precipitous retreat' to Herbeumont. At 2330 it could assemble only 1,278 EM and 14 OFF. 9 RI was in equally bad shape. During the night the remnants retreated as far as the Chiers.

German IR81

IR81 had its home station in Frankfurt am Main. The Grand Duke of Hesse, although a Lieutenant General, had insisted on accompanying his regiment in combat, while the regimental commander was Prince Friedrich Karl of Hesse.[7] The German aristocracy still knew how to fight.

By 1430 the regiment had reached the crossroads in the middle of the Fôret de Luchy. Two companies, 5/81 and 8/81, were marching down the rail line to the south, providing flank cover for 21 ID. When the advanced guard made contact, the regimental commander went forward on reconnaissance. On returning he ordered the regiment forward. I/81 was to move down the road to directly support the left flank of IR88, but 1/81 and 4/81 became engaged and extended IR88's right flank north of the road. 4/81 detected French artillery in a clearing and used the cover provided by the gorse to march at double-time directly into the battery position; the French gunners, who could not see 4/81 approach, fired over their heads. When the German infantry appeared in the middle of their battery position, the battery surrendered.

At 1515, I/Foot Artillery 3 opened rapid fire against the French 65th Brigade infantry 1,000m to 1,500m away, point-blank range for heavy howitzers.[8] The battery commanders stood on the caissons to direct the fire. The howitzers reported operating in a target-rich environment, with thick clumps of French infantry moving in the open. After half an hour there were no targets left and the howitzers bounded forward to fire on Bertrix. French infantry appeared everywhere at 600–800m range, even in the howitzer battalion rear, were engaged by one or two salvoes, and then disappeared.

2/81 and 3/81 moved south of the road with III/81 on their left flank. The two companies reached the treeline and saw French infantry 600m to their front and attacked, supported by 4/FAR 63 and 6/63, which had set up directly to their rear. The light howitzers engaged the French infantry at 600m to 1,200m range with 'visible effect'. When his troops had advanced to within 150m from the French, the III/81 battalion commander ordered his two companies to fix bayonets. II/81 attacked to the left of III/81, with the Prince, who had commanded the battalion in peacetime, accompanying the standard. The attack met little resistance: the III/81 battalion commander said that the artillery had mostly taken out the French; the remnants surrendered. The commander of 2/81 was killed during the fight for a French battery. The men of 2/81 were very bitter, and would have killed their prisoners had a senior NCO not prevented them from doing so.

The French 65th brigade began to retreat, pursued by IR 81 and the howitzers of II/63. The gunners brought their heavy farm horses to a canter, probably for the first time in their lives, and unlimbered directly behind the advancing infantry. 5/FAR 63 operated almost independently, at one point forming a 'hedgehog' to engage targets in three directions. The pursuit was joined by II/FAR 27, which moved forward by bounds to engage targets at 1,000m to 1,200m range. As the pursuit reached the rail line, the French made a last stand. The 2nd gun of 4/27 was brought forward to provide flanking fire at point-blank range, which caused the French severe casualties. Because the gorse severely restricted visibility, the MG company of IR 81 did not fire a round all day. However, IR 81 did receive support from two platoons of IR 88's MG company. The regiment bivouacked in the open to immediately to the north of Bertrix.

Casualties

The French 33rd DI divisional artillery had been destroyed; only a few guns escaped, and casualties amongst the gunners were heavy. The French 20 RI lost 66 OFF and 1363 EM; the regimental standard was captured by German 21 ID's engineer company, 1/21st Engineer Battalion. 11 RI lost 25 OFF and 1,000 EM. The 66th Brigade had taken over 30 per cent casualties and an even higher proportion of its officers; the fragments of the brigade had to be withdrawn to Mouzon on the Meuse to reorganise. 65th Brigade was a demoralised wreck. IR 7 was not reconstituted until 24 August. It had lost four OFF and only 6 EM KIA, five OFF and 55 EM WIA and 8 OFF and 609 men MIA (!) After 25 minutes of intense German fire, 7 RI had disintegrated.

The German casualties seem to have been about 1/3 those of the French. The most heavily engaged German unit, IR 88, lost 21 OFF and 436 EM KIA and WIA. The regimental history noted that the regiment had already taken more casualties than in the entire Franco-Prussian War.

IR 81's officer casualties were high: 3 company commanders and 5 lieutenants had been killed, 1 battalion commander, 2 company commanders and 7 lieutenants wounded.

Conclusions

Once again, the French did not know what had hit them: the commander of the French 33 DI artillery was intellectually so far removed from being able to comprehend the requirements of mobile warfare and the meeting engagement that he thought that the Germans had sprung a well-prepared ambush.

Two factors were decisive in the destruction of the 33 DI at Bertrix. First was the excellent German operational and tactical cavalry reconnaissance, coupled with the utter ineffectiveness of the French cavalry reconnaissance. The second was the German artillery. The Germans handled their guns like tanks, audaciously combining mobility and firepower with the protection provided by their armored gun shields to continually bring the guns right behind their own infantry to engage the French infantry at close range. The German gunners were able to do so because of the high level of crew training and the initiative and aggression of the leaders at gun commander and battery commander levels. The Germans won all the gun duels with the French artillery. I/18 RA was destroyed in place. The annihilation of II/18 RA as it moved at high speed across Hill 471 had more in common with a tank battle than First World War artillery tactics. In both cases, the Germans overwhelmed the French 75s with a high volume of accurate fire. In the pursuit of the 65th Brigade the German artillery again acted in a most tank-like manner, moving quickly and freely over the battlefield to put close-range fire on the disintegrating French brigade.

23 August

22 August, which had been extremely hot, gave way to a bitter cold night, which the troops spent in the open. Early on 23 August, 21 ID moved east towards Neufchâteau to assist XVIII RK. At 0400 IR 81 had already begun movement towards Orgeo.[9] The route of the French retreat was easy to follow from the equipment, packs and weapons that the French troops had thrown away.

The French held Orgeo with a rear-guard. IR 81 deployed and began a standing firefight. Occasionally the regiment received heavy French artillery fire. At about noon, after the heavy howitzers had softened up the town and the 41st Brigade began to turn the French left flank, IR 81 went over to the attack and pursued the withdrawing French to St. Medard, then Straitmont and finally Chiny. 9/80 took 30 casualties from French artillery fire. 9/81, which had been left at Bertrix to police up the battlefield, took 100 French stragglers prisoner.

The French XVII CA war diary said that the corps was in such a state of disorder that, while it was recognised that there had been considerable casualties, the exact number could not be ascertained until several days after the battle.

7
Maissin-Anloy

On the left flank of the French 4th Army, beginning at 0300 the XI CA marched in two columns, with 21 DI, the corps artillery and corps headquarters, on the left moving on a route from Paliseul to the west of Maissin. Naturally, 21 ID sent out a strong flank guard to Porcheresse to the north, consisting of two battalions of 137 RI, a battery and a half-squadron of cavalry. 22 DI moved on the right to Maissin. By 1100 the advance guard regiment of 22 DI, IR 19, was entering Maissin with I/19 and III/19, while II/19 as right flank guard was advancing through Anloy to Moulin de Villance.

The German 25 ID was deployed in assembly areas south of Libin. VIII AK, which was on 25 ID's right, was far to the north and had the mission of covering the left flank of the 3rd Army. On 21 August VIII RK was far to the rear, at Bastogne, and was to move to St. Hubert on 22 August. 25 ID was in an exposed and isolated position. The commander of 25 ID wrote that on the morning of 22 August no one thought that there would be a battle that day.[1]

Maissin

That morning the German 6th Dragoons sent a stream of reports concerning the approaching French forces. A French cavalry column appeared west of Maissin and German cavalry patrols reported that they had received fire from the town. The 25 ID commander ordered 50th Brigade in Villance to occupy Maissin with a battalion. I/IR 118 and the MG Company were given the mission. It advanced with its left flank on the road from Villance to Maissin, 3/118 on the left, 4/118 in the centre, 1/118 on the right and 2/118 in reserve and followed by the MG Company. The leading companies were deployed in several waves of thin skirmisher lines.[2] FAR 25 opened fire on Maissin in support of I/118 and began to move forward by bounds to positions 600–800m west of Villance.

At 1200 I/118 took fire from Maissin, as well as from Hill 398 and from Bournon Bois, although the enemy was invisible. Initially the French fire was ineffective. The battalion advanced in long bounds, crossed the 'rather wide and deep' Lesse stream and by 1230 had reached the east side of Maissin. 1/118 entered Maissin without encountering significant resistance, 3/118 had to crawl the last few metres because of the French salvo fire. In keeping with German doctrine, 1/118 pushed through the village and set up a defence on the west side, supported by all six MG. A standing firefight developed with the infantry of the French 22 DI west of the town. Fighting with bypassed French troops in Maissin continued throughout the entire afternoon.

2/FAR 25 advanced to Hill 367, directly east of Maissin, and occupied a very exposed open position in order to provide direct fire support. It lost twenty-three horses to enemy fire during the approach march, so that initially only two guns could be brought into action. It engaged withdrawing French infantry at 600–800m range, suppressed French fire from Bournon Bois, and engaged infantry and MG south of Maissin at between 1,600m and 2,000m range. It was later joined by 5/25. Most of the French artillery counter-fire went over the batteries and landed near the limbers 300m to the rear, killing twenty more horses.

At 1145 III/ IR 118 was committed to the right of I/118 to take Hill 398. II/118 followed echeloned to the right rear of III/118, to protect the right flank against French forces that were (incorrectly) reported to be in the Chapmont forest. III/118 advanced south of the Chapmont forest to the Maissin–Tellin road, which it reached at 1400, but only at the cost of heavy casualties from enemy small arms fire as well as friendly artillery fire. The batman of the commander of 10/118 had to run back to the German artillery to get them to cease fire. The regimental commander committed 8/118 to reinforce III/118 directly, and 6/118 to extend the right flank. Nevertheless, IR118 could not advance. At 1500 the regimental commander committed his last two reserve companies to hold the south and southwest sides of Maissin.

At 1130 II/117 and III/117 were committed to the south of Maissin to take the Bournon Bois. First they had to move through the thick underbrush of Figéohay woods, which took thirty minutes.[3] On the western treeline they took weak fire from the mill at the east edge of Burnon Bois. As the regiment continued the attack the fire grew much stronger, forcing it to stop and take cover. In general the regiment was able to advance only slowly: 5/117 lost all of its officers. On the other hand, 8/117 arrived at 1230 in Maissin almost without casualties and moved to reinforce IR118 on the north side of the town. III/117, on the left, had difficulty crossing the woods; units became intermixed and got lost. By 1430 the III/117 battalion staff, a platoon of 10/117 and the machine gun company had reached the west end of Bournon Bois and engaged French forces south of Maissin. They tried to continue the advance but quickly took so many casualties that they were forced back to the treeline. The French fire was so intense that

The Battle of the Frontiers

only one MG could be brought back up the steep hill to the woods. The bolts were taken out of the rest of the guns and the MGs themselves were hidden and recovered the next day. 9/117 linked up with IR 115 in the Derrière Houmont, where it had excellent observation and fields of fire towards Maissin and the terrain south of the town, and was able to inflict significant casualties on French troops trying to enter the town.

Soon after 1400 the French 21 DI began the attack with its right-hand 42nd Brigade moving on Maissin while the left-hand 41st Brigade marched through the Bolet Bois against the right flank of the German 25 ID.[4] The French division right was formed by the 93 RI and one battalion of 137 RI, which the division commander said attacked too soon 'against well-prepared trenches' and suffered 'considerable' casualties. The 21 DI said that the 41st Brigade on the left was better led and 'was able to hold its positions'. At 1515 the French 21 DI artillery opened fire on the tree line of Bolet Bois. This was hardly the offensive à outrance.

To block this French attack, at 1530 I/117 was committed in the Bolet Bois on the right of IR 118. 4/117 reinforced IR 118 directly and soon had taken about 100 casualties. The rest of the battalion pressed on to the western treeline of Bolet Bois, just in time to see lines of French infantry attack from the woods about 700m to the west. 1/117 and 2/117 occupied the treeline and brought the attack to a halt with their fire, while 3/117 guarded the right flank. A lively firefight developed. Then the French artillery shelled the treeline so that the two companies had to withdraw 100m into the woods. Reinforced by 3/117, the treeline was reoccupied. French artillery and MG fire again forced 2/117 and 3/117 back into the woods, but they later occupied it for the third time.

1/ FAR 25 was ordered to move to the right flank to provide close support to the infantry. The battery worked its way forward over difficult terrain under enemy fire, unlimbered on the reverse slope of the hill, and the gunners manhandled the guns onto Hill 398 between I/117 and IR 118, still in a half-covered position, with the gunners standing on the guns to aim them. The guns arrived at 1730, just in time to engage attacking French infantry at 700m range. The French managed to close to within 400m before their attack collapsed in the face of 1/25's rapid fire. 1/FAR 25 did not take any French artillery fire, probably because of the half-covered position.

The rest of FAR 25 began to take more accurate French counter-battery fire, including a direct hit on one gun that wounded seven men. Shells falling behind the gun shields were particularly dangerous for the crews, and FAR 25 was spared worse casualties because the gunners had immediately dug revetments to the rear. As the regimental history said 'we learned from the first day that digging in paid off'. German counter-battery was also effective. Two French batteries at Bellvue Farm were engaged by German artillery. The French batteries were forced to withdraw, leaving behind two guns. The German 25 ID commander also personally observed how German artillery fire broke up French infantry attacks.

The French steadily pressed the attack, especially against III/118 north of the town. The French also began to push I/118 and II/117 out of Maissin, in spite of taking heavy casualties from the fire of IR 118's MGs and the cannon fire of FAR 25. There was no French 'bayonet charge': the French infantry used the terrain well and covered their attack with small arms and MG fire, which caused I/118 significant casualties. At 1800 a French infantry attack, supported by artillery and MG fire, forced I/117 to retreat out of Bolet Bois.

The IR 118 regimental commander was forced to order all three battalions to withdraw to Villance. The German retreat had to be made against heavy resistance from the French troops in the town that had been bypassed and now fired from houses and the church. The retreat was conducted in good order, led by the surviving officers. A battalion-strength group formed a line east of the Lesse stream, about 1,200m west of Villance. At 2200 the remnants of the regiment assembled on the Maissin-Villance road and bivouacked there.

Anloy

At 1100 the 49th Brigade, at Glaireuse, was ordered to take the high ground west of Anloy. The brigade designated Bournon Bois–Anloy as the initial objective and deployed IR 115 on the right, with IR 116 on the left. The Lesse stream was crossed at 1300. Both regiments marched with two battalions on line and one in reserve. The initial objective was reached without contact with the enemy. The rolling terrain, covered with standing grain and small copses, did not offer long-range observation or fields of fire, which made the fire-support mission of FAR 61 especially difficult.[5] As the 49th Brigade advanced farther, it took close-range French small arms fire. The French troops were II/19 RI, two battalions of 118 RI and 357 RIR (reserve infantry regiment), which by 1200 had occupied a line south from the Bournon Bois. French artillery near Bellvue Farm put 'not very strong' fire on the 49th Brigade.

IR 115 attacked with I/115 on the left, III/115 on the right, II/115 and the MG Company in reserve. I/115 had three companies on line and one in reserve, III/115, one of whose companies was guarding II/FAR 61, advanced with all three remaining companies on line.[6] Given the terrain, the battle was conducted at platoon and company levels: small-unit tactics *par excellence*, fire and manoeuvre against individual copses or groups of French troops. By 1500 the regiment had crossed the Anloy–Maissin road. Once the French troops had to move and expose themselves their red trousers made fine targets. II/115 was committed to fill a gap in the centre; the MG Company was committed on the left flank. IR 115 pushed into the Bois de Derrière Hautmont and overran a French battery after a vicious fight with multiple counterattacks by both sides. By 1700 the regiment took the Bois de Hautmont. The French 42nd Brigade launched a counterattack from Bellvue Farm. The group of IR 115 troops in the Bois de Derrière Hautmont included the regimental MG

The Battle of the Frontiers

Company, whose flanking fire broke up the 42nd Brigade's attack with heavy casualties. An indication of the methodical nature of the fight is the fact that in eight hours of continual combat IR 115 had advanced slightly over 2km. It now stood in the rear of the French troops at Maissin. However, the regiment was aware that the German 50th Brigade had fallen back from Maissin to Villance. The situation elsewhere was uncertain. In addition, the regiment was completely disorganised and the regimental commander was dead. It was decided to pull back to Anloy and reorganise. The regiment bivouacked near Anloy. This is the sort of thing that one did during a peacetime exercise. A risky but potentially high-reward course of action would have been to hold in place, blocking the road out of Maissin. As it transpired, the French night withdrawal out of Maissin was chaotic – 19 RI was not even notified and realised only the next morning that it had been left behind. Had IR 115 remained in Bois de Derrière Hautmont and put fire on the route of withdrawal the 22 DI might have collapsed completely.

IR 116 on the brigade left was only 400m from the French troops when they opened fire.[7] The French were invisible and aimed return fire was impossible. Nevertheless, the German infantry attacked: as the division commander said, the troops got the bit in their teeth and pushed forward, disregarding casualties, throwing the French out of the wheat fields and copses in a series of assaults. The regimental right flank advanced 'at a headlong pace'. The French counterattacked against the regimental centre and initially IR 116 fell back, but the situation was stabilised by a platoon of machine guns and an engineer company. Another counterattack against the regimental right flank was parried by a group of 100 stragglers gathered up by the adjutant of II/116. The divisional left flank was completely in the air and I/116 had been echeloned behind the regimental left flank to cover it. As it came out of a sunken road southwest of Anloy it was met by intense fire. The lead companies deployed by squads to the left and moved forward through standing grain against an invisible enemy.

At around 1600 the French launched an attack by several battalions supported by a battery of artillery against I/116 to turn the 25 ID left flank. This was probably the 68th Brigade of the French 34 DI, composed of 59 RI, 88 RI and a battery of 14 RAC. I/FAR 61 put the battery out of action at 2,600m range before it was able to fire. I/FAR 61 then engaged French infantry at 1,600m range. The IR 116's MGs were deployed on the left and were a vital factor in the successful defence against French attack. Nevertheless, it appeared that the French would still turn the left flank when the IR 116 regimental commander personally brought forward two guns of FAR 61 and set them up 600m from the right flank of the French attack, which then collapsed with heavy casualties. At 1600 FAR 61 began a systematic bombardment of the copses held by French troops across the regimental front. The IR 116 attack continued to gain ground, though often only after intense hand-to-hand combat.

Collapse of French 34 DI[8]

The French 34 DI had had attacked to the right of XI CA against the German 25 DI, with no success. But due to the destruction of the 33 DI in the Fôret de Luchy, the 34 DI was ordered to retreat, front to the east towards the German 21 ID, which was pushing into its rear area. This, on top of the pounding that the division had taken from 25 ID, caused a panic. The division collapsed, with only two battalions and two groups of artillery turning to face 21 ID. The rest traversed the woods and retreated as far as Florenville, even passing the debris of the 33 DI.

VIII RK

VIII RK was bivouacked at Bastogne on the night of 21–22 August. Its objectives for 22 August were St. Hubert and Vesqueville, a march of about 25km. When they arrived there at 1300 the corps commander was informed that 25 ID needed support, and VIII RK continued the march. The 15 RD arrived at Libin at 1800 and its artillery fired on Maissin and Hill 398. The 16 RD marched to Anloy and its advance guard regiment, RIR 28, appeared behind the IR 116 front, having completed a 45km forced march on bad roads and in the August heat. Together, the two German regiments, after more close combat, threw the French out of their last position. The withdrawing French passed a few hundred metres in front of I/116, suffering 'terrible losses' from I/116's flanking fire.

German 25 ID Situation

To the 25 ID commander, the situation that evening appeared grim. The 50th Brigade had been defeated and as a consequence the 49th Brigade had fallen back to Anloy. Initial strength returns for the infantry showed an average of 50 per cent casualties, with officer casualties up to 80 per cent. The actual casualties were far less, and the figures reflected the disorganisation of the division and the difficulty in reestablishing units in the dark, but the division commander had no way of determining exactly what condition 25 ID was really in and feared for the worst. During the night the division operations officer worked to reorganise the unit. More important, large numbers of lost soldiers found their way to the field kitchens! The strength of the division rose.

French 21 DI Situation Report[9]

At 2030 21 DI sent in a situation report that said that the Germans had waited for the French in prepared positions. The Germans had taken considerable casualties from French artillery and cold steel, and the division could renew the attack the next morning if his flanks were covered.

The Battle of the Frontiers

French 22 DI Situation Reports,

At 1645 XI CA reported to 4th Army HQ that it had been heavily engaged at Maissin since 1230 against an all-arms German force. The corps intended to hold Maissin 'in spite of heavy losses'.[10]

At 1900, the 22 DI reported that, after heavy combat, the division, assisted by the 41st Brigade of 21 DI, had taken Maissin and the high ground to the north, but had not crossed the Lesse. The division right flank had been pushed far back from Anloy and the road to Paliseul was threatened. An attempt by the 42nd Brigade to gain some breathing space here 'did not succeed'. The division had taken the Hessian Guard uniform emblems for those of the Prussian Guard, which surely would be grounds for anxiety. The left flank guard of the 21 DI had been thrown out of Porcheresse by troops of the German 15 ID and it had to be assumed that strong German forces were approaching from the northeast, while XVII CA to the south was withdrawing. The 22 DI had suffered very heavy losses and the troops were exhausted. At 2000 XI CA ordered 22 DI to withdraw to Paliseul, and at 2100 21 DI was ordered to do the same.

23 August

On the morning of 23 August 15 RD (VIII RK) marched in the fog towards Maissin. 25 ID (XVIII AK) continued to reorganise and dug trenches against a renewal of the French attacks. At around 1200 the division received an air reconnaissance report that stated that at 0800 French columns with vehicles had been seen retreating towards Bouillon. Only at 1200 did the division begin the pursuit by advancing towards Maissin. As the regiment passed the former French positions the effect of German artillery fire was evident. Once again, the route of the French retreat was marked with discarded weapons and equipment. At 1400 the troops halted to eat and rest. At 2100 the march was resumed in the dark. The march was halted when the advanced guard reached Bertrix on the morning of 24 August. The division bivouacked, exhausted. IR 116 marched for 16 hours without catching up with the French. 9/116 was assigned to bury the dead. They counted five to six French dead for each two German.

Casualties

There are five war cemeteries near Anloy–Maissin. In them are buried 988 German and 2,240 French soldiers. The 25 ID commander said that his division lost 1,100 dead.

IR 118's losses were extraordinarily high. The regiment lost 307 killed, including the commander of III/118, the adjutant of II/118, the adjutant of III/118, 3 company commanders, 4 lieutenants, and 567 wounded, including the commanders of I/118 and II/118, the regimental adjutant, 4 company commanders and 7 lieutenants. On 23 August I/118 had 384 men, II/118 577, III/118 344 and the MG Company 80, a total of 1,385 men out of the original 3,200.

IR 117 lost 8 OFF KIA, including the commander of III/117 and all the officers of 5/117, and 113 EM. 11 OFF and 239 EM were WIA and 67 MIA. Hardest hit were 4/117 and 5/117. IR 115 lost 11 OFF and 70 EM KIA, including the regimental commander and the commander of I/115, and two company commanders, and 16 OFF and 395 EM WIA. IR 116 suffered more casualties on 22 August than it would on any other day in the war: 13 officers and 340 EM were KIA, 20 OFF and 599 EM WIA, 72 EM MIA.

FAR 25 had fired 1,639 rounds.

Conclusions

The German 25 ID was outnumbered 2–1 in infantry and 5–3 in artillery, and both of the division's flanks were in the air. Nevertheless, it inflicted twice its own casualties on the enemy. The only explanation for such a result is superior German tactical doctrine and training. This was the conclusion reached by the officers of 25 ID themselves.

The first words in the FAR 25 regimental history proclaimed that in 1914 'in terms of training the regiment stood at the height of its powers'. The regimental historian's conclusion was that on 22 August the training proved itself 'brilliantly':

> 'The course of our baptism of fire brought our batteries into the most varied situations, which were mastered in every case, so that on the evening after the battle, leaders and gunners gratefully had the complete conviction 'We are the best!'. All movements were executed with the exactitude of a training exercise.... this brought the troops a feeling of security and confidence in our peacetime training, and created the best possible basis for the unparalleled triumphal march of the coming weeks'.[11]

The historian of IR 115 said that during the firefight at Anloy the French consistently fired too high, and that 'superior German tactical training and marksmanship came into its own.'[12]

The 25 ID commander attributed the ability of his division to stand up to superior enemy forces to the difference between German and French artillery tactics. The Germans used open or half-covered artillery positions and were therefore able to place fire directly on their targets. He had personally seen several French attacks collapse under accurate German shrapnel fire. On 30 August the 25 ID captured a French hospital, whose senior doctor told the division commander that 50 per cent of the French losses at Maissin had been due to German artillery fire. The French, on the other hand, generally used covered positions, behind woods, and must have had great difficulty adjusting fire, for they usually used area fire. None of the German after-action reports mentioned significant losses due to French artillery.[13] The FAR 25 regimental history said that the German 'ladder' (bracketing) method of adjusting fire was complex, but also effective, especially in counter-battery fire.[14]

The 50th Brigade held off superior French forces for an entire afternoon, in spite of taking terrific casualties. Even more impressive was the performance of the 49th Brigade, which defeated three French brigades in succession and pushed in the right flank of the French 21 DI.

The performance of the French XI CA was far less impressive. Three French brigades, enjoying a massive superiority in artillery, should have been able to make short work of the German 50th Brigade. But the French never attacked the 50th Brigade's open right flank, perhaps because they did not want to try to manoeuvre through the Bolet Bois, and it took the XI CA far too long to wear down the 50th Brigade and force it to retreat. The corps artillery could not find suitable firing positions and never fired a shot.[15] German superiority in a mobile battle was evident at Anloy. First the right flank of the 21 DI was pushed back. Then the Germans outmanoeuvred the counterattacks by both the French 68th Brigade (34 DI) and the 42nd Brigade. In all three actions it was the initiative, mobility and combat power of German units at the platoon and company/battery levels – and the inferiority of the French at these levels – that was decisive.

8
Virton[1]

German 9 ID

On 20 August the German V AK, on the right flank of the 5th Army, marched only 15km west to Etalle. On 21 August the corps stood fast, mostly bivouacked in or near towns. This lack of movement on the roads and the difficulty of detecting troops in towns would surely have made French air reconnaissance much less effective and contributed to the lack of French intelligence concerning the location of the German 5th Army.

To the west and south of Etalle lay a wooded zone 9km deep. For local security, 9 ID established an outpost line at the edge of the forest, 2.5km from the bivouac, using I/IR 19, II/IR 19 and III/IR 58. 1st *Uhlan* Regiment sent patrols beyond this zone to the south in the direction of Meix devant Virton, Robelment, Virton and Éthe, and to the west of the woods towards Florenville. At 1200 on 21 August 1st *Uhlan* reported a column of all arms marching from St. Mard, 1km southwest of Virton, in the direction of Latour, and another about 12km south of Etalle. At 1400 French infantry was reported dug in at Robelment. At 1300 a column of all arms was seen at Houdlément, some 5km to the left front of the XIII AK. Between 1230 and 1600 the German 3 KD fought with two to three battalions of French infantry west of Jamoigne, about 12km or 13km due west of Etalle. Foot patrols from the German 17th Brigade reported detecting French infantry at Virton and Robelmont and artillery in Virton.

One of the 15-man 1st *Uhlan* patrols was led by Lieutenant Freiherr Manfred von Richthofen, the future Red Baron.[2] Richthofen sighted a French dragoon patrol and, in keeping with German cavalry doctrine as well as his own personal inclinations, charged. The French cavalry disappeared and Richthofen's patrol ran into French infantry. Only Richthofen and four men were able to escape on horseback; others showed up later on foot, and some were killed or wounded. Richthofen later wrote that 'This baptism of fire was not as much fun as I thought.'

Upon hearing of the advance of French forces, the V Corps commander sent a warning order at 2000 on 21 August, telling the divisions to occupy alarm quarters just to the north and east of the large band of forest, and to be ready to move on short notice. This involved considerably difficult night marching, but from the new location V Corps was as far forward as possible while remaining out of the forest, and thereby retaining full freedom of movement. Once the corps began marching through the woods, changes in direction would be impossible.

The Germans patrolled intensely. Richthofen was sent out with another patrol. At 0130 on 22 August he reported that he had taken fire north of Virton from what he thought was the security detachment of the French troops bivouacked in Virton. 10/IR 58 was sent out as a night patrol to Bellevue. At 0155 on 22 August it reported by bicycle messenger that one of its patrols had taken fire on the road to Virton 1km south of the tree line. The sketch attached to the report showed five German infantry or cavalry patrols and an infantry security detachment in the immediate vicinity of Robelmont and Bellevue.

V AK would serve as the pivot for the attack of the rest of the 5th Army. The V Corps order instructed 10 ID on the corps left to take and hold the high ground between Virton and Robelmont. 9 ID, on the corps right, was to hold the heights at Bellevue above Éthe. Movement would begin at 0400, 22 August. Due to clogged roads, the vehicle bringing the V AK attack order corps order had taken two hours to cover 18km; the order reached 9 ID at 0150. 9 ID HQ immediately issued fragmentary oral orders to put the advance guard and the lead elements of the main body in motion. 1st *Uhlan* was sent forward to secure the exit from the forest into the open ground above Virton; at 0445 IR 58 would be detached with a cavalry squadron and an artillery battery from I/FAR 41 to guard the division right flank at Robelmont, which at 0100 had been reported by 10/58 to be occupied by the French. In spite of the late receipt of orders, fatigue and movement in total darkness, the advanced guard crossed its start point at 0400. This was a textbook example of effective troop leading. 9 ID was motivated by the knowledge that in war every minute counts, and this attitude paid handsome dividends: 9 ID was able to seize the vital terrain at Bellevue minutes ahead of the arrival of the French advance guard. The French were surprised in good part because 9 ID had been able to cover so much ground in the dark.

Terrain

Bellevue sits on top of a flat, high plateau covered with potato fields, standing grain, and meadows. The plateau drops off very gently towards Virton and the Basse Vire to the south; the field of fire from near Bellevue to Virton is excellent. To the west and southwest from Bellevue the plateau is flat for about 1km, offering an excellent field of fire, then drops off rather abruptly towards the valley, providing a covered avenue of approach. There is little concealment and the cover on the plateau aside from minor accidents in the terrain, such as slightly sunken farm roads, which are therefore tactically significant.

French IV CA, 20–21 August

The French IV CA was composed of the 8 DI and the 7 DI. The Corps Commander was 67 years old and a veteran of the Franco-Prussian War. The corps also had two reserve infantry regiments, 315 RIR and 317 RIR, each with two battalions.

On the night of 20–21 August the French 3rd Army had crossed the Othain, headed for Arlon. On the left flank of the 3rd Army was IV CA, which on 21 August was to reach Latour with 7 DI on its right, while 8 DI on the left was to reach Virton.

The only maps of Belgium that the corps possessed were on the scale of 1:200,000, which is practically useless for tactical operations. The maps of Germany were on the much more serviceable scale of 1:80,000.[3] In a small way, this is an indicator of the direction that the French Army thought operations were going to take.

The four active-army squadrons of the corps cavalry regiment, 14th Hussars, were employed together for corps reconnaissance. The two reserve squadrons of 14th Hussars were attached to the divisions, 5/14 Hussars to 7 DI, 6/14 to 8 DI.

The 14th Hussars had a hard day on 21 August. It was continually in contact with German security detachments, which delayed its advance so much that by the end of the day it had been unable to cross the Ton or Basse Vire Rivers. The commander of the 14th Hussars complained that the German cavalry continually drew his men into fire traps, and for that reason the regiment had been unable to conduct any reconnaissance. Nevertheless, the IV CA commander was convinced that there were no significant German forces in his area of operations.

The 14th Hussar Regiment had been opposed by the German 10 ID cavalry regiment, 1st *Jäger zu Pferde*, as well as the 27 ID cavalry regiment, 19th *Uhlan*. In addition, the XIII AK commander had pushed III/IR 123 forward to Virton and the Basse Vire to reinforce the cavalry with infantry outposts. It was no wonder that the 14th Hussars made no progress. The German security forces withdrew only under pressure from the 7 DI advance guard, which slowed the march of the division main body.

French 8 DI

The advance of 8 DI on 21 August was conducted according to Bonnal's emphasis on 'security', which Grandmaison had so despised and derided. The 14th Hussars stayed close to the 8 DI infantry, while the infantry employed numerous company and battalion-sized detachments to comb out the woods and towns near the route of march. These detachments advanced cross-country in tactical formation. Grasset cited this procedure to refute accusations that the French neglected security and had been surprised on 22 August. This proves only that even in 1930, 16 years after the event, the French army did not understand the tactical problem in 1914.[4] At best such use of oversized local patrols would only have prevented an outright ambush, which was not the threat at hand. Combined with the lack of long-range reconnaissance, this procedure slowed the march considerably, but provided no security at all against fast-moving German operational manoeuvre, which was the real threat.

Masses of Germans were reported everywhere. The local population told the cavalry that 1,500 Germans were at Robelmont, so without further ado it stopped to wait for the advanced guard infantry to come up. If there were any Germans in the town, it could not have been more than a patrol. A local man told the cavalry that there were 500 Germans in ambush at Virton; the cavalry took fire and in turn reported that there were 1,000 Germans in Virton, so the advanced guard commander deployed to attack, telling the division commander that there were 2,000 Germans in Virton. The squad-sized German security detachment at Virton fell back in front of the French advance guard.

8 DI bivouacked in and southwest of Virton at 1600. The division deployed RI 115 to provide local security north of Virton, with 12/RI 115 at Bellevue. Neither the 14th Hussars nor the patrols of RI 115 passed beyond the tree line north of Virton.

The contrast between German and French reconnaissance and security was stark. The German recon forces operated aggressively, day and night, one terrain feature (the woods between Etalle and Virton), some 10–15km, from their main body. The French cavalry was completely stymied. The French infantry security line at Bellevue was about 2km from the main body at Virton; indeed, Virton is visible from Bellevue.

The French IV CA order for 22 August, which had been issued at 2400, 21 August, arrived at 8 DI HQ at 0300, 22 August. It said that weak German forces were in the area of Etalle–Virton; stronger German forces were supposed to be in Luxembourg. 7 DI on the right was to march to St. Léger, 8 DI on the left to Etalle. 8 DI was to begin the march at 0415 from a starting point (the crossroads about 1km west of Virton), with a mission of counter-attacking against any threat to the right flank of II CA.

French troop leading did not reach the German standard. The corps order was issued too late and took too long to reach the division. Below the division level, the problem was compounded. The messengers carrying the divisional orders, mostly on bicycles, took some time to find the units in the fog, and many had difficulty finding them at all; RI 117 was alerted at 0455, forty minutes after the

Virton

division was to begin its march. Troops were hastily assembled and began movement, without any coffee. The cavalry learned at 0400 that they were to get to the start point by 0430 to lead the column. There was difficulty getting the march organised in the thick morning fog. At 0500 the advanced guard battalion of 130 RI left the north edge of Virton, about forty-five minutes late.

Bellevue Farm

Shortly before 0400 a French outpost north of Bellevue Farm made contact with a German patrol and withdrew to the farm. The commander the French security company, 12/115 RI, reported this to his battalion commander, who moved 9/115 RI and the regimental MG company forward towards Bellevue at around 0500. A thick fog covered the area, reducing visibility to a few feet.

At about 0520 1st *Uhlan*, moving south on the road to Virton, took fire at Hill 310, about 1km northeast of Bellevue on the road to Etalle. 1st *Uhlan* reported making contact with an enemy platoon, which was correct; it was an outpost of the French 12/115 RI. 1st *Uhlan* then took fire from Robelmont. As the firing moved towards Bellevue the German 9 ID commander, who was forward with the advanced guard, decided at 0555 that the enemy was weak and had to be attacked with the entire 18th Brigade in order to quickly take Bellevue, the division objective. IR 7, the advance guard regiment, whose commander was Prince Oskar von Preussen, the 26 year-old fifth son of the Emperor, would attack on the right, with two battalions of IR 154, the first regiment in the main body, swinging to the left, the last battalion of IR 154 was held back as the brigade reserve. The fog was still thick and the attack would, for all intents, be conducted as though it were a night attack; to maintain orientation and control, formations would have to be much thicker than usual. The French and German forces were probably within a few hundred metres of each other, though they did not know it.

IR 7 deployed with III/7 on the left: 8/7, the point company, was on the east of the road. II/7, on the right, moved to the southwest. I/7 was in reserve. III/7 ran into the French 12/115 IR, at Bellevue farm, and the French 12/115 RI, which was still deploying. The Germans immediately laid down a high volume of fire and advanced on the farm itself, while other elements pressed on to the left of the farm. Both French companies took serious casualties, and both French company commanders and the battalion commander were hit. 9/115 RI was practically destroyed and at 0700 the remnants ran for the rear, uncovering the right flank of 12/115. The commander of the lead French brigade had sent 8/130 RI forward to reinforce Bellevue; it too was overrun just south of the farm. IR 7 also took heavy French fire and III/7 ran forward to a road embankment opposite the farm, which offered cover. About 0900 the fog began to lift and it was discovered that the French were on the other side of the embankment. 1/IR 7 and 4/7 were committed on the right of the road to fill the gap between II/7 and III/7. With great difficulty, two MGs were brought forward, and their fire was decisive. At around 1030 2/7 was committed, and IR 7 went over to the assault over the road embankment, which contained about 100 French dead, and Bellevue was taken. The regiment advanced west to Hill 295 and set up a defence along a sunken farm track. IR 7 estimated it had been engaged with two battalions, when in fact there had been three French companies near Bellevue farm.

Advance Guard, French 8 DI

As it neared the woods north of Virton the cavalry point troop of 8 DI reported hearing a single shot to the front, followed by voices in German ordering cease fire. The French point element fell back and troop commander reported the contact. The commander 130 RI responded by shrugging his shoulders. The cavalry point, accompanied by the advanced guard officers, was ordered to resume the march in the fog and again took fire that forced it to retreat.

The choice of 130 RI as the advance guard regiment is hard to understand. The regiment had taken heavy casualties at Mangiennes on 10 August and the losses had been replaced with older reservists. 130 RI was therefore not a well-trained or cohesive unit. I/130 RI, the point battalion of the French 8 DI, was 500m from Bellevue and still in march column when it took fire from the elements of IR 7 that had passed to the east of Bellevue. I/130 RI quickly took heavy casualties, its battalion and all of its company commanders were killed, a panic broke out and the battalion was strewn to the four winds.

At 0645 the French 15th Brigade and advanced guard commander sent a report to the division commander saying that the Germans were undoubtedly not numerous, but were tough and holding well. He was going to manoeuvre a company to the right, which he thought would suffice.

II/130, next in column, deployed to the left of the remnants of I/130. Grasset says that this battalion was also effectively engaged by German artillery, lost all but three officers, and by 0730 was streaming back to Virton. Three MGs were destroyed. The first two companies of the next battalion in the column, III/130, took 50 per cent casualties, lost all their leaders and were pinned in place by German fire. The following two companies came on line and were greeted by a wall of bullets and shells, but managed to constitute a firing line. When the fog began to lift and German artillery fire began to fall on them, a panic broke out and the battalion fled. By 0730 the commanders of both 130 RI and the 15th Brigade were dead. 130 RI, said Grasset, had melted as if in a furnace.[5]

In Virton town, chaos reigned. Waves of beaten troops from 115 RI and 130 RI flowed to the rear, while 124 RI tried to make its way forward. The 8 DI division artillery was stuck on the road between the north exit of Virton and the rail crossing to the north of Dampicourt. Not only did it block the road, but it was nowhere near a place from which it could provide fire support.

German IR 154

IR 154 had been ordered to swing left of IR 7 to take the high ground near Hill 265 and the reservoir about 1km north of Virton.[6] III/154 led the regiment to the left of the main road through the thick undergrowth of the Bois de Virton. At the tree line the regiment oriented itself on the farm road that led to north side of Virton, III/154 to the right of the farm road, I/154 to the left, MG Company in reserve. III/154 had 10/154 and 9/154 in the first line, 12/154 and 11/154 in the second. The two lead companies in turn deployed two platoons in the first line and two in the second and moved out up the hillside, across the fields lined with hedges and barbed-wire fences, past grazing cattle. Soon, both lead companies spread out and had all four platoons on the first line. In the fog, 10/154 swung far to the right, towards Bellevue farm and extended the left flank of III/IR 7. Continuing straight ahead, 9/154 found itself within 200m of the high ground that was its objective, where it took French fire. It attacked and took the hill at the cost of heavy casualties; one platoon leader was killed and two were wounded. With the help of 1/5th Engineer Battalion the company then dug in. 12/154 was deployed to extend 9/154's right flank and bend it back to face the southwest, and then 11/154 extended the right flank further.

III/154 had already taken the high ground by the time that I/154 began its advance. I/154 ran into the French 8/115 RI, which had outpost duty on hill 265; the French company was enveloped on both flanks and forced to withdraw. Two platoons of 4/154 advanced as far as the reservoir but were driven back by intense French fire at 200m range. The rest of 2/154 and 3/154, moving in the fog, veered to the right and were drawn into IR 7's battle at Bellevue. The brigade reserve, II/154, was also committed at 0730 to assist IR 7. Most of the brigade was now oriented to the southwest and west, and there was a considerable gap between IR 7 and IR 154.

The brigade defended in place for the rest of the day. Small variations in the otherwise flat terrain provided the infantry significant cover: the sunken road on the right, a hollow by Hill 295 and the reverse slope of the high ground on the left.

5/154

5/154's battle is typical for the combat experienced by German units at Virton, which revolved around firepower and the careful use of the terrain. At 0730 the brigade commander ordered 5/154 to move south on the east side of the road to Virton to close the gap between IR 7 and IR 154. 5/154 extended the right flank of III/154 and took fire from Hill 260, about 400m to the front. 5/154 engaged these French forces in a firefight, inflicting casualties on French reinforcements. The commander of 5/154 decided to take the French position on Hill 260, using his reserve platoon. His battalion commander agreed and gave him an additional platoon from 12/154. Both platoons made one long bound forward, and then advanced slowly by low-crawling or bounding forward in small groups through hedges and barbed-wire fences. The commander of 5/154 noted that his troops fired 'calmly and with determination and [he] was later able to ascertain its devastating effect.' When his troops had approached to within 40m he ordered rapid fire, with the result that the French abandoned the position, leaving behind many dead and wounded. The company commander and a lieutenant ran forward with a few men to occupy the position and were met by intense fire from hayricks about 50m away; the lieutenant was killed and the company commander wounded in the arm. For thirty minutes he signalled for reinforcements to come up, until a squad finally came forward and cleared out the hayricks, which by now also harboured a French MG, with their fire. The 5/154 company commander was wounded a second time by a ricochet through the nose and mouth. His group was joined by a patrol from 11/IR 7 and two squads of IR 154, which had taken took some prisoners en route. Finally, two complete platoons came forward and contact was established with the right flank of III/154, which had also advanced. These troops began to take French artillery fire. Reluctantly, the commander of 5/154 ordered the bulk of the troops to pull back 30m to 40m to the reverse slope of the hill, leaving observation posts at the top. This manoeuvre was executed with difficulty but in good order. When the French fire slackened, 5/154 reoccupied the hill, which drew the attention of the French artillery, at which point the German infantry pulled back again. This procedure repeated itself several times. Finally the German infantry, under fire from the French artillery, began to dig in, and between 1500 and 1600 the French fire died away.

MG Company IR 154

The MG crews unloaded their guns from the carts at 0630 and carried them with considerable difficulty through the thick undergrowth of the Bois de Virton and then advanced to the south, parallel to the farm road leading to Virton. As the fog lifted, four guns went into action, engaging targets at 1,200m with continuous fire and 'devastating results'. The guns then followed III/154 and fired on French MG that were going into action with 'visible effectiveness'. Two guns were moved to the left flank, led by the MG Company commander, and engaged targets to the southwest with such effect that they drew French artillery fire, killing the platoon leader of the adjoining infantry platoon and causing confusion amongst the troops. The MG company commander re-established order and ordered the men to dig in, so at the end of the day the foxholes were ¾ of a metre deep. A MG platoon was left with III/154 and it fired on French infantry as they attempted to advance from Virton, inflicting heavy casualties. Later attempts by French forces to move north were smothered by MG fire. Two MGs were sent to reinforce 5/154, and together they poured fire into the right flank of French infantry attacking IR 7 at Bellevue. By 1600 this platoon had fired off all of its ammunition. As the French counter-battery fire suppressed the German artillery, the MG fire became an even more important element to the defence. By the end of the day the MG Company had fired 18,000 rounds.

IR 154 captured four French MGs and during the day took over 100 POWs from four French regiments. This number of prisoners increased during the night as unwounded French soldiers who had played dead were discovered in the regimental rear.

German 9 ID Divisional Artillery[7]

I/FAR 41 deployed with the advance guard, but initially could not fire due to the fog. It was quickly followed by II/FAR 41 at 0630, I/Foot Artillery 5 at 0745 and I/FAR 5 at 0830. All of these units had to occupy a restricted and exposed position between Bellevue and the Bois de Virton.

The adjutant of I/FAR 41 wrote a detailed account of his section's battle. He said that the section (minus 3/41, which was supporting IR 58) deployed in a cabbage field behind IR 7, which was engaged with French infantry at Bellevue. The French bullets hitting the cabbages made an unusual sound. The French were still defending the interior of Bellevue and the verges of the road were filled with French and German dead and wounded as the two batteries of FAR 41 galloped past to take up firing positions 150m south of the farm. The fog began to lift and the skirmisher line of IR 7 became visible 200m to the front. Beyond them, in skirmisher line and columns, appeared the French infantry. The adjutant, on his observation ladder, had a panoramic view of the action. He assumed direct control over two guns of the leftmost battery, then two more. He directed their fire against French infantry at 300m to 350m range and against a column 500m to the front; he could clearly observe, with 'wild joy', the effect of his shells on the target. The batteries began to receive small arms fire from both the front and bypassed French infantry in the rear and took casualties. When the fog lifted completely, I/41, in an open position on the plateau, became the target of French counter-battery fire. 2/FAR 41 was wiped out, the last gun crew firing until was destroyed by a direct hit and small arms fire. 1/41 took heavy casualties but continued to fire with reduced crews. The adjutant climbed down from his observation ladder just before it was destroyed by a direct hit. Finally it was decided to withdraw the remaining I/41 crews from the guns and pull them back into the woods. The crews of II/41 followed soon thereafter. FAR 41 had been completely suppressed and the crews did not return to the guns until after dark. The next day only 8 of the 12 guns of 1/FAR 41 and 2/41 could be made operational.

I/FAR 5 occupied a shallow depression at point 310 northeast of Bellevue at 0850. 3/5 was brought immediately to the rear of the infantry to provide close support with 'devastating effect'. The French conducted counter-battery fire against 3/5 all day without being able to suppress the battery.

The Battle of the Frontiers
French 124 RI

The French 8 DI was in a very dangerous tactical position. The lead two regiments had been wrecked. The division artillery, which had been marching immediately behind 124 RI, was stuck helpless on the road. The town of Virton and the terrain near it were in a valley and were indefensible, and if the Germans continued the attack, then the artillery was lost. When the Germans brought up their heavy howitzers, Virton would become a death trap. The 8 DI and IV CA commanders could hardly have known that the German 9 ID had orders to hold Bellevue, and had no intention of attacking Virton. They therefore decided to continue the attack in order to push the Germans away from Virton.

At 0800 the French IV CA commander ordered 124 RI to move forward to hold Virton, while he committed 117 RI to attack on its left. 124 RI, which had been following 130 RI, was able to deploy successfully just north of Virton, with III/124 in the centre, I/124 on the right and II/124 on the left. 2/154 occupied a strong defensive position in the churchyard on the northeast side of town. III/124 deployed with 10/124 astride the road and 11/124 on its right, both companies with two platoons in the first line, two in the second. 9/124, initially in reserve, was moved to the regimental left flank, with 12/124 following. The regiment advanced, but as the fog lifted it began to take fire and was pinned down. Fortunately, the German shrapnel burst too high. Since the troops did not have entrenching tools, they tried to dig in with their mess kits. Under these circumstances, the III/124 battalion commander decided to find cover farther forward, and ordered the battalion to advance. The two lead companies moved quickly, but were stopped at a thick hedge reinforced with barbed wire. In spite of the fact that there were no wire cutters, some of the troops were able to force their way through the obstacle. The lead companies then ran into the German IR 154 line, reinforced with MG, at a distance of 100m and were decimated. The remnants withdrew to the reverse slope. II/124 made three bounds forward and was stopped after advancing 50m. 8/124 was committed to try to push the attack forward, making 15m to 20m bounds forward, but was soon stopped too. After the battalion had taken about 50 per cent casualties, including most of its officers, it broke for the rear. The rest of I/124 charged up the hill in the dissipating fog, but it encountered small arms, MG and artillery fire that forced it to take cover about 150m north of the reservoir. Under heavy German fire the remnants of the regiment began to crumble and fall back to Virton

II/115, which had occupied the eastern end of the outpost line, had reassembled to the east of Virton. It was ordered to 'reoccupy' its positions on the crest. By this time, the fog had lifted, and when II/115 advanced on the right of 124 RI it was met by German small arms and MG fire that pinned it to the ground and rendered 1/3 of the battalion casualties. The battalion fell back to Virton.

At 0900 117 RI, the last intact regiment of 8 DI, was deployed to the east of Virton with orders to attack Robelment. When it moved out, 8 DI had one combat-effective battalion remaining, I/115 RI, with 2/124 defending the cemetery.

Four battered battalions held the 'line' north of Virton, huddling behind whatever cover they managed to find. Anyone who exposed himself was hit, and the French troops had practically stopped firing. 130 RI had been reduced to debris. The division artillery was disentangling itself from Virton and was moving to firing positions on Hill 280 southwest of St. Mard. The IV CA commander had moved to the same hill to set up his CP, from where, the battlefield being empty, he could see nothing. He was soon joined by the 8 DI commander.

French II CA

The II CA, to the left of IV CA, had bivouacked on the night of 21–22 August on the road from Meix devant Virton in the north to Montmédy in the south in a column 18km long, with 4 DI in front followed by 3 DI. The IV CA column began movement from 0200 to 0400 on 22 August, so that the advance guard might reach its start point at Bellefontaine at 0600. Movement was slow in a thick and cold fog; the road was full of artillery and ration vehicles and there were frequent halts. The troops were tired and had had neither breakfast nor coffee.

There now obtained a curious situation in which the German 9 ID was heading southwest towards Bellevue while the French 2 CA was heading north about 3km to the west. The danger that Moltke had warned 5th Army against had come to pass; 9 ID was engaged against the French 8 DI to its front, while three brigades of the French II CA were free to attack the open German right flank.

On the II CA line of march the road between Beauregard and Meix devant Virton lies deep in a valley, dominated by the high ground to the east and west. If the Germans held the heights near Robelmont they could interdict the road, cutting the II CA column in two and preventing movement to the north. The French II/147 RI of the 4 DI had bivouacked at Robelmont and its security detachments were pushed back at 0630 by the German IR 58. However, at this time the order arrived to withdraw to Meix devant Virton in order to march north and II/147 whose commander, showing a striking lack of initiative, pulled back, reaching Meix at 0800. The Germans were now in a position to occupy Robelmont unopposed.

German IR 58[8]

IR 58, with 3/FAR 41 in support, had been detached to secure Hill 305 east of Robelmont; the town was known to be occupied. By 0700, III/58 deployed on Hill 305 with 9/58 and 11/58 on line, 12/58 in reserve. I/58 occupied a covered position to the left of III/58, II/58 a covered position to the right. An officer's patrol from II/58 had taken fire from Robelmont. A cavalry patrol from 1st *Uhlan*, attached IR 58, discovered the French 4 DI column on the road at Meix. At 0845 8/58 was ordered to occupy a position north of Robelmont, opposite Meix devant Virton. An order from 9 ID, which arrived at 1000, instructed IR 58 to move forward to occupy Robelmont and protect the division right flank. The regiment advanced and found the town free of French troops. I/58 occupied Robelmont, II/58 the heights to the north of the town, while French artillery fire forced III/58 to dig in on the east side of Hill 305. Between 1100 and 1200 French infantry advanced from the west to within 1,100m of Robelmont but were taken under fire and approached no closer.

3/FAR 41, which was supporting IR 58, set up in an open position north of Robelmont by 0900. The battery commander established his observation post on the west end of the village, directly behind the infantry, communicating with the guns by telephone, and engaged French infantry in the valley at 1,800m range. 3/41 also took French counter-battery fire that destroyed a gun, an ammunition caisson and forced the gun crews to take cover.

French 117 RI

At 0900 117 RI, the last intact regiment of the 8 DI, was ordered to attack on the division left to take the heights near Robelmont. The advance in the low ground between Houdrigny and Virton was in dead space which prevented German observation and fire, and proceeded without difficulty, but as the regiment reached the plateau it was met by rifle, MG and artillery fire from the front as well fire from German troops on the right flank. By 1200 117 RI was pinned down. The regiment was about 600m from the Germans, who were themselves deployed on an open field, but the French troops could see nothing of the enemy.

French 3 DI

The French 3 DI marched behind the 4 DI on a single road. The problems inherent in marching a corps on one road made themselves felt. By the early morning of 22 August 3 DI had already been held up for two and a half hours due to the inevitable march delays resulting from putting so many troops, guns and supply vehicles on one road.

At 0900 German small arms and artillery fire began landing on the road west of Robelmont, which quickly rendered the road impassable. The French unit on the road at this point was 91 RI, the last unit of 4 DI. The II CA column was cut neatly in half. The commander of 91 RI decided to attack uphill towards Robelment. The regiment moved up out from the valley to the north of Houdrigny towards the high ground south of Robelmont, I/91 on the left, III/91 on the right, II/91 in reserve. The two lead battalions were soon pinned down by rifle, MG and artillery fire. II/91 was committed between the lead battalions and by 1000 all of 91 RI was immobilised. The troops hardly fired their weapons, in part due to a lack of identifiable targets.

The fog lifted and the 3 DI divisional artillery, 17 RAC, went into action on the heights above Houdrigny, while German 15cm shells began landing in the general vicinity. At 1015 the commander of the 3 DI committed two battalions of 87 RI to the right of 91 RI. This was a poor tactical decision: there was no room for 87 RI to deploy. III/87 advanced on the left and soon became intermixed with 91 RI while II/91 on the right became intermixed with 117 RI. 87 RI did nothing but thicken up the target array for the German infantry and artillery. Halfway up the slope to Robelmont–Bellevue the lead companies, still in column, took fire and deployed by bounds. At the cost of serious casualties they reached the plateau but the fire there was so intense that the lead companies fell back down to the slope, where the support companies joined them. By 1200 91 RI, I/117, III/117, III/87 and II/87 were jumbled together on a line 600m long along the slope halfway up to the plateau.

The 3 DI commander ordered 51 RI to move north cross-country from Sommethonne to occupy Meix devant Virton. I/51 took 45 KIA and 140 WIA in the process, apparently from flanking fire by II/IR 58 to the east of the town. 128 RI and 72 RI, plus the corps artillery, were still marching towards Sommethonne.

The II CA commander had great difficulty forming an appreciation of the situation. He returned to Sommethonne to get information concerning the 4 DI, and learned that it was engaged at Bellefontaine. He also received a report that there were German forces at Saint Léger, which led him to the conclusion that the Germans were going to attack to separate 4 DI from 3 DI. This made the II CA commander cautious. Only at 1100 did he decide to send 128 RI and half (two sections) of 29 RAC, the corps artillery, to attack Robelmont, and as a consequence any chance of a coordinated attack by II CA and IV CA on the German 9 ID slipped away. Staff coordination between the French corps was non-existent, and a face-to-face meeting between senior officers of the French II and IV CA, which were only a few kilometres apart, never took place. In fact, the German unit at St. Léger was German XIII AK, which had left St. Léger the morning of 22 August headed southwest, to Bleid and Mussy la Ville, not west. The right-hand brigade of XIII AK was engaged with the other IV CA division, 7 DI

French IV CA Artillery

The IV Corps artillery regiment, 44 RAC, which was marching behind the 7 DI, received orders to turn around and march several kilometres to the high ground south of St. Mard in order to support 8 DI. Since 7 DI was also in contact, the corps artillery commander left one section to support 8 DI and marched to St Mard with the rest. Only at 1000 did the French artillery engage German infantry (probably II/IR 19), moving east of the Etalle-Virton road in a westerly direction. Robelmont, which was assumed to be occupied by the Germans, was also bombarded. A suspected German battery on the tree line was also fired on, as was a positively identified battery near Robelmont.

The Battle of the Frontiers

The 1st section of the 8 DI artillery regiment, 31 RAC, set up to the west of Virton, but the 2nd and 3rd sections could not find suitable positions and had to push their way through the clogged roads to positions west of the corps artillery, north and northwest of the village of Harnoncourt. It could not fire until 1045, when it engaged suspected enemy artillery on the tree line and immediately received counter-battery fire that caused considerable damage to the limbers and caissons. After 1130 the German IR 7 reported taking heavy artillery fire that caused numerous casualties.

By the time that the French 8 DI and IV CA artillery opened fire, the infantry of the 8 DI had already been destroyed by a combination of German rifle, MG and artillery fire. The German 9 ID, thanks to its superb unit and officer training fought as a combined-arms team. The French 8 DI did not.

French IV CA Situation Report

Sometime after 1030, IV CA sent a situation report to 3rd Army. It said that 'The enemy had deployed out of the woods to the north of Virton.' No indication was given as to German strength or whether the Germans were attacking or defending. The report said that it did not appear that the Germans had more than three artillery sections. Concerning 8 DI, the report said that fight was being conducted on the front Houdrigny –Virton, that the division had engaged all four regiments, and that the French artillery was in position and seemed to possess fire superiority. There were too many troops massed in Virton and the excess troops were forming a fall-back position on the south bank of the Ton. Combat activity seemed to be dying down. The corps commander said that he had the general impression that the 8 ID would not be able to resume the offensive towards Etalle.

The 3rd Army liaison officer (LNO) assigned to IV CA submitted his own report at the same time. He said that the German attack did not seem to be determined, and if the 7 DI attacked on the 8 DI right that 'the matter would be on the right track.' Grasset found the LNO's report to be 'factually correct' and 'masterful'.[9]

Both reports failed to mention that the infantry of the 8 ID was wrecked and the real question at hand was whether the division could hang on to Virton or not. These reports prove that the senior leadership in the IV CA had no idea of the actual tactical situation.

A second corps situation report at 1115 acknowledged that the corps had been defeated. It began by saying that 'We still hold Virton.' In fact, there were only two intact companies in Virton, 11/115 RI and 2/124 in the cemeteries. Any visible French movement drew the attention of the German MGs. The report said that all 8 DI troops, except one battalion, were engaged. The 'sorely tried' troops of 130 RI and 124 RI were being regrouped. These troops were no longer capable of offensive action. 7 DI had suffered a defeat before it had reached Éthe. IV CA had sent a reserve infantry regiment to Éthe. The corps reported that it expected it could hold a line from Hill 280, where the corps' HQ stood, to the town of Ruette.

At 1200, IV CA ordered 8 DI to withdraw from Virton to Hill 280 south of the Ton. Due to German fire and the loss of leaders, 124 RI was no longer a combat-effective unit, command and control had collapsed, and the elements of 124 RI that were still in contact withdrew with difficulty. The withdrawing troops became a leaderless rabble. The remnants of 130 RI consisted of a captain, 7 lieutenants and 200 stragglers collected near St. Mard. About 300 130 RI men remained somewhere in Virton. A defensive line of sorts was cobbled together on Hill 280 in front of the artillery.

German V AK

At 0945 9 ID reported to the Corps HQ that Bellevue had been taken. Shortly thereafter the V AK commander arrived at the 9 DI HQ: he clearly believed that this was the critical point in his corps sector. Both he and the 9 ID commander were most concerned about the division right flank, since the gap to VI AK, marching to Tintigny, was covered only by 3 KD. They were admonished repeatedly by 5th Army HQ to guard this flank, proof that the Army HQ was well aware of its weakness.[10]

At this time a report from 10 ID arrived, saying that it was engaged at Éthe. German patrols made it clear to the 9 ID and V AK commanders that the French were massing west of Robelmont. At 1045 the V AK commander reported to 11 ID, which was moving on Tintigny, saying that enemy infantry and artillery were attempting to turn 9 ID's right flank. At 1200 a report from VI AK said that the corps was in contact at Tintigny and Rossignol and that the intent was to swing the corps left wing from Izel and Tintigny to the west. 3 KD was also in contact the woods between Saint Marie and Bellefontaine.

The German V AK and VI AK were separated by an army boundary, which can easily become a weak point due to lack of coordination, but the senior leadership of the two German corps took particular pains to insure that this did not occur. In contrast with the French II CA and IV CA, the German leadership had a good grasp of the tactical situation, identified the problem areas and communicated with each other.

German IR 19[11]

At 1000 the 9 ID commander, concerned by the French threat to the weak right flank, sent the 1st *Uhlan* Regiment to the north of Robelmont. It was followed by I/IR 19, the MG Company of IR 19, and II/FAR 57, which were sent to reinforce IR 58. These units began arriving at 1400. I/IR 19 moved into Robelmont, the artillery set up east of the town. French artillery fired continually at the town and the surrounding area.

The Battle of the Frontiers

Since the field of fire from the west edge of Robelmont was not very good, the I/19 battalion commander sent a platoon from 2/19 and two MG platoons forward to ground that offered wide visibility into the valley to the south and southwest. This was a brilliant use of the MG, which could deliver maximum firepower while presenting a small target. The movement the three platoons was noticed by the French artillery, which put accurate fire on them, but the losses were not severe because many of the French shells were duds (over fifty were found the next day), and every time the French artillery adjusted their fire onto German position, the small detachment was able to move to another position that was just as good. The fire of one MG platoon against a French battalion attacking from the west was 'visibly effective' and the French column fell back.

II/FAR 5 was initially held in reserve. At 1030 6/5 was deployed east of Robelmont to support IR 158 and engaged French infantry attacking southwest of the town. At 1115 it was joined by 4/5 and at 1200 by 5/5. Around 1200 the battle reached its peak, as French infantry pressed the attack and the French shifted their counter-battery fire to FAR 5. 1/5 and 2/5 avoided the French artillery fire with a slight shift of position: 6/5 had to manhandle the guns 40m to the rear so that they could be limbered up. The artillery situation for 9 ID improved considerably when the corps heavy howitzer battalion went into action in the afternoon, disrupting the French artillery.

9 ID also kept II/IR 19 in reserve. When III/19 arrived, it became the reserve and II/19 was sent to reinforce IR 154. IR 19 also had to send two of its MG ammunition wagons to IR 7, whose MG Company had fired off all of its ammunition. II/IR 19 moved to directly reinforce the IR 154. A platoon leader of 6/19 described the firefight. He said that after a difficult approach march the platoon made one long bound forwards and came to the firing line. The enemy was 900m away. It was necessary to conserve ammunition, for it was only early afternoon. Nevertheless, the troops were in their first engagement and began firing rapidly and nothing could slow them down. Only after the lieutenant had put his sabre on the individual weapons and shouted himself hoarse could he obtain a steady rate of fire. Around 1300 the troops dug skirmisher holes with their entrenching tools. The troops were now firing carefully at identified targets. The lieutenant picked up a French rifle and began firing. The troops lay in their position until dark.

A platoon leader from 7/19 said that the company had to make its way through hedges and wire fences with axes and wire cutters:

'As we had practiced a hundred times on Apple Tree Hill on the Labau local training area, the riflemen deployed on the reverse slope and crawled to the top, where there was a field of fire. With long bounds we went forward a few hundred metres to the line of the '154' men, who called out 'Range 600' to us as we arrived. It worked just like in training. There wasn't much to be seen of the enemy; he fought in groups, seeking cover behind hayricks or bushes. We had trouble controlling the distribution of fire, but on the other hand the expert riflemen came into their own. Our precisely aimed fire stopped every attack at 400m range. German rifle marksmanship training celebrated a triumph. Around midday we began to move forward again. Our advance with very short bounds and mutual fire support worked flawlessly ... Then the order came to dig in, and the entrenching tools flew out at once, and soon everyone had dug a skirmisher hole and set up his pack in front to support his weapon.'

The lieutenant commented on the fact that French carried their shining silver mess kit on the top of their packs, which was a fine target that was fatal for many French soldiers. He noted that the French canteens he inspected were all empty and smelled of alcohol. While gathering the dead, he said that the destructive power of German rifle and MG fire was plain to see: a French machine gunner corporal had died with a rosary in his hand, with the rest of his crew around him.

An NCO from 5/19 described running up the last slope and joining the firing line: 'It was as calm as a manoeuvre. Each man aimed carefully and squeezed the trigger. The old soldiers now and again said 'Hit'... The movement by bounds worked perfectly.' At the end of the day on 22 August the IR 19 regimental historian said that morale was 'excellent'.

Afternoon, 22 August

The last units of the French II CA, 128 RI and the II CA artillery, 22 RAC, were directed to manoeuvre to the left and deploy on the heights southwest of Meix devant Virton, where they arrived at 1400. The artillery engaged IR 158 at and north of Robelmont. 128 RI was ordered to attack to the south and east of Meix devant Virton. Then, at about 1630, a report reached 3 DI that a large body of German troops was advancing to the north of Meix devant Virton. A virtual panic set in. 128 RI's advance was stopped in the valley and the artillery of 22 RAC was pulled back to the north of Sommethonne. The report later turned out to have been false, but the damage had been done and these two units were out of the battle.

The German IR 7 and IR 154 held in place and continually dug in their fighting positions, aided by 1/5th Engineer Battalion. This was all the more necessary since from about 1100 on they began to take heavy French artillery fire.

By 1300 the only intact French infantry on the battlefield were the elements of 117 RI, 87 RI and 91 RI pinned down on the open plain east of Houdrigny, taking fire from the entire German line, principally from IR 7 and IR 58, but also long-range fire from II/IR 19 and IR 154. French troops advancing from Beauregard were engaged at 1,500m and 1,600m range by IR 154 on Hill 265.

The Battle of the Frontiers

German artillery fire on the French infantry was continual and caused serious casualties. The noise was deafening. II/117 RI lost 1/3 of its troops. 10/117 broke and ran for the rear. II/117 lost a machine gun while trying to bring it into action; III/117 couldn't get the MG into firing position at all. In 91 RI, several incidents of panicked flight to the rear were stopped by the officers only with considerable difficulty. In this confused situation, 5/91 tried to advance, was cut down by German fire, and then the company disintegrated in flight. The German troops were invisible; 87 RI fired back almost at random.

At 1815 a platoon leader in 3/117 RI ordered his troops to advance in order to stop a retreat. The rest of 1/117 advanced too, then I/117, then the entire regiment. The Germans replied with rifle and MG fire. The French reached some German IR 7 foxholes, but the German troops had pulled back to the tree line. The firefight had been intense, but lasted only ten minutes. It soon became dark, the German troops had ceased firing and there was mass confusion in 117 RI, which began to make its way down the slope to rejoin the division. Grasset said that the attack of 117 RI was a spontaneous act, the result of the spirit of offensive *à outrance* inculcated by the 1904 infantry regulation, that is, the regiment was motivated by offensive training that predated anything that Grandmaison had ever written.[12]

The order to withdraw was sent forward to all three regiments at 1900. 87 RI was in such a bad state that it could not even pull back; the units were intermixed, the losses in cadres had caused control to collapse and the men were utterly exhausted. II/87 finally pulled back with 400 men. III/87 never received the order to withdraw at all; when elements of III/87 and 91 RI began to fall back the battalion commander, in order to halt the retreat, sounded the charge. 5/87 7/87 and 8/87 attacked, took heavy casualties and then retreated.

German 3 KD[13]

The 3 KD spent 22 August completely inactive at St. Marie, between VI AK on its right and V AK on its left. V AK requested that the division operate against the flank of the French forces at Meix devant Virton to relieve the pressure on 9 ID. The cavalry division replied that it appeared impossible to move through the woods. A similar request from 11 ID was turned down for the same reason. The division also refused a request for support from FAR 6 against French troops advancing on Orsainfaing. That evening the division returned to the control of HKK 3 and moved to Esch, about 18km east of Longwy. The division was convinced that it was hemmed in by wooded terrain, which was unsuitable for cavalry, and that the only course of action was to stay in the open ground near St. Marie.

3 KD was used to plug the gap between 4th Army and 5th Army during the approach march, and then to fill the space between V AK and VI AK during the

Virton

battle. Performing this mission put 3 KD in such a position that it was immobilised by terrain and the enemy and friendly infantry corps. The cavalry division commander reconciled himself with this situation and exercised no initiative or imagination in trying to make his unit useful, either during the battle or in pursuit.

French Situation Reports

During the night of 22–23 August IV CA sent a situation report to 3rd Army. It listed the condition of each of the major units. The good news was that one and a half battalions of 115 IR were still cohesive. 117 RI, which had fought remarkably well for the entire day, still had one exhausted battalion. 124 RI had been decimated, two battalion commanders were dead, one was wounded, and the regiment was now the strength of one battalion. 130 RI had taken serious losses, particularly in officers, and was demoralised. One brigade commander was dead, the other dead or wounded. The divisional artillery had lost several caissons and a gun.[14]

The report of the 3rd Army LNO at 1630 said little except that the fighting had died down. The LNO offered the opinion that the situation was 'relatively good, if the enemy does not launch a strong attack on the IV CA front.' Such reports clearly sought to downplay the seriousness of the situation and show once again why the French senior commanders had difficulty forming an accurate estimate of the situation.

Casualties

The four infantry regiments of the French 8 DI had been destroyed. 130 RI had lost its regimental and battalion commanders, most of its captains and lieutenants and had been reduced in strength to a weak battalion, commanded by a captain. 124 RI had lost all three battalion commanders, almost all its officers and 770 EM. 117 RI had lost 775 OFF and EM, I/115 RI was reduced to two companies.

The two German regiments opposing them suffered far fewer casualties. IR 154 lost 6 OFF and 113 EM KIA and 18 OFF and 357 EM WIA. IR 7 casualties were probably of the same order of magnitude. II/IR 19 had very few casualties. The casualties in the French 3 DI were relatively light. 87 RI lost 11 OFF and 196 EM KIA, 349 OFF and EM WIA.

The German IR 58, which had been engaged all afternoon with the French 3 DI and the artillery of II CA, lost only 1 OFF and 18 EM KIA, 4 OFF and 91 EM WIA. 11 EM were MIA. The French infantry had not approached closer than 600m and the French artillery fire had not been particularly effective.

The German FAR 41 took extraordinarily heavy losses for an artillery unit: 35 EM KIA, 11 OFF and 122 EM WIA, 66 horses lost. These were the highest one-day losses that the regiment took during the entire war. FAR 5 lost 16 EM KIA, 8 OFF and 72 EM KIA, 29 horses killed and 21 injured. Four ammunition caissons had been blown up. The German artillery had deployed in the open in order to support the infantry, which it did very effectively, but this left it vulnerable to French counter-battery fire.

23 August

The French IV CA operations order for 23 August, issued at 2330, 22 August, was quite matter-of-fact. It said that the enemy had held his positions north of Virton and that the 7 DI had withdrawn to the southeast. On the left, II CA had advanced to the north, on the right; V CA had withdrawn a short distance. From this wildly inaccurate summary, one would think that all had gone well with the 3rd Army. The order then said, without further comment, that the corps would defend on the west bank of the Chiers, with rear-guards holding the towns of Dampicourt, Rouvroy, Harnoncourt and La Malmaison on the east bank. In other words, the corps was on the start line of 21 August.

The German 9 ID held in place during the night, with officers and NCOs of all grades pushing the troops to dig in. The division was informed that it would defend in place on 23 August. Numerous night patrols were sent out, which even entered Virton and interrogated the inhabitants. They established that the French had withdrawn all along the front. They also identified the regiments by the French dead, and thereby determined that they had been fighting the French 4 DI and 8 DI

By daylight the IR 154 holes were deep enough for standing soldiers. Good, tough leadership paid off: at 1100 the French artillery began an intense bombardment that lasted until 1700. Nevertheless, there were no casualties. FAR 5 conducted an artillery duel with the French artillery during most of the afternoon. The German regiments patrolled aggressively. IR 154 patrols established the location of French artillery batteries and infantry. The patrol reports made it clear that the French were withdrawing.

Conclusions

Superior German reconnaissance and troop-leading procedures gave the German advanced guard, IR 7, perhaps thirty minutes head start on the French advance guard, 130 RI. These thirty minutes were absolutely decisive. They allowed IR 7 to deploy and attack Bellevue while 130 RI was 500m away from the farm and still in march column. IR 7 then engaged 130 RI, which offered no effective resistance and was quickly destroyed. IR 7 was able to seize the decisive terrain at Bellevue and hold it.

The rest of the battle consisted of a daylong firefight dominated by German rifle fire, supported by the German MG and artillery. Both the German and

Virton

French infantries were lying in open fields, although the fact that the German infantry had entrenching tools gave them an advantage. The French 8 DI battered itself to pieces trying to retake Bellevue. Four German infantry regiments, under attack from the west and south by seven French regiments, maintained fire superiority for the entire day and inflicted disproportional losses on the French infantry. At the height of the battle the German 9 ID was defending a line 4.5km long. All the division's infantry had been committed to the firing line with the exception of three companies, which constituted a very small division reserve.

The regimental historian of IR 154 said that the regiment's success was due for the greatest part to its high state of marksmanship training and outstanding fire discipline, which was supervised in combat by leaders of all grades. His conclusion was right on the mark, and applied equally to all the German regiments. In after-action reports, the German troops said that the French were tough and brave in the defence and particularly adept at using the terrain. However, the French infantry generally fired too high.

The French infantry was unable to coordinate fire and movement. Instead of supporting movement by fire, time after time the French infantry advanced until it was pinned down in an exposed position that offered no possibility for effective return fire. German rifle and MG fire dominated the battlefield.

The German artillery was outnumbered 2–1 and was being fired upon from the west and south. It occupied a very restricted area and was firing from open positions and was therefore easy for French artillery observers to find. The German artillery suffered heavily and its fire was not decisive. The German 9 ID artillery found the accuracy of the French artillery 'particularly the heavy artillery' was 'unpleasant'. The Germans had the impression that the French knew the terrain intimately. They said that the French batteries were well sited and difficult to find, and had such long range that sometimes the German heavy artillery could not reach them.[15] This complaint would be repeated frequently during the entire Marne campaign. We encounter it for the first time because the previous artillery duels had generally been close-range gunfights – which the German artillery usually won.

In fact, the French did not know the terrain any better than the Germans, the French did not have any heavy artillery at Virton and the maximum range of the French field gun was not significantly different than that of the German – and nowhere near the range of the German heavy howitzer. The principal difference between the two artilleries seems to be that the Germans emphasised open gun positions in order to provide close infantry support whereas the French artillery preferred covered gun positions. In the resulting artillery duels the German guns were exposed, while the French guns were practically impossible for the Germans to locate. On the other hand, the adjutant of I/FAR 41 said that the French artillery set up so far to the rear that it could not distinguish between friendly and enemy forces and for that reason could not effectively support their infantry.

The Battle of the Frontiers

The German 5th Army's decision to attack on 22 August put the German 9 ID in a potentially fatal position, exposed to attack by two French divisions, which were supported by two corps artillery regiments. The 9 ID had to seize the plateau around Bellevue and hold this exposed terrain against everything that the superior French forces could throw at them for the rest of the day. The 9 ID succeeded because of almost faultless tactical decision-making and the superb execution of combat tasks by the infantry and artillery.

9 ID was aided by a succession of French errors, beginning with poor reconnaissance. For two hours after the fog lifted the Germans fought a combined-arms battle against French infantry that had no artillery support. There was no coordination between the attacks of 8 DI and 3 DI. 3 DI was committed in driblets, one regiment after the other. The inability of the French 3 DI, supported by the II Corps artillery, to make any headway whatsoever against two German regiments (IR 154 and a battered IR 7), speaks volumes of the French inability to conduct an encounter battle.

9
Éthe and Bleid[1]

French 7 DI

Due in large part to the 14th Hussars' inability to push back the German security units, 7 DI reached its bivouac areas so late that it was not possible to send its own security forces north of the Basse Vire. 103 RI established the outpost line on the north side of the Bois des Loges, the Jeune Bois and Gomery. It does not appear that even night patrols were sent to Éthe or north of the Ton. The division bivouacked in column: 104 RI in Ruette, 13th Brigade at Malmaison and the rest of the division as well as the corps units further to the south.

The IV CA order for 22 August arrived at 0200 that morning. 7 DI was to march through Éthe and then turn east through Saint-Leger. It was to counterattack north against any German offensive against the right flank of the II CA. Start time from Éthe was 0500. The order of march was 14th Hussars, then 104 RI as advanced guard, followed at a 2km interval by the main body, led by 103 RI, then the division artillery, and finally the 13th Brigade. The corps engineers and the corps artillery, protected by 317 RIR, would follow 7 DI. The cavalry had apparently not conducted any patrolling either that night or during the morning.

Éthe lies in a bowl in the Ton valley. North of the town the ground, consisting of pasture and farmland, rises gradually for 150m to a plateau. From this plateau only the tops of the houses of Éthe are visible. To the southeast is a hill near Gevimont, which was pastureland. To the south are more hills, covered at the top by woods. While artillery set up to the north of Éthe cannot place observed fire on the town itself, it has excellent fields of fire on the hills to the southeast and south. The ground was covered by a thick fog, which began to lift at around 0830.

14th Hussars, leading the 7 DI column, made contact at 0500 in Éthe with a patrol of the 19th *Uhlans*. The Germans initially defended the railway station, and then fell back. At this time, unknown to the French, the lead elements of the German 10 ID were 1500m north of Éthe moving south, and 53rd Brigade from the German XIII AK was 3,500m northeast of Gomery moving southwest.

Grasset, the French military historian, who was an officer in 103 RI at this time,[2] recommended that the division should stop; one battalion should hold Éthe while the 14th Hussars reconnoitred to the front. This emphasis on 'security' was straight out of Bonnal and would have given Grandmaison fits. The 7 DI commander said that such a procedure would have required the division to halt (at its start point!) for two hours and expose the flank of the 9 DI on the right. He also said that if the Germans attacked Éthe, one battalion would not have stopped them.[3] He was completely correct on both counts. The real problem was 14th Hussar's lack of interest in separating itself from the infantry to conduct long-range patrols, a problem that it was too late to solve at this point. This small incident shows how prevalent Bonnal's tactics still were in the French army, and how weak was the influence of Grandmaison's ideas.

At 0530 the commander of the 7 DI sent III/101 RI to Bleid to guard the division right flank. Once again, this was a 'security detachment' straight out of Bonnal. The division commander employed a battalion where a platoon patrol would have served just as well, while exposing the isolated battalion to destruction in detail.

The 14th Hussars marched down the road to Saint Leger, just in front of the advance guard infantry, and at 0600 encountered German infantry in strength. By 0645 III/103 RI had gone to the Hussar's assistance and deployed on a line 2,500m long between Hamawé and Gévimont, far too great a frontage for a battalion. The French had run into the *Uhlans* again, this time reinforced by the engineer company of 27 ID.

The advance guard of 7 DI began to fan out. II/103, expecting only enemy cavalry, spread out in company-sized detachments all along the north edge of Ethe. In 15 minutes they made contact with the lead elements of the German 10 ID marching from the north. This was completely unanticipated. In response, I/104 occupied the rail embankment to the east of Éthe, a massive earthwork four metres high and five metres across, and II/104 deployed on its right.

At 0745, the lead brigade commander reported personally to the commander of 7 DI at the bridge south of the town, saying that the firing was probably due to contact with German patrols in the town, and that he had ordered the buildings to be searched. Like all the other senior French commanders on 22 August, the general officers of the 7 DI had not the slightest idea of the actual size of the German force opposing them.

The CG of 7 DI entered Éthe and began to give orders to platoon leaders. He sent a platoon of 5/103 and four or five hussars to attack the Germans entering Éthe from the north. The platoon was cut to ribbons by German fire and the platoon leader killed. He then directed two platoons of III/104 to guard the

Éthe and Bleid

north side of Éthe. At this time, the commander of 7 DI says he decided to hold Éthe 'at all costs'.[4] This may be an *ex post facto* rationalisation. There is every reason to believe that he had no idea that serious German forces opposed him and expected to quickly pass through Éthe. He therefore let matters drift. If he actually made a decision to defend Éthe, it was a fundamental tactical mistake: Éthe lies at the bottom of a river valley and was indefensible. If the 14th Brigade was seriously engaged while in Éthe it was almost certain to be destroyed. It might still have been possible to disengage the 14th Brigade in the fog and defend the woods south of the town with a unified division, which is where the 7 DI might have established a line. But even this position was precarious, for here the 7 DI right flank was completely in the air, guarded at Bleid by a single battalion.

German IR 50

Like 9 ID, 10 ID conducted a night march to occupy a forward assembly area. The troops finished the march tired and wet and found whatever dry spot they could to take off their packs and sleep. Their rest was soon ended by a silent alarm. The troops drank their coffee from the field kitchens and then began their march, except for 9/50, which had been on outpost duty. As a 9/50 squad leader said, the troops were 'freezing and tired…the troops' attitude was not rosy…The company commander called out, as he often did in peacetime when everyone was exhausted, 'Heads up, people! The coffee will be replaced by perfect military bearing!' and the old joke gave the troops comfort'.[5]

At 0520 the advanced guard of the 10 ID, IR 50, began its movement towards Éthe, about the same time as, 10km to the south, the advance guard of the French 7 DI started its movement north. 2/IR 50 left the wood line north of Ethe at 0630.[6] The fog was very thick. The point platoon entered Ethe at 0715, took fire and fell back on the advance guard company. The advance guard battalion deployed 4/50 to the left of 2/50, 1/50 to the right, 3/50 remained in reserve. The battalion was soon involved in a close-range firefight and took heavy casualties. At 0750 the regimental commander ordered I/50 to push through to the south side of Ethe to the west of the road to Gomery. III/50 was committed on the left with 11/50 and 12/50 in the first line and 9/50 and 10/50 following in echelon left. I/50 fought through Éthe house by house and pushed on to the south side. The battalion began to run out of ammunition, but the munitions wagon raced through the enemy fire and delivered ammunition straight to the front line. At 0750 the IR 50 MG Company was on the hill engaged behind I/50. It took fire from the platoon of the French 6/103 RI, which had been sent as flank security to Belmont. The MG Company changed front to the west to engage them, losing its first man KIA. At 800m range the French were clearly visible and 'just like on the firing range' in short order the French infantry was suppressed. The MG company then shifted front back to the south and for the rest of the day 'engaged many worthwhile targets (staffs, infantry, cavalry, a MG in the church tower) in Éthe and out to the Bois de Loges.' III/50 assumed a firing position north of Éthe and as the fog lifted was involved in a firefight with French troops on the rail embankment east of the town. Since the French seemed to be extending their line to the east, at 0800 9/50 and 10/50 were committed on the firing line. By 0830 most of II/50 was on line intermixed with III/50.

Destruction of the French 14th Hussars

At 0830 the French II/104 and III/103, which were in a firefight with German forces to their front near Hamawe, began to receive artillery fire from their rear, which came from the German I/FAR 56 north of Éthe. The lead French elements were now clearly in trouble.

The 7 DI commander ordered I/104 to attack across the rail line to the north. The terrain in front of the battalion rose slowly for 150m to the plateau, which was the limit of visibility. The ground was covered with ripe grain. The battalion moved out at 0830 and took casualties as it advanced with 30m bounds until it reached the crest, where it was met by a blast of German rifle, MG and artillery fire. 2/104 lost three-quarters of its strength. 1/104 was unable to cross over the crest of the hill, one platoon lost 48 of 58 men. A platoon of 3/104 took 75 per cent casualties. The remnants of the battalion were pinned down and by 1100 their position was untenable. The 100 or so men remaining were unable to return the German fire and the battalion commander ordered them to withdraw to the rail line.

Once contact had been made, the 14th Hussars fell back behind the lead infantry battalions, with unsuitable terrain on all sides. The only tactically sound course of action was to have withdrawn the cavalry regiment under the cover of the fog to the south side of the Jeune Bois – Le Mat and then perhaps move it to cover the division right flank at Bleid. The commander of the 14th Hussars was Lieutenant Colonel Hauteclocque, whom Grasset says was one of the two best students in his class at the French War College, the other being Weygand, the head of the French army in 1940. If true, Hauteclocque must have been a far better strategist than he was a tactician. Hauteclocque apparently decided that pulling back would look like he was avoiding a fight, so he decided to launch a mounted charge against the German forces north of the rail line. The only way to reach the north side of the rail embankment was through a tunnel east of Éthe. Hauteclocque put himself at the head of his regiment, cried "En avant! Pour la France!" and charged through the tunnel. He immediately had his horse killed from under him and the troopers behind him stopped in their tracks. Hauteclocque remounted and charged through the tunnel again. A platoon of cavalry following him succeeded in reaching the open ground north of the embankment but was destroyed by German fire. The rest of the regiment stopped south of the tunnel. Only Hauteclocque,

Éthe and Bleid

wounded, and a captain rejoined the regiment. Hauteclocque told the captain to take the regiment in open order through the town to the south side of the Ton. But the squadrons had become intermixed, the noise was deafening, and command and control collapsed. The captain could only get the attention of about a hundred troopers in his immediate vicinity; these made a wild ride through Éthe and, still hidden by the fog, raced up the hill to the Jeune Bois and all the way back to Ruette. The rest of the regiment wasn't so lucky. Led by the regimental executive officer, to avoid German fire they crossed the Ton 200m to the east of the bridge. The fog lifted and the regiment tried to make a break for the Jeune Bois across the open hillside. The German I/IR 50, accompanied by two MGs, had already penetrated to the south side of Éthe, the rest of IR 50, including the remaining four MGs, were in firing positions just north of the town. IR 50 was presented with the target straight out of a gunnery range. The 14th Hussars were effectively destroyed – on 23 August it could assemble 10 OFF and 180 EM. Accompanied by his orderly and a trooper, Hauteclocque passed on foot through Ethe and crossed the Ton, but all three were killed trying to climb the slope to the Jeune Bois. A squad leader in 9/50 wrote of the battle:

> '…. the August sun drove the fog completely away and the heat began to be quite uncomfortable. Sweat poured down our faces…. The troops took off their packs and used them as rifle rests. Well-aimed fire finally began to shake the will of the French on the rail embankment. Then – we could hardly believe our eyes – French cavalry charged towards us…. we opened fire at close range: now all that mattered was to fire as fast as possible. My shoulder was sore – the next day it would be black and blue – but shoot, shoot. The French cavalry couldn't take this murderous fire. The ones that had not been put out of action turned around and disappeared into the woods on the other side. Some of the riders had approached to within about 20m from our position. The French continually brought up reinforcements. Every French attack failed in the face of the well-aimed fire of our infantry. Repeated rapid fire led to a shortage of ammunition, which we relieved at first by taking the ammunition from the dead and wounded. First Sergeant Petersen came over from the left flank and pointed out to us the heads of the enemy as they appeared over the rail embankment. The cries for ammunition drew Captain Killmann to the front line. Just as the first sergeant raised his arm to show the captain the enemy location, his arm sank to the ground: 'our Petersen' was dead. Weeping, the company commander closed the eyes of the first sergeant, no longer leader and subordinate, but comrades.'

German 10 ID Artillery[7]

I/FAR 56 was tasked with supporting the advance guard.[8] At 0730 it set up just beyond the tree line, on both sides of the road, 2km north of Éthe. The section

The Battle of the Frontiers

began to take small arms and artillery fire. The fog was lifting, but Éthe was invisible in the valley and there was no room in I/FAR 56's current position to deploy the rest of the artillery. The divisional artillery commander requested and received permission to deploy all his guns well forward on the slope above Éthe.

The divisional artillery commander ordered the entire 10 ID artillery brigade forward, using the cover of the fog as much as possible, to occupy an open position on the slope above Éthe. He instructed each artillery regiment to assign one section to fire on Éthe, Belmont and the hillside to the south. The other section would conduct systematic area counter-battery fire of the suspected French artillery positions on the reverse slope of the hill south of Éthe. Two batteries in each counter-battery section would fire shrapnel; one would fire high explosives.

As the FAR 56 regimental historian said 'The disadvantages of a mostly open position had to be accepted. The first priority was to be able to provide effective fire support.' 2/56 and 3/56 set up 800m north of Éthe to the west of the road, 1/56 to the east. From this position, both the town and the opposite slope could be engaged. The section opened fire at 0800.

II/FAR 56, the light howitzer section, galloped forward under fire. 4/56 set up in an open firing position to the right of I/56 and immediately engaged French MGs. 5/56 and 6/56 found covered positions further to the right.

FAR 20 raced forward under French rifle and artillery fire at the same time.[9] It was a wild ride over uneven ground. Guns and caissons tipped over; the infantry helped in setting them upright. The regiment began to take casualties. Some guns moved into their positions without difficulty; some got stuck and had to be pushed up the last incline by gunners and infantrymen. I/FAR 20 set up to the east of the road, with II/20 on its left, level with the infantry and sometimes in front of it. Most of the batteries were in open positions, with only the standing grain offering some concealment. Except for 5/20, which could engage the western edge of Éthe, the town was in defilade. By 0930 both German artillery regiments were in action.

While the battery command position of 5/20 was setting up: 'The NCO in charge of the battery command scope got his first chewing-out; the eyepieces had not been correctly adjusted. Any tension in the battery disappeared; we could just as well have been on an exercise at the MTA in Neuhammer or Lawica'.[10]

When the fog in the valley lifted, the slope to the south of Éthe presented itself to the German artillery as an immense panorama. The red trousers and the flapping coats were of the advancing French infantry were clearly visible to the gunners; there were so many targets that the batteries could not fire as units and they had to be engaged by platoons or even by individual guns.

Éthe and Bleid

Destruction of the 7 DI Advance Guard Artillery

At 0800 the lead battery (7/26 RAC) of the 7 DI advance guard artillery was stuck in a traffic jam, the lead elements stopped in the main crossroads in the centre of Éthe, unable to move forward because of the infantry combat to the north and east, unable to find suitable firing positions, and with the road to its rear blocked by 8/26 RAC, which had stopped just north of the bridge over the Ton. The next battery in the column, 9/26, and the ammunition caissons were on road all the way up to the Jeune Bois. The detachment commander instructed 7/26 and 8/26 to find firing positions where they were; 9/26 was to turn around. He was too late.

At 0845 the fog lifted and a hail of rifle and MG fire descended on the French artillery. The German artillery joined in, firing at maximum rate. The German infantry and gunners could hardly miss; the French artillery was parked nose-to-tail on the hillside at point-blank range. At the same moment, 14th Hussars made their death ride across the hillside. Practically every German bullet or shell must have hit something. Grasset said 'in a few seconds there was a horrible slaughter'.[11]

Three gun teams and their crews were destroyed on the road. The other nine guns of advanced guard artillery managed to reach cover in Éthe, but could not find suitable gun positions and could not see the Germans. Since the ammunition caisson horse teams had all been killed, the caissons were stranded in the beaten zone of the German fire, leaving the guns in Éthe with very little ammunition.

7 DI Advance Guard Cut Off

The 14th Brigade of the 7 DI was now cut off in Éthe. It was not surrounded by German troops; the Jeune Bois to the rear was still in French hands and would remain so for the rest of the day. Rather, the 14th Brigade was cut off by German rifle, MG and artillery fire, which prevented reinforcement or withdrawal. Ammunition could not reach the brigade, nor could the wounded be evacuated.

Lt. Kruse of II/FAR 20 described the German barrage:[12] 'Red trousers appeared out of the tree line on the horizon: we'd gotten here at just the right time (he probably saw the French I/103 RI, the last unit of the 14th Brigade). Defying death, the French stormed forwards, although in addition to 5/20, 4/20 and 6/20 directed their fire against their ranks. Wave after wave broke from the protective cover and into the open. In front of the forest was a stubble field, beyond that a hedge, which was the boundary between life and death. In front of us was our infantry, firing rapidly; beyond them, the French. It was a massacre. Every salvo from the three batteries reaped a dreadful harvest. Ten minutes after we had begun firing the French called off their advance. Here and there individual Frenchmen could be seen fleeing into the woods'. FAR 20 found a report, probably by the commander of I/103 RI, to his regiment, which said that it was absolutely impossible to attack out of the Jeune Bois or Bois des Loges to Belmont, and that his battalion was completely out of control.

This may be the first time in modern warfare that a major manoeuvre unit would be cut off and destroyed solely by firepower, without an infantry assault. Éthe demonstrates that the German army had drawn the appropriate conclusions from the technological progress – smokeless powder, the magazine-fed rifle, the machine gun and quick-firing artillery – that had led to an exponential increase in the effectiveness of firepower and expanded the depth of the battlefield, while the French were still essentially thinking in terms of the smaller Napoleonic battlefield

The 7 DI commander, the division staff and division artillery commander were located with the advanced guard and therefore could not effectively communicate with the second brigade and the remainder of the division artillery. Nor could the division HQ send a situation report to corps. Command and control in the 7 DI had collapsed.

On the other hand, at 1200 the German V AK reported to 5th Army that it had taken Belmont and Laclaireau, demonstrating that the German command and control system was functioning far better.[13]

Artillery Duel

From map analysis FAR 20 determined that French artillery (the rest of the 7 DI artillery and the IV CA artillery) was probably firing from defilade positions south of Éthe –Gomery. Two French artillery batteries were also thought to be firing from Hill 293 north of Latour. These guns continually overshot FAR 20. The German regiment also suspected that there was at least another French battery behind the Jeune Bois. Two French guns were identified by a thin cloud of smoke and suppressed. The French forward observers had to be on the northern tree line of the Jeune Bois.

The German artillery therefore began firing a planned counter-battery program. German counter-battery doctrine emphasised that such unobserved area fire required a great deal of ammunition and might not yield any results, but in this case it was very effective: the French artillery suffered significant casualties from the 10 ID counter-battery fire, and the commander of 26 RAC was killed. German artillery fire on the tree line must have suppressed the French FOs; even though the German guns were in open positions, the fire from the French artillery was so uncontrolled it appeared to be practically random.

A French battery attempted to escape from Éthe. It was immediately engaged by 4/FAR 20 and 5/20 and destroyed. The regimental historian wrote: 'A moving enemy battery at 1,200m range! What a rare target! It is unlikely that anyone was able to escape the annihilating fire of the two batteries. A few individuals attempted to crawl along the road ditches to the rear. In vain! Our shrapnel got them. The riders who tore like mad across the open field towards the woods were no luckier. On the next day the enemy battery presented a truly terrible picture: guns, horses, drivers and gunners, all cut down!'

Around 1300 French artillery fire became murderously effective. Just south of the junction of the tree line and the road a large concentration of German troops had carelessly assembled. French artillery singled them out and killed the General Staff officer of 10 ID, the commander of IR 6 and his adjutant and caused a panic in the massed vehicles of the IR 6 MG Company and trains, FAR 56 caissons, field hospital and other assorted support units.

FAR 56 also took heavy French artillery fire. 4/56 was hit by 'a hail of shells' and took heavy casualties, 3/56 was deluged by 'hundreds of shells'. The commander of II/56 was wounded; the surgeon of I/56 lost an eye but continued to treat the wounded. In accordance with peacetime doctrine the caissons and limbers had set up 200–300m behind the guns, on the tree line, crowded around what little cover was available. The French artillery fire landed with 'fearful effectiveness'. The horses panicked and ran away, vehicles were overturned. The losses in men and horses were heavy. At the same time, 4/56 engaged a French battery trying to set up below the Jeune Bois and destroyed all but one gun.

To add to the FAR 56's difficulties, at 1345 the French 5/104 RI, cut off by the advance of the 53rd Brigade and trying to escape to the north, appeared behind the batteries and opened fire, causing even more confusion in the rear areas. 1/56 and several guns of II/56 swung around and, helped by an engineer company that happened to be in the area, pushed the French back into the woods.

On the other hand, 4/FAR 20 evaluated the effectiveness of French counter-battery fire as 'miserable', in spite of a massive expenditure of ammunition. The battery suffered three WIA. The next day the German artillery officers, always professionally curious, looked at their position from the French point of view and established that it was difficult to distinguish the German II/FAR 20 position half-way down the slope from the tree line behind it. The French had therefore shelled the tree line, thinking that they were engaging the German guns. This fire was hard on the staffs and caissons near the tree line, but left the German guns completely unsuppressed and free to engage a succession of targets practically at leisure.

German IR 47[14]

The regiment was awoken by silent alarm at 0330, drank its coffee in the dark and marched behind IR 50 at 0400 as the first unit of the division main body. At 0800, with IR 50 engaged at Éthe, 10 ID ordered 20th Brigade (IR 50 and IR 47) to take Éthe, while the 19th Infantry Brigade (IR 56 and IR 6) swung to the right towards Belmont.

IR 47 deployed with I/47 and III/47 to the east of the road, II/47 to the west. At 0815, II/47 was sent to extend the right flank of IR 50 and maintain contact

The Battle of the Frontiers

with the 19th Brigade on the right, while the rest of the regiment was to move through the woods to approach Éthe from the northeast. Shortly after the regiment moved out, French artillery fire landed in the spot that they had just vacated.

The 20th Brigade commander personally directed a platoon of 10/47 to extend the left flank of III/50, which was about 500m north of Éthe and had begun to dig in. The platoon linked up with III/50 with little loss. III/50 was delivering a quick rate of fire against the rail embankment 400m to the front and the platoon of 10/7 joined in. The platoon leader wrote about the fight:

'The heads of the French were easily recognizable when they aimed and fired. I was pleased to see that my people were firing calmly and exactly. In front of us there was an underpass in the rail embankment and a signalman's house… Around 1400 the enemy fire became weaker. Fire continued to pour out of the signalman's house. I had three squads fire several salvos at the door and the windows, and soon a white flag appeared. I approached the house with my platoon, the door opened and about 20 Frenchmen came out. They were horribly terrified, because their lives were at stake; many threw themselves down in front of me, seized my knees and hands and begged me for mercy for the sake of their families. I quieted them down and had them marched away. Then we climbed the rail embankment and could see that our marksmanship had been outstanding. Almost all of the French that lay there had been shot in the head; the prisoners told us that they hadn't dared to expose their heads in order to aim.'

To the left, 9/47 came out of the tree line in time to see French infantry advancing in thick skirmisher lines and in squad columns. The French were thrown back by the company's fire, but the enemy found cover behind the rail embankment. In the ensuing firefight the soldiers of 9/47, who were in a field with standing grain and clover, had to kneel in order to fire and took considerable casualties.

The 1st Platoon of 11/47 crossed the rail line, ran into advancing French infantry in a field 75m away and began a close-range firefight. Sergeant Barufke remembered how calmly one of his soldiers, Hermann Miethe, fired:

'Just like at home on the rifle range, he said to himself at every shot 'Aim – Squeeze – Unload – Load'. A bullet shot his glasses off his nose. He carefully bent them straight, cleaned the unbroken right lens with his thumb and forefinger and put them back on his nose and then continued 'Aim – Squeeze' in the same monotone. Suddenly his head was pulled upwards; his helmet slid onto the back of his neck – a bullet had taken off the point on the helmet. But even this did not disturb him.'

It would be hard to find a better example of the value of drill in combat.

More and more troops, and finally an MG joined the platoon. The Germans gained fire superiority. Individual French soldiers ran to the rear and were followed by others; finally the rout became general. Few escaped 'because the fleeing soldiers were excellent targets'. The battle here had lasted three hours. 11/47 and 12/47 tried to pass through a tunnel in the embankment in column, but were pushed back by French fire from the tree line on the opposite side. The companies then began the firefight from positions on the rail embankment. The 12/47 company commander had been killed and the first sergeant went to the left flank to take charge. The first sergeant observed how French soldiers crawled along a sunken road to seek cover behind a wall. Gathering three riflemen, they killed or wounded 15 of these soldiers with well-aimed rifle fire. 100m to the front was a walled farm. With three squads the first sergeant moved by rapid bounds under heavy fire across the meadow that led down to the farm. With the last bound he shouted '*les armes à bas!*' and found that he had captured 83 French soldiers.

The Cauldron at Éthe

The only unit opposing the advance of IR 47 at Laclaireau was 8/103. Massively outnumbered, by 1000 8/103 had been destroyed, along with a platoon from 10/104 and another from 11/104 that had been sent to reinforce it. This exposed the right flank of the French II/104 RI, which was defending along the rail line to the east of Éthe. By 0930 the firefight here was fierce, and at 1030 MG fire from IR 47 to the north enfiladed the French line. The withdrawal from the exposed position became a panic and II/104 disintegrated, with the men fleeing towards Éthe.

The French troops at Hamawé were now cut off. 5/104 tried to escape at 1115 by marching to the north. It ran into the caissons of the German artillery, whose fire forced the French troops back into the woods. These troops wandered around in the German rear areas until 24 August, when they were rounded up.

On the west end of Éthe the German IR 46 broke up the companies of the French 103 RI defending there and pushed the remnants into or south of the town. FAR 20 went on a systematic search for the French MG in Éthe, sending out FOs who found and suppressed them.[15]

Between 1000 and 1100 the debris of the French 14th Brigade was forced, in small groups, usually without officers, back into Éthe. The largest remaining organised unit was 4/103. By 1200 the 14th Brigade was no longer a combat-effective unit and the commanding general of 7 DI decided to break out and resume command of the rest of his division – about three hours too late.

By 1100 the artillery fire lifted the pressure on IR 50 significantly. At 1200 the French began to attempt to reach the woods to the south of Éthe. IR 50 engaged them with pursuit fire, but in accordance with higher orders IR 50 did not pursue beyond Éthe itself. It seems quite likely that the commander of the 10 ID recognised the pointlessness of street fighting in Éthe or a frontal attack on the Jeune Bois and therefore did not press the attack. According to Grasset, who may on this one occasion be right concerning German motivation, at 1300 the commander of the German 10 ID thought that Éthe was only an advanced French position, and that the French main line of defence was along the Jeune Bois.[16] This was a naturally strong position, which he was unwilling to attack until IR 46 had turned the French left flank and had taken the Jeune Bois from the west. Then the remaining French troops in Éthe could be attacked from the front and rear. Nevertheless, by 1700 most of Éthe was in German hands. The battle wound down during the afternoon to the degree that FAR 20 sent troops into Éthe to requisition food, and several cattle that were found on the battlefield were slaughtered and cooked.

German XIII AK[17]

The unit to the left of the German 10 ID was the XIII Corps. XIII AK was part of the army of the state of Württemberg, which, like those of of Saxony and Bavaria, had its own administrative apparatus separate from the Prussian army. All of its unit records below corps level have therefore survived in the state archive in Stuttgart, including the corps and division war diaries. The Württemberger are famous amongst Germans for their industriousness, which is saying a very great deal indeed, so the war diaries and *Gefechtsberichte* (combat after-action reports) from company to division level are of especially high quality. In sum, the records for the XIII AK are the best available for this period, equalled only by those of the XIV AK archives at Karlsruhe and the Bavarian army archives at Munich.

Cavalry Patrol

On the afternoon of 21 August the XIII AK cavalry regiment, 19th *Uhlans*, sent out several patrols to the west and southwest. One such, consisting of an NCO and 10 men, led by Lt. Ebner, departed from Meix-la-Tigne. He reported that once his patrol has passed through the woods southwest of Meix he ordered the troopers to spread out. Keeping a sharp eye out, the patrol passed from one hill to the next, leaving Bleid on the right, until it reached the main Musson –Virton road, about 10km from his point of departure. There he set up an observation post in a farm on high ground that offered excellent visibility to the south. After a time he saw a long French column of infantry and cavalry approaching St. Remy, 1km to the south. He sent two couriers by different routes at a gallop to report to division HQ; his is the first report of contact with a major French unit. His patrol was eventually detected and drew fire, at which time he pulled back.

This was a textbook piece of patrolling. It was made possible by the failure of the French cavalry to establish a counter-reconnaissance screen; Ebner reported that in the column he had seen the French cavalry was staying close to the infantry. On the other hand, the French cavalry conducted no such long-range reconnaissance patrols.

Rommel's Infantry Patrol

On 21 August, in addition to the patrols of 19th *Uhlan*, 27 ID sent out several officer foot patrols, one of which was led by Lt. Rommel, of 7/124, who wrote an account of his patrol which is a small masterpiece.[18] Early on the morning of 21 August he and several other officers reported to the regimental commander, who personally gave them their patrol orders. Each patrol was to consist of an officer and five men. They were to move from Meix le Tigne past Barancy and Gorcy towards Cosnes near Longwy, a distance of about 8km, to determine enemy locations and strength. Rommel said that the patrol was conducted even more carefully than was usual on manoeuvres, leaving Meix by moving in the ditch beside the road. Barancy had been reported occupied by weak enemy forces the day previously, but Rommel now found that there were no French troops there. He crossed wheat fields and passed through the Bois de Mousson, covered by the patrol of Lt. Kim in overwatch. On the Cosnes-Gorcy road he found signs that French had moved towards Cosnes. Moving yet more cautiously through the undergrowth along the road, he reached a copse 500m west of Cosnes and stopped to observe the town with his binoculars, but saw no French troops. Moving towards Cosnes, he questioned an old woman working in the fields, who said that the French had left Cosnes an hour previously, headed for Longwy. The patrol worked its way through fields and orchards into Cosnes, entering the town with extreme caution. There were no French troops in the town and the inhabitants confirmed the old woman's story. They also brought the German soldiers food and drink, which Rommel made them taste first to ensure they were not poisoned. He then seized six bicycles, giving the owners quartermaster receipts, and rode towards Longwy for a ways, before returning on the road to Gorcy and Barancy, the men spaced at wide intervals, to report to the regimental commander at Meix. Even though Rommel had not seen any French troops, his observations had produced much valuable information.

More Reconnaissance and Counter-Reconnaissance

Even the artillery got involved in patrolling. FAR 13 sent out three artillery officer patrols.[19] The high number of German patrols, and the fact that they were led by such promising officers as Rommel, speaks volumes about the German dedication to reconnaissance and counter-reconnaissance.

In addition to the patrols, III/123 was dispatched at dawn on 21 August towards the Basse Vire between Virton and Ruette.[20] The battalion spread out on a 5km front and sent patrols to the south of the river. After short firefights at Ruette and

The Battle of the Frontiers

Virton, the battalion returned to the regiment at 1600. It had been able to establish the direction of march of large bodies of French infantry as well as prevent the French 14th Hussars from accomplishing any useful reconnaissance.

By 1500 21 August the XIII AK had received reports of French columns moving from from St. Pancré towards Ville Houdlement, probably in regimental strength, a similar column moving from St. Mard towards Virton, and from Tellancourt towards Longwy, finally a column moving from Tellancourt to Gorcy. The XIII AK anticipated a battle on 22 August near Bleid, so much so that a General Staff officer was sent to the area on 21 August to familiarise himself with the terrain. The divisions were alerted. At 1630 27 DI moved forward into assembly areas, with the 53rd Brigade at St. Léger and the 54th Brigade on its left at Gennevaux, dug in again and sent out patrols. At 2130 21 August a corps order was issued for an attack at 0400 22 August. The 27 ID would attack Bleid and Signeulx, 26 ID, with only one brigade (the other brigade was covering the bombardment of Longwy) would advance with the right wing aiming for Houdlemont, the left wing towards Gorcy. The initial objective was to throw the French back across the Virton-Musson rail line. The corps chief of staff said that the corps situation was favourable. The corps had been resting for 20 hours before it was alerted on the evening of 21 August. It moved forward at dusk, undetected by the French, and then was able to get some further rest in warm weather that night. The corps HQ was connected by telephone with both division HQs.

French II/101 RI at Bleid[21]

We have detailed accounts of the fight at Bleid from both French and German sources which disagree on an important point: the French say that the Germans attacked in the fog, while most of the German sources say that they waited to attack until the fog lifted. Since these two accounts cannot be reconciled, they are both presented as is.

The French account says that at around 0710, 6/101, the advance guard company of II/101, had marched slowly in a thick fog through Bleid and had reached a hillcrest around 1km east of the town. The company was in an echelon right formation, with a platoon leading on the left, the centre platoon astride the road and a third platoon on the right rear. All the squads were deployed. The company was suddenly attacked at about 40m range by dense lines of German skirmishers, which also turned both company flanks. The company ran for the rear and ended up at the eastern tree line of Le Mat. When the fog lifted, it was taken under fire by German artillery. The company had lost the leading platoon but the rest successfully withdrew to Gomery. At the same time the lead company of the battalion main body, 7/101, was 500m north east of Bleid when a group of hussars came racing to the rear, shouting 'The enemy is here, less than 100m!' The German line, I/IR 124 and III/124, surged out of the fog and the company was practically annihilated, losing all of its officers, NCOs and fifty per cent of its enlisted men almost at once. The two German battalions continued their attack, hitting 5/101 near Bleid in the front, flank and rear and annihilating the company in the town after some stiff street fighting. 8/101 was surrounded in a small wood to the west of Bleid and wiped out. The speed and violence of the German attack were terrible. Each French company was caught isolated and in the open by a force some six times its strength and crushed. There were about 800 French troops at Bleid; 150 from 6/101 made it back to Gomery, 583 were KIA, 60 were POW. The dangers associated with Bonnal's use of battalion-sized security detachments had been amply demonstrated.

German 53rd Brigade[22]

On 22 August the German 27 ID attacked with the 53rd Brigade on the right, reinforced by I/FAR 49 and all but one squadron of the 19th *Uhlan* regiment and 2/13th Engineer Battalion, and 54th Brigade on the left with FAR 13 and 5/19th *Uhlan*. II/FAR 49, I/IR 120 and II/120 were in division reserve. The 27 ID order of 0015 hours 22 August gave the 53rd Brigade the mission of crossing the line of departure, which was the road St. Léger–Gennevaux, at 0400 to take the town of Bleid and the heights to the north of it. Further advance would probably be towards the south of Latour.

The 53rd Brigade operations order instructed IR 124 to attack on the left, IR 123 on the right, the middle of the brigade aiming at the crossroads 500m northwest of Bleid. French infantry was thought to be in this area. IR 123 was to echelon right, IR 124 left, so that the brigade would be moving in a wedge-shaped formation.

The XIII AK conducted its approach march on the morning of 22 August in thick fog. The divisions were initially instructed by the corps HQ to occupy attack positions before making contact, in order to wait for the fog to lift, which would allow the artillery to support the infantry. According to patrol reports, the French had occupied a line from the northwest of Bleid to Mussy and then Barancy. At 0530 the corps commander ordered the attack to begin, fog notwithstanding. 53rd Brigade, however, waited for the fog to lift.

53rd Brigade was advancing against two French battalions, and enjoyed 3–1 superiority in infantry. The brigade's supporting artillery was also ready to open fire, whereas the French artillery was still in march column. This unequal contest could have only one conclusion.

The first unit to make contact was 19th *Uhlan*, moving down the road to Éthe. It was first engaged by the French 14th Hussars and then the French advance guard infantry, which pushed the *Uhlan*s back. The presence of strong French forces on this road was unexpected and threatened the flanks of both the 10 ID and 53rd Brigade. 2/13th Engineer Battalion, which was following 19th *Uhlans* on the road, took up a defensive position and the two units were able to stop the French advance guard.

German IR 123[23]

At 0400 22 August the 53rd Brigade moved to occupy an attack position at Hill 319, 1,200m northeast of Bleid. The enemy was known to be in artillery range, perhaps prepared to attack. Visibility in the fog was less than 50m. IR 123 deployed a skirmisher line while the rest of the regiment remained in march formation behind it, with II/123 on the left, I/123 on the right, III/123 echeloned right behind I/123. The regiment advanced cross-country using compasses, as in a night movement, over water meadows, through woods with thick undergrowth and down steep hills. By 0515 IR 123 had reached its assigned area and halted. Patrols were sent out, moving with difficulty through the dense fog. They took fire north of Bleid, but no action was taken due to the lack of visibility. It appeared to the patrols that the enemy was digging in. At 0530, I/FAR 49 deployed behind Hill 325.

The regiment reached the Gevimont–Bleid road at 0900 without a shot being fired when the fog began to lift and IR 123 saw a strong force of enemy infantry advancing 800m to the front, from the woods at Le Mat and across the high ground to the north, probably the French III/103. The German artillery opened fire at once, soon joined by the lead companies of I/123, II/123 and the MG Company; it was plain to see that the German fire, especially that of the MG, was causing the French serious casualties.

After a half-hour firefight, at 0930 the 53rd Brigade order to advance reached IR 123. II/123 on the left attacked with 7/123 and 6/123 in the first line, the other two companies following, I/123 on the right with three companies in the first line. Fire was coming from the Sur Rogène hill in particular, so 3/123, followed by 5/123, moved north through the woods east of the hill and from positions on the tree line engaged elements of the French II/104 on Sur Rogène; the German companies were prevented from advancing further by flanking fire from Hamawé. The two companies were joined by III/123.

Meanwhile, II/123 advanced by bounds in successive dense waves of skirmishers, supported by the MG Company, (Moser called the attack 'a truly pretty picture')[24] probably against the French 6/101 and 7/101. The MG Company could not identify the enemy position, so all six guns engaged the tree line at Le Mat, which immediately resulted in a weakening of the French return fire: the regimental KTB said that the MG fire was 'particularly effective'. French troops could be seen withdrawing towards Le Mat, leaving the ground strewn with their dead. Lt. Strauss described the firefight:

'Now and then I looked down the skirmisher line at my men. They held their weapons in an iron grip, aimed, fired, ejected the spent round, aimed and fired again. They did not look to the right or left, their lips were pressed together, stern, determined. In their hard faces was written: victory must be ours; it must! Death howled and blew and rattled and whizzed and thundered through the air, so that the earth shook and the ground sprang up in pure horror. Death raged in our ranks, broke skulls and bored through hearts. Our nerves were stronger than those of our enemies. They broke and ran in panic flight and our machine guns kept up a continual ear-splitting rattle after them. The French stumbled like drunkards…and fell, shot in the back'.[25]

II/123 assaulted at 0945 and the French pulled back to the edge of the forest. The battalion pursued, taking 30 prisoners in a wood west of Bleid and reaching a sunken road in front of Le Mat, formed a firing line, which thickened as they were joined by 2/124 and 4/124. The IR 123 MG Company could observe the heavy casualties their fire caused.

German IR 124[26]

IR 124, minus III/124, which was brigade reserve, was to the left of IR 123. It had to make a 3km to 4km approach march to the attack position at Hill 325, which took three hours across rolling, wet terrain, cutting down barbed wire fences. The II/124 KTB says that the fog lifted at 0700, the regimental history 0745. To the front the terrain dropped into a shallow valley and rose gently up the opposite slope, which was covered with grain and potatoes, and on which a line of French skirmishers was visible. At the top of the slope was a wood (Le Mat) and a second line of skirmishers. Without waiting for brigade orders, II/124 attacked, with 6/124 and 8/124 in the first line. The II/124 KTB noted that the German artillery support was excellent. The French fell back into a copse and were shelled by the artillery.

At 0805 I/124 was ordered to take Bleid. 2/124 assaulted directly into Bleid, while 5/124 and 7/124 attacked the town from the north. After some bitter street fighting the French fled towards a small wood on the west side of the town. This brought them into the zone of fire of the MG Company, which shot them down.

Attack on Le Mat

II/123 assaulted towards Le Mat with II/124, reinforced by 9/124 and 11/124 on their left. The attack was covered by fire from the IR 123 MG Company. The German artillery was shelling the tree line, but apparently took the IR 123 and IR 124 troops for retreating French and shelled them too. The companies fell back to the valley, reorganised, got in contact with the artillery and renewed the assault, but now under French artillery fire and probably also fire from V AK artillery. The German units became completely disorganised, so 10/24 and 12/124 were committed to move the attack forward and the heights were stormed. When the German infantry got to the top, they found it strewn with French dead; the German MG fire had swept down the French defensive line.

The FAR 49 regimental history said that the fog had lifted enough by 0830 that I/49 could open fire on Le Mat (II/49 was in division reserve and saw little action). I/FAR 49 advanced to keep up with the attack, with 1/FAR 49 bounding forward to a firing position north of Bleid and 2/49 to a position 500m further to the west. However, when 2/49 and 3/49 attempted to set up firing positions 600m northeast of Bleid to support IR 123 against the French on Sur Rogène, they took such heavy artillery fire, the majority of it probably friendly fire from 10 ID, that the two batteries and an ammunition column were immobilised.[27]

The infantry assault on Le Mat halted on the tree line. The Germans began to police up the battlefield, taking prisoner a considerable number of French who had been feigning death. While this was going on, the German troops on Le Mat began to take artillery fire from Signeulx to the south. Moser said that the troops took heavy casualties because they were unused to reacting to artillery fire. The troops sought cover in the Le Mat forest and dispersed in the woods. The II/124 commander collected some of his troops and moved west through the forest, eliminating French stragglers. III/123 had fragmented to such a degree that commander did not feel that he had enough troops under his control to attack Éthe from the rear. Most of II/123 and II/124 eventually swung north towards Sur Rogène. The tree line of Le Mat is higher than Sur Rogène and the French infantry on the hill was clearly visible. The German fire, especially that of the MG Company (against the French 9/103), was murderous, but the German troops in turn took heavy artillery fire which caused serious casualties and forced them to pull back into the woods. One German MG was destroyed.

Rommel at Bleid

Rommel's superiors clearly thought that he was an especially reliable officer, for they kept him employed during the entire night of 21–22 August carrying high-level orders. By the morning of 22 August he had been awake for 24 hours and was exhausted. Nevertheless, the II/124 battalion commander sent him ahead to scout the route to Hill 325 with map and compass in the fog.

When the battalion reached the hill there was an exchange of gunfire between German and French patrols. I/124 came up on the battalion right and Rommel's platoon was deployed to make contact with it and then to advance southeast on Bleid. Rommel's platoon advanced in skirmisher line down the slopes northeast of Bleid, over potato and cabbage fields, with visibility still only 50–80m. Suddenly Rommel's platoon received a volley of rifle fire and the troops threw themselves flat on the ground, as other volleys whizzed over their heads. Rommel could not see the enemy, but rushed forward with his men anyway, to find only the tracks left behind by the French troops in the fields. This procedure repeated itself several times: the French fired, the Germans charged, the French withdrew. Finally the French broke contact completely and the platoon advanced for about 1km without taking fire. Rommel's platoon was probably far in advance of both his battalion and I/124 on the right. They reached a hedge, where Rommel stopped the platoon. He went forward with a sergeant and his two range estimators to conduct a reconnaissance of a farm on the other side of the hedge. He saw another house, and he knew he was on the northeast side of Bleid. Fifteen metres to his front were 15 or 20 Frenchmen (from the 6/101 RI) talking and drinking coffee on the road. Rommel and his three men jumped from behind the building and opened fire, killing or wounding several Frenchmen, but the rest took cover and a firefight ensued. Rommel said that there were about ten French men left and he gave the order to his men to rush them, but in doing so they received such heavy fire that the Germans retreated back to the hedge, without loss.

Rommel's platoon on the hedge began taking fire from a house on the opposite side of the road. Rommel employed textbook German tactics, which would stand him in good stead twenty-five years later in Africa. He directed his 2nd Section to provide covering fire from the hedge while he and the 1st Section swung around to the right to take the enemy in the flank and rear. A battering ram beat down the door and flaming torches were thrown into the room, which contained grain and straw. The defenders were killed or surrendered. The same procedure was used on successive buildings. Other elements of I/124 and II/124 joined in. The Germans began to take casualties in heavy street fighting.

The fog had lifted in the valley, though it still covered Hill 325, when Rommel collected his men 300m to the northeast side of the town in order to rejoin his battalion. While conducting a leader's recon to the front he saw French troops (7/101 RI) and brought up his platoon to engage them. 'Our deployment behind the ridge, our movement into position, and the opening of fire by the platoon was carried on with the composure and precision of a peacetime manoeuvre' wrote Rommel. The platoon 'delivered a slow and well-aimed fire as they had been taught to do in peacetime training'. The French return fire was too high and the first fifteen minutes of the engagement the French had only hit a mess kit. When Rommel saw friendly troops on Hill 325 to his right and was therefore assured of support, he ordered his troops to advance by fire and movement 'a manoeuvre we had practiced frequently during peacetime'. The French fire was still too high and the platoon still had not taken any casualties. The platoon reached a depression that provided cover within assaulting distance from the French and Rommel's men fixed bayonets. The French fire ceased entirely and when Rommel's platoon advanced they found only French dead and tracks leading through the man-high grain towards Le Mat. Rommel said that once again he and his platoon were far ahead of the other German troops, so he instructed

The Battle of the Frontiers

his platoon to hold in place while he conducted another leader's recon. After 400m he reached the Gévimont–Bleid road and followed as it rose to the north, when about 150m to the north 100 French troops could be seen moving west through the grain, the sun glinting off the mess gear strapped to the top of their packs (6/101 RI again). Rommel and his two companions opened fire on the French, forcing them to disperse and inflicting several casualties, without taking any return fire, even though the Germans had to fire standing.

Rommel's platoon moved up the road to join IR 123, which was advancing to the west. Along the way they took about fifty prisoners from 6/101 RI and 7/101, including a captain and a lieutenant. Rommel began to orient his platoon towards Le Mat when he blacked out from fatigue. When he came to, he saw German troops retreating from Le Mat because of French artillery fire. He stopped them and had them dig in. Fifteen minutes later the regiment was assembled by bugle call west of Bleid.

What stands out most strongly in Rommel's account was the 'empty battlefield'. Rommel rarely saw other German troops; the enemy could be detected only at short range. Visibility was initially very limited due to the fog, but even when the fog lifted it was restricted by the terrain and vegetation. Rommel, and the other German troop leaders as well, overcame these difficulties with a combination of aggressive action and good small-unit tactics.

Attack on Sur Rogène

By 1100 all of IR 123 as well as the 53rd Brigade reserve, three companies of III/IR 124 and a IR 124 MG platoon, were engaged in a firefight against the Sur Rogène hill and taking losses. Nevertheless, IR 123 began to gain fire superiority. At 1130 53rd Brigade ordered the regiment to hold in place, preparatory to marching to the southwest. But the French on Sur Rogène were taking small arms fire from the front and flank and artillery fire from the rear and were visibly weakening. At 1145 the commander of 5/123 began the assault on the hill, carrying the rest of the troops with him.

5/123 took heavy casualties due to the flanking fire from the French 11/103 RI and 5/104 RI with two MG at Hamawé, but the German troops swept up and over the hill. The only French to be found there were dead or wounded; the remnants of the French II/104 and III/103 had fallen back to Éthe. But heavy artillery fire from a French battery at Éthe and other batteries south of the Jeune Bois killed a captain and two lieutenants and forced all the German troops on Sur Rogène except 5/123 to seek cover on the southeast slope. The 53rd Brigade sent another order for the troops to assemble north of Bleid for employment elsewhere, but the commander of 5/123 sent back a message that the hill had been taken and needed to be held. At 1230 the regimental adjutant had to personally haul the troops back to Bleid.

Éthe and Bleid

IR 123 had fired 90,000 rounds of infantry ammunition and 11,950 rounds of MG ammunition, which illustrates clearly that most of the regimental firepower was the product of rifle fire. The regimental KTB said that the superiority of German marksmanship training was obvious; the French dead lay in rows. The French were, however, very skilful in the use of cover and it had been extraordinarily difficult to see their skirmisher lines.

The IR 123 KTB said that due to the fact that V AK and XIII AK had no communication with each other (the woods between the two corps being full of French troops) IR 123 had been shelled so badly by 10 ID artillery that the regiment had taken heavy casualties and been rendered combat ineffective. The FAR 20 (10 ID) regimental historian admitted that the regiment had fired on targets at Sur Rogène and Le Mat, but denied that these could have been 53rd Brigade troops. The regimental history then acknowledged that in mobile warfare friendly fire is sometimes unavoidable.[28] Had the 10 ID artillery not fired on IR 123, the regiment would have been perfectly positioned to engage the French forces along the rail line and in Éthe from the rear and destroyed them.

The IR 123 regimental historian admitted that not everyone on the battlefield is a hero. The visible effect of the German fire on the French infantry was shocking. But almost everyone did his duty, motivated by the example of the leaders and the spirit of comradeship.

Reorganisation at Bleid

Gradually the firing died down. No one knew where the French had gone or what the situation was. At 1300 orders were received to assemble at Bleid. The field kitchens came forward, the troops were fed, and a report was received that the French were in full retreat. Moser described the scene at Bleid:

> 'The horrors of war had swept over this town in the middle of nowhere. Many houses had been shot to pieces or were in flames; the bodies of French and German soldiers and Belgian civilians lay everywhere. The terrified populace had sought cover in cellars or had fled with wives and children to hide in gardens or bushes. In the middle of all this there were hundreds of thirsty German soldiers who drank water, wine or lemonade like animals and then, after hours of the most intense exertion, often fell into a state of complete apathy… That was war, whose overwhelming power had in a few hours shown the best troops that we had ever had, filled with fresh and optimistic idealism, the true nature of raw reality. But they were proud of their baptism of fire, which had ended with the retreat of the enemy…'[29]

Modern combat put such a mental and physical strain on the troops and generated such disorganisation and confusion that conducting a direct pursuit after a successful battle was practically impossible.

The commander of IR 124 recommended that the Brigade reserve, I/124, take Gomery. Such an attack might well have cut off the French 13th Brigade, had only the 53rd Brigade commander acted on it. But the battle at Bleid-Sur Rogène had pulled the 53rd Brigade to the west while the rest of the rest of the XIII AK was marching southwest. With 52nd Brigade engaged at Longwy, XIII AK had no forces for other missions and wanted 53rd Brigade to catch up.

At 1200 XIII AK ordered the 27 ID to hold in place, and only ordered the attack to resume at 1410. The German 27 ID issued the order for the pursuit at 1500. During this three-hour delay the XIII AK lost contact with the French, who were able to withdraw out of reach. 53rd Brigade moved behind 54th Brigade at 1730, IR 124 in the lead. Movement was slow and difficult; the roads were clogged with artillery, supply columns and automobiles, which forced the infantry to make frequent halts. The 27 ID did not make further contact with French troops. The 53rd Brigade arrived; the troops exhausted, at St. Remy and Ruette, only 3km from Bleid, at 2100, where it bivouacked. This was 4km short of the division's objective, Tellancourt.

French IV CA

Because the French 7 DI commander and his staff were trapped in Éthe, the division did not send any situation reports to the IV CA. At 1000 a IV CA staff major encountered a staff captain from 7 DI who said that the division advance guard had had been surprised, that in order to break contact two regiments had attacked with the bayonet and been massacred by German machine guns, and that the division commander was dead. The staff captain said that he was the sole survivor of the division headquarters.

This report contains practically every cliché used by soldiers who had panicked and run away from the battlefield: bayonet charges, massacre by machine guns and sole survivor foremost among them. Nevertheless, the IV CA staff major sent the captain's report to his headquarters and even embellished it further, saying that the 7 DI had been surprised; the commanding general was dead, and for good measure that the division had been routed and the artillery lost. The inability of French officers to give accurate reports was reaching absurd levels.

German IR 46[30]

At 0900 10 ID sent a report to 9 ID which said that the division intended to attack to seize the high ground between Gomery and Latour. IR 46 manoeuvred right towards Hill 300, 1,300m north of Belmont. Two officers were sent to reconnoitre a route through the woods, where the undergrowth was so thick that the regiment was forced to march single-file on a footpath for much of the way, slowing it so much that it did not reach the tree line until 1000. There it deployed

Éthe and Bleid

with I/46 on the right, III/46 on the left, II/46 and MG Company in reserve. The regiment took little enemy fire, moving across country, through hedges and barbed-wire fences, until it reached Hill 300 at 1135. There the regiment waited while the artillery conducted preparatory fires against Belmont and Éthe, chasing off some French infantry on the south side of the Ton. IR 46 continued the march to Belmont, which it entered at 1320 with no resistance, and crossed the Ton. IR 6, following IR 46, would later take 80 French POWs in Belmont who were hiding 'in places that no one suspected them'.[31] 1st *Jäger zu Pferde*, which was patrolling to the front, reported that there was an enemy battery and weak infantry in Latour. Through his binoculars the regimental commander could see French columns withdrawing. French artillery began firing at the regiment from positions to the right front. Most of III/46, the lead battalion, evaded the fire by moving forward, while I/46 and 10/46 took cover in the Bois de Bampont. The shelling lasted twenty minutes, and then stopped. In the course of the next hour the regiment would be shelled four times.

On its own now, III/46 got the bit in its teeth and pushed forward quickly in long bounds. 9/46, with elements of two other companies, reached the Basse Vire valley between Latour and Chenois, from where they were able to engage French troops retreating to the south. A French artillery battery, 2/26 RAC was caught trying to withdraw and destroyed, with a lieutenant colonel and 50 EM KIA. 11/46 and most of 12/46 became involved in street fighting in Latour.

When a force estimated at three French companies was seen advancing west from Gomery and the Basse Vire, the battalion commander withdrew most of the troops in Latour to a sunken road northeast of the town, from which they engaged the French at 700m range. The firefight lasted two hours, during which the battalion commander was killed and the adjutant assumed command. The III/46 troops were also taken under fire by its own regiment's MG, which forced them to take cover and allowed the French to make several bounds forward. Nevertheless, the French did not succeed in closing and their attack failed. An NCO from 3/46 told of the fight:

'I ordered my 18 men to set their sights at 600m, and when it became clear that this was too short, 800m. Through my binoculars I could observe the casualties and confusion in the enemy column. Then the 1st platoon of 3/46 under Lt. Schulz joined our skirmisher line. Hearing the rapid firing of our two squads, they had run up to the high ground. When Corporal Schneider entered the line to my left I told him what range we were using, and he repeated it to his left and right. Lt. Schulz took over fire distribution and fire control. We put heavy fire, at times rapid fire, on the enemy, who was apparently retreating. There was no question that we had inflicted heavy casualties. I could also see through my binoculars several enemy artillery pieces approach and go into position.'

The Battle of the Frontiers

Two salvoes of artillery shells landed near the position:

> 'I heard a cry and saw a man thrown into the air, lose his nerve, leave the line and run downhill. It was a miracle that there were no other casualties. The next salvoes caused our fire to be unsteady and weaker'.

The regimental commander came up to the firing line and ordered the company to find cover in the Bois de Bampont.

> 'The enemy artillery now conducted area fire into the woods. It was a critical situation for the 3rd Company. The bursting of the shrapnel directly over our heads, and the resulting rain of shrapnel balls, which, clacking and rattling, shredded the leaves over us and cut into the trunks of the trees and the leaves on the ground, rubbed our nerves raw and was a real test of our strength. First Sergeant Krüger, who lay not far from me, time and again found comforting words for the company; his unshakeable calm and undaunted conduct contributed significantly to the fact that discipline was fully upheld. We suffered our first casualties. In my squads Musketeers Laverenyz and Milinski were the first to fall. Comrade! Comrade!'

French 13th Brigade

By 0845 the lead element of the 13th Brigade, I/101 RI, had reached Gomery and prepared to defend there. 26 RAC deployed west of Gomery and began to take German counter-battery fire. At 0900 it was joined by half of the corps artillery regiment, 44 RAC. At about 0800 the commander of 7 DI sent an order to the commander of the 13th Brigade to attack Belmont, which apparently did not arrive until 1000. This order was repeated at 1030 and 1200. The first units of 13th Brigade needed an hour to march forward, deploy and engage, the last units needed two hours. The brigade commander ordered 101 RI to occupy the Jeune Bois, with a battalion of 102 RI to its right; another battalion of 102 RI was to move into the Bois de Loges. I/101 and II/102 attempted to advance from the Jeune Bois but were stopped by German artillery fire. This fire smashed 11/101 and 12/101; all the officers but one became casualties and only 30 men remained uninjured.

At noon 6/101 appeared at Gomery and the company commander reported that II/101 had been destroyed at Bleid and that there was a German brigade in that vicinity, which caused the 13th Brigade commander to fear for his right flank – a justifiable concern, as it would turn out. Had 13th Brigade succeeded in entering Belmot, the entire 7 DI might well have been destroyed when XIII AK moved from the east against the 7 DI line of retreat. The 13th Brigade commander decided at 1230 to fall back 10km to defend Malmaison, which was tantamount to leaving the 14th Brigade to its fate.

Éthe and Bleid

The 13th Brigade and the attached artillery had already begun its rearward movement when the 7 DI commander finally reached the south edge of the Jeune Bois, saw 13th Brigade withdrawing and ordered a counter-march. The division CP was established at Gomery and the rest of the division artillery redeployed. One battery of French artillery retreating along the Basse Vire was engaged by fire from the German I/ IR 46 and the guns had to be abandoned. Between 1300 and 1400 successive French detachments were destroyed trying to stop IR 46's march on Latour.

At about 1300 the entire 13th Brigade was reoriented to face the new threat presented by IR 46 at Latour. By 1430, 9 companies of the French 102 RI and I/101 RI were engaged facing west between Latour and Gomery, while three companies watched the tree line of the Jeune Bois to the north. In a throwback to bad mid nineteenth century tactics, four more companies were organising a fall-back position along the rail line to the south. Elements of the German IR 123 and 124 began a firefight with three French companies at Gomery.

The French 13th Brigade attack on IR 46 made practically no progress in the face of German rifle fire, in spite of the fact that the French were far stronger. The advance of a group of two companies of III/102 and one of I/102, supported by an MG platoon, took heavy casualties and was stopped 500m from the German position. German artillery fire from both Éthe and Bleid was unable to stop the attack of I/101 supported by 9/101, but they could proceed no further than the 102 RI against IR 46 small arms and MG fire.

French Withdrawal

At 1600 the commander of 7 DI decided that the 13th Brigade needed to withdraw to Malmaison, and by 1730 the French troops in the Jeune Bois began to fall back. Immediately after dark, at 2030, the remnants of the 14th Brigade began to withdraw. Of the five French battalions in Éthe, only 500 men and 8 guns escaped.

The French IV CA situation report to 3rd Army during the night of 22–23 August said that of the 7 DI units, 104 RI had been decimated; the other regiments were scattered and intermixed between Allondrelle and Villers le Rond. The 7 DI artillery had lost two (of three) sections. The 14th Brigade commander was probably dead. The corps artillery had lost a section fighting with 7 DI. The corps cavalry regiment, 14th Hussars, had been reduced to 200 horses (from 750). In sum, the 4 CA combat power had been 'extraordinarily' reduced.[32]

Poor reporting from IV CA, and 7 DI in particular, had left the 3rd Army HQ out of touch with the situation at the front. Grasset noted that the 3rd Army HQ's appreciation of the situation was divorced from reality and its orders during the battle had been irrelevant. For example, during the afternoon 3rd Army had no idea the terrible condition that IV CA was in, and wanted IV CA to shift forces to its right in order to assist V CA.[33]

The Battle of the Frontiers

V AK Command and Control Problems

The French command and control problems were not unique. The German V AK had focused its interest on its right flank at the expense of 10 ID on the left. At around 1730 the 10 ID, apparently lacking information from V AK and acting on rumours that 9 ID was in difficulty, ordered its units to fall back to the north of Belmont and Éthe and dig in; the artillery was directed to shell Éthe. Both the IR 46 commander and his brigade commander had seen the advantages of keeping IR 46 in place at Latour. Had 10 ID not withdrawn the regiment, the escape of the remnants of the French 14th Brigade would have been much more difficult. Remarkably, 10 ID still had an entire regiment available, IR 6, which had hardly been engaged. Had the 10 ID reinforced IR 6 with artillery and cavalry and committed it to exploit IR 46's success and continue the advance, then the integrity of the French IV CA would have been in danger. The German V AK would also have been in a position to conduct a highly effective pursuit the next day. Had XIII AK on the left also conducted a vigorous pursuit that afternoon, the entire French 3rd Army front would have been blown open.

The friendly fire casualties in IR 123 caused by 10 ID artillery also point to a failure of command and control by the 5th Army, V AK and XIII AK. It was the job of the all three headquarters to inform each other of the locations and actions of their divisions. As a result, both V AK and XIII AK failed to capitalise on the possibilities that the troops had provided them. In particular, a push by even small units of the 53rd Brigade or the XIII CA cavalry reinforced with artillery against the French 7 DI flank and rear could have led to the collapse of the entire French IV CA.

French Fantasies

Both Grasset and Trentinian were convinced that Éthe was a French victory, because at the end of the day the French still held Éthe. The fact that the French abandoned the town as soon as it was dark was not mentioned. Grasset said, without any justification, that the 10 ID artillery had been wiped out. FAR 56 had suffered 'enormous losses in men and material' and FAR 20 had been 'almost destroyed.'[34] Trentinian also thought that the 53rd Brigade had been caught while in column of march, and that the entire German V AK had conducted a 'precipitate retreat', uncovering its right flank and rear, which the 7 DI unfortunately could not exploit. He said that the French IV CA could have attacked the right flank of the German XIII AK (53rd Brigade) and defeated it.

Both Grasset and Trentinian displayed an astounding incomprehension of what had happened at Éthe and why it had happened. Neither officer bothered to inquire as to the V AK mission, actions or casualties. Both rated holding terrain to be more important than fire or manoeuvre. Most enlightening is Trentinian's unprofessional comment that 'a meeting engagement is nothing like a war game'.

Éthe and Bleid

Had Trentinian played more war games, he might not have lost the 14th Brigade. With tactical judgment like this, the French defeats in August 1914 are easier to understand. Neither Grasset nor Trentinian came up with any useful lessons learned, which also makes the French defeats in 1940 easier to understand.[35]

French Casualties

In the five military cemeteries around Éthe-Bleid 573 German and 2056 French soldiers are buried, giving the general ratio of German to French casualties, which was a little less than 1:4.[36]

The 7 DI lost 124 OFF and 5,200 EM. The 14th Brigade had been destroyed, several batteries of artillery had been lost and the 13th Brigade roughly handled. The worst hit unit was 101 RI, which was wiped out. Two other regiments had taken approximately 50 per cent casualties: 103 RI lost 29 OFF and 1,760 men and 104 RI 25 OFF and 1,689 EM.

German Casualties

IR 50 lost 13 OFF and 261 EM KIA. 231 IR 50 soldiers are buried in the military cemeteries in the division's area of operations. The remaining soldiers died of wounds and were buried near the hospitals. 19 OFF and 425 EM were WIA, one-quarter of which soon returned to duty. Most of the casualties were due to infantry fire. French artillery fire destroyed two ammunition wagons and three field kitchens. In the entire Franco-Prussian War the regiment had lost 23 OFF and 323 EM KIA, 16 OFF and 649 EM WIA.

IR 47 lost 6 OFF and 50 EM KIA, 5 OFF and 161 EM WIA, 16 EM MIA. IR 46 lost 2 OFF and 24 EM KIA; 69 EM MIA (many of which were later determined to be KIA) and 5 OFF and 133 EM WIA. One battalion commander was KIA, one WIA. FAR 56 took relatively heavy casualties for an artillery unit: 3 OFF and 15 EM KIA, 6 OFF and 43 EM WIA, 7 EM MIA.

The other regiments in the 10 ID sector took significantly fewer fatal casualties: IR 6 eight, FAR 20 two, 19th *Uhlan* three, 1st *Uhlan* two, 1st *Jäger zu Pferde* three, 5th Engineer Battalion (3rd and 4th Companies) eight, fourteen unknowns, for a total of 355 EM KIA.[37]

The 53rd Brigade casualties were heavy. IR 123 lost 7 OFF and 73 EM KIA, 18 OFF and 510 EM WIA, 37 EM MIA. IR 124 lost 5 OFF and 42 EM KIA, 5 OFF and 380 EM WIA

23 August

The remnants of the French 7 DI had fallen back 13km to the Cheirs on the night of 22–23 August. On 23 August 8 DI held the high ground southwest of

The Battle of the Frontiers

Virton, relying on massed artillery fire to keep the German infantry from advancing, and supported by II CA on its left.

At the end of the day on 22 August the situation was not clear to the 10 ID, which dug in on the high ground above Éthe, prepared for French attack. The next morning German patrols discovered that the French had gone.

On 23 August V AK had little room to manoeuvre. About 15km to the southwest was the old fortress of Montmédy, which both the 5th Army and V AK gave much more respect than was warranted. Both headquarters were unwilling to allow 9 ID to approach within range of the fortress artillery. The problem of Montmédy was just another consequence of 5th Army's decision to attack on 22 August instead of withdrawing to the north. V AK also had to contend with the French II CA, which was relatively undamaged and still on its right flank at Sommethonne.

At 0825 on 23 August the 5th Army issued its operations order. V AK was to be prepared to support the left flank of the 4th Army in the area of Tintigny and also to begin the encirclement and bombardment of Montmédy fortress. The Army intent was clearly that V AK push southwest towards Montmédy.[38]

Nevertheless, 10 ID advanced very slowly. The German official history says that V AK wanted 10 ID to occupy the high ground south of St. Mard, but 10 ID did not do so because it was waiting for 9 ID to take Virton – which didn't happen. During the day V AK came to the conclusion that the French were defending with 'considerable forces' on the line Meix–Dampicourt–St. Mard.[39]

IR 47 moved into Éthe on 23 August, where it received fire from French stragglers and Belgian civilians. The regiment searched Éthe and found French soldiers who had been hiding there as well as armed Belgian civilians, who were executed. After clearing Éthe it then advanced only as far as the Jeune Bois south of the town. The hillside south of town and the road to Gomery were strewn with French dead and wrecked artillery equipment. The regiment remained there the entire afternoon, until between 1700 and 1800 the march continued again, the 20th Brigade advanced towards St. Mard behind a skirmisher line. When the Brigade reached Latour it became clear by questioning the civilian population that the French had not been in the area since the previous day. The brigade continued the advance in march column to Chenois, where it bivouacked. An abandoned French battery supplied welcome replacement horses for the division and the regiment captured a number of French bicycles.

On the morning of 23 August the 53rd Brigade field kitchens came up. The brigade began movement only at 1000, had a short firefight west of St Remy and bivouacked at Malmaison, having advanced 10km. 10 ID took 100 POWs and captured 6 MGs in Latour. Moser said that there were French stragglers everywhere, individuals and groups in up to battalion size. 100 French troops came in a body to surrender.[40]

Éthe and Bleid

24 August

To avoid Montmédy, 9 ID marched to the east, following 10 ID. 10 ID did not move out until 0830, reaching Malmaison by 1315, where it rested for two hours. At this time a 5th Army order arrived, which instructed V AK to envelop the French left flank.[41] This was a fantasy. The slow and uncertain German advance over the last two days had forfeited any possibility that V AK could even catch up with the French, much less envelop their flank. On 24 August the French IV CA crossed to the south bank of the Cheirs.

Conclusions

Grasset was scathing concerning the performance of French strategic cavalry reconnaissance: 'The entire 4th Cavalry Division, three brigades strong, operated since the 7th of August in the area of Attert (8km north of Arlon), Arlon and Longwy. It never succeeded, even with the assistance of the local population, in obtaining anything more than vague information.' The German counter-reconnaissance screen, made up of cavalry and bicycle infantry and set up along water lines, had stopped French cavalry reconnaissance cold. French air reconnaissance failed in the wooded terrain.[42]

The contrast between the tactical effectiveness of the German 10 ID and the incompetence of the French 7 DI is stark. The German division conducted its meeting engagement battle drill perfectly. The infantry and artillery deployed smoothly from march column into combat formation. Each regiment then acted as the situation demanded. IR 50 and IR 47 conducted methodical attacks, while IR 46 pressed deep into the French rear. The German artillery support and counter-battery fire would be rated excellent, were it not for the friendly fire incidents. The French 7 DI was caught in march column and never recovered. Command and control in the 7 DI collapsed, the 13th Brigade and the surviving artillery were powerless to prevent the destruction of the 14th Brigade. The Germans were in control of the battle from beginning to end.

The effect of this German tactical excellence was reduced by a lack of vision, coordination and aggressiveness by the German division and corps commanders at the operational level, who seemed to be satisfied to see that the battle proceeded satisfactorily at the tactical level. Lack of coordination between division and corps HQs led to serious friendly-fire incidents. Lack of operational aggressiveness led 10 ID to miss the opportunity to penetrate practically unopposed on 22 August deep into the French IV CA rear. Granted, the V AK mission was to defend Éthe-Virton, but opportunities such as those that 10 ID had on 22 August do not present themselves twice.

In 1920 the commander of the 53rd Brigade, Moser, said that the infantry might have fired longer, and might have waited for the artillery before advancing, but nevertheless it advanced by bounds with 'with speed and precision and wild joy' regardless of the holes torn in their ranks. What leader, he asked, could fault such brave troops?[43] He said that the attack on Le Mat was 'a joy to see how all arms cooperated', with the infantry being supported by covering fire from the MG and artillery. There were 50 per cent casualties among the company commanders and 33 per cent of the enlisted men were killed or wounded.

Moser was one of the most important German writers on tactics, but by 1927 it was clear that Moser's brigade had taken heavy casualties for little result. Moser was now ready to blame the troops. He said that the battle brought the German infantry the 'severe lesson': that it had attacked too boldly, heedless of French fire. The result was 'heavy and bitter casualties'.[44]

The real problem was that the 53rd Brigade had slipped from Moser's control, and instead of attacking southwest, as the corps order prescribed, into the undefended French IV CA flank and rear, or west through the Forest of Le Mat, which offered cover and concealment, it attacked northwest to Sur Rogène, a naked hilltop which offered neither cover nor concealment. The brigade thus became involved in a bloody frontal attack that brought it no tactical advantages.

10
Longwy

Longwy Bombardment Force[1]

On 20 August 'Attack Group Kaempfer' was created to quickly overrun Longwy. The attack group included two major XIII AK units, the 52nd Brigade and II/FAR 65 from the 26 ID, and the 23rd Brigade from 11 RD, reinforced by the 12th (21cm) Mortar Regiment. Longwy was an obsolete fortress, built about 150 years previously in the Vauban manner and only slightly modernised since then. General Kaempfer was not in the XIII AK or VI RK chain of command, but was directly subordinate to 5th Army HQ, a cumbersome if not outright dangerous arrangement.

The reasoning behind this attack on Longwy is difficult to understand. The equivalent of a reinforced active-army infantry division was being pushed forward in an attempt to quickly overrun an obsolete fortress. The fortress was not an obstacle and could have been isolated using *Landwehr* troops. But once 5th Army attacked it, active-army forces were diverted and the fort displayed an unexpected strength in passive resistance. Throughout the Marne campaign the German General Staff repeatedly showed that it overrated the importance and combat power of fixed fortifications.

The 52nd Brigade conducted the approach march towards the north front of Longwy on the night of 20–21 August, with IR 121 pushing in the fortress security detachments and occupying Autrux on the northeast side of the fortress, 600m from the gate. I/IR 122 and II/IR 122 held the tree line of the Forêts de Monts to the west. The 23rd Brigade held the high ground to the east. II/FAR 65 opened fire on Longwy at noon, followed by the mortar regiment. The bombardment continued through the night.

The attack group received a report at 1400 on 21 August that a French column was located at Ville Houdlemont and St. Pancré. During the evening, I/122 came

The Battle of the Frontiers

into contact with two companies of the French 89 RI advancing from Gorcy, probably conducting a reconnaissance in force.

21 August, German IR 127[2]

On the morning of 21 August the regiment (minus II/127) was formed into a task force with a platoon of 19th *Uhlans* and a battery from FAR 13 to take Mousson and the high ground to the south in order to cover the movement of the heavy mortars towards Longwy. By 0445 the regiment occupied positions near Musson and sent out infantry and cavalry patrols. The foot patrols encountered French patrols, the cavalry reported a French column, probably an infantry regiment with cavalry, 8km to the south at Tellancourt, marching north. At 1400 the outpost company, 2/127, could see the French infantry advancing, and were astounded to find that the French still wore their red trousers. At 1600 a firefight developed that lasted until dark, when the French withdrew. The regiment lost 7 KIA and 23 WIA.

The French now knew that the Germans were in force in front of Longwy, the only time during the fighting in the Ardennes that the French identified a German unit in place. The French V CA therefore focused on attacking the German 52nd Brigade at Longwy.

French V CA[3]

The French V CA consisted of the 9 DI and 10 DI. The V CA had a difficult march on 21 August and its units arrived at their bivouac areas so late that it was not possible to get the troops fed – the lack of a field kitchen showed itself to be a severe disadvantage. The jumpy French outposts fired at nothing throughout the night, while the German bombardment of Longwy was clearly audible.

The corps order for 22 August said that there were German bivouacs between Etalle and Arlon, which is to say that the V CA thought the German main body was 15km away when in fact by the morning of 22 August XIII AK was within 5km. The order noted that German artillery at Musson was firing on Longwy and the German infantry held the Fôret de Monts east of Longwy. The corps mission was to attack the German infantry dug in at Bel Arbre near Longwy. On the right, 10 ID, reinforced by two sections of corps artillery, would attack with its right flank along the Chiers with its centre of gravity on the line Gorcy –Musson. This would bring them against the German 26 ID. On the left, 9 DI would attack towards Baranzy and Gennevaux. This would bring it into contact with the German 54th Brigade, that is, the German brigade would be outnumbered almost 2–1. 9 ID would give up the 82 RI, which with two sections of corps artillery would form the corps reserve. Both divisions would cross the line of departure at Signeulx–Gorcy–Cosnes at 0500.

French 9 DI

The French 9 DI attacked from Signeulx (included) to Gorcy (excluded) with 18th Brigade on the right and 17th Brigade (which consisted of only the 4 RI, 82 RI being the corps reserve) on the left. The division artillery deployed on the heights near Houdlemont. The 18th Brigade attacked in heavy fog at 0530 with 113 RI on the left and 131 RI on the right, and was soon stopped dead in its tracks by German small arms fire. The V CA war diary said that the French infantry advanced in formations that were too dense. It thought it had encountered German infantry dug into prepared positions, which was completely wrong. The French infantry suffered 'enormous' losses. When the fog dissipated the French guns found that they had chosen naked, exposed positions and two batteries that were not able to withdraw in time were lost. The 9 DI infantry began to run short on ammunition and the caissons with infantry ammunition could not make their way forward through roads clogged with supply wagons and ambulances. The 9 DI situation quickly became critical. Between 0800 and 1100 the corps commander reinforced 9 DI with the two artillery groups from the corps reserve, then the two corps artillery groups attached to 10 ID, then 331 RIR and the corps infantry reserve, 82 RI. Nothing helped. The corps artillery tried to set up near Grancourt–St. Remy, but due to the nature of the terrain and German counter-battery fire 'was unable to operate effectively'. By 1100 the 9 DI had been thrown back to the plateau at Tellancourt. The 9 DI had attacked a force half its size and had been routed in about six hours.

131 RI's tactics had nothing to do with the offensive *à outrance*. The regiment employed Bonnal's tactics, which would have given Grandmaison apoplexy: only four companies attacked, one company was on the defence and seven were in reserve! I/131 was on the right. 1/131 and 4/131 attacked near Cussigny, 3/131 defended the town of Cussigny (500m north of Gorcy) and 1/131 was in battalion reserve. III/131 attacked on the left with only two companies, because the other two companies were in regimental reserve, and all of II/131 was in brigade reserve. By 0815 III/131 was heavily engaged and asked for reinforcements, which were sent forward but never arrived due to the intense German fire. When the fog lifted the French artillery began to fire on Baranzy. By 1100 the 131 RI had taken heavy losses and began to retreat, and it did not stop until it had reached the Chiers at Longuyon.

At 1100 the V CA commander instructed the 10 DI commander to suspend his attack. The corps artillery moved back towards Longuyon and prepared to cross over to the south bank of the Chiers. At 1200 the corps HQ displaced to the rear and set up 3km north of Longuyon. About this time the infantry began to flow to the rear, the units completely intermixed, including numerous stragglers from the VI CA on the right. The corps artillery was stopped before it could cross the Chiers and ordered back north to Tellancourt to cover the corps retreat.

The Battle of the Frontiers
French 4 RI

After the war, the commander of the 4 RI wrote down his impressions of the battle.[4] The 4 RI commander said that the 17th Brigade order for 22 August, which he received only at 0400, stated that the Germans seemed to be withdrawing behind rearguards. 4 RI was cross the line of departure (LD), the Signeulx–Gorcy road, at 0500 to take Mussy la Ville, but the late arrival of the orders meant that the regiment did not cross the LD until 0600. The regiment then waited for I/4 RI to arrive from Malmaison and did not really get moving until 0830. (In any army, failure to meet the LD time is a cardinal sin. It was the job of 4 RI to protect the left flank of the 18th Brigade; since 4 RI lagged behind, the 18th Brigade flank was now exposed). Around 0730 wounded soldiers of the 113 RI began arriving in Signeulx. They said that they had attacked German trenches protected by barbed wire in front of Baranzy, that their attack had failed and that the Germans had then counter-attacked. 4 RI had been advancing for 15 minutes when the fog lifted suddenly and the two leading battalions, II/4 RI and III/4 (I/ 4 had been left in Signeulx) were hit with intense German small arms and artillery fire and pinned down. The French artillery was not firing. The battalions stayed pinned down for the next two hours, taking 50 per cent casualties; one battalion commander was killed, the other wounded three times. The debris of both battalions fell back to Signeulx at 1100, covered by the fire of the French artillery, which had since gone into action. I/4 took up a defensive position behind the rail embankment. The withdrawal of the 113 RI uncovered the battalion right flank and I/4 fell back at 1200, about the same time that the Germans entered Signeulx. The division reserve, the 82 RI, was ordered to counter-attack (*retour offensif*) from Saint Remy towards Signeulx at 1400, but 'made little progress' and the Germans occupied Saint Remy at 1600. The 17th Brigade regrouped at a farm to the north of Longuyon. The regimental commander said that the Germans did not pursue aggressively. He did not mention that part of the reason for this was that the French had quickly fallen back 12km, which would have made it difficult for the Germans to catch up with them. The regimental commander concluded that the French mistake had been to attack without artillery support, which overlooks the fact that, until the fog lifted, the Germans didn't have artillery support either.

German 54th Brigade[5]

From 1800 until about 2000 on 21 August the second brigade of the German 27 ID, the 54th Brigade, moved from Saint Léger to Gennevaux. Half-left an enormous pillar of fire could be seen – the city of Longwy burning under the German bombardment. The 54th Brigade attacked to the left of the 53rd with the objective of taking the town of Signeulx. The Brigade normally consisted of IR 120 and IR 127, but I/127 had been detached to 26 ID and I/120 and II/120 were division reserve. The 54th Brigade was left with only three infantry battalions, but was supported by all of FAR 13. The brigade advanced with II/IR 127 on the left, III/127 on the right, III/120 in Brigade reserve.

The terrain was rolling farmland, a succession of low ridges separated by wet valleys. The fields were still covered in standing grain and there were numerous hedges and small groups of trees.

The right-flank company, 12/127, moved towards Mussy, the left-flank company, 5/127, towards Signeulx, the companies advanced in the fog in successive waves of skirmishers. At 0530 the companies began encountering French patrols. Ten minutes later they ran into French infantry at 100m range on the high ground southeast of Mussy and threw the French back after a short firefight. The regiment advanced to the high ground southwest of Mussy at 0630 when the fog lifted somewhat and a firefight began with French infantry occupying the opposite hill. The two forward battalions had spread out and the IR 127 adjutant reported to brigade at 0810 that the regiment had committed its reserves and was running low on ammunition. I/120 was therefore attached to IR 127, with two companies carrying the contents of an ammunition wagon forward for IR 127. The I/IR 120 war diary said that the battalion advanced through the fog with two companies in front in a skirmisher line and the two following companies in successive waves of skirmishers. At 0845 the battalion intermixed with the IR 127 line, mostly on the IR 127 right flank. III/120 was released from the brigade reserve and moved forward to the right of IR 127. IR 127 was still under fire from an invisible enemy to the front.

At around 0900 the fog lifted completely and French skirmisher lines could be seen on the high ground between Mussy la Ville and Houdlemont, as well as on the road north of Signeulx. Until 0920 the IR 120 and IR 127 soldiers conducted a violent firefight with the French. The weather was now clear and sunny and the effect of the German was could be observed: individual French soldiers got up and ran to the rear through the standing grain towards the hill behind them. The bright colours of the French uniforms contrasted against the dark lanes stomped in the grain and provided excellent targets. The German MG now went into action 'which quite visibly made a strong impression on the enemy. The superiority of the German MG over the French MG was clear in the first minutes.'[6] More French troops fell back and the French fire became weaker. After 30 minutes' firefight the German line began to advance. IR 120 and IR 127 were so intermixed that the companies and platoons had dissolved. Each officer gathered the nearest troops around him together and led them forward – a testimony to German discipline and training. The French committed reinforcements, which could not stop the German advance. The French artillery also opened fire, but the IR 127 historian noted that a high proportion of the French shells were duds. At about 1045 the two regiments began the assault on the hill held by the French. The French withdrew to the southwest before the Germans could close with them, leaving about 150 unwounded prisoners. II/127 pushed the pursuit as far as

The Battle of the Frontiers

Signeulx, taking the rail station after a short firefight. By this time, the French had completely disappeared. In accordance with orders, the regiment then held in place and did not resume movement until 1630. The regiment was able to report at 1500 that it had been engaged with the French 113 RI. The advance resumed with the battalions deployed tactically, the forward companies in skirmisher lines, and continued until 1800, when the regiment bivouacked.

The war diary for I/IR 120 said that the offensive spirit of the troops and their confidence in their leaders had been confirmed. It admitted that it could also be said that the troops had gotten the bit in their teeth and had outrun their artillery support. The French infantry had made little impression on the batallion; it not fought well and its defence had been weak. A lieutenant was killed when a French soldier, playing dead, shot him in the back.

FAR 13[7]

At 0400 on 22 August FAR 13 occupied an overwatch position northwest of Gennevaux. At 0615 French bugles and the cry of '*en avant*', followed by infantry fire, could be heard 600m to 800m to the front and small arms fire began to land in the battery positions. At 0750 the guns were moved into open battery positions and by 0815 the fog had lifted enough to allow the entire regiment to open fire. The German infantry had already advanced some considerable distance and the regiment began to advance by bounds to catch up. The regiment set up first on a ridge 1500m west of Gennevaux, then bounded forward to another position on a ridge west of Baranzy, while under fire from French artillery, whose shrapnel burst too high to cause casualties. Occupation of the position was made more difficult by the necessity of avoiding the large number of French dead and wounded in the area. The regiment opened fire from the new position just as the infantry attack had begun to stall. The regimental history said that its shells set up a 'smoke screen' of dust and dirt that allowed the infantry to resume its advance. The battle reached its peak when two French batteries appeared immediately to the east of Signeulx. 5/FAR 13 and 6/13 immediately shifted to the new targets 'just like in a firing exercise', putting one French battery out of action after it had fired a few rounds, and the other before it could fire at all. At 1000 the regiment advanced by bounds to positions on the high ground between Signeulx and Bleid. In a short time there were no more targets to be seen, except at extreme long range.

Since the infantry advanced so quickly, the requirement for the artillery was to reconnoitre new firing positions, move forward and occupy them, and engage targets, all in rapid succession. The batteries always fired from open positions. The regiment had been trained to meet just such a situation, and it felt that the baptism of fire had been a success.

The regiment had only three wounded. When the regimental surgeon went forward to tend to the infantry, he encountered infantrymen who swore they had

Longwy

been fired upon by German artillery, and then extracted French copper casings from their wounds.

French 10 DI[8]

The French 10 DI was to attack at 0500 along the axis Gorcy – Bel Arbre. The 19th Brigade attacked on the left towards Musson, 20th Brigade attacked on the right towards Bel Arbre, an old outer work of the Longwy fortress. Two battalions were in division reserve. The 19th Brigade in particular ran into difficulties and was unable to advance beyond Gorcy and Vaux, stopped by the right flank of the 26 ID, the 51st Brigade.

46 RI had the mission of attacking Gorcy.[9] I/46 and two companies of II/46 would attack Gorcy itself, while III/46 and a battalion of 89 RI supported them on the right, attacking from Romains to Vaux. The other two companies of II/46 had fought the IR 127 task force the previous day and were 'reorganising'. I/46 made good progress until instructed to withdraw at 1400. III/46 and the battalion of 89 RI were not so fortunate, first being pinned down by superior enemy forces and then forced to evacuate Romains. The regimental war diary said that the regimental commander covered the withdrawal with the divisional engineer company, not 46 RI troops, a good indicator that 46 RI was no longer a coherent unit. At 1800 the colonel had succeeded in rallying the 'debris' of II/46 and III/46 on a plateau, which was under violent fire from German heavy artillery. The regiment then retreated 13km, to a point just north of Longuyon. The German 52nd Brigade halted the 20th Brigade at Longwy; 10 DI was forced to send its reserves to assist the 9 DI. By afternoon, the 10 ID was in retreat, and the troops could be rallied only at Fresnois-la-Montagne, south of Tellancourt and 8km west of Longwy

German 26 ID[10]

When the mobilisation order reached the 26 ID on 1 August the division had just returned from holding its first division FTX (field training exercise) at Münsingen, and the author of the division history said that the division was in 'the best condition imaginable'.

After detaching the 52nd Brigade to attack Longwy on 20 August, the 26 ID consisted of the 51st Brigade (IR 119 and IR 125), three sections of artillery and the division troops. 21 August was a rest day until late in the afternoon, when the division moved forward to an attack area at Rachecourt. The corps attack order for 22 August attached I/IR 127 from 27 ID to 26 ID. The division ordered I/127 to attack on the right towards Ville-Houdelmont while the division left flank attacked past Musson to Gorcy. At 0520 the division received a verbal order from the corps HQ to begin the attack. At 0855, III/IR 122 and II/IR 121 were detached from the 52nd Brigade in front of Longwy and attached to 26 ID.

The Battle of the Frontiers
German IR 119[11]

At 0225, 22 August, IR 119 received the order to occupy its attack position. I/119 was on the right, III/119 plus 7/119 and 8/119 were on the left, 4/119, 11/119 and the MG company were regimental reserve, with 9/119 and 10/119 as brigade reserve. The company ammunition wagons arrived and the ammunition was distributed in bandoliers for the troops to hang over their necks. At 0545 the regiment moved out in a thick fog, behind a screen of skirmishers. It was difficult to maintain direction and orientation in the fog. The troops had to push through hedges and cut down barbed-wire fences, passing to the north of Baranzy and stopping with I/119 to the north of the road to Signeulx, III/119 to the south, and sent out patrols. About 0645 a firefight developed against a largely invisible enemy.

The fog lifted to reveal French troops at close range in the standing grain to the front. The regimental historian said that it was just like the end of an exercise on the Cannstadt meadow: the signal for the assault was given and the troops attacked at a run against the mill west of Baranzy and the heights 1,200m west of Signeulx. Both positions were taken and the regiment stopped to reorganise, as the fog and combat had caused several regiments to become intermixed.

The regiment could now see that the fog had allowed it to cross 2km of completely open ground. French artillery had not been a factor, either blinded by the fog or suppressed by German counter-battery fire. The first battle, the regimental history said, had shown the regiment that it was superior to the French infantry.

At 1430 the regiment began the pursuit, advancing about 5km to the south side of the Bois du Pas Bayard. The march continued in the dark through the woods, navigating by compass, which was 'awful'.

An IR 119 officer related his combat experiences in the regimental newsletter in 1924. He had just led a patrol to make contact with the 27 ID and joined 5/127's skirmisher line. There was continual French small arms fire. He began to look for the French through his field glasses when a soldier pointed them out in the fog, 100m to the front. The signal 'Fix bayonets' was sounded and then 'Charge!' He passed dead French soldiers, ran across a stubble field and a meadow to a hedge at the top of a hill. A soldier fell next to him and he picked up the man's rifle, firing offhand. A bullet struck the rifle stock. He ran forward to the next hedge, saw three French *kepis* and emptied the magazine of his pistol at them. He ran forward through the hedge until he saw a French skirmisher line at close range. The French were all dead or wounded and the attack continued past them and then to the top of the next hill and stopped there, at about 0800, with men from 5/127, intermixed with others from 1/119 and 10/119. The German troops took fire from the French they had bypassed and a few German soldiers went back to silence them.

Suddenly the fog lifted to reveal a meadow to the front and Signeulx in the distance. In the meadow there were large groups of French troops. Immediately the fire commands were given: 'Straight ahead in the meadow! Two companies assembling! Range 800! Fire at will!' To the left German MGs also opened fire. The French were mown down and the Germans began to advance by bounds. Having already taken two minor wounds, the officer was hit in the right arm, but continued forward. The French return fire had ceased. To the left, 1/119 and 10/119 stormed the mill, while 5/127 attacked west along the road to Signeulx and took fire once again. The French used *rafale* fire tactics, rising out of cover to fire off their magazine (eight rounds) and then ducking under cover again. Usually their fire was too high, but because the German units were intermixed and the supports had all come forward, their skirmisher line was too dense and there were casualties. The Germans took up the firefight at 1,200m and advanced by bounds. The sound of the French MGs, firing their 25-round strips, was easy to distinguish and 'didn't impress us much'. German artillery fire landed in the French position, and covered by this fire 5/127 made another bound forward. The officer used his binoculars to detect some French soldiers and instructed the troops near him to put fire on them. Then the Germans then made another bound forward. The officer mentioned that this was bloody and sweaty work. It should be remembered that it was a hot summer day and the troops were carrying their packs and a combat load of ammunition.

The officer kneeled down behind some riflemen, one of whom had carefully laid his weapon over his lower arm, and then taken a slice of bread out of his bread sack, followed by a piece of sausage, and began to eat. The officer asked him sharply why he wasn't firing. The soldier replied reasonably, in his Swabian dialect, 'I can't just shoot all the time; I need to have a little snack, too!'

Gradually the enemy began to crumble. Individuals could be seen jumping up and running to the rear; or rather, as the officer said, attempting to do so. He did not see any that succeeded in evading the German pursuit fire.

The officer said that the dreaded French 75mm gun had little effect on the battle. At one point two French batteries tried to go into action 1,700m from his position, but were smothered by MG and artillery fire.

5/127 had approached to within 600m of the French when someone called out that the troops on the right were beginning an assault. That was the sign for the company to sound 'Fix bayonets!' and 'Charge!' The officer said that it was an indescribably glorious sight, as the entire line, three waves deep, followed by the supports, company and platoon leaders in front, rose up and moved forward, not at a run but in an even walk, and singing '*Deutschland über alles*'. They advanced over meadows and through standing grain; everywhere fallen French troops lay in masses. They crossed a road embankment where the French dead had been hit at 600m to 800m range by German rifle fire. There was seldom any hand-to-hand combat. The surviving French troops threw away their weapons and cried: 'Pardon! Pardon! Camarade!' The troops reached the next high ground, gasping for breath, when the battalion adjutant arrived, telling them to hold in place.

Another German officer noted that the French were miserable shots and wasted ammunition, which reflected badly on the quality of French marksmanship training.

The battle had lasted all morning and IR 119 had advanced under fire for 5km, pushing the French steadily back. This was not one engagement, but a series of engagements that the Germans won in a convincing display of tactical excellence. All ranks continually pressed forward, the leaders retained control of the troops, even when they belonged to different units, and resistance was crushed by a combination of small arms and artillery fire, the fruit of the training that IR 119 had received at home station, in the Münsingen MTA, and in field training exercises.

German IR 125[12]

On the morning of 22 August III/IR 125 was attached to IR 119, while I/125 and II/125 were the 26 ID reserve. III/125 attacked on the left of IR 119 towards Baranzy. As of 0630 it was engaged in a firefight, although the visibility in the fog was 30m. Only at 0830 could the troops begin to see French troops moving. Advancing to the east of Baranzy, the battalion took fire from the Bois de Plainsart and the attack stalled. At 1000 the fog lifted and the German artillery immediately began shelling the woods, which allowed III/125 to resume its advance. The French withdrew and III/125 pursued to Ville Houdlemont, where it halted.

II/125 was sent forward to join the 51st Brigade and reached Baranzy just in time to assist I/ IR 119 in storming the village. Again, the French withdrew, to take up a new position on the high ground 1000m west of Signeulx. When the battalion had approached to within 600m from the French, German artillery fire drove the French off their position. The battalion continued the advance as far as the Signeulx rail station.

While assembling near Signeulx the regiment came under violent French artillery bombardment, which lasted only ten minutes, when the French guns were silenced by FAR 13. The MG Company was instructed to police up the equipment of the French battery that had been destroyed. It found a war chest with 9,000 francs and a 'unauthorised load of food and wine in the ammunition caissons, which was quite welcome.' The company also captured 'thirty magnificent French artillery horses, some of which are still in service with the MG Company in Bad Cannstadt today (1923!)' When the pursuit resumed that afternoon III/125 encountered a French artillery battery in the woods east of St. Pancré and captured four guns, two ammunition wagons and a large number of horses.

A senior NCO in 10/125 gave his impressions of the battle. In peacetime training every combat order began with the 'Situation': the enemy situation, neighbouring friendly units and orientation on the terrain. Knowledge of the 'Situation' was a question officers frequently put to their troops on exercises. The sergeant, a professional soldier, noted sourly that in real combat nobody at the unit level knew what the 'Situation' was. Nevertheless, on 21 August it was clear that the company would receive its baptism of fire the next day. 'To tell the truth, our mood at this moment was quite serious, you could see in each other's faces the inner struggle that was going on, but you could also see how each man came victorious out of this fight and how a solemn determination forged an invisible, but for that reason even stronger, bond between comrades'. Finally the troops were told that the company would attack the enemy, who was deployed on both sides of the Musson–Baranzy road. Two platoons would form a skirmisher line; the third would march in column behind them. The company moved out in fog so thick that only a few men to the left and right could be seen. 'Nevertheless, thanks to our outstanding training, we stayed in formation'. A few rounds went over their heads, but the advance continued, until the command 'Halt! Defensive position!' The company lay on the grass. Then a command 'To the rear, march!' was heard. The troops, confused, began to slowly move to the rear when the company commander roared 'Where did that idiotic order come from? The 10th Company will remain in its positions!' The sergeant said that the company commander's quick and decisive action ensured the troops that come what may, they had an energetic leader in whom they trusted completely. Then French soldiers appeared in the fog and were shot down:

'Now there was no more hesitation. Individually, in squads and in half platoons we worked our way forwards, exactly as we had learned in our long peacetime training. Then the sun tore apart the veil of fog and presented a scene before our eyes that we will certainly never forget'.

The company lay on somewhat higher ground and could see far and wide. On lower ground, IR 119 was advancing by bounds in heavy fire. To the front, especially on the road from Signeulx to Houdlemont, the French were visible, furiously attempting to dig in. The German artillery opened fire, much to the troop's surprise and pleasure, and a French company, still in column, was caught in the open and destroyed. A French battery appeared, and the company watched in horror as it headed for the company left flank, from where it could fire with murderous effectiveness. The range was too long for it to be stopped by German rifle fire. The French battery had only a few hundred metres to go when the third shell fired by a German artillery battery hit a French ammunition wagon, which blew up with a spectacular explosion, disorganising the French movement. This shell was followed by one direct hit after another until the French battery was destroyed. The company cheered, although, as the sergeant said, the spectacle that had been played out before them was in fact quite horrible. The company objective was Ville Houdlemont, which the French held strongly. In spite of the fact that the French wore blue coats and red trousers, they hid themselves quite well in the town. Two French MGs in some bushes that could fire on the company left flank, however, presented the biggest problem. With every bound the French MGs sent death and destruction like a storm wind into the German ranks. A look to the rear showed a sad picture of a number of dead of or badly wounded German soldiers. Although the troops were already numbed by the stress of combat, the news that the company commander had been killed 'was like a stab in the heart'. But these sacrifices were not in vain. As the German line approached the French position, French courage sank. From time to time red trousers could be seen disappearing to the rear with 'unbelievable speed'. The closer the Germans got, the more often this happened. When the Germans approached to within assaulting distance of the edge of town, 'the rest evaporated with a nimbleness that commanded our admiration.' Patrols were sent to follow the French, who threw away packs, weapons and anything that weighed them down and quickly left the Germans behind. The sergeant said that 'We could be proud that we had acquitted ourselves so brilliantly in our baptism of fire, and we were … Truth be told, one has to admit that after a fight the first order of business for most of the troops was getting something to eat.' The subsequent events on the grim battlefield then unrolled just as though the company were on a manoeuvre 'after taking the objective', to the astonishment of all concerned. The signal 'General Halt!' was played, then 'Stack Arms!' One comedian even sounded 'Return to Quarters!' The troops sat down next to the stacked weapons and ate whatever they could get their hands on.

German XIII AK[13]

XIII AK ordered the corps to halt in place at 1200 'because the situation of the neighbouring corps and to the front had to be clarified'. 27 ID had reported at 1100 that 54th Brigade had taken the heights between Bleid and Signeulx, but did not want to advance further because contact with 53rd Brigade had been lost and the division HQ thought that the high ground northeast of Bleid was still in French hands, when in fact the French had never held this ground. The Division HQ thought the 53rd Brigade was fighting at St. Leger, where it had started its march on 21 August, and did not know that the brigade had taken Bleid.

This constituted a serious failure of command and control, leading to a loss of contact with the enemy and an ineffective pursuit. The job of both the corps and division HQ was to keep each other informed, so that the corps did not have to stop while the HQ sorted out the situation.

The corps wanted the advance to resume at 1445. When the 51st Brigade hadn't begun to advance by 1530, the corps headquarters bypassed the 26 ID HQ and ordered the brigade to move out. In the 26 ID sector the movement was slowed because the units went through the Bois du Pas Bayard rather than around it. By evening the corps had no communications with 26 ID HQ. On the morning of 23 August, XIII AK HQ learned the 26 ID had stopped at the south edge of the

Bois du Pas Bayard, instead of advancing to the Chiers. In the 27 ID sector the advance was slowed by artillery and supply columns moving on the same road as the infantry. Clearly all the units in the division knew that the French were nowhere in the vicinity and the artillery and supply units were racing forward to get the best billets for the night: the infantry failed to reach its assigned objectives.

German 52nd Brigade[14]

Since there was no return fire from Longwy, early in the morning of 22 August General Kaempfer ordered an immediate infantry assault on the fortress with I/IR 122 and II/122, to start at 0800. Both battalions and the engineers sent out patrols to find if there were any gaps blown by the artillery in the walls. III/IR 121 was to hold Autrux and protect II/FAR 65; I/121 and the MG Company 121 were to attack on the right to take Bel Arbre. The organisation of the attack was hasty and resulted in a lack of coordination: in order to provide fire support, the commander of II/122 sent 5/122 to occupy Bel Arbre, supposedly the objective of I/IR 121. The French had not defended Bel Arbre and 5/122 reached it without difficulty by 0745. Both Bel Arbre and the town of Romain lie about 500m to 600m south of the tree line of the Bois de Chadelle. The farmland around Bel Arbre and Romain consisted of standing grain and fields of potatoes.

The assault was still being organised at 0830 when the brigade was completely surprised to hear rapid fire from 5/122, followed by a signal flag report that 5/122 could see five French infantry battalions with artillery advancing from the southwest against Bel Arbre. At the same time, an *Uhlan* patrol made a similar report. It would appear that there had been a serious failure of German staff work. There is no evidence that the attack group Kaempfer had been kept current on the enemy situation in the XIII AK area, perhaps because it had been detached on a special mission under a general officer who was directly subordinate to 5th Army HQ.

The 52nd Brigade immediately issued an attack order: 'Strong enemy forces advancing from Cosnes on Romain. The brigade will attack. The centre of the brigade will orient on the small tree 200m west of Bel Arbre, IR 122 on the right, IR 121 on the left. IR 121 will leave two companies behind the centre as brigade reserve.' At 0855 XIII AK ordered III/122 and II/121 to reinforce 26 ID, reducing 52nd Brigade to four battalions.

The brigade had been deployed to assault Longwy and had to reorient itself to the right front against Romain. It was essential to take the town as quickly as possible; if the French held Romain, there was no possibility that 52nd Brigade could take Longwy. The German companies moved independently through the woods southwest towards Romain, with the troops of I/122, II/122 and I/121 becoming intermixed. The troops had taken off their packs for the assault, and therefore moved quickly. The long-range fire from 5/122 on the advancing French slowed their movement and forced them to deploy. At the same time that the German

The Battle of the Frontiers

infantry broke out of the tree line, French infantry occupied the north edge of Romain. Moser wrote:

> 'Now our infantry showed what its magnificent offensive spirit could accomplish. The platoons advanced in perfect bounds to close with the enemy, in spite of the terrible holes torn here and there in their advancing ranks by French machine guns'.

The MG Company of IR 121 set up in a quarry near Bel Arbre and provided very effective fire support. French artillery caused heavy casualties, while the German artillery could not find suitable firing positions. Nevertheless, the French were thrown on the defensive. By 1000, 8 /122, 6/122 and 2/122 had reached Romain. The centre of French resistance was the walled churchyard, which was the scene of bitter fighting. By 1100 the French troops were retreating and the French artillery ceased fire. The remaining French troops were pushed out of Romain. During the entire fight the garrison of Longwy was completely inactive. After the French withdrew, the brigade held in place to continue the bombardment of Longwy, which fell on 26 August.

The 52nd Brigade's fight at Longwy was not a shining hour for German generalship. The brigade seems to have been forgotten by both 5th Army and XIII AK and therefore had no idea that strong French forces were advancing in the immediate vicinity. General Kaempfer's decision on the morning of 22 August to assault Longwy was premature: there were no breaches in the walls and the fortress had by no means been softened up. Kaempfer did not plan the attack, but made a last-minute decision that he expected would be executed immediately, without any preparation or coordination. As the IR 122 history said, had the assault had been conducted, there would have been a disaster. For that reason, the attack by the French 10 DI was actually a stroke of good fortune. It was also sheer good fortune that 5/122 had gone forward to Bel Arbre, from where it detected and slowed the French advance. Had the German infantry attacked Longwy and then been struck in the flank by an attack from Romain, the 52nd Brigade would surely have been destroyed. The German infantry was thrown into an attack at Romain without any coordination and without artillery support. The only credit the German army drew from this battle was due to the performance of the battalion and company commanders and the individual infantrymen, which once again was beyond all praise. On the other hand, the French for once knew where the Germans were and launched a coordinated attack. This attack might well have succeeded. It was only the defeat of the 9 DI that forced the V CA commander to order the 10 DI to withdraw. In addition, had the garrison of Longwy demonstrated any initiative at all, the 52nd Brigade would have been defeated.

Longwy

23 August

The French V CA war diary said that by the morning of 23 August the corps had been more or less reformed and deployed on a defensive line north of the Chiers. The troops were tired and hungry. When the Germans began to put pressure on the corps the situation quickly became critical and the corps withdrew in good order to the south side of the Chiers, covered by the artillery.[15] On the night of 23–24 August the corps commander was relieved of his command.

On the evening of 22 August the German XIII Corps HQ had no idea where the French had gone and decided to prepare for a French attack on the morning of 23 August, particularly because it had no hard information concerning the neighbouring German corps but expected that their situation was less favourable than its own.[16] The XIII AK did not even know the situation in its own area of operations: it thought that Cosnes, 3km west of Longwy and in the middle of the corps sector, was still occupied by the French, even though 20th *Uhlan* bivouacked there that night.

The corps was held in readiness on the morning of 23 August to receive an enemy attack. The extent of the corps' victory became apparent only during the course of the morning; the corps established that on 22 August it had taken 2,000 POWs and the 27 ID found that the roads to its front were covered with discarded French weapons, packs, equipment, artillery caissons and guns, all of which pointed to a French rout.[17] The order to begin the pursuit was issued at 0930.

As on the afternoon and evening of 22 August, on the morning of 23 August valuable time, which was could have been used to plan and to issue orders, had been lost because of failures in command and control at the army, corps and divisional levels. These delays also gave the French time to recover: when the 27 ID did move out, it immediately encountered French artillery fire at Tellancourt that forced the lead elements to manoeuvre away from the road.

IR 127's objective was the Chiers. The regiment reported seeing French infantry falling back, pursued by German artillery fire. But the French artillery was very active in covering the retreat. The IR 127 regimental historian said that the troops were worn out from the previous days' exertion and by the hot weather on 23 August. The regiment bivouacked that night on the high ground north of the Chiers.[18]

Casualties

268 German and 884 French soldiers are buried at the war grave at Barancy
IR 127 lost seven OFF and 102 EM KIA, 11 OFF and 266 EM WIA.
I/IR 119 lost one OFF and 19 EM KIA, four OFF and 139 EM WIA.
I/IR 120 lost three OFF and 10 EM KIA, one OFF and 77 EM WIA
III/IR 120 lost three OFF and 18 EM KIA, four OFF and 151 EM WIA.
IR 125 lost a total of 11 OFF and 100 EM KIA and WIA.

The Battle of the Frontiers

IR 121 lost three OFF and 38 EM KIA, two OFF and 95 EM WIA.
IR 122 lost seven OFF and 157 EM KIA and 14 OFF WIA. I/122 and II/122 took twenty-six per cent casualties.

Conclusions

XIII AK had an opportunity to turn French defeat into French disaster. The superb Württemberg troops had crushed the French 9 DI by 1100 in the morning. The lead brigade of the French 7 DI on the corps right had been destroyed and the second brigade was in full retreat by early afternoon; there was a gaping hole in the French centre and a half a day left to exploit it. Longuyon was 12km from Signeulx. A vigorous pursuit could have completed the destruction of the 9 DI and put the German XIII AK in the position to break up the entire French front.

Instead, the XIII AK 'waited for the situation to clarify itself', which in combat is the antithesis of decisive action. The fog of war is inherent in military operations. Decisive action requires risk-taking in spite of the lack of clarity. There were plenty of indicators that the 54th and 51st Brigades had crushed their opponents, the foremost being the 5km fighting advance they had made in a matter of hours. The casualties in both brigades were relatively low. If, as the corps maintained, it was concerned that the situation was not rosy in the neighbouring corps sectors, the best way for the XIII AK to assist those corps would have been to rupture the enemy front. The French infantry had been routed; a vigorous pursuit would have turned the rout into an uncontrollable panic.

Instead, XIII AK opted for 'safety first': XIII AK wasted the afternoon of 22 August and the night of 22–23 August in waiting. It may well be that the corps feared that it had only beaten the French advance guard, and that the French were manoeuvring for their vaunted '*retour offensivf*'. By the time the corps started moving late on the morning of 23 August, the French artillery had recovered its poise and its fire slowed the German advance considerably.

At the unit level, the German infantry and artillery had accomplished all that could be expected and more. The quality of German unit training was demonstrated, in extremely difficult conditions. The French infantry had once again been shattered before the French artillery could intervene. Moser too said that the first battle gave the German troops a feeling of superiority over the French.[19]

11
The Battle South of Longwy

Unknown to either side, the situation to the south of Longwy was more favourable for the Germans than it was any other area in the Ardennes. The French VI CA, with three divisions on a 25km front, faced the German VI RK and the XVI AK, with the V RK rapidly approaching from the rear. To make matters worse, the French right flank was 'in the air' – completely exposed. The only factors operating in favour of the French were first, that the VI CA was a border security unit and accounted to be one of the best corps in the French army, and second, that the Germans had to be conscious of the threat that French units might attack from the protection of Verdun against their own left flank.

The mission of the German VI RK was to attack towards Longuyon-Pierrepont. The XVI AK was to attack towards Joppécourt-Anderny, and not to cross that line, a reflection of the 5th Army's concern for its left flank. This left a large gap between the two corps, to be filled by V RK, the army reserve, which had to execute a forced march from its assembly area to the west of Luxembourg to reach the front line.[1]

The French VI CA was oriented on the German force attacking Longwy. The corps had deep objectives. The 12 DI on the left was to attack north of Longwy to Aubange (6km northeast of Longwy). 42 DI was to attack to Mexy and Villers de Montagne, to the southeast of Longwy. The 40 DI would act as flank guard, with one column advancing from Joppécourt to Fillières, the second from Higny to Mercy-le-Haut. The corps would begin its advance at 0500. The French 7 DC would guard the Army right flank.[2]

As of 17 August the reserve divisions on the right wing of the French 3rd Army had been placed under General Paul Durand with the mission of defending the Meuse between Toul and Verdun and of eventually investing Metz from the north. Durand's group was to remain under the orders of the 3rd Army commander, who expected that at least two of these divisions would cooperate in his offensive.[3] On the other hand, Durand was still receiving instructions from GQG which told him to remain on the defensive. Durand did not report this to the 3rd Army commander, probably because on 19 August he was placed under the orders of the commander of the new Army of Lorraine, Maunoury, who did not arrive at the Army HQ in Verdun until late on 21 August. The Army of Lorraine had the same strictly defensive mission as had Durand's group of reserve divisions. Indeed, the Army of Lorraine was oriented towards the progress of the 2nd Army, not the 3rd. GQG did not inform 3rd Army of the command changes. Both the HQ of 3rd Army and the HQ of the Army of Lorraine were located in Verdun, but they didn't talk to each other: when the commander of the 3rd Army left Verdun for his forward command post on the morning of 22 August, he thought that the reserve divisions were still under his orders and would move to cover his right flank; they did not. It would be hard to find a worse example of high-level staff work.

German VI RK[4]

The VI RK was a Silesian unit and included the 11 RD and 12 RD. The 11 RD included the active army 23rd Infantry Brigade (IR 22 and IR 156) as well as the 21st Reserve Infantry Brigade (RIR 10 and RIR 11), 4th Reserve Hussar Regiment and Reserve Field Artillery Regiment (RFAR) 11. 12 RD included 22nd Reserve Infantry Brigade with RIR 23, which had only two battalions, RIR 38 and 6th Reserve *Jäger* (light infantry) Battalion, and the 23rd Reserve Infantry Brigade, made up of RIR 22 and RIR 51 (with two battalions). The 12 RD also included the 4th Reserve *Uhlan* Regiment and RFAR 12. The corps included about 32,000 men, while an active army corps had 44,000 men. VI RK composed of older reservists and *Landwehr* men. Like all reserve units, it was created during mobilisation; for the most part the officers and men had never worked together before. The regimental commanders, battalion commanders, company commanders and the adjutants were regular army officers; the platoon leaders were reserve officers or warrant officers.

The commanders of German reserve units used every available moment during mobilisation, deployment and the approach march to conduct tactical training. RIR 10 had received and organised all its personnel and issued its equipment by 7 August and used 8 and 9 August for company and battalion road-march and tactical training, before beginning the rail march on the evening of 9 August. It unloaded at Saarbrücken on 12 August, marched to its assembly area by 16 August and conducted further tactical training on 17 August. On 18 August the German right wing began its advance. 21 August was a rest day for the 5th Army, which RIR 10 used in part to conduct more tactical training.[5] RIR 51 conducted marksmanship training at the firing range on 7 August, tactical training on 8 and 9 August and on 10 August a road march, including the combat and field trains, followed by field training.[6]

The Battle South of Longwy

When the German V RK met the French 12 DI and 42 DI, according to the pre-war calculations the active-army French units should have cut through the German reserve units like a hot knife through butter. The troops of the French divisions were almost all young active-duty soldiers: as a border-security unit, the French VI CA was kept at nearly full-strength in peacetime. The German VI RK had 72 field artillery pieces; the two French divisions, given a proportional slice of the corps artillery, should have had 104 guns, a 40 per cent superiority. VI RK was an exception and did have a heavy howitzer battalion (16 howitzers).

It is therefore remarkable that the German VI Reserve Corps, in combat on 22 August with two first-rate French active army divisions, gave just as good as it got. The real surprise was not that the Germans used reserve units like active-army units, but that the German reserve units were able to stand their ground.

At 1700 on 21 August 5th Army HQ notified the commander of VI RK that strong French forces were 15km to his front, headed in his direction. A half-hour later he received the same report from his own cavalry. The VI RK commander moved the 11RD on the corps right front to Hussigny, and the 12 RD on the left to Tiercelet. In accordance with the 5th Army operations order, the VI RK ordered the corps to attack west, with 11 RD on the right towards Cutry-Laix, to the south of Longwy, while 12 RD on the left attacked the high ground northeast of Villers au Montois. RIR 51, which had only two battalions, and the 6th Reserve *Jäger* (Light Infantry) Battalion were detached from 12 RD (23rd Reserve Brigade, which now included only RIR 22) to be corps reserve.

The commander of the VI RK confronted a leadership problem, the consequence of modern communications, which still bedevils combat leaders to this day. The Corps HQ was connected to the Army HQ by landline telephone. When the fighting began, the corps chief of staff recommended to the corps commander that he remain at the headquarters so as to be able to communicate instantly with Army HQ. The Corps commander disagreed, saying that he had to move closer to the front, to receive reports from the troops on a real-time basis and to be able to see the action for himself. The Corps Commander therefore left his HQ at Villers la Montagne and moved forward to Chénièrs.

Modern communications could be as much a hindrance to good combat leadership as they were a help, because they tied the commander to an unfavourable location far from the action. Israeli commanders noted the same problem in the 1973 Yom Kippur War, when many commanders stayed at their HQ because of its long-range radio communications with higher headquarters, rather that going forward to be closer to the troops and see the terrain.

This brought into question the corps commanders' mode of transport on the battlefield. He said that riding in an automobile limited him to the roads, where he would often get stuck in traffic. For that reason he still preferred the horse, which allowed him to move across country quickly.

At Chénièrs he met the commander of the heavy howitzer battalion, which opened fire on French columns at 7,000m range, slowing the French advance considerably.

French VI CA[7]

On the French 12 DI left, near Cutry, the 23rd Brigade and elements of the 24th Brigade ran into elements of the German 11 RD. Battered by German artillery, the French were not able to advance beyond Lexy and could hold onto the high ground west of Cutry only with great difficulty until midday, when they were forced to withdraw, at the same time as the 10 DI to their left. On the 12 DI right, the 24th Brigade (132 RI and elements of 106 RI) supported by a group of corps artillery, advanced on Caure Ferme but were stopped.

The 42 DI advanced guard (151 RI and a group of corps artillery) encountered German forces while leaving Pierrepont at 0800, 8km south of Cutry. 42 DI was soon 'heavily engaged' on the north tree line of the Bois de Doncourt. The enemy 'strongly held' the area of the Bois de Latrimont. The division commander manoeuvred 162 RI and a second group of artillery at 0910 to attack the Bois de Goemont. At 1030 he committed 94 RI and the third artillery group on the right to attack Boismont and Baslieux; the attack did not reach Baslieux. The division commander reported that the fire of enemy artillery was very effective. In spite of frequent counterattacks the division was pushed back almost everywhere.

A brigade of 40 DI, which was holding Bazailles, attempted to take Ville au Montois. The corps liaison officer reported that the fight was a tough one and the situation did not look good. This was apparently the last report that VI CA received from any of the divisions. Nor did the corps seem to have issued any useful orders to the division. Command and control in VI CA had collapsed.

German VI RK[8]

On the corps right, 11 RD attacked with 23rd Infantry Brigade (IR 22 on the right and IR 156 on the left) on the right, 21st Reserve Infantry Brigade (RIR 11 on the right and RIR 10 on the left) on the left. The division made good progress and took the forest de Lauromont south of Cutry from the French by 0900. The 11 RD attack was then stopped at Cons and the Bois de Doncourt.

12 RD attacked with the 22nd Reserve Brigade, which included only RIR 22, RIR 51 being the VI RK reserve, from Laix on the right and 23rd Reserve Brigade on the left, with RIR 23 on the right and RIR 38 on the left. This put RIR 38 on the corps left flank, which was completely in the air until V RK would arrive.

The 12 RD was also stopped at the Doncourt woods, in spite of heavy artillery support. A French counterattack at 1700 forced the 22nd Reserve Brigade at 1730

The Battle South of Longwy

to withdraw to Laix, followed at 1830 by the 23rd Reserve Brigade. The French did not pursue.

IR 22[9]

I/22 had been left at Longwy to guard the heavy artillery. III/22 deployed to the south of Mexy with 9/22 and 10/22 in the first line, 11/22 and 12/22 in the second, II/22 and the MG Company echeloned to the right rear. When the two lead companies reached the high ground east of Cutry they took heavy small arms fire. The companies deployed skirmisher lines and at 600m range took up the firefight with French infantry on the edge of Cutry, whose red trousers stood out like poppies in the gardens and fields of grain. 11/22 was deployed on the regimental right, the MG Company on the left. At 0830 II/22 moved to the right of III/22 and advanced on Lexy and Rehon. III/22 did not wait for the German artillery, but assaulted Cutry, supported by the MG, which inflicted severe losses on the French. 11/22 took an entire French company with three officers prisoner. 8/22 took Heumont Ferme and pushed on to the north.

The regiment, reinforced now by I/22, continued the attack to the north, climbed with difficulty out of the ravine south of Lexy and surprised the French troops in the town, who fled in disorder. The German troops scrambled to the top and engaged the French with pursuit fire, many kneeling or standing. III/22 pushed another kilometre to the west, but due to the difficult situation RIR 11 was in, I/22 and III/22 were pulled back to Cutry. Most of III/22 assisted IR 156 in the attack on Ugny. The regiment spent the night digging in near Cutry, in expectation of a French attack the next morning

IR 156[10]

IR 156 was an Upper Silesian unit; ninety per cent of the troops were Polish-speaking. Most were coal miners and, as the regimental historian said modestly, 'not bad soldiers'. The regiment marched on the left of IR 22. It moved out at 0230, marching to Haucourt, and then deployed to advance on Chénières, with III/154 on the right, I/154 on the left, preceded by a skirmisher line, II/154 and the MG Company in the second line. At 0630 the regiment reached Chénières and continued the advance on Cutry, believed to be occupied by the French. As the regiment crossed the high ground 1km to the northwest of Chénières, it took heavy small arms fire. The regiment immediately ran forward to a firing position and engaged the French on the edge of the town at 900m to 1,000m range. The supports moved forward by bounds to thicken the firing line. The MG Company went into action between the leading battalions and the regiment had soon obtained fire superiority. Nevertheless, the French position was too strong for the regiment to be able to advance.

The Battle of the Frontiers

At 0740 RFAR 11 opened fire on Cutry.[11] The town was soon covered in a cloud of smoke and dust. An enemy battery was destroyed as is attempted to displace to a safer position. French infantry, easily identifiable in their red trousers, attempted to advance from the Bois de Lauromont south of the town and were taken under effective artillery fire.

The artillery support was decisive; the infantry resumed its advance, entire companies advancing by bounds. The French broke and ran, leaving 100 unwounded POWs. Several men in civilian clothes shot at the troops of IR 156 and were dealt with. II/156, in reserve, was deployed to protect the right flank of IR 22 for the rest of the day but made no contact.

IR 156 reorganised in Cutry and was ordered to resume the advance towards Cons-la-Grandville–Ugny. The regimental history said that the French were numerically superior, well positioned and invisible. Lacking specific targets, the regiment had to employ area fire. This time, no artillery support was forthcoming – RFAR 11 was supporting the 21st Reserve brigade – and the advance was slow and difficult. The French therefore launched their counterattack – *retour offensif* – but were met by murderous fire from IR 156, delivered 'as cold-bloodedly as on the firing range', which forced the French back to their start line. By this time, the regiment had shot off all its ammunition, when two ammunition wagon drivers brought their vehicles to the front line and the ammunition reserve was unloaded. Immediately after being resupplied, I/156 renewed the attack and at 1630 successfully assaulted Ugny.

4/ IR 156

A senior sergeant from 4/156 recorded his impressions of the battle. The troops were awakened at 0300 and took their breakfast of coffee and bread from the field kitchen, shivering in the morning chill. The company commander made a short speech and at 0400 the company moved out. At 0445 the company left the road, the ammunition wagon came forward and the combat load was distributed to the troops, who stuffed extra clips in their pockets and bread sacks, and the rifles were loaded. The fog lifted and the day was sunny and clear. The company began to advance, one platoon in skirmisher line far to the front, the rest in platoon column. The company encountered a man-high garden wall. Now the reason for all the climbing drills in training became evident. The active-duty troops helped the somewhat less fit reservists over the top. The skirmisher platoon climbed a hill to the northwest of Chénières and took up firing positions, with the other two platoons in defilade on the hillside behind them, when the French opened fire. The company commander ran to the top of the hill and deployed the 2nd Platoon in support; 3rd Platoon began in reserve, but was soon ordered to the firing line too. The sergeant and his men moved by bounds through the tall grain. He lay down next to a man who had been shot in the lower body and was groaning.

The Battle South of Longwy

The enemy was invisible; the grain blocked his view of anyone but the man to his left and right. In a few seconds he counted six French bullets that landed so close that they threw dirt in his face. Lying in enemy fire, unable to fire back, was 'horrible'. The sound of the French bullets going past and the humming of the ricochets were nerve-wracking. He called to the soldier next to him, only to find that the man had been shot in the head and was dead. The man with the lower-body wound had also died. The sergeant rose to one knee to see the terrain and then bounded forward, followed by his men, while French bullets struck the ground around him; one round passed between his outspread fingers, glancing against his wedding ring, and he stumbled over a wounded German soldier. He could now see the red trousers of the French in the village gardens and the commander of 4/156 walking upright behind the firing line. He made more bounds down the hill, over the wheat fields and meadows. German artillery fire began to land in the town and the French fire weakened suddenly. At 0900 horn signals, drums and shouts of the German troops rose to a 'hellish concert' and 4/156 advanced into the village in skirmisher line at a walk, the company commander five paces to the front glowing with pride, past French dead and wounded. Every hayrick was prodded with a bayonet to insure the French were not hiding in it, waiting to shoot the German troops in the back. Twenty paces to the sergeant's rear, a 4/156 man discovered a Frenchman in this manner and shot him. The troops assembled in the village and the roll was called. Each man was trying to make sense of the events of the last few minutes.

> 'What was that? Is it possible that a few days ago we were riding on the train through Germany? Haven't months or years passed since then? We were no longer the same men that we were then. Deep seriousness was plain in the face of every man. The soldiers carried their heads prouder and higher. After his first battle he was conscious of his own worth. This experience had made him into a complete man.'

Between 1200 and 1300 the company moved out in column south of the road to Ugny and soon took fire. 1st and 2nd Platoons deployed into skirmisher line, bounded forward several times and then formed a firing line. Our sergeant was now leading the 3rd Platoon; all the officers other than the company commander had been wounded. The 3rd Platoon followed by squads or half platoon column. The platoon took cover in a water-filled ditch and a French machine gun opened continuous fire that passed directly over their heads. Losses mounted on the firing line and the company commander ordered the platoon to the left of the firing line with three-pace interval between skirmishers. The sergeant ran forward, threw himself down on the ground and then looked back

'It is simply good to relate how the troops came running forward, the squad leaders in front and the musketeers behind, the rifle in the right fist and in the left the bayonet and entrenching tool. They gasped for breath under their heavy packs and came forward, heads bent to the ground. I thought, just like the training area at Heidau. In truth, I laughed and was happy to have been allowed to be a troop leader.'

The advance continued by squads and by individuals, carefully using the terrain. Commands were hardly necessary; the troops flowed forwards on their own. Most of the French fire was too high, but a ricochet tore away the top half of the skull of one of the sergeant's range estimators, splattering him with the man's blood. French artillery shelled the area to their rear. Ammunition began to run short when a sergeant and a corporal raced forward with ammunition wagons to resupply the firing line. The ammunition sergeant became the first enlisted man in the regiment to be awarded the Iron Cross 2nd Class. The 3rd Platoon made several bounds forward, past German dead and wounded, to the firing line. At 1700 men from IR 22 and RIR 10 joined them, and new squads and platoons were organised on the battlefield. The attack penetrated into the village and about a platoon of French soldiers were captured, while with binoculars the rest could be seen to be withdrawing.

The first sergeant assembled the company on the road, calling out '4/156 over here!' The company commander was not to be seen, and it was feared that he had been killed or wounded, when someone called out 'Here comes our Starzik' (Polish for 'old man') and he walked out of the darkness, a rifle slung over his back, accompanied by an NCO and several soldiers. He was greeted with cheers, and several men impulsively shook his hand. He was visibly moved. When he then said 'Now that we're all together, I imagine you're hungry'. A musketeer, a good Upper Silesian who in garrison had often been sent to the guardhouse for drunkenness, gave the company commander a large piece of French white bread, saying 'Here, Herr Hauptmann, booty from the village where we started the attack.' The first roll call showed 3 NCOs and 8 EM dead, 2 officers, six NCOs and 32 EM wounded. The company moved back to high ground and dug in. The field kitchen arrived at 0030 with hot food.

RIR 10[12]

The 21st Reserve Infantry Brigade attacked on the 11 RD left, with Chénières the objective of RIR 11[13] on the right and RIR 10 moving on the left south of the town. I/RIR 10 was held as division reserve. II/R 10 deployed with each forward company on a 100m front, 7/R 10, 6/R 10 and 8/R 10 on a 300m front on the regimental right, III/R 10 deployed 11/R 10 and 12/R 10 on a 200m front on the regimental left, with two companies in the second line. The terrain was

The Battle South of Longwy

rolling and dotted with small copses. The regiment moved over five hills in its hour and a half-long approach march. RIR 11 on the right became engaged in a firefight in Chénières and RIR 10 swung to the northwest in support. By 0800 it was taking French small arms fire.

The regimental historian was sharply critical of French marksmanship. He said that while German peacetime training took great pains to teach the troops to aim and fire carefully, French squads, half platoons and platoons would spring up from cover on command, rapidly fire off their magazine and then disappear under cover again (*rafale*). The result was that while the French fired off masses of ammunition in salvos that initially were quite impressive, the German troops quickly learned that the French rarely hit anything.

By 0830 the regiment had reached the Bois de Lauromont where it was stopped by French artillery fire. In contrast with the ineffectiveness of French rifle fire, the regimental historian said that the accuracy and thoroughness of the French artillery made a strong impression on the troops. III/R 10 also took effective infantry fire from the Bois de Doncourt. All companies suffered heavy casualties. II/R 10 tried to advance, but in addition to the enemy fire took friendly fire from IR 22 and German artillery. All along the regimental front small groups tried to continue the advance but gained only a few hundred metres at the cost of heavy casualties. The French attempted to conduct a counterattack, which quickly broke down in the face of German small arms fire.

4/RFAR 11 and 5/R 11 displaced forward 600m at 0930 and engaged French infantry north of the Villers–Longwy road. At 1100 5/R 11 and 6/R 11 displaced to the south of the Bois de Lauromont to support the 21st Reserve Brigade and were soon followed by I/RFAR 11. They engaged French infantry in woods south of Ugny at 1,000–1,600m range.

At noon the VI RK was heavily engaged. The front 23rd Infantry Brigade ran from Lexy to the east of Ugny, and the brigade was in good shape. The 21st Reserve Brigade was under pressure from French attacks and would be forced to give up Caure Ferme in the next hour, but held the western tree line of the Bois de Lauromont. The 12 RD was in heavy combat at the Bois de Doncourt and the Bois de Goemont, and the left flank was in the air and in danger of being turned.

At 1300 a division order reached the RIR 10, ordering it to take the town of Ugny about 1,000m to 1,500m to the front. At 1400 the line swept forward without halting, led by the brigade commander in person. The advance outran the French artillery fire, only to come under German artillery fire again. The German troops turned back and could be stopped by the surviving leaders only with difficulty. The German units were mixed together. III/R 10 had collected troops from every regiment of the 12 RD to the south; there were several soldiers from RIR 11 with II/R 10. As night fell the troops were reorganised and dug in where they stood.

The Battle of the Frontiers
RIR 51[14]

RIR 51, the corps reserve, had only two battalions. At 1330 I/R 51 was committed to plug the gap between 11 RD and 12 RD. At 1430 II/R 51 and the MG Company were pulled back to secure the corps HQ, a misuse of the MG Company as well as a sign that the corps commander did not think that things were going well.

I/R 51 deployed from the Bois de Lauromont in a wedge formation, 3/R 51 in front as the point of the wedge, 1/R 51 on the left, 4/R 51 on the right, 2/R 51 in overwatch dug in at the woods. The battalion took fire but could not detect where it was coming from, so the troops worked their way forward to RIR 10 and RIR 11 as quickly as possible, bringing them extra ammunition. The ground between the Bois de Lauromont and the Bois de Doncourt was under fire from a French artillery battery, but the troops soon saw that they could run forward in the intervals between each four-round salvo.

The commander of 3/R 51 requested artillery support from II/RFAR. 4/11 moved to an open position southwest of the Bois de Lauromont and began firing on thick French skirmisher lines, but in ten minutes was engaged by French counter-battery fire and almost all of the gunners became casualties.

A lieutenant of 4/R 51 with his platoon, plus men of 3/R 51 and 6th Reserve Engineer Battalion, attacked Caure Ferme using the same tactics Rommel had used at Bleid; half the platoon provided frontal suppressive fire, while the other half manoeuvred through a woods to the right to attack the farm in the flank. The entire platoon then assaulted and drove the French from both the farm and the woods.

The attack by 3/R 51 made only slow progress at the cost of serious casualties. Due to the length and intensity of the firefight, ammunition began to run short until supporting troops, each carrying two or three bandoliers, came forward. Nevertheless, the attack stalled completely.

On the left, two platoons of 1/R 51 were engaged in a firefight when troops from RIR 38 and RIR 11 were seen withdrawing from the Bois de Doncourt, while the French entered the woods in strength. French fire on 1/R 51 intensified and the company commander committed his reserve platoon to the firing line and attacked into the Bois de Doncourt, where the fight continued at point-blank range and with the bayonet. The French ran out of the forest to the rear and 1/R 51 pushed on to the far tree line. The French received reinforcements and attacked again, forcing 1/R 51 to evacuate the woods. The troops from RIR 38 and RIR 11 who had fled were assembled by the RIR 51 adjutant and brought forward, and together with 1/R 51 pushed the French back out of the woods again. Both sides had fought bravely and taken heavy casualties; the woods were strewn with French dead and 1/R 51 had been reduced to the strength of a platoon.

At 1500 6/RFAR 11 was attempted to occupy an open position on the southwest corner of the Bois de Lauromont, and drew French artillery fire which

The Battle South of Longwy

caused serious personnel casualties and put almost all of the horses out of action.

By 1600 the I/R 51 attack at Caure Ferme had been gaining ground. At 1630 intense German artillery fire was heard to the southwest and French artillery fire on I/R 51 fell off significantly: V RK had reached the battlefield. I/R 51 used this opportunity to press the attack against the high ground north of Caure Ferme, with elements of 3/R 51 and 4/R 51 advancing 1km to put pursuit fire on the withdrawing French.

I/R 51 was ordered to occupy a defensive position at the southeast corner of the Bois de Lauromont. The field kitchens came forward and the troops ate a well-deserved hot meal and then began digging in. The battalion spent the night in their position, wrapped in their coats, with listening posts to the front.

The regimental historian said that the battalion had acquitted itself well in its baptism of fire. Its quick and energetic attack had stopped the French advance. Peacetime training and 'old-Prussian discipline' had proven their worth, and the troops of all ranks had demonstrated initiative and a spirit of self-sacrifice.

A corporal who was a range estimator for a platoon leader in 4/R 51 provided an example of the determination of the men of RIR 51. The platoon was advancing by bounds and driving the French out of a copse near Caure Ferme when a bullet tore open the corporal's right cheek, which began to bleed profusely. He nevertheless continued to advance with his unit for 1km and had reached the road south of Ugny when he was hit for a second time in the right shoulder; the pain becoming so intense that he had to take off his pack, but he moved forward with his unit to the next hill. A major told him to go to the rear to receive medical attention, but the corporal replied that enemy artillery fire made that impossible. The major then began to stand up and was hit in the chest; dying, he gave a last letter to his wife to a nearby sergeant.

Friendly artillery fire began to fall on 4/R 51 and the order was given to fall back. The corporal turned his head to the left to repeat the order and a bullet hit him in the mouth, knocking out two teeth and passing through the opposite cheek. A fourth bullet then hit him in the hand and he lost consciousness due to loss of blood. He awoke the next day in a field hospital and was told that he had been brought in by an engineer patrol. He was loaded with other wounded onto a wagon and transported to Diedenhofen. At a halt in Villrupt, where 4/R 51 had bivouacked on the march west, he was recognised by a French girl who, with the help of a doctor, tried to give him some cognac, but his mouth was too filled with dried blood. The corporal convalesced in Germany until the spring of 1915, when he returned to his old unit, 4/R 51. 'To my great pleasure', he said, 'I was awarded the Iron Cross 2nd Class'.

The Battle of the Frontiers

Casualties

IR 156 lost an officer and 53 EM KIA, 2 OFF DOW, 4 OFF and 248 EM WIA.
IR 22 lost 24 EM KIA, six OFF and 118 EM WIA.
RIR 10 took much heavier casualties: seven OFF and 111 EM KIA, 19 OFF and 583 EM WIA. Two company commanders were killed and two wounded.
RFAR 11 lost an officer and 12 EM KIA, an officer and 44 EM WIA. The regiment fired 2510 shells.

German 12 RD

12 RD began its advance at 0600, initially encountered little resistance and moved quickly forward, with RFAR 12 following by bounds. On the 12 RD left RIR 38 advanced with II/R 38 to the north of Baslieux, I/R 38 (minus 2/R 38 and 3/R 38 in regimental reserve) through the town and III/R 38 to the south.[15] There were no German units to the left of RIR 38, whose flank was therefore completely exposed. West of Baslieux the regiment encountered French outposts and patrols. Shortly before 1000, 12 RD encountered French resistance at the Bois de Goemont.

The French fire was heavy. RIR 38 took serious casualties and could advance only by short rushes. The French were invisible, even to the German leaders who kneeled or stood in the fields of grain to search the terrain with their field glasses. The German troops in the grain had to fire kneeling against suspected enemy positions on the tree line and the edges of fields. The French, on the other hand, occupied higher ground and could see the Germans. A French battery fired into the regiment's flank, while RFAR 12 fired on the tree lines.[16]

On the regimental right, II/R 38, with elements of RIR 22, and the 6th Reserve *Jäger* battalion, pushed through the Bois de Goemont, but had to fight off continual counterattacks and took such heavy fire that the were forced to withdraw. On the left III/R 38 suffered 'extraordinary' casualties. It was reinforced by 2/R 38 and 3/R 38 and II/RIR 23 but still was only able to hold its position. The right was reinforced by 1/R 38 and II/RIR 23 but again could do no more than hold its position. At 1300 the brigade ordered its units to dig in. The Germans began to run out of ammunition, as it was impossible to bring resupply forward over the open ground to their rear, and the French gained fire superiority. The ammunition wagons took fire in Baslieux until the *franc-tireurs* were eliminated. At 1400 RFAR 12 began bounding forward, and was able not only to provide effective fire support but also to destroy a French battery. At 1500 RFAR 12 began to run low on ammunition, forcing it to conserve shells, something that almost never happened in regular German army regiments.

In the early afternoon I/R 38 and III/R 38, unable to continue the firefight and concerned for their open left flank, withdrew to the southwest of Baslieux. The regiment now began to take fire in the rear from Baslieux, which was silenced by

The Battle South of Longwy

patrols that flushed out the *franc-tireurs*. The withdrawal was covered by RFAR 12, which had just received ammunition resupply. Massed artillery fire brought the French pursuit to a halt.

The French were strangely slow to turn the open German left flank, and when they did so, the manoeuvre was weak and too shallow. A French all-arms force moved from Joppecourt towards Ville au Montois at about 1100, but did not attack towards Baslieux until late afternoon, when RIR 38 was in position there and V RK was approaching. The French then broke off the envelopment.

The French did not attack the regiment's position at Baslieux and late in the afternoon the firefight died down. Nevertheless, at 1730 the brigade ordered a withdrawal to a new position astride the Laix–Baslieux road, 600m to the west of Laix. Since the units were thoroughly intermixed, officers took charge of the group of soldiers around them. The French did not pursue and their fire was ineffective.

The commander of 12 RD reported to the VI RK commander near the end of the day that he did not think that the situation was very favourable and that that attack on Baslieux was bleeding his division. This was only generally correct; the 12 RD was taking heavy casualties, but it had advanced beyond Baslieux. It is significant that he did not mention any pressure on his open left flank. The VI RK commander, counting on V RK to arrive on his left, told the 12 RD commander to stop and dig in.

What is significant about this exchange is that the division commander was badly informed about what was happening at the front, and that the corps commander's order had no effect on the conduct of the fighting troops. Only the leaders at brigade level and lower could stay current with the tactical situation, and theirs were the only orders that the troops carried out.

4/ 38

The RIR 38 fight is well-illustrated by the actions of 4/R 38. It should be remembered that this was a German reserve infantry unit, though from its combat performance it is indistinguishable from an active-army unit. Bois de Goemont was French right flank strongpoint and at 1030 the RIR 38 regimental commander ordered 4/R 38 to take it. The company was able to use a gully to approach and enter the woods undetected. The undergrowth in the woods was very heavy and the company advanced with the leading platoon in a thick skirmisher line, maintaining direction by compass, with the rest of the company 50m to 100m in column behind. The company pushed French troops back, passing the French dead and wounded. As 4/R 38 neared the northwest edge of the wood, German artillery began to shell the area and the troops had to advance by running from tree to tree. Reaching the far tree line, the company found the battlefield spread out before them. To their right, RIR 38 was advancing across a

The Battle of the Frontiers

plain that ascended like a glacis. The French defenders in their red trousers were visible in three lines on the slope. They would spring up in the standing grain, empty the magazine of the weapons and drop back down. 4/R 38 opened fire on the flank of the lower French lines at 400m to 500m range and the French stopped jumping up. The rapid fire of fire of 4/R 38 destroyed the lower line of French troops. This gave RIR 38 some relief and the commander of 4/R 38 could see his regiment advancing by short bounds or crawling. At the same time, 4/R 38 took both friendly and enemy fire. Upslope and to the left the French still held the tree line. From this point it would be possible for 4/R 38 to engage the upper line of French troops. The company commander ordered his men to crawl backwards into the woods and then move uphill along the tree line. By this time he had lost control of all but about twenty-five men. They encountered French troops advancing down the tree line with the same intentions that the Germans had. The woods consisted of mature trees and man-high bushes. The German soldiers discovered that if they lay on the ground behind the trees they could see the French far better than by standing. They allowed the French to approach to within a few metres and then shot them down. The effect of such close-range fire, the company commander said, was 'awful'. The Germans then advanced from tree to tree until they again encountered French troops, and shoot those down also. The procedure was repeated several times. The Germans did not take any losses; the company commander said that his men were shooting 'like poachers'. Finally they reached the same elevation as the highest line of French infantry. Half of the German troops took this line under fire at 400m range, receiving French rifle and MG fire in return. The French continually sent reinforcements to this line, which the 4/R 38 troops engaged at 500m to 600m range: the company commander said that 'not many made it.' The other half of the 4/R 38 troops formed a line at a angle to the left to hold off a French attack along the tree line.

The 12 RD troops had taken the first and second French positions, but the attack stalled there and the troops dug in. The French artillery fire caused serious casualties, while the German artillery continued to fire on the French positions that the 12 RD troops now occupied. A few 12 RD troops fell back, then more, until the infantry was in full retreat.

The French made four counterattacks against 4/R 38, which repeated the tactics it had used in taking the hill: the Germans hid themselves at the base of the trees; the French would be first visible at 50m range, but the Germans allowed them to approach to 5m to 10m before opening rapid fire, mowing the French down. 4/R 38 was joined in the Bois de Goemont by two MGs from RIR 22 and infantrymen of every regiment in 12 RD. The last French attack was made in squad column led by a major with drawn sabre, and was shot to pieces. More men from 4/R 38 came forward, and the company commander now had 80 soldiers. A close-range firefight now developed and the Germans began to take casualties: both MG gunners were shot in the head and killed, the MG ran out of ammunition and withdrew. The company commander ordered his men to crawl back 50m and dig in; for a considerable time the French fired into the vacated German position.

The company commander could see to his right that 12 RD was in full retreat with the French in pursuit, which could not stopped by fire from 4/R 38. At 1800, with the sun setting, the commander of 4/R 38 reluctantly decided that he had to withdraw. He pulled his troops back in skirmisher line and when they had broken contact marched them in column down the path, covered by a rear-guard. French troops had advanced into the gully south of the woods and the German troops had to shoot their way past them. The residents of Baslieux shook their fists at the withdrawing Germans and shouted curses. 4/ R 38 stopped on the high ground south of Baslieux and occupied defensive positions. German stragglers found their way to the company, and 4/38 grew to 500 or 600 men, which the company commander organised into ad hoc units. It was now dark and patrols were sent out. Of course, the field kitchens had no idea where the company was, and the troops had to make do with radishes they dug out of the fields.

RIR 38's casualties were 'extraordinarily severe': seven OFF, including two company commanders, and 76 EM, were KIA. Eight OFF, including a company commander, as well as 442 EM, were WIA

German V RK

The difficulties encountered by the 12 RD were ameliorated by the arrival of the V RK on the battlefield. V RK consisted of the 10 RD with the 77th Infantry Brigade (IR 37 and IR 155) and 18th Reserve Infantry Brigade (RIR 37 and RIR 46) and 9 RD with the 17th Reserve Infantry Brigade (RIR 6 and RIR 7) and 19th Reserve Infantry Brigade (only RIR 19 and Reserve *Jäger* Battalion 5). The corps had begun a night march from its bivouac area west of Luxembourg at 0130 on 22 August. As a reservist NCO wrote later to his family:

> 'Our regiment had to make a long night march, which is never pleasant; you can't see where you're putting you feet and you stumble, getting a friendly shove from your comrades, then the column stops and starts off again at a run. But you can get accustomed to anything and you learn how to cope.'[17]

In the early morning the units took a short rest and the value of the field kitchens once again proved itself, as they provided the troops with hot coffee. 10 RD was ordered to attack at 0830 on the corps right towards Ville au Montois, the 9 RD on the left towards Fillières. This corresponded to the intent of the army order, which arrived at 0900, instructing the corps to advance to the Crusnes between Pierrepont and Joppécourt and defend there.

The Battle of the Frontiers
German IR 37[18]

The lead element of 10 RD was IR 37, which around noon took artillery fire first from its own divisional artillery, RFAR 10, and shortly thereafter from the artillery of the division on the left, RFAR 9. The second friendly fire incident caused casualties and the adjutant of II/37 had to ride over to the guns to get them to cease fire. IR 37 moved quickly, with two platoons screening to the front while the rest of the regiment remained in march column. The point took fire from the edge of Ville au Montois at 1440. III/37 deployed to attack the town, with I/37 following echeloned to the left rear. II/37 was released from the reserve and followed III/37. III/37 advanced by fire and movement against weak French return fire. I/37 was ordered to attack left of III/37 in order to take the wooded high ground south of Ville au Montois and then to continue the attack to Bazailles. I/37 deployed 1/37 and 3/37 in the first line, followed by 4/37, with 2/37 echeloned behind the left flank. III/37 reported to the brigade commander 'three or four times' that it was taking fire from German artillery. The regimental commander sent his adjutant to division HQ to fix the problem. A reservist sergeant wrote in a letter home in August 1914:

> 'Our artillery now began to shell the village, and our captain ordered a platoon to form a skirmish line and advance. When we reached the high ground to our front, our platoon leader ordered us to lie down and we observed the village, which we knew was occupied by the enemy. We had already set our sights at 700m, for the dance had to begin soon. We couldn't see anything, but when we resumed the advance the crackle of rifle fire came from the town. We began to fire too. Our platoon leader called out to us 'Aim at the windows and all the gaps in the town' and all of us understood what we had to do. Shot after shot, well aimed, was sent into the houses and the walls. But now from the left the French artillery began to shell us, which was truly terrible. We were under artillery fire for the first time and we had to accustom ourselves to it. You cannot imagine how awful this shrapnel fire was. We were hit first here and then there by salvoes. The French must have gotten the range exactly, because they shot damn well and we took many casualties. My squad mate Meier was badly wounded next to me. We worked our way gradually towards the edge of the village. Support troops frequently joined the line, and II/37 brought ammunition up. The enemy rifle fire slackened, a sign that we had hit them well in spite of their good position … The French infantry fired off lots of ammunition, but their aim was bad.'

4/37 and 2/37 were committed to the firing line. When III/37 and I/37 approached to within 200m of the town 'Fix bayonets!' was sounded and at 1500 IR 37 stormed into Ville au Montois and, in keeping with German street-fighting doctrine, quickly pushed through to the opposite side of the town. The French defended only a few houses; most either fled in the direction of Bazailles or hid

The Battle South of Longwy

in cellars and were flushed out when the Germans set fire to the houses. Many were taken prisoner that evening by German cavalry. The streets of the town were littered with discarded French packs, weapons and pieces of uniforms.

As soon as groups of IR 37 troops reached the west side of Ville en Montois they set off towards Bazailles. In spite of the French fire, and the fact that the companies were by now completely intermixed, the deployment into skirmisher line 'went just like on the training grounds'. While the troops were in Montois the French artillery fire had ceased. It now resumed, as effectively as before. Nevertheless, at 1630 the regiment assaulted Bazailles and by 1645 the town had been taken. Now the regiment came under German artillery fire; the German guns had not been informed of the rapid advance of IR 37 and took them for French troops. The best solution was to outrun the friendly fire by continuing the attack towards the regiment's final objective, Boismont.

The right flank of IR 37 reached the Boismont–Baslieux road under a hail of French shells and took cover in the ditches. There was no enemy infantry fire. The strain was too much for some of the German troops' nerves and they began to run back towards Bazailles, followed by the entire right wing. Near the edge of Bazailles they were met by the regimental commander with drawn sword, shouting 'Children, we must advance!' A corporal bugler ran to the colonel's side and played the signal 'March forwards!' The line turned about, ran back across the road through the French artillery fire to the hill on the other side, where they began to take French small arms fire. 'You will not believe me when I tell you' wrote the reserve sergeant 'that we considered this fire to be a blessing, for we now had an enemy in front of us again on whom we could vent our rage, which was not inconsiderable'. The French counterattacked against the regimental left flank. The dense French lines were met by well-aimed rifle fire and were stopped with 'extraordinarily heavy losses'. At this moment RIR 7 and 5th Reserve *Jäger* Battalion from 9 RD came to the aid of the hard-pressed IR 37. Together, by 1900 they had taken Boismont.

IR 37 took very heavy casualties: 15 OFF were KIA, 26 WIA, 41 in total, or about 2/3 of the regimental officer corps. The regimental commander had been hit three times by rifle bullets and once by a shell splinter. 1/37, 4/37 and 10/37 lost all of their officers; 1,403 EM were KIA or WIA. I/37 lost 527 EM, and III/37 594 EM, which is more than 50 per cent of their strength. The regiment had been under continual French artillery fire, which the V RK artillery was too weak to suppress. Once again, the German reserve corps's deficiency in artillery had to be made good by the infantry, and at the cost of heavy casualties.

German IR 155[19]

IR 155 attacked on the right of IR 37, with II/155 on the right, I/155 on the left and III/155 behind as reserve. The regiment advanced across an 'endless' field of

The Battle of the Frontiers

oats towards the woods north of Bazailles. IR 155 took fire from groups of French troops that did not occupy a continuous line but hid themselves in the oat fields and woods. The French were invisible, so IR 155 fired at suspected locations, with some success, for they found French dead as they advanced. On the left flank 2/155 saw French infantry on the northern edge of Ville au Montois at 800m range. The French fired too high; the regiment learned later from French prisoners that they had set their sights for 1,300m. The regimental historian said that the French artillery knew their job and accurately engaged IR 155 from the left front. The best reaction to artillery fire was to try to run out from under it, all the more so because the German artillery was also firing at the regiment. The regiment therefore pushed forward in long, quick bounds. In the ditches of the Baslieux – Bazailles road sixteen French soldiers were taken prisoner. IR 155 continued to race forward, entering the woods east of Pierrepont, where they found many French dead and wounded.

Both French and German artillery shelled the woods, so IR 155 continued its wild career forward. Boismont drew troops like a magnet, until it was being attacked by elements from IR 155, IR 37, RIR 37, RIR 46 and 5th Reserve *Jäger* Battalion. As the Germans took Boismont, artillery fell on this town too and some German troops detoured around the town while others pushed through it quickly towards the Crusnes stream, but were halted by orders from the commander of RIR 46, who in peacetime had been assigned to IR 155.

The troop's canteens were by now empty. Some soldiers slaked their thirst eating peas out of the fields. Three IR 155 men heard a cow mooing in a field near Boismont. With French shells whizzing overhead, acting as though it were the most normal thing in the world, one soldier grabbed the cow's horns, a second held his mess tin under the cow, and the third milked her. As the regimental historian wryly noted, everyone was happy, the cow and the three IR 155 men together. Darkness fell:

> 'The tension dropped away as we came to the realisation that the gift of life had been granted to us. We greeted our comrades and congratulated them for still being alive. One man gave another a piece of bread, a cigarette or a shot of alcohol (which clever troops found in the neighbouring village). But we could not amuse ourselves for very long with such material or philosophical concerns. The units had to be reorganised and security detachments sent out ... It should be mentioned that when darkness fell several nearby units sang the old hymn, '*Nun danket alle Gott*' (Now all give thanks to God) probably remembering the memorable Battle of Leuthen on 12 December 1757. The hymn resonated solemnly over the battlefield. The field kitchens did not arrive, so the troops dug up turnips and ate them.'

The Battle South of Longwy

The commander of I/155 described the battle:

> 'The advance went forwards quickly. It was, of course, our first battle. Our motto was 'Go get 'em', reinforced by the fact that it was impossible to lie down in one place for long. As soon as an advancing group lay down, enemy artillery shells landed on them or shrapnel burst over them. Our advance was also given wings by our own artillery, which fired on us thinking that we were French troops retreating. We would never have thought that an attack could be made at such speed. Everything colluded to accelerate the pace, and the French positions in the woods and to the south of them were taken at a tempo that would have been criticised in peacetime manoeuvres. We also had numerous casualties in our units which were at full war-strength ... At a dead run, with heaving breast and bathed in sweat in the August sun, we nevertheless reached our objective roaring 'Hurrah!' and threw the French out... French artillery fire immediately began to fall... We went forward another 600m or 700m to a point halfway between Bazailles and Boismont. The French ran like hares and threw away anything that hindered their running. The German skirmisher line pursued them with fire, while the fastest German runners got the bit in their teeth and pursued the French on foot in order to stay right on their heels. I continually sent orders for the troops to pursue by fire and reorganise, but I have no idea whether the messengers got through. One who I am sure did reach the forward line was the battalion adjutant, Lieutenant von Ravenstein, but not only did he not stop the troops, he charged on with them, along with Lt. Marx and his men, as far as Boismont ... The *furor teutonicus* had seized them ...They would neither rest nor be satisfied until darkness put an end to their wild advance. I could not reprimand any of them ... Rather, the hotheaded Lieutenant von Ravenstein was rewarded for his boldness with one of the first Iron Cross 2nd Class, and later the *Pour le mérite* ... That was our first day in combat! ...We were proud of conduct on the battlefield, mixed with mourning for those who were gone from us, but also the now well-founded hope that we would win.'

IR 155 had lost 21 OFF and 567 EM KIA and WIA.

German RIR 46[20]

The 18th Reserve Infantry Brigade, which consisted only of RIR 46, RIR 37 being the corps reserve, was committed to the right of IR 155 at 1400. The regiment advanced with III/R 46 on the left, II/R 46 on the right and I/R 46 and the MG Company in reserve.

III/R 46 deployed 10/R 46 and 9/R 46 in the first line, 11/R 46 and 12/R 46 followed 300m behind. The lead companies soon took fire, but advancing by bounds moved quickly over fields of oats, wheat, rye and potatoes across the

Bazailles–Baslieux road and assaulted into the woods at 1600, which the French evacuated. Still moving by bounds, and mixed in with troops from I/R 46 and IR 155, the battalion reached Boismont at 1700. III/R 46 was luckier than the other 10 RD regiments: the French artillery dropped their rounds behind III/R 46, which was encouragement enough to keep the battalion moving forward, without inflicting the casualties the other units suffered.

On the right, 9/R 46 and II/R 46 pushed through the dense undergrowth of the woods east of Pierrepont and the battalion lost all cohesion, elements of II/R 46 taking part in the assault on Boismont. I/R 46 was ordered to push through the woods to the other side. Orientation was lost in the woods and the battalion ended up on the north tree line, from where it assaulted the mill of Baslieux and took three officers and 20 EM prisoners at the cost of light casualties. The MG Company was prevented from coming into action by French artillery fire, losing two OFF and 14 EM KIA or WIA as well as 19 horses.

After a 2km assault the troops were thirsty, but afraid to use the wells for fear they might be poisoned. When barrels of wine were found widespread drunkenness occurred, which led to 'unheard of' measures by the leadership to re-establish discipline. In addition, the units were completely intermixed: several soldiers from XVI AK remained with the regiment for months because there was no way to return them to their units.

The regiment lost an officer and 26 EM KIA, 7 OFF and 137 EM WIA and 188 men MIA, most of whom later returned to duty having dropped out during the march or become separated from the regiment in the battle. The regimental historian, who was present during the battle, acknowledged that these were light casualties, especially considering the thick skirmisher lines that the regiment employed. This was due to the fact that the French forces opposing it were weak (apparently a battalion of bicycle infantry) with few MGs. French artillery fire was also ineffective; on the other hand, the German artillery support was 'thoroughly weak'. RIR 37, which was corps reserve for most of the day, lost one OFF and one EM KIA, one OFF died of wounds.[21] Each regiment in the 10 RD fought a different battle on 22 August.

German 9 RD

The 9 RD attacked to the left of 10 RD The first unit to go into action was RFAR 9, which supported the 68th Brigade (34 ID) of XVI AK, in attacking Fillières.[22] As it went into position it was immediately engaged by French artillery for a half an hour until the French withdrew. The lead brigade of 9 RD, 19th Reserve Brigade, joined in on the assault on Fillières. RFAR 9 then bounded forward to positions east of Ville au Montois to fire on the retreating French. As II/R 9 began to occupy its positions it once again drew violent French artillery fire.[23]

The Battle South of Longwy

The second brigade in the division column, 17th Reserve Brigade, was committed at 1400 to the right of 19th Reserve Brigade, to the north of Fillières, with RIR 7 on the right and RIR 6 on the left. RIR 7 had already conducted a 60km road march, much of it at night. It was now instructed to advance north of the Ville au Montois–Fillières road, which would bring it behind 10 RD.[24] The combat power of V RK was now massed on the axis of advance Ville au Montois–Bazailles–Boismont.

RIR 7 deployed skirmisher lines with two pace intervals, II/R 7 on the left, III/R 7 on the right, I/R 7 following. The officers dismounted and the regiment pushed about 3km over fields of standing grain and clover towards Boismont. The regiment received accurate artillery fire and the regimental history acknowledged that the French gunners were quite good at hitting moving targets. RIR 7 entered Boismont at dusk. The regimental history noted that during the night rumours of wildly exaggerated casualties circulated. RIR 7 was supposed to have lost 1/3 of the regiment killed, including the regimental commander. Rumours of catastrophic casualties would have deterred the army and corps leadership from immediately ordering a vigorous pursuit. Only later was it possible to establish that the regiment had suffered considerable, but nevertheless not particularly heavy, losses. Initial reports showed two OFF and six EM KIA and one OFF and 204 EM WIA. There were also 443 MIA, 72 of which were later determined to be KIA; most of the rest rejoined the regiment.

German XVI AK[25]

The initial mission for XVI AK was to guard the army left flank and maintain contact with Diedenhofen. The corps was therefore not to pass beyond the line Joppécourt – Anderny, and the initial objectives were, for the 34 ID on the right, the line Serrouville – Beuvillers, and for 33 ID on the left Beuvillers–Sancy. This line was reached at 0800 without enemy contact, and the XVI commander ordered 34 ID to advance to Fillières–Malavillers, 33 ID to the high ground on both sides of Anderny.

The 34 ID operations order said that the French were marching columns of all arms from Spincourt to Longuyon. The division deployed the 86th Infantry Brigade, FAR 70 and II/FAR 69 on the left, towards Audun le Romain, with 68th Infantry Brigade with I/FAR 69 on the right towards Fillières.

At 0930 the division issued its attack order. French columns were reported marching towards Mercy le Haut and Ville au Montois. II/IR 145 and III/IR 145 were held back as division reserve. 86th Brigade on the left was to take Mercy le Haut, 68th Brigade on the right was to take Joppécourt. The advance would begin immediately.

Fillières

IR 67[26], supported by I/FAR 69, conducted the 68th Brigade attack. I/145 was in brigade reserve, the other two battalions were the division reserve. IR 67 halted its approach march at Aumetz, where the field kitchen gave the troops hot coffee. The troops were told at 0700 to 'lock and load', and the regiment advanced carefully, preceded by patrols. In Serrouville the patrols reported that the French had been located 4km to the west in Fillières. IR 67 deployed with II/67 on the left, III/67 on the right, I/67 in the second line, minus 1/67 and 2/67, which were regimental reserve. The regiment moved through a wood in the ravine located to the east of Fillières. I/145 followed. The tree line was 600m from Fillières, with the ground gently rising to the town. The grain in the fields had been partially cut and stacked, in between were potato fields. French advanced positions could be seen in front of the town, but the main line of defence seemed to be the town itself. 3/67 and 4/67 were ordered to outflank the town on the right.

At 1100, using the map to establish the range, 2/FAR 69 engaged the French infantry outside Fillières, and when these fled into the town, shifted fire there.[27] The town began to burn. 'What happened next' said the IR 67 historian 'was very much reminiscent of the combat exercises at Frescaty (training area)'. IR 67 opened fire and the platoons advanced by long bounds. 'Our troops, carefully trained in peacetime, fired calmly, as if at the range. But the first losses also appeared, especially in places where the troops bunched up.' 3/67 and 4/67, outflanking the French from the north, reached the town first.

To the south of the town the French had established advanced positions as far as the ravine. 5/67 and 6/67, enveloping the town from this direction, had a particularly difficult time. 7/67 was committed, as were the regimental reserve, 1/67 and 2/67, and the MG Company. The regiment entered Fillières from three sides. When the German artillery was shifted out of the town, the Germans assaulted and heavy street fighting ensued as they cleared it house by house. French artillery rounds began to fall and continued to do so for the rest of the day. By afternoon the town was in German hands. When the infantry had taken Fillières, 3/FAR 69 bounded forward to the high ground on the west side and engaged the retreating French infantry.

I/145 advanced south of IR 67, with three companies in the first line and one in reserve.[28] As it climbed out of the ravine and reached the tree line it encountered French infantry in a stubble field 50m to the front. With a few quick bounds forward the battalion broke into the enemy position and engaged the French hand-to-hand. Most of the French fled and I/145 pursued them to the west, passing to the south of Fillières. It was engaged by French artillery fire that caused significant casualties; I/145 bounded forward quickly and ran out from under the barrage.

The German 9 RD had arrived on IR 67's right flank. The battalions of IR 67 were thoroughly intermixed and out of contact with brigade HQ, so the commander of II/67 continued the attack to the west on his own initiative at 1400

The Battle South of Longwy

with a *Kampfgruppe*, as the regimental history put it, made up of most of I/67, his own 8/67, III/67 and the MG Company. They were shelled by French artillery, but evaded this fire by rapid bounds forward. The *Kampfgruppe* made careful use of the terrain, moving on the tree line north of the ravine, which shielded them from observation by the French. 9 RD was attacking Bazailles from the west and IR 67 swung right to strike from the south, now joined by I/145, and near dark pushed into the town.

The rest of IR 67 moved south. The commanders of 6/67 and 7/67 detected a French skirmisher line extending on the left down to the ravine south of Fillières, and opened fire. Gradually the two companies were joined by more and more German troops, and after a long firefight the French withdrew down the ravine to the west. The commander of 7/67 had been killed and the commander of 6/67 severely wounded. This part of IR 67 crossed the open ground south of Fillières, which was under heavy French artillery fire, to a ravine, which offered protection from the French artillery. The regimental commander joined the group. A patrol was sent further south and discovered a French skirmisher line in a meadow on Hill 370, 700m in front. The group advanced and began the firefight anew, soon joined by the MG Company of IR 145 and the troops from the 5th Reserve *Jäger* Battalion, while elements of IR 173, IR 30 and IR 145 attacked from the east and south.

I/FAR 69 moved to a covered position behind a low rise in the ground, with the 1/69 and 2/69 battery commanders in an OP behind a hedge to the right front, which offered them a panoramic view of the battlefield, connected to their battery positions by field telephone. The artillery section commander also had telephonic communications with the infantry, which was used to pass requests for fire. The two batteries reopened fire at 1330 at ranges from 1,700m to 2,500m. The French infantry began to run when the first bracketing rounds landed, and when the batteries fired for effect the entire French unit broke for the rear. Lines of dead or wounded French skirmishers lay on the ground. The artillery continually found new targets. At 1600 the French launched a large deep counterattack from Joppécourt consisting of four or five successive skirmisher lines; the dark French uniforms stood out in the light stubble fields and 'offered an unusually good target'. The two battery commanders coordinated their fire: 2/69 engaged the attacking column, while 1/69 fired on Joppécourt.

The 2/69 commander estimated the range from the map and fired his first bracketing rounds at 4,400m range, behind the target, because the infantry had told him that the artillery was firing short. At 3,700m he bracketed the target to the front. The first line of French troops stopped 'like on a badly-executed parade'. He then ordered 'Battery, one salvo, 3,800'. 'The effect was astounding; part of their first line collapsed, part turned and ran, which spread through the other waves as if by command, and then entire mass streamed back to Joppécourt.' 2/69 then walked salvoes from 3,800m to 4200m range into the retreating French, while 1/69 blocked the edge of Joppécourt with fire. The effect was 'extraordinary'. The French artillery fired continually but ineffectually, as their shells went over the battery and to the left and right. The French shrapnel burst too high: I/69 lost only one man dead and one wounded. I/69 suspected where the French artillery was located, but had so many infantry targets that it was never able to engage it. It did fire on one French artillery forward observer (FO) – in 1915, FAR 69 learned from prisoners that the opposing French artillery unit had been 46 RAC and the FO was the commander of 6/46 RAC, who had been killed.

As darkness fell the French withdrew and the Germans dug in. I/FAR 69 bounded forward over paths reconnoitred by the 14th *Uhlan* Regiment and occupied positions in the former target area, moving with difficulty to avoid dead and wounded French and exhausted German infantry. The brigade commander, who had observed the fight from the front line, remained there during the night.

IR 67 lost 6 OFF and 65 EM KIA, 10 OFF and 368 EM WIA, 45 EM MIA, most of whom were probably KIA. This was about 18 per cent of the regiment's combat strength. The regiment had taken more casualties than it had during its magnificent fight at Gravelotte in 1870. The losses were very unevenly distributed: 4/67 had lost 14 EM WIA, 11/67 12 WIA, while 2/67 lost 83 EM and 10/67 75 EM, about 1/3 of their strength. The regimental history said that 50 per cent of the casualties could be attributed to French artillery, adding that the German troops quickly learned to fear the French guns, but that French rifle marksmanship was not good. I/IR 145 lost 26 KIA, 121 WIA and 23 MIA. Looking at the French battery positions the next day, the commander of 2/FAR 69 drew the conclusion that:

> 'The empty battlefield is of course misleading; the great masses of troops must be somewhere – in order to find where they are hiding themselves it is necessary to use map reconnaissance. We need to shoot tactically and not only against the targets that have just become visible'.

German IR 173[29]

The 86th Brigade order, issued at 0715, 22 August said that the French were at Joppécourt and Mercy le Haut. IR 173, supported by II/69, was to attack on the brigade right; IR 30 supported by FAR 70 on the left.

From heights east of Mercy le Haut, French troops were seen approaching the town. IR 173 therefore advanced fully deployed, with the MG Company on the left flank, then II/173, III/173 and I/173 all on line. Each battalion kept a company in reserve. About 1,200m from the town IR 173 took up positions and opened fire. The French were clearly being reinforced: their fire grew stronger and stronger, and French MG went into position on the south side of the town. The German troops could not fire prone due to the standing grain and had to fire kneeling or offhand;

The Battle South of Longwy

this led quickly to German casualties. 2/16th Engineer Battalion advanced behind the regiment in open order and filled the gaps in the I/173 and II/173 lines. Due to the terrain, II/FAR 69 could not follow IR 173 and had to follow IR 30 instead. This left IR 173 without direct artillery support. Under these circumstances, IR 173 prudently did not try to advance; the standing firefight continued the entire day. Near dark, French forces were seen withdrawing from Mercy le Haut. Foot patrols were sent into the town to confirm that the French had left, but IR 173 dug in where it stood. IR 173 had lost about 50 KIA and 200 WIA.

Faced with a very strong French position, IR 173 had reacted exactly as German doctrine prescribed: it did not attempt to advance until it gained fire superiority. In the event, this resulted in a daylong firefight and the regiment did not occupy its objective until the following day. In spite of its exposed position in a field of grain in the open the regiment's casualties were not severe, probably because the firefight was conducted at such long range.

German IR 30[30]

At 0630 the regiment began its advance in column, deploying west of Beuvillers with I/30 on the right of the road to Audun, II/30 on the left of the road, III/30 and the MG Company following behind the middle. The regiment advanced with a line of skirmishers, followed by supports and then reserves in column, 'just like it had been taught in peacetime and on manoeuvres', moving at a walk or by bounds across the fields of standing oats. At 0900 took fire from Audun and the tree line to the north: the French units were later identified as bicyclists from the 15th, 26th and 29th Light Infantry Battalions.

FAR 70 had taken up an overwatch position north of Beuvillers at 0800.[31] When it was notified that Audun le Roman was occupied by the enemy at 0850, II/70 moved into a covered position northwest of the town, but did not open fire until 0945, with 4/70 engaging the town while 5/70 and 6/70 fired on the tree line: IR 30 had to wait more than 45 minutes for artillery fire support from FAR 70, which is not good. 1/70 moved to the south of Beuvillers and conducted counter-battery fire against French guns 2km east of Malvillers, while 4/70 shifted to unobserved area fire behind these French guns.

The light howitzers of II/FAR 69 supported the attack by the 86th Brigade on Audun from covered positions just west of Beauvillers. Only the tops of the houses and the church tower were visible, but the section was able to adjust its fire onto the town without difficulty.[32] IR 30 now had the luxury of fire support from four gun and three howitzer batteries.

II/30 attacked Audun while III/30 attacked the tree line. In the high grain the troops could only fire kneeling or standing; the French delivered a high rate of badly aimed fire. By 1100 I/30 was only a few hundred metres from the tree line, while II/30 pushed into Audun and the French withdrew.

The Battle of the Frontiers

IR 30 had engaged a large French security force. It is hard to see how the French derived much benefit from this fight, in which a smaller French force was pitted, unsupported, against a superior German force backed up by plenty of artillery. The time gained was surely outbalanced by the pounding inflicted on the French infantry.

IR 30 continued the advance towards Malavillers while FAR 70 moved forward behind it to Audun. II/30 took fire when it was 400m east of Malavillers. III/30 deployed on its own initiative to the left of II/30, and I/30 attacked from the north. At 1330 the regimental commander ordered IR 30 to assault the village, which the French defended with determination. The French strongpoint was a large combination farmhouse and barn at the east side of the village, which 11/30 set on fire. French artillery began to fall, one shell hitting the farmhouse, at which point French resistance ceased.

The rolling terrain offered II/FAR 69 no observation of the enemy, so the section used unobserved area fire against suspected enemy locations, while the French artillery used unobserved area fire against the German infantry; fortunately for the Germans, the French shrapnel again burst too high to be effective.

IR 30 immediately continued the attack, making a difficult change of front to the north, moving on both sides of the road towards Mercy le Haut. The regiment began to take accurate French artillery fire, causing the first serious casualties. The entire regiment was now dispersed in open order and the battle was in the hands of the company commanders. A firefight began with the defenders of Mercy le Haut. FAR 70 pulled into position north of Malavillers and at 1220 bounded forward under French artillery and infantry fire to positions close behind IR 30. FAR 70's fire was frequently directed at targets other than Mercy le Haut proper, which led the infantry to complain that they were not being supported. IR 30 continued the advance through fields of grain by platoons, half platoons and squads, with FAR 70 bounding forward, and by 1700 the infantry had taken the French advanced position about 400–500m south of Mercy le Haut. The German infantry and MG fired against suspected locations but casualties mounted:

'Thank God, the French usually fired too high, while our people gave well-aimed fire, like on the Elsenborn firing range. Careful, methodical German marksmanship training bore fruit, as did the initiative fostered by the German army, without which command and fire control in the deafening noise of combat would have been unthinkable.'

A particular problem was a French MG whose position could not be found. As the infantry advanced II/FAR 69 bounded forward until it could fire on Mercy le Haut. The effect of the light howitzer fire on the town was once again 'extraordinarily great', especially after they began to employ flat-trajectory fire with delayed-action fuses, which had a 'massive effect' when they exploded inside the houses. Statements from prisoners, the inhabitants of the town and observations of the German infantry all show that the howitzer fire demoralised the French infantry. It was probably this fire that finally silenced the troublesome French MG. At dusk the firing died down patrols established that the French had withdrawn and IR 30 entered Mercy le Haut.

At 1510, III/145 from the division reserve was committed to attack on the left flank of IR 30. As it advanced, II/145 was committed at 1750 on its left. There was no French resistance and, probably due to the French withdrawal and the gathering darkness, the two battalions advanced faster than in any peacetime exercise. The skirmisher lines coalesced and the formation began to resemble a battalion column. When it became fully dark, the two battalions halted. It would appear that the division held on to its reserve far too long and committed it so late that these two battalions could contribute nothing. This was a cardinal sin in German tactical doctrine.

On 23 August III/30 was tasked with clearing up the battlefield. It buried about 100 German and 223 French soldiers.

German 33 ID

During the early morning of 22 August IR 135 was 'plinking away' at French flank security units in Audun and Beuvillers until around 0900, when it was ordered to swing south about 4km to Sancy le Haut, where it would turn west.[33] IR 144 would move on its left. At 1135, 5th Army HQ decided that V RK was not making progress. In addition, reports from 6 KD on the army left flank showed that there were no large enemy forces there. 5th Army ordered XVI AK to attack to assist V RK by manoeuvring 33 ID right to attack through Murville against the French flank.

By late afternoon 33 ID approached Murville. On a report that the French held Murville, FAR 33 shelled the town with its light howitzer section.[34] IR 135 reached the high ground northeast of Murville at 1630 and deployed. It was soon followed by FAR 34, which moved quickly into the German skirmisher line and immediately opened fire on French infantry deployed on the road Mercy le Haut –Higny–Xivry. A French battery that attempted to go into action at Xivry was shot to pieces before it could fire. IR 134 and IR 144 attacked at 1700 and entered Higny after dark. IR 135 lost 22 WIA. FAR 35 had fired 667 rounds, FAR 33 693 rounds. Neither artillery regiment suffered any casualties.

German Failure to Attack French Right Flank

The lack of coordination between the French VI CA and the reserve divisions that were supposed to protect its right flank had left that flank completely unprotected and presented the German 5th Army with the opportunity on 22 August to begin rolling up the French 3rd Army. The 5th Army had the opportunity to add a deadly operational manoeuvre to what was otherwise a purely frontal attack.

The Germans did not do so because they were transfixed by the danger posed by Verdun: the possibility that the fortress might harbour strong French forces that would sortie and attack the German left flank. Elaborate precautions were taken to guard against this threat: 6 KD was ordered to reconnoitre in this direction and 33 ID was held back to protect the flank. The result was that neither unit accomplished anything useful on 22 August. 33 ID never made serious contact with the enemy. 6 KD ended the day at Landres, tied tightly to the XVI AK left flank.

This was massive overkill. The German flank was in the immediate vicinity of the immense Metz – Diedenhofen fortress complex, and any French force attacking the flank of XVI AK had to be worried about being taken in the flank itself by German forces in the fortress. In fact, the German troop strength in Metz –Diedenhofen was not inconsiderable and was growing larger.

The reason that 5th Army HQ did not know what French forces were near Verdun was that it decided late on 21 August to attack on 22 August. There was insufficient time to reorient assets for the necessary deep operational reconnaissance. The question of French strength on the German left flank was to be resolved on the morning of 22 August, while the attack was moving forward.

Fundamentally, the 5th Army HQ operational priority was that of 'safety first'. This meant that it was more interested in avoiding defeat than it was with taking risks to win a decisive victory. Indeed, 5th Army HQ never recognised exactly how vulnerable the French flank was because its reconnaissance assets were focused on the non-existent threat to its own left flank.

Had the German 6 KD been given an offensive orientation to the west instead of a defensive orientation to the south, it would have detected the weakness of the French flank very early. It also would have been presented with a cavalry commander's dream, the opportunity to raid deep into the enemy rear area. Had 33 ID moved aggressively forward to the west at the same time as 34 ID, it would have found nothing to its front and could have ended the day deep in the French VI CA rear. Given the pounding that VI CA had taken, the 33 ID envelopment would have resulted in the destruction of the French corps. The French 3rd Army would have been cut off from its pivot at Verdun, and its retreat would have been a footrace against the German XVI AK, one of the most mobile units in the German army.

French Situation, Evening, 22 August[35]

An order arrived from 3rd Army at about 1900, directing VI CA to hold north of the Chiers, preparatory to renewing the attack. The corps chief of staff said that this hardly corresponded to the actual corps situation. VI CA had lost contact with all three divisions. The chief of staff admitted that the corps headquarters had been 'unable to exercise any control over the three divisions in spite of the

The Battle South of Longwy

perfection of the multiple means of modern communication at its disposal: telephones of all kinds, wireless, couriers, signals, aircraft, pigeons, observers, etc. etc.' Officers had to be sent forward by horse and in automobiles, and even the use automobiles eventually required long marches on foot.

There was no news from 12 DI. He said he had the impression that 42 DI was scattered in front of Pierrepont. 40 DI appeared to be in as bad way. On the right flank, 7 DC had long ago disappeared and the reserve divisions had not arrived.

VI CA wanted 12 DI to hold Viviers; the problem lay in finding the division commander. 42 DI was to hold Pierrepont and assemble the division at Saint Supplet, while 40 DI was to hold Joppécourt. The corps HQ fell back to Rouvrois sur Othain. At some point the corps commander ordered his last reserves, 132 RI, the 25th and 8th *Chasseur* (light infantry) battalions, the corps engineers and a group of corps artillery, to hold Arrancy as a rear-guard. Around midnight the corps began to receive reports from the divisions.

12 DI had been broken apart, but was located roughly where the corps wanted it to be, with the main body at Viviers sur Chiers, about 3.5km north of Longuyon and the 24th Brigade 5km to the south at Arrancy. 12 DI reported that 10 DI on its left had withdrawn 'with more than a little disorder'.

42 DI reported that it had suffered 'heavy losses' and that the Germans had taken Xivry on its right flank. In the words of the VI CA war diary, 42 DI 'initially reformed in the area of the Haute Borne between Han devant Pierrepont and St. Pierrevillers'. The 42 DI after-action report said that both the 40 DI and 12 DI had retreated past it in the direction of the Othain, forcing 42 DI to withdraw to the region of Nouillonpont–Muzeray that is, 42 DI conducted a night withdrawal of about 8km beyond its assigned position to the next major terrain feature, the Othain river.

The corps learned that the commander of 40 DI was at Nouillonpont with a little infantry and two artillery groups, but had lost contact with the rest of his division. The division had been flanked by German troops attacking from Mercy le Haut and scattered. The corps war diary said that 40 DI fell back to the area south and west of Xivry and then 'rallied during the night in the area of Nouillonpont–Spincourt' to the southeast of 42 DI. An officer arriving at corps HQ from Verdun reported finding 40 DI troops near Etain, 30km to the rear. The Germans captured abandoned vehicles from the 40 DI divisional staff, including the map supply with maps of Germany as far as the Eifel and the Rhineland. 40 DI had been wrecked and was no longer combat-effective.

The chief of staff of VI CA maintained that the VI CA plan, given the information available at the time, was correct. To complete the corps mission, it was necessary to advance on Longwy with two divisions. It could not be foreseen that 40 DI would have its right flank exposed by the departure of the 7 DC and the inertia of the reserve divisions and be overwhelmed by superior enemy forces. The corps had been surprised while in movement to its expected area of operations.

The Battle of the Frontiers

German Situation, Evening, 22 August[36]

The VI RK commander knew that V RK had covered his left flank, and heard that XIII AK on his right had forced the French to retreat. The 12 RD commander reported that he could not hold his positions, a judgment that the VI RK commander thought had no foundation. The corps had lost about 150 OFF and 4,500 EM. The VI RK commander was also able to determine that he had been engaged against 'significant elements of the French V and VI Corps ... their best troops'.

5th Army's evening order (which was not mentioned in the 5th Army war diary) announced that the army had been 'victorious along the entire line' and instructed VI RK to dig in. There was no mention of pursuit. It would seem that 5th Army thought that it had won the battle on 22 August, but the French were clearly able to renew the attack the next day.

French VI CA Situation, 23 August[37]

The French 3rd Army order for 23 August directed VI CA to establish a defensive line on the Crusnes, with its right at Mercy la Bas (which had long since been lost), and to be prepared to resume the offensive when 54 DR and 67 DR had come up to cover the corps right flank.

At 0800 VI CA reported to 3rd Army that 12 DI was at Arrancy, that 42 DI was at Saint Pierrevillers, covered by the corps cavalry brigade (in fact, it was 8km to the rear on the Othain), and that 40 DI was 'far from being reformed'. VI CA had no idea of the situation on the rest of the French 3rd Army front.

On the morning of 23 August VI CA ordered the 23rd Brigade of 12 DI to move forward 4km to Montigny. 24th Brigade was given the 24th battalion of *Chasseurs* (light infantry), some corps artillery and the corps engineers and told to hold Beuville, though in fact this was actually a rear-guard. The additional units were apparently necessary to carry out this mission, for 24th Brigade itself stayed at Arrancy. 42 DI was ordered to defend the Othain on the line Muzeray–Nouillon Pont–Rouvrois sur Othain–Châtillon. 40 DI was in bad condition and reorganising in the army rear at Billy sous Mangiennes–Loison (8km west of Nouillon Pont). During the morning the 23rd Brigade on the Chiers was 'violently attacked' and by 1300 was falling back to the Crusnes. None of the other VI CA units came in contact with German forces.

German Situation 23 August

In the V RK sector on the morning of 23 August, IR 155 began to dig in 1km east of Boismont at 0200. No one knew anything concerning the situation, but 'the word' was that the French would attack. At 0900 an officer arrived from division HQ, saying that the French were not going to attack and work on the trenches was stopped. The troops warmed themselves in the sun, and then moved to a

The Battle South of Longwy

bivouac at 1130 and the field kitchens arrived. The regiment had to displace when French artillery landed closer and closer to the bivouac, but when the French ceased fire it reoccupied the old location.

The field kitchens reappeared at the I/RIR 51 (VI RK) defensive position, bringing hot coffee. The troops cleaned their weapons and equipment and wrote postcards home while patrols were sent to find the wounded and dead. The commander of I/R 51 told the battalion that 'I congratulate you, men; the enemy is fleeing in panic and you have contributed to the victory!' These words, the regimental historian said, were most satisfying, because the troops were still troubled by the impressions of the previous day's combat and did not understand that they had won. The Corps Commander ordered 1/R 51 to assemble, praised the company for saving the day and awarded the company commander the Iron Cross 2nd Class.

The VI RK leadership watched French columns retreating, pursued by German heavy howitzer fire. The commander of 11 RD said that the French had taken heavy casualties, but the corps commander was sceptical, maintaining later that he had not recognised the extent of the French losses, which had been obscured by the tall grain. A 5th Army order arrived at 1100 ordering the VI RK to begin the pursuit, but the corps commander ordered the advance to begin at 1400 to give the units time to complete their reorganisation.[38]

RIR 38 guarded the 12 RD left flank and marched on Pierrepont, and I/ R 38, the point element, took fire from the direction of the town. I/ R 38 had formed a bicycle section, and this was sent forward and quickly rousted out the French.

By 1430 the lead element of RIR 51 reached Doncourt where it took fire. After a short fire preparation the regimental commander personally led 4/R 51 in an assault on the town. The troops broke into the barricaded houses, rounded up the inhabitants and collected them in a large garden and burned the buildings. Several young men armed with pistols and shotguns were killed. The residents of the town were then released. RIR 51 had a few wounded and a horse in the MG Company killed. A youth was sent to the next town, Beuville, with instructions that the inhabitants open their doors and windows and stand in front of the houses, which they did. There were no incidents.

When the point element, 5/R 51, moved out of Beuville it took fire from the rail embankment 700m to the front. French artillery fire began to fall on the point company and Beuville. 23rd Reserve Brigade ordered RIR 51 to take Arrancy, and I/R 51 was deployed to the left of the point, II/R 51 to the right with the MG Company in support. The regiment began the attack at 1730 and had advanced 500m when it was stopped by heavy French artillery fire and the lead troops dug in. The brigade headquarters called off the attack, recognizing that no progress could be made until reconnaissance and artillery preparation had been conducted. After dark II/R 51 pushed listening posts 400m to the front and both battalions and the MG Company sent officer patrols 600m beyond them towards the southwest, which reported the area free of French troops.

The Battle of the Frontiers

As the 34 ID infantry advanced, FAR 69 occupied overwatch firing positions, ready to give immediate fire support.[39] As the infantry advance continued, the guns bounded forward to new positions. When 2/FAR 69 occupied an assembly area, it did not park in the open, but to avoid aerial observation moved to the tree line and the guns, caissons and teams were covered with greenery cut from the trees. The battery was invisible from the air. The only problem was that the horses attempted to eat the camouflage.

French VI CA Situation 24 August[40]

12 DI was defending the Crusnes at Arrancy, 42 DI at Muzeray. The 40 DI was 'beginning to reorganise' at Billy sous Mangiennes (between the Othain and the Loison), and in fact it would take three days to reassemble 40 DI. 54 DR was at Spincourt. At 0700 3rd Army ordered the corps to fall back to the Othain in the general direction of St. Laurent and Spincourt, but the Germans attacked before the order could be executed. 12 DI was pushed out of Arrancy under pressure towards the Othain. 42 DI was ordered at 0800 to attack towards St. Pierrevillers and Han devant Pierrepont, probably to assist 12 DI in breaking contact. By 1000 the attack was 'progressing with difficulty'. 42 DI was then forced to fall back to the Othain. The corps broke contact during the night and continued the withdrawal.

Arrancy 24 August

Arrancy and the hills adjoining it above the Crusnes formed a very strong position. The Crusnes valley was broad, open and offered no cover. The fact that the French 12 DI only had enough troops to hold a strongpoint at Arrancy and the immediate vicinity, and that both of the flanks of this position were uncovered and could be enveloped by the Germans, is powerful evidence of the terrible shape that its infantry was in on 24 August.

At 0230 the German 23rd Reserve Brigade sent out more officer patrols to determine the enemy strength and positions at Arrancy. One patrol of an officer and five men was able to enter Arrancy without encountering any French security forces. The patrol leader ordered his men to split up and each to investigate a street; he took the main street and observed French troops washing and shaving as if on an exercise. He determined that a French infantry regiment, a MG section and some artillery were in the town.

12 RD established that the French had occupied a defensive position at Arrancy and on the high ground to the north and south. The division decided to conduct a double envelopment of Arrancy and the adjoining high ground. In contrast to the meeting engagement on 22 August, the division had the time to prepare a coordinated attack. The 22nd Reserve Brigade would fix the French by attacking

The Battle South of Longwy

Arrancy from the east with RIR 51. RIR 38 would envelop the French from the southeast and the 23rd Reserve Brigade from the north and northeast. RFAR 12 would conduct a preparatory bombardment, supported by I/10th Heavy Howitzer Regiment, a XVI AK unit.

Just before dawn, at about 0400, RIR 51 occupied the rail embankment on the eastern side of the Crusnes opposite Arrancy with II/R 51 on the right, the MG Company behind the right flank, and I/R 51 on the left. By 0430 the regiment was in position. II/R 51 had two companies on the rail embankment and two about 500m to the rear in reserve, I/R 51 had two companies on line, one in reserve and one company was protecting the artillery at Beuville.

At 0600 the German artillery preparation began and steadily became more and more effective. The RIR 51 troops could observe the shells and shrapnel exploding near the French trenches. Occasionally a direct hit would force the French infantry to flee the position. At 0800 the French artillery also opened fire, with little effect against RIR 51, but with more success against the artillery and staffs at Beuville. A direct hit on the brigade staff killed the brigade adjutant and shell-shocked the brigade commander so badly that he had to be replaced by the commander of RIR 51.

RIR 51 was to engage the French with fire, but to wait until the pressure on the flanks made itself felt before attacking. At 0600 the MG Company opened fire, at 500m to 1,200m range, against French infantry on the northeast corner of Arrancy as well as in front of the town. At 0630 6/R 51 and 8/R 51 engaged French infantry on the rail embankment east of the town and on the hill to the northeast at 800m to 1,200m range. 6/R 51 was able to successfully engage a column of French infantry at very long range (1,200m to 1,400m) that was incautious enough to expose itself. The commander of 6/R 51 could observe the effects of his company's fire: the French scattered and then ran back towards the town. The firefight lasted until afternoon and the day was hot. Water was scarce, but in compensation the troops found a field of carrots. 5/R 51, in reserve, had dug in and thereby escaped a barrage from French heavy artillery with few casualties.

RIR 38 moved out from Pierrepont towards Arrancy at 0530. It deployed on the reverse slope of the hill southeast of Arrancy, but on crossing over the crest took such intense fire that further advance was nearly impossible, even with skirmishers in very open order. In particular, the French MGs kept up continuous converging fire that swept through the fields of grain. Nevertheless, several platoons of III/R 38, on the regimental right, succeeded in crossing over the crest by running and crawling and advanced several hundred metres in order to begin the firefight at 150m range against the French troops in the houses of Arrancy and along the rail embankment. Under intense fire from invisible French MGs the attack stalled again.

The Battle of the Frontiers

II/RFAR 12 manhandled its guns up the steep slope of the high ground south of Arrancy to support RIR 38. It required the personnel of the entire section to bring the first four guns of 5/RFAR 12 into position. Careful reconnaissance then revealed paths up the hill that were used by the rest of the section. II/RFAR 12 detected a French battery in march column and destroyed it.

A forward observer team from II/RFAR 12 came running over the crest to the III/R 38 firing line, hauling all of its equipment and unreeling a telephone wire. It set up an armoured plate to protect the FO, as well as his observation scope and hooked up the field telephone to the wire. As French bullets pounded off his armoured shield, the FO sent his call for fire back to the artillery regiment. The commander of III/R 38 came forward and directed the artillery fire against the church tower and the upper stories of the nearby houses, which resulted in a significant reduction in the French fire.

At 1000 RIR 51 could see RIR 38 approaching from the south and RIR 22 from the north. RIR 51 began its own attack, advancing by squad and platoon bounds. The French artillery shells impacted regularly 50m apart, permitting the German infantry to move forward in the gaps. Following the infantry, three MGs bounded forward to the edge of the town while three provided covering fire.

The artillery regiment now occupied direct fire positions that offered excellent observation over Arrancy and the terrain behind it. Nevertheless, the old problem of infantry-artillery cooperation resurfaced. The 12 RFAR historian complained that the infantry failed to maintain contact with the artillery. At 1020 some senior officers observed French infantry leaving the town and assumed that German troops had entered Arrancy. They therefore ordered the artillery to shift their fire to the area behind the town. The German infantry hadn't entered the town and was therefore robbed of fire support. Only at 1130, when the infantry reported to the artillery that it was still outside the town, was fire redirected to the town itself and the rate of fire increased to support the attack. As RIR 51 entered Arrancy, German rounds continued to fall on the town. A platoon leader in 5/51 tied a handkerchief ('that was hardly white anymore') to a rifle and swung it back and forth. This finally attracted the attention of the gunners, and a mounted artillery officer came forward, at which point the artillery fire ceased.

RIR 23 and 6th *Jäger* Battalion came up on III/38's right. The attack now began to make good progress. At 1200 the French began to withdraw. II/R 38 came up on the left of III/R 38. RIR 38 and RIR 23 crossed the rail embankment and penetrated into the town, with RIR 51 on their right. RFAR 12 shelled the retreating French troops and the batteries of I/RFAR 12 moved forward on their own initiative to the high ground northwest of the town, from where they were able to fire into the 'thick masses' of retreating French troops. I/RFAR 12 occupied ground that it had shelled twice during the battle: French dead and wounded and abandoned French machine guns testified to the effectiveness of its fire.

The French turned to make a stand in the fields of grain on the high ground southwest of Arrancy, with RIR 38 in hot pursuit. After a short but violent firefight RIR 38 assaulted and the French withdrew again, with RIR 38 still on their heels, as far as the Longuyon–Rouvrois road, where the regiment halted and conducted a pursuit by fire.

The advance of RIR 38 resulted in considerable mixing of units and many I/R 38 soldiers, echeloned to guard the open regimental left flank, were convinced that the German troops to their front were French. Only energetic action by the I/R 38 commander, his adjutant and the commander of 4/R 38 prevented a serious friendly-fire incident. To re-establish control the commander of I/R 38 assembled the nearby troops, fell them into squad columns and marched them forward, in step, singing, stopping frequently to lay down. He then deployed a thin skirmisher screen and pushed the French in front of him as far as the road.

5th Army ordered VI RK to hold in place. II/R 51 had received its baptism of fire, at the cost of one OFF and 26 EM KIA and two OFF and 106 EM WIA. RIR 38 lost the commander of II/38, a lieutenant and 30 EM KIA, five OFF and 198 EM WIA.

Conclusions

The performance of RIR 38 on 22 and 24 August was exemplary. On 22 August its attack protected the open left flank of the VI RK. The regiment had taken about 15 per cent casualties and been forced to retreat. Nevertheless, on 24 August it attacked again, against strong resistance, pushing the French off their position and pursuing them for over 3km. In three days of combat RIR 38 had taken about 760 casualties. It continued to perform effectively during the pursuit across France and the battle of the Marne. Such professionalism, discipline and morale would have been laudable in a regular army unit. It is almost incredible that it was exhibited by a unit that did not exist until 3 August, less than three weeks prior to its first battle.

Indeed, the reserve infantry regiments of the German VI RK had acquitted themselves exceptionally well, proving to be as good or better than the elite border-security active-duty infantry regiments of the French VI CA. The weakness of the German reserve corps was exactly where it was to be expected: the reserve corps had too little artillery, and the gun batteries were not as proficient as regular army batteries. This meant that the reserve infantry regiments received too little artillery support, and artillery support it did obtain was too slow in arriving. There was also a high incidence of friendly fire, due to a lack of infantry-artillery cooperation, itself the result of a lack of practice between the artillery and infantry commanders.

The most significant observation to be drawn from the fight between the German VI RK and the French 12th and 42nd DI was that in an equal fight the French active army regiments were unable to defeat German reserve regiments;

indeed, frequently it was the German reserve units which defeated the French active units. Prior to the war, this would have been considered practically impossible.

Comparing the German active-army 23rd Infantry Brigade to the 21st Reserve Infantry Brigade, fighting beside it with the same lack of artillery support, shows that, good as the German reserve infantry units were, the German active army infantry regiments were even better. The most significant gains in the German VI RK sector were made by IR 22 and IR 156, which rolled over the French troops opposing them. The ability of both regiments to move quickly and fluidly across such a lethal battlefield was remarkable, and their infantry and MG firepower was murderous. IR 156, like so many other German regiments, reported that the first battle convinced the German infantry of their superiority over the French infantry, an opinion that the regiment maintained to the last.

12
Conclusions

Recapitulation

Joffre's plan had been to concentrate superior forces in the French 4th Army sector and attack the weak German centre, break through and cut off the German right wing. The 3rd Army would protect the 4th Army's right flank. Upon learning that the French were advancing in its sector, the German 5th Army immediately attacked. Neither the German 5th Army nor its right-hand neighbour, 4th Army, were concentrated for combat; one corps in 5th Army and two in 4th Army were a day's march behind the leading corps. Therefore, Joffre's plan succeeded: five corps of the French 4th Army faced three corps of German 4th Army.

In the French 4th Army area of operations, II CA was stopped by a German brigade at Bellefontaine and a German regiment at Robelmont. This left the right flank of the 3 DIC exposed and the division was destroyed, as was the 5th Colonial Brigade to its left. XII CA, which was between the Colonial Corps and XVII CA, had been practically inert. In failing to reach its objectives, it had uncovered the flanks of both neighbouring corps. 33 DI of XVII CA had also been enveloped and destroyed. 34 DI, the second division of this corps, disintegrated. On the 4th Army left flank the XI CA had failed to inflict a decisive defeat on an outnumbered and exposed German division. Indeed, the second brigade of that German division had crushed three French brigades and forced XI CA to retreat.

On the left flank of the French 3rd Army, all four infantry regiments of 8 DI had taken such heavy losses that they were no longer combat-effective and one brigade of 7 DI had been wiped out. The next division on the right, 9 DI, had been defeated by 1100 hours. 10 DI had been ordered to retreat. Of the three VI CA divisions, 12 DI had been forced to retreat, 42 DI had retreated even further, and 40 DI had been smashed. All of the remaining divisions in both French

The Battle of the Frontiers

armies had broken contact with the Germans and retreated during the night to escape destruction

Due to superior German reconnaissance and troop-leading procedures, the Germans had almost always seized the key terrain and deployed first. The German infantry and artillery gained fire superiority. French units were often caught in march column and the French artillery was slow in supporting the infantry. German units were able to manoeuvre on the battlefield; the French were not. The German reserve infantry units had proved themselves to be at least as effective as the French active-army units. The German units had proven themselves to be superior to the French in every regard.

The corps and army HQ on both sides lost control of their units. Many of the German units could have pursued on 22 August but never received orders to do so. The situation was unclear to German leaders at division level and above, and they preferred 'safety first'. When the extent of French defeat became evident in late morning on 23 August, the French were out of range and recovering from their defeat.

French casualties overall had been three or four times higher than those they had inflicted on the Germans. Nevertheless, German losses had been significant and these, as well as the exertions of hard marching, combat and a night spent digging defensive positions, had worn down the German soldiers, who on 23 August were physically and mentally exhausted.

Army HQs, 22 August
German 5th Army[1]

Crown Prince Wilhelm wrote that the leadership of AOK 5 knew intuitively that they had won the battle on the entire front. But the tremendous tensions that arose during the day from the continual stream of messages, issuing orders, and the associated feelings of anxiety and satisfaction, had given rise to grave concern. The massive casualties suffered tempered the elation of victory. The intensity of the battle and lack of information concerning the French – AOK 5 did not know how badly the French had been hurt – left the possibility that the French might attack on 23 August. AOK 5 did not know the situation in the 4th and 6th Army sectors. It also wanted to await the arrival of five *Landwehr* brigades from the Metz garrison. AOK 5 was concerned that the French could have already massed a large force at Verdun to attack the 5th Army left flank. AOK 5 reported to OHL that it had won the battle, but that did not intend to advance on 23 August. The German 5th Army clearly felt that it had not decisively defeated the French. Given the high casualty rate in 5th Army had suffered, the possibility of a French *retour offensif* had to be guarded against.

Conclusions

French 3rd Army[2]

The French 3rd Army, which opposed the German 5th Army, reported around noon on 22 August that it had taken heavy casualties but its situation was good and that the enemy had suffered just as severely. The GQG liaison officer to 3rd Army reported at 2200 that the 3rd Army commander, Ruffey, had briefed him on the situation. Ruffey said that the 3rd Army held the same line as it had that morning, from Virton to Joppecourt. The army had made only limited progress because 7 DI of IV CA and 9 DI of V CA had been surprised and taken serious losses. The situation had been stabilised by the French artillery, which had established a 'significant superiority' over the German artillery. The LNO praised the 'calm and *coup d'oeil* of General Ruffey'. The 3rd Army attack had run into enemy troops 'in solid defensive positions'. The enemy seemed to have intended to mask Longwy while turning the army right flank, that is to say, VI CA and 7 DC. Ruffey complained that the 7 DC had not covered the VI CA right flank. In addition, Ruffey complained that 54 DR had not covered the right flank of VI CA, as he had ordered. Closer examination reveals that the division's leading elements were at Spincourt, exactly where Ruffey had ordered them to be, about 15km behind 40 DI. Ruffey's mission for the reserve divisions had been to cover a German attack from Metz to the south. Only after the battle did Ruffey contend that he expected them to operate towards the east.

On 22 August 3rd Army reported that it had been engaged with the German VI AK, XVI AK and a brigade or a division of XIII AK. That the army (seven divisions) had taken such punishment at the hands of, at most, five German divisions would have been alarming.

After the war Engerand said the 3rd Army had fought outnumbered seven divisions against ten: Engerand was explicitly saying that the German reserve divisions were the equals of French active divisions. He maintained that the French 3rd Army had inflicted such heavy casualties on the German 5th Army that it was immobilised for 24 hours. This was incorrect. For most of the day the odds were practically equal, fourteen French active brigades against thirteen German active brigades and three reserve brigades. In the afternoon four more German reserve brigades appeared. At the end of the day many, perhaps most, of the German units were still quite capable of offensive operations; none of the French brigades were. What had been immobilised was not the German manoeuvre units but the mindset of German 5th Army HQ.

German 4th Army[3]

For the entire day on 22 August the German 4th Army was in a precarious position. The army right flank was in the air. There was a gap between XVIII AK on the right and XVIII RK in the centre, leaving XVIII AK isolated. XVIII RK and the corps on the left, VI AK, faced superior numbers of enemy forces. It was absolutely necessary to protect the right flank and concentrate the army. At 1400 AOK 4 ordered VIII RK to push towards XVIII AK as far as possible. VIII AK was to swing south towards XVIII AK. 4th Army sent situation reports to OHL, AOK 3 and AOK 5. At about the same time, an order arrived from OHL, instructing AOK 4 to move its right flank units to the west, south of Dinant, to cut off the French forces facing the German right wing. This order bore no relation to the situation on the ground; AOK 4 disregarded it and VIII AK maintained its march south.

French 4th Army[4]

Langle de Cary reported to GQG on the evening of 22 August that the results of the day's combat were 'not very satisfactory'. There had been serious reverses at Rossignol and Ochamps, which negated the successes gained by XI CA and XII CA. Nevertheless, at 2330 he ordered the Colonial Corps, XII CA and II CA to hold their present positions while XVII CA and XI CA resumed the attack to the north, supported by the newly arrived IX CA and 60 RD.

At 0130 on 23 August 4th Army sent a sobering report to GQG. In II CA the 3 DI was in good shape at Meix devant Virton, but the 4 DI had been thrown out of Bellefontaine and had been 'sorely tried'. The 3 DIC and 5th Colonial Brigade had also been 'sorely tried'. XII CA was in good shape and had not even engaged its corps artillery, but was falling back. XVII CA was in poor condition, 33 DI had lost its artillery, 34 DI had been thrown back. XI CA had pulled back to the Semois.

More French Fantasies[5]

Both Ruffey and Engerand asserted that, had only the 54 DR and 67 DR attacked, and the 7 DC acted energetically, then the French 3rd Army would have turned the flank of the German 5th Army, perhaps cut it off from Metz, and the French would have won a great victory, which, Engerand maintained, would have had 'the greatest consequences for the entire front', and doubtless the entire German position in Belgium would have been shaken. At the very least, the right flank of the 3rd Army would have been secured.

That all this did not come to pass, according to Engerand, was due solely to GQG's mishandling of the Army of Lorraine. GQG changed the organisation and commanders of the Army of Lorraine and removed it from 3rd Army control – without notifying 3rd Army – on the very day it launched the 3rd and 4th Army offensives. Simultaneously, GQG gave the Army of Lorraine a purely defensive mission, instructing it only to prevent the enemy from marching on Verdun, which contradicted the offensive mission it had been given by 3rd Army.

It is curious that Engerand argues that Ruffey intended to use reserve divisions

Conclusions

in an offensive role, while so many other French apologists claim that the French were beaten solely because they had not planned to use reserve divisions in anything other than secondary roles.

In any case, the leading elements of the of 54 DR were 15km behind VI CA; it was unlikely that 67 DR, which was even further to the rear, could have reached the battlefield on 22 August. Even if the two reserve divisions could have attacked, they would have run into the German 33 ID, supported by a cavalry division, which was waiting for just such a French operation, and the outcome for the French reserve divisions would not have been good.

23 August
GQG

At 0730 on 23 August, Joffre sent his evaluation of the situation to the Minister of War, Messimy.[6] He divided the front in half at Virton – Longwy. To the right of that line, the French were advancing slowly, although they enjoyed a significant numerical superiority. The French artillery had silenced the German artillery. On the left of this line the terrain was unfavourable and the French advance had met with 'great difficulties' in spite of a considerable numerical superiority. The French were attacking the Germans who were still in march column and the Germans must also be in a difficult situation. The French task was to continue the fight, utilizing their numerical superiority.

The 1800 intelligence summary said that GQG had no information concerning enemy forces on the 4th Army front. 3rd Army had made contact with the German VIII and XVI AK and elements of XIII and XXI AK.[7] This report was mostly wrong: VIII and XXI AK were nowhere near the French 3rd Army sector, but V AK, VI AK and VI RK were.

GQG was completely out of touch with the real situation on the 3rd and 4th Army sectors. Had these armies been dependant on guidance from GQG, they would have been destroyed. The French troops, however, had taken matters in their own hands and as a matter of simple self-preservation had retreated out of the range of the German armies.

French 3rd Army[8]

Ruffey's orders for the night of 22–23 August instructed the 3rd Army to defend north of the Chiers. 'The enemy had not followed V CA and had suffered as badly as we had'. At 0030 he ordered 3rd Army to resume the offensive on the morning of 23 August. When GQG expressed the desire at 0245 to have 3rd Army resume the attack, Ruffey responded that he had already given the orders to do so. At 0810 3rd Army submitted a situation report that showed how little the army HQ knew. It said that 40 DI had withdrawn to Nouillonpont; some elements had 'arrived' in Etain. IV CA was in good shape. General Trentinian was at the head of 7 DI (not dead), of which two regiments had been reduced to a battalion each (a rosy evaluation). There were no precise reports from VI CA, which was 'strongly established' on the Crusnes, but when these reports arrived 3rd Army would renew the attack with IV CA and V CA.

Then the reports from the corps began to arrive. VI CA said that its right flank had been threatened with envelopment and it had withdrawn to the Othain. V CA reported that the troops were incapable of conducting a defence and requested to withdraw over the Chiers. At 0930 Ruffey gave up the idea of attacking. Until 0930 on 23 August the 3rd Army HQ was divorced from reality and exercised no control over the situation.

IV CA reported at 1100 that the situation was 'very good'. Both divisions were reorganising. 8 DI had already reconstituted five battalions (of twelve!), 7 DI had six battalions. It is hard to see how divisions that had lost half their infantry could be in good condition.

At 1300, 3rd Army sent a report to GQG: the army's situation was good. The reconstitution of IV CA and V CA was proceeding well. The enemy had been 'severely tried'. IV CA was behind the Crusnes to the east of Montmédy and not under pressure. 8 DI had reconstituted itself reasonably well, 7 DI had been 'severely tested by the preceding day's combat'. V CA was on the Othain to the west and south of Longuyon; most of the corps had been 'severely tested'. VI CA was just north of the Othain, to the south of Longuyon. It too had been 'severely tested' but was 'preparing to resume the offensive'. 'The debris of the 40 DI were in reserve at Pillon (8km due south of Longuyon) ready to counterattack.' 54 DR was supporting the VI CA right flank and 'the counterattack by 67 DR, 73 DR and 75 DR was being prepared under favourable conditions'

But then harsh reality set in. In a telephonic report that the army gave GQG at 1330, 3rd Army said that 'the debris of V CA was conducting a major withdrawal to the Loison'. The artillery was in good condition, but the infantry was no longer able to hold its ground due to casualties and fatigue. The enemy was not pursuing vigorously.

The 3rd Army intelligence summary sent in at 1700 shows that the army literally did not know what had hit it. It said that it had identified in its sector the German XVI AK, XVI RK, VI RK, XXI AK and elements of XIII and XII AK. This was mostly wrong. XVI RK did not exist; XII AK and XXI AK were not in the 3rd Army sector. The army had failed to identify V AK, VI AK and V RK.

French 4th Army[9]

At 0500 on 23 August Langle ordered the 4th Army to withdraw to the Chiers, covered by 2 DIC. He reported to GQG that the morale in XVII CA was not good. Its retreat had forced XI CA to withdraw to the Semois, which was not an

Conclusions

obstacle to a German attack. Both corps needed to be pulled out of the woods and into open terrain. XII CA had both flanks in the air and had to fall back to Florenville, but it and the Colonial Corps would also have to move even further back, and the whole army might well have to retreat to the Chiers or the Meuse.

Joffre replied at 0830 that according to the reports he had received, there were only three German corps on the 4th Army front. He told Langle to resume the offensive as soon as possible. Joffre was absolutely correct; on 22 August the French 4th Army had faced only three corps, and one of those was a reserve corps. Langle issued a pro-forma order for IX, XI and XII CA to resume the advance. Nevertheless, the 4th Army had been so badly beaten up that it was incapable of doing anything other than retreat.

GQG[10]

At 1900 on 23 August Joffre reported to the War Minister that 'the offensive between Longwy and the Meuse had stopped momentarily.' This was due to the failure of several individuals who would be dealt with. Three divisions had taken particularly heavy losses. Joffre said he would attempt to resume the offensive.

Four French armies had taken the offensive and been badly beaten. Nevertheless, Joffre's official explanation was that there were no systematic problems; all that was required was to eliminate some incompetent officers. Joffre had not mentioned that on 24 August the 3rd and 4th Armies would begin to withdraw to the Meuse.

German 5th Army[11]

During the night of 22–23 August AOK 5 received reports from the corps which gave a picture of complete French defeat: the French units had been broken up, the French troops were retreating in great disorder, and French command and control appeared to have collapsed. AOK 4 reported that its fight at Rossignol and Tintigny was 'not unfavourable'. A LNO sent to XVI AK reported that the French had been completely routed and that there were no signs of French troops west of Metz. Wilhelm wrote that these were 'unforgettable hours'.

At 0600 5th Army received an operations order from OHL granting the army full freedom of movement, that is to say, the army no longer was required to maintain contact with Metz-Diedenhofen. OHL wanted the left wing of 5th Army – XVI AK – to push the French right wing to the north, away from Verdun. The AOK 5 operations order at 0625 23 August said that the French were in 'panic flight to the Meuse' and directed the corps to 'energetically pursue the enemy, push him away from Verdun and transform yesterday's victory into a catastrophe'. At 0730 AOK 5 reported to OHL a 'Complete victory yesterday to the south of Longwy. I am pursuing...'

The Battle of the Frontiers

However, Wilhelm admitted that there was no effective pursuit by 5th Army on 23 August. The troops had been further exhausted constructing defensive positions during the night. The loss of so many leaders necessitated extensive reorganisation and this consumed time. The tactical leadership waited for reconnaissance reports to clarify the situation. Once that was accomplished and the advance began, it was stalled by French rear guards. The terrain gained was insignificant.

In the V AK sector, 9 ID defended in place and 10 ID gained little ground, but XIII AK attacked early in the morning and made the most progress, gaining 15km, an indicator of what it might have accomplished on the afternoon of 22 August. During the day it appeared that the French were going to make a stand on the Othain. The spook of a French counterattack from Verdun materialised again, as French columns were seen advancing towards Spincourt and Etain. The XVI AK commander stopped the corps at 1330, before it entered Spincourt, and began orienting it, as well as the 6 KD and two newly arrived *Landwehr* brigades, to the south, ending the possibility that the 5th Army would turn the French right flank.

German 4th Army[12]

At 2040 on 22 August, 4th Army issued an operations order renewing the attack at 0500 the next morning with all five corps. At 0630 a similar order arrived from OHL. Air reconnaissance revealed that the French were withdrawing in good order to the Semois. On the army right flank VIII AK, which had hardly been engaged on 22 August, gained only 6km against French forces that had recently arrived. VIII RK attacked, supported by 21 ID, but 25 ID did not move at all. In the XVIII RK sector, 21 RD moved out only at 1200, 25 RD at 1400. VI AK began to advance at 0900, made contact with the 2 DIC, which was still relatively undamaged, and gained only 2km. Due to the heat and the exhaustion of the troops caused by combat and forced marches on 22 August, the 4th Army pursuit produced no results other than occupying terrain. At 1425 AOK 4 reported to OHL:

> 'We were completely victorious! We have taken thousands of prisoners, including general officers and many guns. Army is in pursuit of the beaten enemy …The troops fought wonderfully. Many units had very heavy casualties.'

French 4th Army

4th Army reported at 0200 on 24 August that it had another hard day on 23 August. The sole remaining units of the Colonial Corps, 2 DIC and the corps artillery, had been attacked and driven out of their first position. In the afternoon,

XII CA on the army left flank had been attacked and forced to retreat, which caused the Colonial Corps to abandon its second position. XII CA reported at 1800 that it needed to reorganise on 24 August and was unable to take the offensive. The corps also required several days rest and replacement officers and NCOs. IX CA on the army left, which had not fought on 22 August, reported at 2000 that it had been pushed back late that afternoon. The 33rd Brigade had 'preserved its cohesion' and the artillery had suffered few casualties but the 36th Brigade was no longer combat-effective. Both 136 RI and 77 RI had lost a thousand men and their morale was poor. 4th Army said that 'under these conditions, the 4th Army offensive found itself temporarily suspended'. Langle reiterated that it would be necessary to fall back to the Chiers and Meuse.

The French View

Engerand's book *Bataille de la Frontières*, published in 1920 on the basis of French primary sources, is broadly representative of the French view of the battle.[13] He was critical of Joffre's offensive strategy and therefore looked kindly on many of the generals Joffre relieved, including Ruffey, the 3rd Army commander and Trentinian, the 7 DI commander. According to Engerand, the 4th Army pushed into the dense forest of the Ardennes without conducting proper reconnaissance and ran into German forces 'completely dug-in'. The French persisted in senseless attacks until the Germans counterattacked and drove them back. Engerand was, however, principally concerned with the 3rd Army sector. Engerand said that V CA in the 3rd Army centre launched three successive attacks, without artillery preparation, against German entrenchments, decimating three regiments. The corps commander, demoralised, ordered a retreat and was relieved (by Ruffey, presumably) in favour of his chief of staff, who stopped the retreat 'and led the troops back to their positions'. The V CA commander also failed to cover the right flank of 7 DI on his left. Fortunately, Trentinian sent out a flank-guard detachment (II/101) and also personally ensured that his advanced-guard held the vital strongpoint at Éthe until 7 DI withdrew from the town on orders. The advance guard of 8 DI, 130 RI, ran into German troops which had been able to construct a defensive position just to the north of Virton without being noticed. 130 RI advanced 'boldly' and the division deployed to prevent being enveloped. When the fog lifted, the German heavy artillery forced 8 DI to abandon Virton. The IV CA commander massed the corps artillery, and the French 75s stopped the German advance. With their support, the French infantry retook Virton and an attack by 117 RI threw the Germans back into the woods. Engerand, like Trentinian, maintained that the withdrawal of V CA prevented IV CA from exploiting its victories at Éthe and Virton.

Langle, the commander of the 4th Army, writing in the mid-1930s, demonstrated a similar capacity for self-deception.[14] He said that the Germans had been fortifying their positions since 20 August and were fully prepared to receive the

The Battle of the Frontiers

French attack. II CA had its march delayed and exposed the flank of the Colonial Corps. The Colonial Corps had been engaged imprudently, with insufficient reconnaissance to the right and had suffered a 'very serious reverse'. According to Langle, XII CA reached its objectives. XVII CA had encountered an entrenched and invisible enemy and suffered the same fate as the Colonial Corps, for the same reasons, although taken somewhat fewer casualties. The XI CA had pushed back the enemy but had sustained 'appreciable losses'. The Germans had taken as many casualties as the French 4th Army and had not pursued. Langle said that the 4th Army had not been seriously hurt and remained capable of continuing its mission. XII CA made a successful counterattack on the afternoon of 23 August. 4th Army withdrew on 24 August only because 5th Army on the left and 3rd Army on the right were withdrawing. Langle said that the real problem was Joffre's insistence that the enemy be attacked wherever he was found. This led to precipitate action. Langle maintained that he was an advocate of methodical, secure operations.

Langle was unable to distinguish between an attack on a prepared position and a meeting engagement. His repeated assertions that the Germans had been digging in for two days betray his complete ignorance of the German situation – 15 years after the battle. At the operational level, the French 3rd and 4th Armies did not have the luxury of a Langle's slow, methodical advance, which would have negated Joffre's strategy, indeed negated the entire Russo-French offensive strategy, as well as giving the German right wing the time to appear in the two armies' rear. Langle's complaint that the corps columns did not coordinate with each other is misplaced: ensuring such coordination was the job of the 4th Army HQ. On a tactical level, the 3rd Colonial Division and 33 DI were not destroyed because they were advancing rashly, but because the Germans counter-reconnaissance had blinded the French patrols, and the Germans manoeuvred at a rate of speed that befuddled the French division commanders.

Bastin says that at Bellefontaine 120 RI took heavy casualties because the German IR 38 was 'well-entrenched'. In reality, it was no such thing. He also mentions French bayonet charges three times. In all three cases it is highly unlikely that any such thing occurred; French bayonet charges are never mentioned in the German sources.[15]

The fascination, common to almost all French soldiers and historians, with German trenches and French bayonet charges has nothing to do with actual combat. It was a means of explaining French defeat that emphasised French heroism and avoided confronting German tactical superiority. For modern historians, German trenches and French bayonet charges provide exactly the correct explanation for French defeat, one that corresponds with the popular 'heroes led by donkeys' thesis, as well as the experience of the next four years of trench warfare.

Strategy and Tactics

The defeat of the French 4th Army by the German 4th Army in the Battle of the Frontiers spelled the failure of the French war plan. Combined with the Russian defeat at Tannenberg, the Entente strategy for simultaneous Russian and French attacks against Germany had also failed. French losses were far higher than German, and the resulting disparity in combat power meant that the French were not even able to hold the last significant terrain obstacle, the Meuse.

These victories were not accomplished by superior war planning or by operational excellence. The French had anticipated the German advance to the north of the Meuse and had devised an excellent means defeating it. The German advance through Belgium was hardly the thing of wonder that it has been made it out to be. That the French plan did not succeed, while the German plan did, had nothing to do with strategy, but was solely the product of German superiority at the tactical level.

There is a school of thought which maintains that the German 'genius for war' was the product of the excellence of the German Great General Staff, that is, German victories were due to superiority at the operational and particularly at the strategic levels.[16] There is no evidence to be found for this proposition either in the Battle of the Frontiers as a whole or in the Ardennes on 22 August. The Chief of the General Staff, the younger Moltke, did nothing to give German planning operational coherence: the seven German armies acted virtually independently of each other. The German 5th Army attack plan for 22 August, written by a General Staff major general, left a corps-sized gap in the army centre that was not filled until late afternoon, and which nearly resulted in a French breakthrough, while the army right flank was hanging completely in the air. The 5th Army plan was not coordinated with the 4th Army. The 4th Army moved to the south on its own initiative at the last minute to cover the 5th Army right flank, in turn leaving the 4th Army's own centre outnumbered and dangerously thin. Due to the 5th Army's poorly thought-out attack, of the ten German corps in these two armies, two corps could only be brought into action late in the day and one not at all, while all the French corps were engaged. The only German senior officer to display sound operational ability in the Ardennes was the commander of the 4th Army, the Duke of Württemberg, a capable professional soldier but also the hereditary ruler of a German state and hardly the prototypical General Staff officer. But the real victors on 22 August in the Ardennes were the officers and soldiers of the divisions of the German 4th Army, which dealt the French 4th Army – the French main attack – the most stinging defeats in the entire Battle of the Frontiers.

The German Army in The Ardennes

The German army's 1906 infantry regulation presented an effective tactical doctrine based on the need to gain fire superiority as well as on offensive action based

The Battle of the Frontiers

on fire and movement. German training in this doctrine was realistic and thorough, and concluded every year by several weeks of live-fire gunnery exercises and tactical problems conducted at MTA. French doctrine did not include the concept of fire superiority and the French did not have adequate training areas. German doctrine and training also emphasised the meeting engagement and individual initiative at the tactical level; the French, on the other hand, emphasised linear engagements tightly controlled at the division, corps and army levels.

The German army won the Battle of the Frontiers because of superior peacetime doctrine and training. German patrolling and reconnaissance were vastly superior to the French. In almost every instance, German reconnaissance provided excellent reports on French movements while blinding French cavalry reconnaissance. French air reconnaissance was largely ineffective in the forested Ardennes; the French senior headquarters formed an entirely erroneous impression of German movements and intentions. On 22 August none of the French divisions had any idea that major German forces were in their immediate vicinity.

On 22 August the two French armies were advancing to the northeast, while the two German armies were attacking to the west. All of the subsequent battles were meeting engagements. German units moved quickly and deployed smoothly. French movements suffered from friction and their deployment was slow and uncertain. Once engaged the Germans smothered the French with rifle, MG and artillery fire and gained fire superiority. If the Germans were on the defence, this fire stopped the French attack. If attacking, the Germans then closed with and destroyed the French infantry by fire and movement. Widespread myths notwithstanding, there were no trenches, and the only barbed wire encountered was that which the Belgian farmers used to fence in their livestock.

German Infantry

Prior to the war there had been considerable concern that the nerves of the troops would not stand up to the terrors of modern combat. As Otto von Moser noted, these battles proved beyond a doubt that the German troops were equal to the task. To Moser's observations it must be added that the French troops were often not equal to the requirements of the modern battlefield; after a few hours of combat, most French units cracked. This was due to inadequacies in French training.

This was not to say that everything went flawlessly. In particular, the infantry often attacked without waiting for the fire support of MG and artillery to soften the enemy up. Losses were even higher than the most sobering peacetime projections: in Moser's units more than a third of the officers and nearly a third of the enlisted men became casualties on 22 August.[17] But French casualties were even higher. As The commander of the 25 ID, speaking of IR 116 and IR 117 at Anloy, said:

'In spite of these (terrain) difficulties, in spite of the casualties and the intense enemy fire our troops worked their way forwards. As was characteristic of our men at this time, they got the bit in their teeth and pushed forward, which cost us a great many casualties ... Nevertheless! Who would dare to criticise the wonderful aggressive spirit of our soldiers?'[18]

In the battle the general was describing, the terrain was very close and the action was taking place at 400m range or less. Artillery support was practically impossible. Using fire and movement, the German troops pushed back the French, one terrain feature at a time. There were no 'bayonet charges'. The German infantry simply kept on battering the French, undeterred by casualties.

The performance of the German infantry on 22 August 1914 was exceptional, the result of high morale, intelligent doctrine, effective training and excellent leadership.

German Artillery

The commander of the VI RK listed the common complaints about the performance of the German artillery.[19] The infantry pushed quickly forward and the artillery was too slow to keep up. The German artillery was especially slow in occupying covered positions. The result was that the German artillery often fired into its own infantry. The French gun had a maximum effective range 2,000m greater than the German gun. The French artillery was better trained and more tactically proficient; the French operated flexibly, by batteries, the Germans employed clumsy three-battery sections.

Most of these criticisms seem to have been coloured by experiences later in the Marne campaign. During the French withdrawal, their artillery was very effective as a rear-guard. During the battle of the Marne the French emptied their magazines, firing prodigious quantities of shells that smothered the German infantry.

But during the meeting engagements on 22 August in the Ardennes the German artillery was almost always superior to the French. If it was sometimes slow to get into action, the French artillery was slower. The Germans were usually able to fight combined-arms battles; the French infantry was often destroyed before the French artillery got into action. The Germans frequently brought individual guns right into the skirmisher line, where they provided highly effective fire support at point-blank range; the French never did so. The German light and heavy howitzers proved their worth.

Both the German and the French artillery soon discovered that frequently the terrain did not provide observation of enemy positions. Rather than do nothing, both artilleries employed unobserved area fire (*Streufeuer*) against suspected enemy locations.[20] This was not provided for in either the French or German pre-war artillery doctrines, because it was felt to be ineffective and wasteful of ammunition. However, both sides used it from the first day of combat on, and to good effect.

German Cavalry

German doctrine emphasised that cavalry needed to be aggressive during the battle in developing opportunities to both participate in the battle as well as to operate against the enemy flank and rear. Doctrine also stated that cavalry was the arm best suited to conduct pursuit.

While the 3 KD and 6 KD had been very effective in the reconnaissance and counter-reconnaissance roles before the battle, during the battle they accomplished nothing. The 3 KD commander decided that the terrain prevented the division from accomplishing anything and resigned himself to inactivity. 6 KD was used to guard the army left flank. Neither division conducted a pursuit, either on 22 or 23 August, although the Colonial Corps would seem to have offered a fine target for 3 KD and the right flank of the French VI CA an even better target for 6 KD.

It appears that the cavalry learned during the approach march that a mounted man presented a fine target and that even small groups of infantry were capable of blocking cavalry movement. By 22 August the senior cavalry commanders were thoroughly intimidated: they avoided serious contact and were unwilling to attempt to move large bodies of cavalry anywhere that they might be subject to small arms or artillery fire. Coupled with the unimaginative operations of the 5th Army headquarters, the timidity of the cavalry leaders cost the cavalry the opportunity to have made a major impact in the battle.

Command and Control

The German army discovered that modern means of communications were unreliable, an observation that would be repeated by practically every subsequent army. This included the telephones that connected army headquarters to OHL, which utilised the seemingly infallible civilian telephone net. As Crown Prince Wilhelm complained, the telephones became so overloaded with traffic that the command and control system at times broke down completely.[21] Nevertheless, German reporting was good and with the exception of the breakdown between V AK and XIII AK German senior HQs kept each other informed.

Liebmann's Evaluation of German Doctrine and Training[22]

In his study of how German doctrine and training withstood the test of combat in 1914, Liebmann concluded that 'In 1914, none of our enemies possessed a doctrine which was superior in combat to that of the German army, even though we must acknowledge that German doctrine had weaknesses'.

'Foremost among these errors was a failure to recognise the effect of firepower, even though German doctrine was based on firepower ... It must also be recognised that even the most conscientious preparation in peacetime does not insulate against similar errors.'

'The German infantry proved itself to be superior to that of the enemy. Its high morale and discipline and its powerful offensive spirit, the product of its traditions and decades of training, allowed it in many cases to simply overrun the enemy infantry'. But Liebmann said that this superiority applied only to mobile warfare, and contended that attacks later in the war against a prepared enemy defence failed disastrously.

Liebmann said that conducting the firefight with thick skirmisher lines was effective and that the casualties incurred were acceptable as were forward bounds by individuals or by squads. Casualties only became serious when long lines bounded forward or entire fronts conducted assaults. And although the German army emphasised fire superiority, gaining and using it in actual practice proved difficult. A much more serious deficiency in German doctrine and training was the failure to recognise the difficulties in infantry–artillery cooperation. In German exercises the problem was glossed over. On the other hand, the German cavalry performed its reconnaissance function everywhere with distinction.

The French army In The Ardennes

French Training and Doctrine

Thomasson listed the reasons for the defeat of the French 3rd and 4th French Armies.[23] Several commanders failed. The cohesion, training, and spirit of sacrifice of some divisions and corps was not adequate. But most important was the insufficient training of certain units and their leaders. They were unable to match the 'brutal and rapid' combat methods of the Germans, in particular the German practice of immediately engaging all available artillery. The Germans engaged their infantry 'progressively and economically', while the French were unable to 'develop the battle methodically'. Dense French formations were too often caught in the open by effective German fire. When French commanders lost sight of their units, they also lost control.

French Command and Control

French reporting was abysmal. The terrific shock effect of German fire and movement was so severe that the French commanders could make no sense of what was happening to their units. At the lowest tactical levels, reporting ceased altogether: so many French battalion and regimental commanders were quickly killed, and movement of messengers on the front line was so difficult, that brigade and division commanders were cut off from their troops. The French senior commanders also recognised that bad news was unwelcome at the next higher headquarters. French commanders always understated the seriousness of the situation and tried to put their units in the best possible light. Their fear that the bearers of bad news would be punished and that the most senior leadership would protect their own positions by sacrificing subordinates as scapegoats was fully justified: Joffre relieved general officers wholesale.

Inaccurate reporting was fatal to top-down French command and control system, which depended on timely and accurate information to permit division, corps and army commanders to form a picture of the battlefield, then conduct manoeuvre and commit reserves. The corps and army commanders were utterly ignorant of the tactical situation and their attempts to manoeuvre were fruitless, even counter-productive. Reserves were committed at the wrong place, too late or not at all. On 22 and 23 August the French troops took matters into their own hands and retreated out of range of German weapons, movements that the senior officers attempted to stop without success.

French Lessons Not Learned

On 16 August GQG had issued tactical instructions to the armies, which 4th Army passed almost verbatim to its subordinate units.[24] In attacking fortified positions, the order said, it was essential to wait for the artillery to provide fire support and prevent the infantry from attacking impulsively. The infantry attack was to be kept under the tight control of general officers (brigade commanders and up) and needed to be carefully prepared.

It is therefore no surprise that by 0930 on 23 August the French 3rd Army had already decided why it had been beaten on the previous day, in spite of the fact that there is no possibility that at this time the army HQ had any actual knowledge of what had occurred at the tactical level.[25] The army bulletin said that the attacks had failed solely because they had not been prepared by artillery fire, not even by infantry fire. It was essential that the infantry attack be preceded by an artillery preparation and that the artillery be prepared to support the infantry. The infantry could not be allowed to conduct bayonet charges without fire support, as it had generally done on the previous day. This evaluation was based on preconceived ideas and peacetime training critiques, not combat experience. The army HQ also needed an explanation for the previous day's defeat that did not implicate the army leadership.

On most of the 3rd Army front (IV CA and V CA sectors) the decisive part of the infantry battle was fought in the fog, when artillery support by either side was impossible. The French had not been beaten because they had launched 'bayonet charges', but rather in hours-long firefights.

Writing in 1937, the French 7 DI commander, General Trentinian, who had been relieved of his command in 1914, drew conclusions from this battle which are representative for those drawn by both the French army and society, and which show that, like Grasset, he was unable to arrive at objective and useful lessons learned.[26] Like most French commentators, Trentinian blamed the defeat of the French offensive on the offensive *à outrance*, that is to say, on Grandmaison and like-minded

Conclusions

young officers as well as GQG and Joffre. The distinguishing characteristic of Joffre's Plan XVII was that it immediately assumed the offensive. This offensive war plan required offensive tactics. A better plan, said Trentinian, would have been that of Michel and Pau, in which the French armies remained on the defensive from the English Channel to the Swiss border until they had determined what the German plan was. Then, the French would go on the offensive.

Trentinian fails to take into account that French strategy was based on the alliance with Russia. Between 1911 and 1913 the French succeeded in convincing the Russians to attack East Prussia on the 15th day of mobilisation with the forces then available, without waiting for the entire Russian army to deploy. The corollary to this Russian offensive was that the French would attack on the 15th day of mobilisation also. Only after this agreement was in place did the French replace the old defensive-offensive doctrine of Bonnal's Plan XIV and XV with offensive strategy of Plan XVII. Had there been no such agreement, that is, had the French adopted Michel's defensive strategy, then the Russians would have been free to follow their own interests, which were to attack the Austrians and stay on the defensive against the Germans. The Germans would then have been free of any distractions in the east, such as the command crisis on 21 August. Nor would Moltke have felt the necessity to send corps to the east, as he did on 24 August.

It is doubtful that French tactics were significantly influenced by Grandmaison's so-called offensive *à outrance*. The tactical manual that implemented this doctrine was issued in 1913, far too late to have any serious effect on training. On 22 August 1914 the French attempted to employ the tactics embodied in the 1904 regulation. It was this regulation and the training that went with it in that failed in 1914, and not the offensive *à outrance*. There is no evidence of the offensive *à outrance* in the tactics employed by Trentinian's own division on that day. In fact, Trentinian's conclusions were pure Bonnal – he says that what the IV CA should have done was to establish a small security detachment (two battalions, a cavalry squadron and an artillery battery) between 7 DI and 8 DI, and 3rd Army should have established a similar detachment between IV CA and V CA. This was exactly the sort of dispersion of strength that Grandmaison was opposed to.

Trentinian was convinced that his corps was victorious on 22 August 1914: 'After vain attacks against the French IV Corps, the German V Corps retreated.' Trentinian's description of 7 DI's victory degenerates into pure fantasy. Since 7 ID was victorious, there was no need to critically examine the division's actions, and Trentinian did not do so. Like Grasset, Trentinian had not taken the trouble to determine, or did not care, what were the mission or actions of the German V AK.

French Army Politics

Trentinian generally faults young General Staff officers at GQG, 3rd Army and IV CA for any mistakes that may have been made. He was particularly bitter because

Joffre, whom he regarded as the cat's paw of the General Staff, relieved over 100 general officers from their commands, including Trentinian himself. These reliefs for cause were 'usually improper, sometimes justified'. We have arrived at the real centre of Trentinian's complaint, which has to do with his career, which he thought had been unjustly and ignominiously cut short by arrogant upstart General Staff officers.

Trentinian was supported in this opinion by Percin, who said that Joffre conducted these reliefs at the instigation of young General Staff officers, who were eliminating officers that stood in their way, principally those promoted by the left-wing Minister of War, André.[27]

Indeed, the argument that Grandmaison's offensive *à outrance* was responsible for the French defeats in the Battle of the Frontiers may have initially been motivated by French army politics. Percin repeats the charge that prior to the war there was a power struggle between General Michel, whose plans were comparable with those of the left-wing politician Juares, and the young Turks and Grandmaison: Michel lost. It would appear that Michel's supporters got revenge by blaming the French defeats in the Battle of the Frontiers on Grandmaison.

1940

French strategy in 1939 and 1940 was determined in large part by the conclusions it drew from the Battle of the Frontiers. The most important of these was that the French army would never allow itself again to engage in meeting engagements or a mobile battle with the Germany army, and in particular not in the Ardennes. The critics of the offensive *à outrance* received full satisfaction: French strategy in 1939–40 would be based on linear defence.

The construction of the Maginot Line made this strategy perfectly evident; it advertised that the French would never attack from Lorraine towards the Rhineland. Since Belgium was again neutral after 1936, the French could not attack Germany through this avenue of approach either. In September 1939 the Germans were free to mass their entire army against the Poles and quickly destroy them without interference in the west, which the Germans defended only with second-rate divisions.

When the Germans attacked in 1940, mindful of the Battle of the Frontiers in the Ardennes in 1914, the French refused to engage the Germans in a mobile battle, conceded the Ardennes and held the obvious line in northern Belgium and on the Meuse River. The German 1914 intelligence estimate said that the French army was not strong enough to form a defensive line all the way to the English Channel, and if they did so, they would have to dangerously weaken their centre.[28] The same calculation applied in 1940. Erich von Manstein based his famous *Sichelschnitt* plan for launching the main German attack through the Ardennes on the fact that the French would be weak in the Ardennes. French defensive strategy in 1939–40, drawing on erroneous lessons learned from the Battle of the Frontiers, was passive and predictable.[29]

Doctrine, Training, Combat and Military History

In modern armies, changes in military technology must be accommodated by changes in tactical doctrine, which then must be taught to the officers and men. In an early 20th-century mass army this was no small undertaking.

The German army mastered this process to a degree not equalled by any other modern army. It drew the correct conclusions from the weaponry revolution occasioned in the mid-1880s by the discovery of high explosives and smokeless powder, the effects of which became evident in the Boer and Russo-Japanese Wars. It codified the concepts of fire superiority and fire and manoeuvre in the 1906 infantry regulation and practiced these tactics at the MTA, and in a broad range of map exercises for the officers. No other army shared the German army's passion for tactical excellence.

The German army did not allow doctrine to be shaped by irrational considerations; their doctrine came from careful observation of the military situation and training was effective and thorough. The French, on the other hand, followed all sorts of false paths, such as red trousers or the notion that racial characteristics and past glory, not good training, were the paramount factors in combat.

The superiority of the German system was evident by the third week of the First World War. The German army more than compensated for its inferior numbers by the fact that, unit for unit, it generated far more combat power than its enemies. In a mobile battle, contact with a German unit was fatal; the surviving Entente units were thrown in headlong flight. The German army had reached a military pinnacle – it knew how to fight outnumbered and win.

Once a military culture has established itself, it develops its own momentum and becomes *Truppenpraxis* – the habitual, instinctive way that an army operates. The German army's culture gave it superiority in the war's initial mobile battles and allowed it to innovate and remain superior to Entente units when the fronts solidified into trench warfare. Indeed, the German army maintained its passion for tactical excellence – and military superiority – for the rest of the century. The power of the German model was so great that even the American army, which had adopted a defective system of *Truppenpraxis* from the British and French in the First World War, when faced with the Cold War problem of fighting outnumbered, converted to some degree in the 1980s to the German system.

It would have been unthinkable for the French to acknowledge that the German system was superior, nor did they. Instead of rationally analysing the Battle of the Frontiers to determine the causes of their defeat, the French invented much more comfortable fictions of German trenches and the offensive *à outrance*, which allowed them to retain their fundamental sense of innate superiority: the

The Battle of the Frontiers

Battle of the Frontiers was an aberration. Having corrected the errors of the offensive *à outrance*, the French imagined that their natural superiority could and did reassert itself. Unfortunately for the French, it was their system that was at fault, as later defeats in the First World War and the 1917 mutiny demonstrated. During the inter-war period, in an era of increasing mechanization and mobility, the French adopted a doctrine of static defence. The French myths concerning the Battle of the Frontiers prevented them from recognizing the advantages of German offensive manoeuvre and virtually doomed them to defeat in 1940.

These same French myths had a baleful influence on American and British military history, which uncritically accepted the French fantasies concerning the Battle of the Frontiers. It was never considered necessary to check the French story against German sources. This was reinforced by an Anglo-Saxon weakness for armchair generalship – little maps and big arrows – which is nowhere more evident than in discussions of the Marne Campaign. The result is a recipe for ill-founded but persistent myth. This study has been an attempt to put the history of the Battle of the Frontiers in the Ardennes back on a firm professional military and historical basis.

Appendix: Laws of War

It is not easy to surrender in a modern battle, and in the Second World War both sides regularly shot soldiers who were trying to surrender or had surrendered. There are no such reports of German mistreatment of French POWs during the Battle of the Frontiers. The French rarely had the opportunity to take German prisoners. The Germans were adamant that when they swept the battlefield they evacuated all wounded, German or French, and gave them equal medical treatment, and buried all the dead.

The IR 19 regimental history gives some of the most common German complaints concerning the French.[1] French soldiers would allow themselves to be bypassed (other regimental histories said they played dead) in order to shoot Germans in the back. There were some French complaints of Germans also playing dead, but since the French so seldom were able to advance, there would not have been much opportunity for the Germans to do so. IR 19 complained that wounded French troops fired upon German soldiers and even stretcher-bearers that were coming to assist them.

The Germans also complained that French soldiers carried or changed into civilian clothes and became guerrillas. Bastin praises the Belgian civilians who aided French stragglers (in civilian clothes) on a massive scale (a French source says that there were 1,000), providing them with food and shelter.[2] This is precisely the charge that German sources made against both the French and the Belgians: the laws of war stipulate that soldiers remain in uniform. Acting on a tip, in January 1915 the Germans caught four French stragglers who were being aided by the residents of Bellefontaine, and fined the village 2,500 Reichsmarks. The mayor of the village complained to the German Governor General that the fine was mass punishment and contrary to the Hague Convention.

Far more has been written the question as to whether Belgian civilians (*franc-tireurs*) fired on German soldiers and if the subsequent German reprisals were

The Battle of the Frontiers

justified, than has been written about the battles themselves. A complete bibliography would take pages. Most important today are: Jean Schmitz and Norbert Niewland, *Documents pour server a l'histoire de l'invasion Allemande dans les provinces de Namur et de Luxembourg, septième partie* (tome VIII) *La Bataille de la Semois et de Virton* (Brussels and Paris, 1924). John Horne and Alan Kramer, *German Atrocities 1914: A History of Denial* (New Haven and London, 2001) is for all intents a summary of Schmitz and Niewland. Larry Zuckermann, *The Rape of Belgium: The Untold Story of World War I* (New York and London, 2004) is unoriginal except that it presents the German reprisals as precursors to the Holocaust. All of these books are apologia in favour of the French and Belgians. They maintain that there were no *franc-tireur* attacks and that thousands of German troops who reported taking fire from armed civilians were hallucinating. German reprisals were therefore really German atrocities. Their thesis is that the German troops were badly trained, poorly disciplined and frightened, none of which is borne out by the combat record of the German army. None of these books made any serious attempt to use German unit source materials.

It is simply not plausible that the judgment of well-trained and combat-experienced German troops could be called into question 70 years after the fact by the unsupported opinions of two Irish academics (Horne and Kramer) who have neither military training nor combat experience.

Horne and Kramer acknowledge (p.128–9) that on 5 August 1914 the Belgian government armed 100,000 civilians, which it termed the 'inactive *Garde Civique* (civil guard)'. They joined the *Garde Civique* proper, which had 46,000 members in 1913. The inactive *Garde Civique* was untrained and had no uniforms. The *Garde Civique* itself was surely little better, but it is impossible to make any accurate assessment, since the Belgian archives contain no records concerning the *Garde Civique* whatsoever: either the *Garde Civique* was so disorganised that it did not keep records of who its members were and whom they gave military assault weapons to, or the records were destroyed by the Belgians. There is no evidence of any kind that the *Garde Civique* as a whole had any training, officers, NCOs or chain of command. The *Garde Civique* was a guerrilla army at best, an armed mob at worst. Horne and Kramer say that on 18 August, that is, the day the German began their approach march through Belgium, the Belgian government disbanded the Garde Civique. They do not say how, given the absence of any organisation, this was accomplished. Nor do Horne and Kramer say where the 146,000 weapons went. Nevertheless, Horne and Kramer are absolutely convinced that none of these 146,000 out-of-control but heavily armed men ever shot at German troops.

René Bastin, the local Belgian historian who lives in Tintigny, related an interesting incident from the fight in Bellefontaine. Some groups of Germans attacked into the interior of Bellefontaine. Seven German soldiers were killed defending the courtyard of the *château*. Bastin says that local tradition has it that it was

Appendix

essential to take the courtyard, which was still held by a German officer. This task was accomplished with the assistance of an 'especially bold' resident of Bellefontaine. Bastin said he thought that the officer was Lieutenant Friedhelm Swoboda of IR 38. He expresses his sympathy for Swoboda's family, which erected a handsome tombstone for their son in the local cemetery, *mais c'est la guerre*: a moving, but perhaps in fact not uncommon incident. In relating this tale, Bastin was surely motivated by the perfectly reasonable desire to show that Belgians were no cowards, but helped the French army defend against German invader. One suspects that similar research would reveal many such events. And there lies the rub: this incident, and its probable counterparts throughout the Ardennes, contradicts the formal assurances of Belgian apologists that Belgian civilians never-ever-not-once fought German troops.[3]

There is no question that German troops shot Belgian civilians as reprisals for *franc-tireur* attacks. Such reprisals are violations of the rules of war. There can also be no question that there were Belgian *franc-tireur* attacks, which were also violations of the rules of war. This observation is confirmed by the fact that in areas where there were no *franc-tireur* attacks, such as the interior of France and the Flemish areas of Belgium, there were no German reprisals.

This book is a study of tactics on 22 August 1914. On a few occasions, alleged *franc-tireur* activity was of minor tactical importance and is mentioned in passing. Otherwise, neither the *franc-tireurs* nor the German reprisals influenced the tactical course of the battle and therefore are not addressed.

List of Illustrations and Maps

1 The trajectory of a rifle bullet at 700m range. The parabolic arc taken by the bullet causes it to pass over a target at 400m away. Courtesy of Heather Wetzel.

2 Beaten zone at 700m. Dispersion of a platoon's fire: with point of aim at 700m, beaten zone extends from 640m to 760m. Courtesy of Heather Wetzel.

3 Breitkopf's attack: the situation at 1300. The attacker's front is 1,000m from the defensive position. The attack is making the most progress on the left. Courtesy of Heather Wetzel.

4 Infantry in a march column. Courtesy of Bernard and Graefe.

5 The infantry is advancing in successive waves with large intervals between each wave. Supporting artillery fire is landing on the objective. Courtesy of Bernard and Graefe.

6 Infantry advancing by bounds. Courtesy of Bernard and Graefe.

7 Infantry advancing by bounds. The soldier on the right has his entrenching tool ready. The two soldiers on the left provide covering fire. Courtesy of Bernard and Graefe.

8 Infantry advancing by bounds. The squad leader observes the enemy.

9 Troops on the firing line provide covering fire while other troops bound forward. In the centre of the picture is the platoon leader (with binoculars). One of the range estimators observes the company commander to the rear, while a second observes forward. Supporting artillery fire lands in front. Courtesy of Bernard and Graefe.

10 Machine-gun team advancing. In the background a second MG provides covering fire. Courtesy of Bernard and Graefe.

11 Infantry in the assault. Courtesy of Bernard and Graefe.

12 A cavalry patrol. The troopers are dispersed and alert, and armed with lance and carbine. Courtesy of Bernard and Graefe.

13 Artillery advancing under fire at a gallop. Courtesy of Bernard and Graefe.

14 Marksmanship training before the First World War. Author's collection.

15 A typical obstacle course before the First World War. Author's collection.

16 The German sFH 02 15cm heavy howitzer. Author's collection.

17 Marching German infantry. Author's collection.

18 Departure from Schwabisch Hall, 14 August 1914. Author's collection.

List of Illustrations and Maps

19 Baranzy from the south (French perspective). Author's collection.

20 Longwy. Baranzy-Signeulx Road from the south (French perspective). Author's Collection.

21 Battery command post 5/FAR 49. Author's collection.

22 Longwy, Baranzy. The German XIII Corps took the town form the French 9th Division. Author's collection.

23 The position of the French and German Army on 17 August. Courtesy of Heather Wetzel.

24 The movement of the French and German Army between 18–20 August. Courtesy of Heather Wetzel.

25 Longlier, 20 August 1914. Meeting engagement between the German 88th Regiment and French 87th Regiment. Courtesy of Heather Wetzel.

26 The position of the French and German Army on the evening 21 August. Courtesy of Heather Wetzel.

27 The position of German VI and V Corps, French XII, Colonial and IV Corps in Rossignol, Virton. Courtesy of Heather Wetzel.

28 German VI Corps destroy the French 3rd Colonial Division at Rossignol. Courtesy of Heather Wetzel.

29 11th Division defeats 7th Colonial Regiment (3rd Colonial Division) and blocks French 4th Division at St Vincent, Bellefontaine. Courtesy of Heather Wetzel.

30 German XVIII Reserve Corps destroys French 5th Colonial Brigade at Neufchateau. Courtesy of Heather Wetzel.

31 The German right flanks holds. The German 25th Division stops the French 21st, 22nd and 34th Divisions. The German 21st Divisions destroys the French 33rd Division. The German 81st and 88th Reserve Regiments stop the French XII Corps. Courtesy of Heather Wetzel.

32 The German 21st Division destroys the French 33rd Division at Bertrix. Courtesy of Heather Wetzel.

33 The German 25th Division holds off the French 21st, 22nd and 33rd Divisions at Maissin, Anloy. Courtesy of Heather Wetzel.

34 The German V Corps defeats the French II and IV Corps at Virton, Ethe. Courtesy of Heather Wetzel.

35 The German 9th Division destroys the French 8th Division and stops the French II Corps at Virton. Courtesy of Heather Wetzel.

36 The German 10th Division and 53rd Brigade destroy the French 7th Division at Ethe. Courtesy of Heather Wetzel.

37 The Battle of Longwy. The German left flank (XIII, VI Reserve, V Reserve, XVI Corps) defeats the French right flank (V Corps, VI Corps). Courtesy of Heather Wetzel.

38 The Battle of Longwy. The German XIII Corps defeats the French V Corps.

39 The Battle of Longwy. The German VI Reserve Corps stops the French 12th and 42nd Divisions. Courtesy of Heather Wetzel.

40 The Battle of Longwy. The German 34th Division and V Reserve Corps defeat the French 42nd Division. Courtesy of Heather Wetzel.

41 The Battle of Longwy. The German XVI Corps destroys the French 40th Division. Courtesy of Heather Wetzel.

42 The German 12th Reserve Division defeats the French 12th Division at Arrancy, 24 August. Courtesy of Heather Wetzel.

Glossary

AK	*Armeekorps*	German army corps
CA	*Corps d'armée*	French army corps
	Chasseurs	French light cavalry or infantry
EM		Enlisted Men
FAR	*Feldartillerieregiment*	German field artillery regiment
FUSS	*Fussartillerie*	German heavy artillery regiment
GDR	*Groupe de divisions de reserve*	Group of French reserve divisions
ID	*Infanteriedivision*	German infantry division
IR	*Infanterieregiment*	German infantry regiment
	Jäger	German light infantry battalion
	Jäger zu Pferde	German light cavalry regiment
JMO	*Journal de marche et d'operations*	French war diary
KIA		Killed in Action
KTB	*Kriegstagebuch*	German war diary
MIA		Missing in Action
OFF		Officers
RAC	*Regiment d'artillerie de campagne*	French field artillery regiment
	Regiment d'artillerie coloniale	Colonial field artillery regiment
RFAR	*Reservefeldartillerieregiment*	German reserve field artillery regiment
RI	*Regiment d'infanterie*	French infantry regiment
RIC	*Regiment d'infanterie coloniale*	Colonial infantry regiment
RIR	*Reserveinfanterieregiment*	German reserve infantry regiment
WIA		Wounded in Action

German Order of Battle

4th Army

Commanding General: General Albrecht Duke of Württemberg
Chief of Staff: Major General Freiherr von Lüttwitz

VI AK
    III/FAR 6 (sFH)
  11ID
    Jäger Regiment zu Pferde 11
    FAR 5
    FAR 41
    21st Bde
      IR 10
      IR 38
    22nd Bde
      IR 11
      IR 51
  12 ID
    Uhlan Regiment 2
    FAR 23
    FAR 44
    24th Bde
      IR 23
      IR 62
    78th Bde
      IR 63
      IR 157

VIII AK

XVIII AK
    I/FAR 3 (sFH)
  21 ID
    Uhlan Regiment 6
    FAR 27
    FAR 63
    41st Bde
      IR 87
      IR 88
    42nd Bde
      IR 80
      IR 81
  25 ID
    Dragoon Regiment 6
    FAR 25
    FAR 61
    49th Bde
      IR 115
      IR 116
    50th Bde
      IR 117
      IR 118

VIII RK
  15 RD

Reserve *Uhlan* Regiment 5
RFAR 15
30th Res Bde
    RIR 25
    RIR 69 (two bn)
32nd Res Bde
    RIR 17 (two bn)
    RIR 30 (two bn)
16 RD
    Reserve Heavy Cavalry Regiment 2
    RFAR 16
29th Res Bde
    RIR 29
    RIR 65
31st Res Bde
    RIR 28
    RIR 68

21 RD
    Reserve Dragoon Regiment 7
    RFAR 25
41st Res Bde
    RIR 80
    RIR 87
42nd Res Bde
    RIR 81
    RIR 88
25 RD
    Reserve Dragoon Regiment 4
    RFAR 25
49th Res Bde
    RIR 116
    RIR 118
50th Res Bde
    IR 168
    RIR 83

XVIII RK

5th Army
Commanding General: Major General Crown Prince Wilhelm of Prussia
Chief of Staff: Major General Schmidt von Knobelsdorf

V AK
    I/FAR 5 (sFH)
9 ID
    Uhlan Regiment 1
    FAR 20
    FAR 56
17th Bde
    IR 19
    IR 58
18th Bde
    IR 7
    IR 154
10 ID
    Jäger Regiment zu Pferde 1
    FAR 20
    FAR 56
19th Bde
    IR 6
    IR 46
20th Bde
    IR 47
    IR 50

XIII AK
    I/FAR 13 (sFH)
26 ID
    Uhlan Regiment 20

Order of Battle

    FAR 29
    FAR 65
  51st Bde
    IR 119
    IR 125
  52nd Bde
    IR 121
    IR 122
27 ID
    Uhlan Regiment 19
    FAR 13
    FAR 49
  53rd Bde
    IR 123
    IR 124
  54th Bde
    IR 120
    IR 127

XVI AK
    I/FAR 10 (sFH)
  33 ID
    Jäger Regiment zu Pferde 12
    FAR 33
    FAR 34
  66th Bde
    IR 98
    IR 130
  67th Bde
    IR 135
    IR 144
  34 ID
    Uhlan Regiment 14
    FAR 69
    FAR 70
  68th Bde
    IR 67
    IR 145
  86th Bde
    IR 30
    IR 173

V RK
  9 RD
    Reserve Dragoon Regiment 3
    RFAR 9
  17th Res Bde
    RIR 6
    RIR 7
  19th Res Bde
    RIR 19
    Res *Jäger* Bn 5
  10 RD
    Reserve *Uhlan* Regiment 6
    RFAR 10
  77th Bde
    IR 37
    IR 155
  18th Res Bde
    RIR 37
    RIR 46

VI RK
  11 RD
    Reserve Hussar Regiment 4
    RFAR 11
  23rd Bde
    IR 22
    IR 156
  21st Res Bde
    RIR 10
    RIR 11
  12 RD
    Reserve *Uhlan* Regiment 4
    RFAR 12
  22nd Res Bde
    RIR 23 (two bn)
    RIR 38
    Res *Jäger* Bn 6
  23rd Res Bde
    RIR 22
    RIR 51 (two bn)

French Order of Battle

3rd Army

Commanding General: General Ruffy

IV CA
    315 RIR
    317 RIR
    14th Hussars
    44 RAC
  7 DI
    26 RAC
  13th Bde
    103 RI
    104 RI
  14th Bde
    101 RI
    102 RI
  8 DI
    31 RAC
  15th Bde
    124 RI
    130 RI
  16th Bde
    115 RI
    117 RI
V CA
  9 DI
    17th Bde
      4 RI
      82 RI
    18th Bde
      113 RI
      131 RI
  10 DI
    19th Bde
      46 RI
      89 RI
    20th Bde

VI CA
  12 DI
    23rd Bde
    24th Bde
      106 RI
      132 RI
  40 DI
  42 DI
    151 RI
    162 RI
    94 RI

Order of Battle

4th Army

Commanding General: General Langle de Cary

II CA
    19th *Chasseurs*
    29 RAC
  3 DI
    17 RAC
   5th Bde
    72 RI
    128 RI
   6th Bde
    51 RI
    87 RI
  4 DI
    120 RI
    147 RI
    91 RI
Colonial Corps
    3rd Regiment *Chasseurs d'Afrique*
    6th Reserve Dragoon Regiment
   3 RAC
  5th Colonial Bde
    21 RIC
    23 RIC
  2 DIC
    22 RIC
  3 DIC
    2 RAC
   1st Colonial Bde
    1 RIC
    2 RIC
   3rd Colonial Bde
    2 RIC
    7 RIC

XII CA
  23 DI
  24 DI

XVII CA
  33 DI
    18 RAC
   65th Bde
    7 RI
    9 RI
   66th Bde
    20 RI
    11 RI
  34 DI
   67th Bde
   68th Bde

XI CA
  21 DI
   41st Bde
   42nd Bde
  22 DI
IX CA

Endnotes

Introduction

1 Guy Pedroncini (ed.), *Histoire Militaire de la France* 3 – *de 1871 à 1940* (Paris, 1992).
2 David G. Herrmann, *The Arming of Europe and the Making of the First World War* (Princeton, 1996).
3 Antulio J. Echevarria II, *After Clausewitz*, (University Press of Kansas, 2000), p.127, 227–8.
4 Carl von Clausewitz, *On War* (Michael Howard and Peter Paret, ed. and trans.), (Princeton NJ, 1976), p.127.
5 *Exerzier-Reglement für die Infanterie* vol 29. Mai 1906. *Neuabdruck mit Einfügung der bis August 1909 ergangenen Änderungen* (Deckblatt 1–78). (Berlin, 1909).
6 General-Inspektion des Militär-Erziehungswesens (bearbeitet), *Leitfaden für den Unterricht in der Taktik auf den Königlichen Kriegsschulen* (Berlin, 1910).
7 F. Immanuel, *Handbuch der Taktik* (Berlin, 1910).
8 Hein, *Kampfesformen und Kampfesweise der Infanterie* (Berlin and Leipzig, 1914). Falkenhausen, *Der grosse Krieg der Jetztzeit* (Berlin, 1909) offers a comprehensive picture of German strategic and tactical doctrine based on the applicatory method – a case study of a Franco-German war. Max von den Bergh, *Das Deutsche Heer vor dem Weltkriege* (Berlin, 1934) offers an interesting but overly critical view, probably as a warning against making the same mistakes in the newly reestablished Wehrmacht. For an excellent, detailed history of the development of European armies from 1900 to 1914, Dieter Storz, *Kriegsbild und Rüstung vor 1914* (Herford, 1992). W. Balck, *Entwicklung der Taktik im Weltkriege* (Berlin, 1920).
9 De Langle de Cary (commander of French 4th Army) *Souveniers de Commandement 1914–16* (Paris, 1935) pp.13–14.

Chapter 1: German Tactics and Training

1 Rudolf von Freydorf (ed.), *Das 1. Badische Leib-Regiment Nr. 109 im Weltkrieg 1914–1918* (Karlsruhe i. B., 1927) pp.17, 742, 754–9; Friedrich von Friedenberg, *Geschichte des Königlich Preussischen Ersten Garde-Regiments zu Fuss: 1871 bis 1914* (Berlin, 1933) p.173.
2 Gebhard Graf von der Schulenberg, *Das Infanterie-Regiment Keith (1. Oberschlesisches) Nr.*

The Battle of the Frontiers

22 im Kriege 1914 1918 (Swinna/ Berlin, 1932) p.24. Otto von Moser, *Die Württemberger im Weltkrieg* (Stuttgart, 1927) p.216.

3   Immanuel, *Taktik II*, p.9. *Leitfaden*, p.105.
4   Clausewitz, *Vom Kriege*, Book 2, Chapter 3.
5   Immanuel, *Taktik II*, p.261–4. *Leitfaden*, p.107–10, 122.
6   Freydorf, *IR* 109, p.759.
7   *Leitfaden*, p.104.
8   *Leitfaden*, p.102–4, 145. Immanuel, *Taktik I*, pp.259–60, 295, *II* pp.10–12, 93.
9   *Taschenbuch des Generalstabsoffiziers* (Berlin, 1914). *Leitfaden*, p.18. Curt Jany, *Geschichte der Preussischen Armee IV*, (Osnabrück, 1967) p.299. *Anhaltspunkte für den Generalstabsdienst*, § 318. Freydorf, *IR* 109, p.926.
10 *IR* 109, p.727.
11 Thomasson, *Le revers de 1914 et ses causes* (Paris, 1919) p.138.
12 Benary, *Königlich Preußisches 1. Posensches Feldartillerie-Regiment Nr 20* (Berlin, 1932) pp.2–19.
13 *Exerzier-Reglement für die Infanterie vom 29. Mai 1906. Neuabdruck mit Einfügung der bis August 1909 ergangenen Änderungen* (Deckblatt 1–78). (Berlin, 1909).
14 Liebmann, 'Die deutschen gefechtsvorschriften von 1914 in der Feuerprobe des Krieges' in: *Militärwissenschaftliche Rundschau 2. Jahrgang* (1937) 4. Heft p.458.
15 Breitkopf, *Die Ausbildung im Gefechtsmässigen Schiessen* (Augsburg, 1907).Voss, *Unsere Infanterie. Ihre Ausbildung und Kampfweise*, (Leipzig, 1914); Friedberg, *1. GRzF*, p.193–4. Joachim Leder, *Geschichte der 3. Schlesische Infanterie-Regiments Nr. 156* (Zeulenroda, 1930) pp.4–11. Dieter Storz, *Gewehr und Karabiner 98* (Vienna, 2006). Eckasrt von Wurmb, *Major Menzels Dienstunterrict des deutschen Infanteriesten* (Berlin 1914)
16 Ortenburg, *Waffen und Waffengebrauch im Zeitalter der Millionenheere* (Bonn, 1992) p.66–73.
17 Döring von Gottberg, *Das Grenadier-Regiment Graf Kleist von Nollendorf (1. Westpreußisches) Nr. 6 im Weltkriege* (Berlin, 1925) pp.V18–19.
18 Storz, *Gewehr und Karabiner 98*, pp.208–9.
19 Immanuel, *Taktik I*, pp.191–2. Byern, *Veranlagung, Durchführung und Beurteilung gefechtsmässiger Abteilungsschiessen und des Prüfungsschiessens für Infanterie und Kavallerie* (Berlin, 1908). Breitkopf, *Vorbereitung, Durchführung und Beurteilung gefechtsmässiger Schiessen in grösseren Abteilungen; Besonderes über gefechtsmässiges Belehrungs- und Prüfungsschiessen. Nur für Dienstgebrauch!* (Augsburg, 1907). Ortenburg, *Waffen und Waffengebrauch*, 144–7. Freydorf, *IR* 109, p.11. Hauptstaatsarchiv Dresden 11359/1389, IR 134, *Ergebnisse des Gefechtsschiessens* (Results of Combat Gunnery Qualification Firing) shows in detail how combat gunnery was conducted and evaluated in 1913. Hauptstaatsarchiv Dresden 11359/1388 *Erfahrungsberichten, Schiessvorschriften* 1907–1909 (Lessons Learned, Combat Gunnery Regulation) gives a detailed analysis of the conduct of gunnery and proposed changes. Friedenberg, *1. GRzF,* pp.177–85.
20 *Exerzier-Reglement….Infanterie*, § 453; *Leitfaden*, pp.27–31, 116–7. *Taschenbuch des Generalstabsoffiziers.* Immanuel, *Taktik I*, pp.298–307.
21 Robert Bruce, *Machine Guns of World War I,* (London, 1997), pp.12–15.
22 Friedenberg, *1. GRzF*, p.190.
23 Immanuel, *Taktik II*, pp.150–65.
24 H. Pantlen, *Das Württembergische Feldartillerie-Regiment König Karl (1. Württembergisches) Nr. 13 im Weltkrieg 1914-1918* (Stuttgart, 1928), p.13.
25 Immanuel, *Taktik II*, pp.211–29. *Anhaltspunkte*, § 227–53. Freydorf, *IR* 109, pp.904–10.
26 Freydorf, *IR* 109, p.776–868. Friedenbach, *1. GRzF*, pp.159–161. Immanuel, *Taktik I*, pp.145, 220
27 Karl Vogt, *3. Niederschlesisches Infanterie-Regiment Nr. 50 1914 1920* (Rawitsch-Lissa i. P., 1931) p.19.
28 The 1st Foot Guard regimental history says 24 kg, IR 109 – the Baden Guard regiment – says 30 kg.

Endnotes

29 Döring von Gottberg, *IR* 6, p.20.

30 *Leitfaden*, pp.83–4, 108–9. *Anhaltspunkte*, § 95–101, 129, 201–10, 236. *Taschenbuch des Generalstabsoffiziers.*

31 Immanuel, *Taktik I,* p.132.

32 *Exerzier-Reglement....Infanterie* § 82–100.

33 *Exerzier-Reglement ....Infanterie*, § 324–351. Breitkopf, *Der Angriff über die Ebene. Nur für Dienstgebrauch!* (For official use only!) (Augsburg, 1907). Immanuel, *Taktik I,* pp.193–246. Freydorf, *IR* 109, pp.742–3, 753–4. Voss, *Infanterie*, 24–31. Friedenberg, 1. *GRzF*. p.172, which calls this 'Burentaktik', not because the Boers or the British used it in South Africa, but because it represented the German army's 'lessons learned' from the Boer War. It was instituted by an army order on 6 May 1902.

34 *Leitfaden*, p.15. 'Cover' is protection from enemy fire, which is normally provided by placing a terrain feature, like a hill, between your own troops and the enemy. 'Concealment' is provided by anything that hides your troops from enemy observation, such as vegetation. Concealment does not provide protection against enemy fire.

35 The author of the IR 109 regimental history said that the 'Boer tactics' introduced into the German army after the South African War consisted of conducting the firefight at the squad level. Freydorf, *IR* 109, p.11.

36 *Leitfaden*, p.22.

37 *Leitfaden*, p.8.

38 Hein, *Kampfesformen*, pp.41–2. Breitkopf, *Die Ausbildung im gefechtsmässigen Schiessen. Nur für Dienstgebrauch!* (Augsburg, 1907) p.39.

39 *Anhaltspunkte*, § 149–67, 293; Immanuel, *Taktik I,* pp.75–85.

40 *Exerzier-Reglement...Infanterie* § 454–465.

41 Moser, *Bataillons und Regiments*, pp.105–6, 119, 240–2. Freydorf, *IR* 109, p.14.

42 Friedenberg, 1.*GRzF*, pp.94–5.

43 Krafft, *Die Aufgaben der Aufnahmeprüfung 1908 für die Kriegsakademie* (Berlin, 1908 and 1910).

44 *Leitfaden*, pp.32–47, 111–2, 159–61. Voss, *Infanterie*, p.25–6. Immanuel, *Taktik I,* pp.309–64.

45 Moser, *Württemberger*, pp.216–7.

46 *Exerzier-Reglement....Infanterie* §451–2.

47 *Leitfaden*, pp.93–5. Voss, *Infanterie*, pp.9–10. Immanuel, *Taktik I,* pp.88–111; *II*, pp.19–20.

48 *Anhaltspunkte für den Generalstabsdienst*, § 178–183.

49 *Leitfaden*, pp.53–8, 113–6. G. Ortenberg, *Waffe und Waffengebrauch im Zeitalter der Millionenheere* (Bonn, 1992), pp. 105–110, 157–66. Hauptstaatsarchiv Dresden 11359/1376. No title; eleven-page perceptive discussion of latest developments in artillery doctrine, 12 April 1906

50 Anon., *FAR* 25, pp.61, 438.

51 *Taschenbuch des Generalstabsoffiziers.*

52 Marx, *Geschichte des 3. lothring. Feldartillerie-Regiments Nr. 69* (Berlin, 1927) pp.10–13.

53 *Leitfaden*, p.71–8.

54 Hauptstaatsarchiv Stuttgart M 1 / 4 Bü 197....*Gefechtsübungen mit gemischten Waffen unter Beteiligung der schweren Artillerie des Feldheeres.* K. P. Kriegsministerium 2. Juli 1904.

55 Franz Nikolaus Kaiser (ed.), *Das Ehrenbuch der Deutschen Schweren Artillerie* (Berlin, 1931) p.19.

55 Voss, *Unsere Infanterie*, pp.40–44.

56 Kaiser (ed.), *Das Ehrenbuch der Deutschen Schweren Artillerie*, p.44.

56 Voss, *Unsere Infanterie*, pp.9–22

57 Anon., *FAR* 25, pp.383–6.

58 Thomasson, *Le Revers de 1914*, p.164.

59 *Exerzier-Reglement...Infanterie* §443–452. Immanuel, *Taktik I,* p.269.

60 Infanterie-Regiment 127, pp.10–11. *Handbuch* p.115.

The Battle of the Frontiers

61 *Exerzier-Reglement....Infanterie*, § 362–374. *Leitfaden*, pp.123–132. Otto von Moser, *Ausbildung und Führung des Bataillons und Regiments* (2nd ed., Berlin, 1912). Voss, *Infanterie*, pp.27–31. Immanuel, *Taktik II*, pp.18–22.

62 Breitkopf, *Der Angriff über die Ebene*. Herrmann Vogt, *Das Buch vom Deutschen Armee* (Bielefeld and Leipzig, 1891) p.38. The Gunnery Schools also set the standards for the annual unit range firing, which was quite similar to that held at the US Army National Training Centres, except that they took place at the Corps Major Training Areas.

63 *Leitfaden*, p.9.

64 *Exerzier-Reglement....Infanterie* § 473.

65 *Leitfaden*, p.9.

66 *Leitfaden*, p.9.

67 If a rifleman is aiming at a point target, a host of variables will cause him to miss: jerking the trigger, poor point of aim, defects in the weapon and ammunition, wind, humidity, etc. This is called deflection probable error. The deflection probable error at these ranges is 5½m. Almost all of his rounds will impact 5½m to the left and right of the target. At closer ranges, the deflection probable error is less, and the intervals between skirmishers can be closed up without an increase in casualties.

68 *Exerzier-Reglement....Infanterie*, § 375–391. *Leitfaden*, 154–9. Immanuel, *Taktik I* p.207; *II*, pp.22–35, 284–7, 294.

69 Freydorf, *IR 109*, pp.758–9,775–8.

70 Marx, *FAR 69*, p.10.

71 Freydorf, *IR 109*, p.11.

72 Friedenberg, 1. *GRzF*, pp.225–6.

73 *Exerzier–Reglement....Infanterie* § 352–361. *Leitfaden* pp.132–6, 207. Immanuel, *Taktik II*, pp.13–18. Generalstab des Heeres 7. (Kriegsgeschichtliche) Abteilung, *Begegnungsgefechte* (Berlin, 1939) pp.1–7.

74 E. Freiherr von Gayl, *General von Schlichting und sein Lebenswerk* (Berlin, 1913)

75 Hein, *Kampfesformen*, pp.96–7.

76 *Exerzier-Reglement....Infanterie* § 392–396. *Leitfaden*, 120–1. Immanuel, *Taktik II*, pp.35–9.

77 *Exerzier-Reglement...Infanterie* § 397–416; *Leitfaden*, pp.24–5, 108–9, 136–46. *Anhaltspunkte* § 311. Immanuel, *Taktik II*, pp.40–55, 70, 287–94.

78 *Exerzier-Reglement...Infanterie* § 417–425. *Leitfaden*, p.149–53. Hein, *Kampfesformen*, pp.110–1. Immanuel, *Taktik II*, pp.54–6.

79 *Exerzier–Reglement...Infanterie* § 434–442. *Leitfaden*, pp.162–3. Immanuel, *Taktik II*, pp.74–82.

80 Immanuel, *Taktik II*, pp.103–16. *Leitfaden*, pp.165–9.

81 Immanuel, *Taktik II*, pp.88–94. *Leitfaden*, pp.171–6.

82 On the training year as seen from the regimental level, Joachim Leder, *Geschichte des 3. Schlischen Infanterie-Regiments Nr. 156* (Zeulenroda 1930) pp.1–11 and Arens, *Das Königlich Preussische 7. Westpr. Infanterie-Regiment Nr. 155* (Berlin-Charlottenberg, 1931).

83 Doerstling, *Kriegsgeschichte des Königlich Preussischen Infanterie-Regiments Graf Tauentzien v. Wittenberg (3. Brandenb.) Nr. 20* (Zeulenroda, 1933) p.12.

84 Otto von Moser, *Die Württemberger im Weltkriege* (Stuttgart, 1927) pp.9–10.

85 For German infantry training, warts and all: Koetsch, *Aus der Geschichte des früheren Kgl. Sächs. 9. Infanterie-Regiments Nr. 133 1881–1918* (Dresden, 1924).

86 Dieter Storz, *Kriegsbild und Kriegsrüstung vor 1914* (Herford, 1992), p.106. Voss, *Unsere Infanterie*, 16.

87 Friedenberg, 1. *GRzF*, p.152.

88 Bayerisches Kriegsarchiv, 1. b. AK (F) 776 Lechfeld. Bayerisches Kriegsarchiv 1. b. AK (F) 778 Grafenwöhr

89 Kaiser (ed.), *Das Ehrenbuch der Deutschen Schweren Artillerie* p.19.

90 Voss, *Unsere Infanterie*, pp.9–22.

Endnotes

91 Liebach, *Bataillons-, Regiments- und Brigade-Uebungen und Besichtigungten der Infanrterie in praktischen Beispielen* (Berlin, 1914)
92 Hauptstaatsarchiv Dresden 11359/2997 *Infanterie-Regiment Nr. 134 Gefechtsbericht.* Hauptstaatsarchiv Dresden 11359/2998 *Felddienstübung des 10. Infanterie-Regiemnts Nr. 134 am 8. Januar* 1914 (Blue's report for the same engagement. Opposing-force exercise. Two Blue companies were to force a river crossing, one red company was to prevent it.). Hauptstaatsarchiv Dresden 11359/1365 *Felddienstbericht des 10. Infanterie-Regiments Nr. 134 am 14. März 1913. Gefechtsbericht Rot* (rear-guard and destruction of a bridge). Hauptstaatsarchiv Dresden 11359/1367 *Bericht über das Gefecht des 10. Infanterie-Regiments Nr. 134 in Gegend Glossen 12. September 1912.* (Day-long regimental exercise: field fortification, attack, withdrawal, bivouac).
93 Freiherr von Gemmingen-Guttenberg-Fürfeld, *Das Grenadier-Regiment Königen Olga (1. Württ.) Nr. 119 im Weltkriege 1914-1918* (Stuttgart, 1927) p.1–2.
94 R. von Freydorf, *Das 1. Badische Leib-Grenadier-Regiment Nr. 109 im Weltkrieg 1914-1918.* (Karlsruhe, 1927), p.10.
95 Doerstling, *IR* 20, p.12.
96 Voss, *Infanterie*, pp.11–12. Hess; von Breitenbuch, *Geschichte 1. Lothringischen Feldart. Regts. 33. Erster Teil: Februar 1890 bis Oktober 1916* (Worms, 1937) pp.25–9. Marx, *FAR 69*, p .8–9. Anon., *Aus der Geschichte des ehemaligen Königl. Preußischen 4. Lothringischen Feldartillerie-Regiments Nr. 70* (Hildesheim, 1937) p.10. Wilhelm Dopheide, *Geschichte des 3. Lothr. Infanterie-Regiments Nr. 135* (Berlin, 1940) p.16.
97 Moser, *Bataillons- und Regiments*, pp.221–2. Voss, *Unsere Infanterie*, 17–23. Leder, *IR* 156, p.8.
98 Hauptstaatsarchiv Dresden, Generalkommando XII Armeekorps 11347. *Korpsmanöver des XII AK im Korpsverbande gegen markierte Feind.* The XII AK units were at peacetime strength – I/102 IR had 10 OFF and 410 EM present for duty – which was considerably less than wartime strength.
99 Alfred Micheler, 'Le 6e Corps d'Armee au début de la Guerre et pendant la bataille de la Marne' in: *Revue d'histoire de la guerre mondiale*, juillet 1934, p.241.
100 A. Grasset, *Le Guerre en Action. Le 22 Août 1914 au 4e Corps d'Armée : Ethe* (Paris, 1927), pp.3–4.
101 Thomasson, *Le Revers de 1914* pp.19–20.
102 Thomasson, *Le Revers de 1914*, pp.206–7.
103 Langle de Cary, *Souveniers*, p.14.
104 Percin, 1914 *Les Erreurs du haut commandement* (Paris, 1920) pp.22, 38.
105 Micheler, 'Le 6e Corps d'Armee' pp.241–2.
106 Immanuel, *Taktik I*, pp.21, 110–2, 169–71, 272–8; *II*, pp.83–7. *Leitfaden*, p.191
107 Ardent du Picq, *Battle Studies* (English trans, Harrisburg PA, 1946)
108 de Grandmaison, *Dressage de l'infanterie en vue du combat offensif* (Paris, 1906) and *Deux conferénces faites aux officiers de l'état-major de l'armée* (février1911), (Paris, Nancy, 1912).
109 It must be noted that Immanuel also maintained that good troops could absorb the casualties and advance without fire superiority. *Taktik II*, p.21.
110 Thomasson, *Le Revers de 1914* pp.20–1.
111 Thomasson, *Le Revers de 1914*, pp.15–6.
112 Thomasson, *Le Revers de 1914*, pp.46–7.
113 De Grandmaison, *Dressage de l'infanterie.*
114 De Grandmaison, *Deux conferences.*
115 Percin, *Erreurs*, p.22.

Chapter 2: Mobilisation, War Plans, Deployment and Approach March

1. Reichsarchiv, *Kriegsrüstung und Kriegswirtschscaft* (Berlin, 1930) p.510.
2. Kaiser (ed.), *Das Ehrenbuch der Deutschen Schweren Artillerie*, p.45.
2. Voss, *Unsere Infanterie*, pp.9–22
3. *Les Armées Françaises* I, I, p.144.
4. Reichsarchiv, *Der Weltkrieg*.I, p.142.
5. Alfons Schubert, *Kriegsgeschichte des 4. Oberschl. Infanterie-Regiments Nr. 63* (1914-1919) (Oppeln, 1926) p.13.
6. Joachim Bunzel, *Das Königlich Preuß. Feldartilerie-Regiment Nr. 41 (2. Niederschlesisches) im Weltkrieg 1914/1918* (Berlin, 1936) p.24.
7. Loosch, *IR* 47, pp.7-13.
8. Zunehmer, *Infanterie-Regiment Graf Kirchbach (1. niederschlesisches) Nr. 46 im Weltkrieg 1914-18* (Berlin, 1935) p.26.
9. Schonfelder, *Das 2. Schlesische Feldartillerie-Regiment Nr. 42* (Berlin, 1938) pp.20-1.
10. Friedenberg, 1. *GRzF*, p.190.
11. Wilhelm Kessler, *Das Königl. Preuss. Res.-Feldartillerie-Regiment Nr. 9* (Berlin, 1938), pp.16-18.
12. Jaspar Kundt, Walter Raschke, *Das Infanterie-Regiment von Courbière (2. Posensches) Nr. 19 im Weltkriege 1914-1919* (Görlitz, 1935) pp.23-4.
13. Prittwitz und Saffron, *Geschichte des Königlich Preußischen Grenadier-Regiments König Friedrich II (2. Schles.) Nr. 11* (Berlin, 1932) pp.13-14.
14. Marx, *Das glückhafte Batterie* (Potsdam, 1937) p.62.
15. A. Von Haldenwang, *Statistik...der Württemberger im Weltkrieg 1914-1918* (Stuttgart, 1936) pp.210-12.
16. Schonfelder, *FAR* 42, p.22.
17. Anon., *Großherzogliches Artilleriekorps, 1. Großherzogliche Hessisches Feldartillerie-Regiment Nr. 25'* (Berlin, 1935) p .15.
18. Haldenwang, *Statistik*, p.211.
19. Percin, *Les Erreurs* pp.8-10, 32, 56-60. Palat, 'Le haut commandement français avant la bataille des Ardennes (20 août 1914)' in : *Revue d'Histoire de la Guerre Mondiale* 3eme année No. 4 Octobre 1925 pp.330-50. Palat says the Germans had the equivalent of 46 corps, including *ersatz* and *Landwehr*.
20. *Armées Françaises*, I,I, p.32.
21. J. Juares, *L'armée nouvelle* (Paris, 1916 edition) p.537.
22. *Armées Françaises*, I,I, pp.20-2, 38-9, 57.
23. *Armées Françaises*, I,I, p.32.
24. *Armées Françaises*, I,I, p.20.
25. Percin, *Erreurs*, pp.41, 66.
26. Thomasson, *Le Revers de 1914* pp.22-3, 114.
27. Grasset, *Ethe*, pp.3-4.
28. Alfred Micheler, 'Le 6e Corps d'Armee' in *Revue d'histoire de la guerre mondiale, juillet 1934*, p.241.
29. *Armies Françaises*,I,I, Annexe, pp.21-31.
30. Reichsarchiv, *Weltkrieg* I, pp.144-5.
31. Kundt, *IR* 19, p.25.
32. Gebhard Graf von der Schulenberg, *Das Infanterie-Regiment Keith' (1. Oberschlesisches) Nr. 22 im Kriege 1914-1918* (Berlin, 1932) pp.23-4.
33. Erhard von Mutius, *Die Schlacht bei Longwy* (Oldenburg i. Gr., 1919) p.11. Leder, *IR* 156, p.25.
34. Gerhard Looch, *Das Königlich preuss. Infanterie-Rgt. König Ludwig III. Von Bayern (2. Niederschl.) Nr. 47* (Zeulenroda, 1932) p.11.

Endnotes

35 Benary, *Königlich Preussisches 1. Posensches Feldartillerie-Regiment Nr. 20* (Berlin-Charlottenburg, 1932) p.29.
36 Meissner, *Das Königlich Preussische Reserve-Infanterie-Rgt. Nr. 37 (im Verbande der 10. Res.-Div.) im Weltkriege 1914/1918 Teil I* (Berlin-Charlottenberg, 1933) p.5.
37 Karl Burchardi, *Das Füsilier-Regiment Generalfeldmarschall Graf Moltke (Schlesisches) Nr. 38* (Oldenburg i. O./ Berlin) p.18.
38 Rogge, *IR88*, p.45-6.
39 *Armées Françaises* I,I, pp.40, 152 ; Annexe , p.142-3.
40 *Armées Françaises* I,I, p.40.
41 *Armées Françaises* I,I, Annexe , pp.166-9.
42 *Armées Françaises* I,I, pp.134-7 ; Annexe , p.272.
43 *Armées Françaises* I,I, p.153.
44 Alfred Micheler, 'Le 6e Corps d'Armee' p.256.
45 *Armées Françaises* I,I, Annexe , pp.257, 307-8, 340, 379-80, 400-1.
46 Reichsarchiv, *Weltkrieg* I, pp.123-4.
47 Reichsarchiv, *Weltkrieg* I, pp.124-6.
48 Reichsarchiv, *Weltkrieg* I, pp.133-4, 183-4.
49 Reichsarchiv, *Weltkrieg* I, p.185.
50 Hermann Pantlen, *Das Württemburgische Feldartillerie-Regiment König Karl (1. Württemburgisches) Nr. 13 im Weltkrieg 1914-1918* (Stuttgart, 1928) p.13.
51 Reinhold Stümhke, *Das Infanterie-Regiment Kaiser Friedrich, König von Preußen (7. Württ.) Nr. 125 im Weltkrieg 1914-1918* (Stuttgart, 1923) pp.8-9.
52 H. Reymann, *Das 3. Oberschlesische Infanterie-Regiment Nr. 62 im Kriege 1914-1918* (Zeulenroda, 1930), p.5.
53 Rogge, *IR88*, p.47-8.
54 Döring von Gottberg, *IR 6*, p.35.
55 Otto Schwalm, *Das Königlich Preußische Infanterie-Regiment Landgraf Friedrich I von Hessen-Kassel (1. Kurhessisches) Nr. 81 im Weltkriege 1914-1918* (Frankfurt, 1932) p.22.
56 Stühmke, *IR 125*, p.9.
57 Ditfurth, 'Die Operationen der französischen 4. Armee vom 18. bis 22. August 1914' in: *Wissen und Wehr 9. Jahrgang* 1928, pp.598-609.
58 *Armées Françaises* I,I, Annexe, p.337.
59 *Armées Françaises* I,I, p.352.
60 *Armées Françaises* I,I, pp.353-4 ; Annexe, pp.406, 423-4, 446-9.
61 *Armées Françaises* I,I, pp.355 ; Annexe , pp.473-4, 496-7, 500.
62 *Armées Françaises* I,I, Annexe , pp.525, 535.
63 *Armées Françaises* I,I, Annexe , p.530.
64 *Armées Françaises* I,I Annexe , pp.531, 559-60.
65 Micheler, 'Le 6e Corps d'Armee', p.252.
66 *Armées Françaises* I, I,, p.370.
67 Micheler, 'Le 6e Corps d'Armee' in: *Revue d'histoire de la guerre mondiale*, octobre 1934, p.343.
68 *Armées Françaises* I,I, Annexe , pp.627, 635.
69 *Armées Françaises* I,I, pp.356, 359.
70 Langle de Cary, *Souveniers*, p.14.
71 Ditfurth, 'Die Operationen der französischen 4. Armee vom 18. bis 22. August 1914' in: *Wissen und Wehr* 1928 (Heft 10) p.604.
72 Palat, 'Le haut commandement français avant la bataille des Ardennes' (20 août 1914) in: *Revue d'histoire de la guerre mondiale* 3me année No. 4 octobre 1925, pp.35, 39-41.
73 *Armées Françaises* I,I, p.370.
74 *Armées Françaises* I,I, pp.356-70 ; Annexe , pp.555-6, 626-7, 634-5, 641.
75 Reichsarchiv, *Weltkrieg* I, pp.255-6, 303, 310.

The Battle of the Frontiers

76 Rogge, *IR*88, pp.56-68.
77 Anon, *FAR* 25, p.21.
78 E. Bircher, *Die Schlacht bei Ethe-Virton am 22. August 1914* (Berlin, 1930) p.31
79 Wilhelm von Hohenzollern, *Meine Erinnerungen aus Deutschlands Heldenkampf* (Berlin, 1923) pp.20-7.
80 Reichsarchiv, *Weltkrieg* I, p.304.
81 Reichsarchiv, *Weltkrieg* I, pp.306-7, 311. Wilhelm von Hohenzollern, *Meine Erinnerungen aus Deutschlands Heldenkampf* (Berlin, 1923) pp.24-5.
82 Reichsarchiv, *Weltkrieg* I, pp.308-9, 313-4.
83 Reichsarchiv, *Weltkrieg* I, pp.317-8.

Chapter 3: Rossignol

1 A. Grasset, *La Guerre en action (6) Surprise d'une Division. Rossignol – Saint Vincent (22 Août 1914)* (Paris, 1932).
2 Jean Charbonneau, *La Bataille des Frontières et la Bataille de la Marne vues par un Chef de Section (8 Août-15 Septmebre 1914)* (Paris, 1928) pp.25-6.
3 R. Allemann, "Das Begegnungsgefecht der 3. französicshen Kolonial-Division und des VI deutschen aktiven Armeekorps bei Rossignol, St.Vincent und Tintigny. Eine taktische Studie", in: *Schweizerische Monatsschrift für Offiziere aller Waffen* 39. Jahrgang (1927) Heft 9 (September) pp.271-8; Heft 10 (Oktober) pp.311-317; Heft 11 (November) pp.343-9; Heft 12 (Dezember) pp.380-7; 40. Jahrgang (1928) Heft 1 (Januar) pp.2-9; Heft 2 (Februar) pp.41-6; Heft 3 (März) pp.V73-80; Heft 4 (April) pp.105-112.
4 Guhr, *Das 4. Schlesische Infanterie-Regiment Nr. 157* (Zeulenroda, 1934) pp.17-23.
5 Grasset, *Rossignol*, pp.94-5.
6 Alfons Schmidt, *Kriegsgeschichte des 4. Oberschl. Infanterie-Regiments Nr. 63 (1914-1919)* (Oppeln, 1926) pp.15-17.
7 Grasset, *Rossignol*, pp.271, 274.
8 Charbonneau, *Frontières*, p.34-8.
9 Langle de Cary, *Souvenirs*, p.13.
10 Grasset had second thoughts about the adequacy of blaming Grandmaison for the French defeats. He says that the Germans won because they applied Grandmaison's principles, moving quickly, without reconnaissance to defeat the enemy by 'shock and awe' *(frappant de stupeur et d'étourdissement)*.
11 Friedrich Uebe, *Das 2. Oberschlesische Feldartillerie-Regiment Nr. 57* (Oldenburg i. O./Berlin, 1923) pp.17-23.
12 *Geschichte des Feldartillerie-Regiments von Peucker* (1. Schles.) Nr. 6 1914-1918 (Breslau, 1932) pp.13-18.
13 Schoenfelder, *FAR* 42, p.31. FAR 6 says the fire came from civilians and uniformed soldiers: p.15.
14 René Bastin, *22 août 1914. 'Un samedi sanglant. Ein schrecklicher Tag' . Tintigny, Saint-Vincent, Bellefontaine. Un combat prématuré.* (Virton, 2004) p.114. Grasset recorded this message but did not see any problems, which were pointed out by Bastin.
15 Grasset, *Rossignol*, p.264.
16 The apologists for the French in 1940 contend that "if only the French had known the Germans were going to attack in the Ardennes, they would have defeated that attack." If only the Romans had known that Hannibal planned a double envelopment, the Romans would have won the Battle of Cannae, etc., etc.
17 Uebe, *Feldartillerie-Regiment Nr. 57*, p.19.
18 Rittau, *Uhlan Regiment Nr. 2*, p.70-1. Tinzmann actually said „*Gruppe hört auf mein Kommando!*" which is a formal order in the German army – indeed, it is a drill-ground

command. There is no equivalent in the American army; the English translation is into the language that a modern American NCO might use, which lacks the formality of the German. Tinzmann was soon promoted to sergeant.

19 Grasset, *Rossignol*, p.153.
20 Grasset, *Rossignol*, p.178.
21 Grasset, *Rossignol*, p.161.
22 Herbert Jancke, *Das kgl. Preußische Feldartillerie-Regiment v. Clausewitz (1. Oberschles.) Nr. 21* (Oldenburg/Berlin, 1923) p.17.
23 Fidel, *IR 23*, p.20-28.
24 Schütz, Hochbaum, *Das Grenadier-Regiment König Friedrich Wilhelm II (1. Schles.) Nr. 10* (Oldenburg i. O./Berlin, 1924) p.25-6.
25 Rittau, *2 Ulan*, p.67.
26 Charbonneau, *Frontières*, p.28.
27 Herbert Nollau, *Geschichte des Königlich Preußischen 4. Niedercleesischen Infnaterie-Regiments Nr. 51* (Berlin, 1931) p.7-10.
28 Bastin, *22 août 1914*, p.188-9.
29 Prittwitz und Saffron, *IR 11*, p.19-22.
30 Schoenfelder, *FAR 42*, pp.32-5.II/FAR 42 fired 4,000 rounds. Grasset does not mention II/FAR 42's support fire and has the details of 5/ II/FAR 42's employment wrong.
31 Grasset, *Rossignol*, pp.205, 212.
32 Windek, *Jäger-Regiment zu Rferde Nr. 11* (Oldenburg i. O./ Berlin, 1929), p.21.
33 *Armées Françaises* I, p.789.
34 Guhr, *IR 157*, p.22.
35 Nollau, *IR 51*, p.10.
36 Uebe, *FAR 57*, pp.21-2.
37 Grasset, *Rossignol*, pp.249-50, lists 9, 476 casualties, but does not include smaller units, such as the division and brigade headquarters and the engineer unit, all of which were destroyed
38 Charbonneau, *Frontières*, p.33.
39 Charbonneau, *Frontières*, pp.44-5.
40 Bastin, 22 août 1914, p.207.
41 Schubert, *IR 63*, pp.17-18.
42 Guhr, *IR 157*, p.23.
43 Nollau, *IR 51*, pp.11-13.
44 Charbonneau, *Frontières*, pp.40-44.

Chapter 4: Bellefontaine

1 E. Bircher, *Die Schlacht bei Ethe-Virton am 22. August 1914* (Berlin, 1930), pp.213-31, Bastin, *22 août 1914*, pp.89-90, 115-195.
2 Schmitz, *IR 10*, pp.22-6.
3 Schoenfelder, *FAR 42*, pp.37.
4 Buchardi, *IR 38*, pp.23-7.
5 Bastin, *22 août 1914*, pp.130-1.
6 Bastin, *22 août 1914*, pp.144.
7 Bircher, *Ethe-Virton*, p.228.
8 The author is very familiar with the terrain near the Lechfeld, the result of numerous exercises, including two REFORGER. He has also walked the terrain at Bellefontaine.

The Battle of the Frontiers
Chapter 5: Neufchateau

1 Grasset, *Un combat de rencontre. Neufchâteau* (22 août 1914) (Paris, 1923) ; *Armées Françaises* I, I, Annexes, pp.996-9. R. Allemann. 'Das Begegnungsgefecht von Neufchâteau zwischen der 5. französischen Kolonial-Brigade und dem XVIII deutschen Reserve-Korps am 22. August 1914. Eine taktische Studie', in: *Schweizerische Monatsschrift für Offiziere aller Waffen* 39. Jahrgang (1927) 3. Heft (März) pp.73-86; 4. Heft (April) pp.107-114; 5. Heft (Mai) pp.138-46. Allemann had access to German after-action reports, now lost.
2 Grasset, *Neufchâteau*, pp.14-5.
3 *Armées Françaises* I,I, pp.394-5.
4 Paris, 26N136, JMO 12 CA.
5 Reichsarchiv, *Weltkrieg* I, p.314.
6 Reichsarchiv, *Weltkrieg* I, p.316.
7 Heinrich von Jordan/Wilhelm von Marcard, *Das Reserve-Infanterie-Regiment Nr. 81 im Weltkrieg*, (Zeulenroda, 1933) pp.7-14.
8 The regimental commander, Heinrich von Jordan, retained command until April 1916 and ended the war as a Lieutenant General.
9 Felix The Losen, *Das Reserve Feldartillerie-Regiment 21 im Weltkriege 1914-18 Erster Teil 1914 bis 1917* (Frankfurt am Main, 1931) pp.9-12.
10 Wahrenburg, *Reserve-Infanterie-Regiment Nr. 83* (Oldenburg i. O./ Berlin, 1924) pp.17-18.
11 Ludwig Sonne, Walter Rodemer, F. CH. Gutmann-Werner, *Geschichte des Großherzoglich-Hessischen Reserve-Feldartillerie-Regiments Nr. 25...im Weltkriege 1914-1918* (Frankfurt am Main, 1930) p.19-20. The regiment fired 563 rounds and took no casualties.
12 Grasset, *Neufchâteau*, p.57.
13 Adolf Soldan, 5. *Großherzoglich Hessisches Infanterie-Regiemnt Nr. 168* (Oldenburg i. O./ Berlin, 1924) pp.11-12.
14 Grasset, *Neufchâteau*, pp.34-5. Grasset's explanation of the tactical events is tendentious; his objective being to denigrate the German infantry. Grasset says that the Germans fired too high, and that their marksmanship was so bad that the two companies advancing on the Bois d'Ospot could continue the march without firing. He says that the two companies were not stopped by German fire but halted only because they were far in front of the rest of the regiment. Since such a decision is suicidal, this explanation seems unlikely.
15 Grasset, *Neufchâteau*, pp.34, 38.
16 Radermacher, *Erinnerungsblätter des Großherzogl. Hessischen Reserve-Infanterie-Regiments Nr. 116* (Oldenburg i. O./ Berlin, 1929) p.10. The regiment lost only one man KIA, one OFF and six EM WIA.
17 *Armées Françaises* I, I, Annexe, p.789.
18 *Armées Françaises* I, I, Annexe, pp.764-6, 817
19 JMO 12 CA.
20 Sonne, et. al., *RFAR* 25, p.20.
21 Losen, *RFAR* 21, p.11.
22 Allemann, *Neufchâteau*, p.112.
23 Grasset said that 992 EM from 21 RIC and 2,050 EM from 23 RIC were not present at the next formation, 3,042 casualties in total. Grasset, Neufchâteau, p.74.
24 Allemann, *Neufchâteau*, p.145.
25 Grasset, *Neufchâteau*, p.28.

Chapter 6: Bertrix

1 R. Allemann, 'Die Begegnungskämpfe im Luchywald und bei Ochamps zwischen Teilen des XVIII deutschen aktiven Korps (v. Schenk) und des XVII französischen Korps

Endnotes

(Poline) am 22. August 1914' in: *Schweizerische Monatsschrift für Offiziere aller Waffen* August 1931 pp.249-57; September 1931 pp.279-88. Hermann Kaiser, *Deutsche und französische Artillerie in der Schlacht bei Bertrix 22 August 1914* (Hanau, 1937).Paris, 26N163, JMO 17 CA.

2 Reichsarchiv, *Weltkrieg* I, pp.312, 314, 327, 331.
3 Rogge, *IR*88, pp.71-82.
4 Hans Hecht, *Das 2. Nass. Feldartillerie-Regiment Nr. 63 Frankfurt im Weltkriege. Erster Teil: Bis zur Sommeschlacht 1916* (Frankfurt am Main, 1924) p.10-12.
5 Bernhard von Fumetti, *Das Königlich Preußische Fusilier-Regt. Von Gersdorff (Kurhessisches) Nr. 80 im Weltkriege* (Oldenburg i. O./ Berlin) pp.28-38.
6 Paris, 26 N579, JMO 7 RI
7 Schwalm, *IR*81, p.26-38.
8 Albert Benary, *Geschichte des Fußartillerie-Regiments General-Feldzeugmeister (Brandenburgisches) Nr. 3* (Berlin, 1937) p .50-3.
9 Schwalm, *IR*81, p.38.

Chapter 7: Maissin-Anloy

1 The commander of 25 ID wrote an account of the battle of Maissin which was included on pp.409-27 of the FAR 25 regimental history.
2 Hans Freund, *Geschichte des Infanterie-Regiments Prinz Karl (4. Großh. Hess.) Nr. 118 im Weltkrieg* (Groß-Gerau, 1930) pp.29-38.
3 Kurt Offnebacher, *Die Geschichte des Infanterie-Leibregiments Großherzogin (3. Großherzoglich Hessisches) Nr. 117* (Oldenburg i. O., 1931), pp.29-40.
4 *Armées Françaises* I,I, Annexe, p.811.
5 Anon., *Das 2. Großherzoglich Hessische Feldartillerie-Regiment Nr. 61 im Weltkriege 1914/1918* (Oldenburg i. O./ Berlin) pp.12-14.
6 Alex-Victor von Frankenberg und Ludwigsdorff, *Das Leibgarde-Infanterie-Regiment (1. Großherzoglich Hessisches) Nr. 115 im Weltkrieg 1914-18* (Stuttgart, 1921) pp.6-10.
7 Albert Hiß, *Infanterie-Regiment Kaiser Wilhelm (2. Großherzoglich Hessisches) Nr. 116* (Oldenburg i. O., 1924) pp.24-8.
8 Valarché, 'La bataille des frontières' in: *Revue d'Artillerie*, Vol. 108, octobre 1931, p.325.
9 *Armées Françaises* I,I, Annexe, p.811.
10 *Armées Françaises* I,I, Annexe,, p.763
11 Anon, *FAR* 25, p.11, pp.37-8.
12 Frankenberg, *IR* 115, p.8.
13 Anon, *FAR* 25, p.425.
14 Anon, *FAR* 25, p.38.
15 Valarché, 'Frontières', p.326.

Chapter 8: Virton

1 Generalstab, *Begegnungsgefechte*, pp.9-57. E. Bircher, *Ethe-Virton*. A. Grasset, *Le 22 août 1914 au 4e corps d'armée* (Paris, 1925).
2 Peter Kilduff, *Richthofen*, (New York, 1993) pp.27-9.
3 Grasset, *Éthe*, p.xiv.
4 Grasset, *Le 22 août 1914*, p.v-vi.
5 Grasset, *Le 22 août 1914*, pp.63-4.
6 Verein der Offiziere „Alt 154", *IR*. 154, pp.95-108.
7 Bunzel, *Far* 41, p.27-35. Siegfried Rubel, *Das Königlich Preußische Feldartillerie-Regt. V.*

The Battle of the Frontiers

   Podbielski (1. Niederschlesisches) Nr. 5 im Weltkrieg 1914/1918 (Berlin-Charlottenberg, 1932) pp.4-7.
8 Walter Schmidt, Otto Winkelmann, Martin Altermann, Das Königlich Preußische 3. Posensche Infanterie-Regiment Nr. 58 im Weltkriege (Zeulenroda, 1934) pp.13-19.
9 Grasset, Le 22 août 1914, pp.94-5.
10 Wilhelm, Erinnerungen, p.29.
11 Kundt, IR 19, pp.40-53.
12 Grasset, Le 22 août 1914, p.175. Grasset's conclusions are worthless. He acknowledges that 87RI, 117 RI and 91 RI were pummeled by German artillery the entire afternoon. Nevertheless, he maintains that the French artillery had fire superiority after 1200, and for that reason the battle was a draw, indeed that the French won a 'moral victory'. Since Grasset was a senior French official historian, his refusal to confront the facts would indicate that the French army was unable to draw any useful 'lessons learned' from this battle, a conclusion that would help explain the miserable performance of the French army in similar battles in 1939 and 1940.
13 Allemann, 'Begegnungsgefecht', pp.44-5.
14 Les Armées Françaises I, I, Annexe, p.748.
15 Bircher, Éthe-Virton, pp.53-4.

Chapter 9: Éthe and Bleid

1 Grasset, Éthe. Grasset was the commander of 5/103 RI. The book does not contain footnotes, but Grasset insisted that all of his information has been checked and was accurate. Bircher, Éthe-Virton. Trentinian, Éthe. La 7e Division du 4e Corps dans la bataille de frontières (10 août au 22 septembre 1914) (Paris, 1937). Trentinian was the commander of 7 DI.
2 Trentinian says Grasset was a battalion commander, in Grasset's book on Éthe he is the commander of 5/103 RI.
3 Trentinian, Éthe, p.67.
4 Trentinian, Éthe, p.40.
5 Karl Vogt, 3. Niederschlesisches Infanterie-Regiment Nr. 50 1914-1920 (Berlin-Charlottenburg, 1931) pp.17-8.
6 Karl Vogt, IR 50 pp.7-15.
7 Benary, FAR 20, pp.39-42. Bircher, Éthe, p.120. Kurt Kruse, 'Einsatz eines Feldartillerie-Regiments vor 50 Jahren in der Schlacht von Éthe-Longwy (Nach dem Kriegstagebuch von 1914)', in: Artillerierundschau 1964 (3. Jahrgang) Nr 3, pp.109-113.
8 Angerstein, Das 2. Posensche Feldartillerie-Regiment Nr. 56 (Oldenburg i. O./ Berlin, 1927) pp.16-21.
9 Benary, FAR 20, pp.35-57.
10 Benary, FAR 20, pp.46.
11 Grasset, Éthe, pp.60-2.
12 Benary, FAR 20, pp.47, 44.
13 Wilhelm, Erinnerungen, pp.30.
14 Loosch, IR 47, pp.7, 14-34.
15 Benary, FAR 20, pp.41-2.
16 Grasset, Éthe, p.114.
17 Hauptstaatsarchiv Stuttgart, M33/2 Bü 884, XIII AK KTB. Fritz von Lossberg, Meine Tätigkeit im Weltkriege 1914-1918 (Berlin, 1939) pp.1-18. Lossberg was the XIII AK Chief of Staff.
18 Erwin Rommel, Infantry Attacks (Vienna VA, 1979) pp.3-5.
19 Hermann Pantlen, Das Württembergische Feldartillerie-Regiment König Karl (1. Württ.) Nr. 13 im Weltkrieg 1914-1918 (Stuttgart, 1928) p.15.

Endnotes

20 Richard Bechtle, *Die UlmerGrenadiere an der Westfront. Geschichte des Grenadier-Regiments König Karl* (5. Württ.) Nr. 123 im Weltkrieg 1914-18 (Stuttgart, 1920) pp.6-7.

21 Bircher, *Éthe*, pp.65-7.

22 Hauptstaatsarchiv Stuttgart, M39 Bü 45 KTB 27 ID; Bü 51 *Gefechtsbericht* (combat after-action report) *21-22 August 1914*. Adolf Deutelmoser, *Die 27. Infanterie-Division im Weltkrieg 1914-18* (Stuttgart, 1925) pp.8-11. Deutelmoser was the division operations officer later in the war. Bircher, *Éthe*, pp.145-6. Moser, *Württemberger*, p.198-204 Walter Oertel, *Die Waffentaten der Württemberger im Bewegungskrieg 1914* (Stuttgart, 1934) pp.37-43. The operations of the German XIII AK against the French 5 CA will be discussed in the next chapter. 53rd Brigade is included here because it was engaged with the French 7 DI.

23 Hauptstaatsarchiv Stuttgart M 94 Bü 89, KTB IR 123; Bü 97 KTB III/ IR 123. Bechtle, *IR 123*, p. 7-11.

24 Moser, *Württemberger*, p.199.

25 Moser, *Württemberger*, p.202.

26 Bircher, *Éthe*, p.146. Hauptstaatsarchiv Stuttgart M95 Bü 49, KTB II/ IR 124. G. Wolters, *Das Infanterie-Regiment König Wilhelm I* (6. Württ.) *Nr. 124 im Weltkrieg 1914-1918* (Stuttgart, 1921) pp.1-6.

27 Eduard Zimmerle, *Das 3. Württembergische Feldartillerie-Regiment Nr. 49 im Weltkrieg* (Stuttgart, 1922) pp.3-5. Moser, *Württemberger*, p.203.

28 Benary, *FAR 20*, p.44.

29 Moser, *Württemberger*, p.201.

30 Zunehmer, *IR 46*, p.31-50.

31 Döring von Gottberg, *IR 6*, p.51.

32 Bircher, *Éthe*, p.102.

33 Grasset, *Virton*, pp.150-1.

34 Grasset, *Virton*, pp.115, 118.

35 Trentinian, *Éthe*, pp.70-4.

36 Schmitz and Niewland, *Semois et de Virton*, p.262.

37 Vogt, *IR 50*, p.14.

38 Hauptstaatsarchiv Stuttgart, M410, Bü 32, KTB 5. Armee.

39 Reichsarchiv, *Weltkrieg* I, pp.341-2.

40 Moser, *Feldzugsaufzeichnungen als Brigade-, und Divisionskommandeur und als kommandierenden General 1914-1918* (Stuttgart, 1920), pp.11-12.

41 Reichsarchiv, *Weltkrieg I*, p.548.

42 Grasset, *Éthe*, p.119.

43 Otto von Moser, *Feldzugsaufzeichnungen*, p.7.

44 Moser, *Württemberger*, p.200.

Chapter 10: Longwy

1 Oskar von Brandenstein, *Das Infanterie-Regiment „Alt-Württemberg"* (3. Württ.) *Nr. 121 im Weltkrieg 1914-1918* (Stuttgart, 1921) pp.3-5. Bircher, *Éthe*, p.204.

2 A. Schwab/ A. Schrener, *Das neunte Württembergische Infanterie-Regiment Nr. 127 im Weltkrieg 1914-1918* (Stuttgart, 1920) pp.1-10. Bircher, *Éthe*, pp.188-95. Hauptstaatsarchiv Stuttgart, M39 Bü 51, 27 ID *Gefechtsbericht 21-22 August 1914*.

3 Paris, 26 N 114, JMO 5 CA. Bircher, *Éthe*, p.196-7. *Armées Françaises* I, pp.374-5.

4 Trentinian, *Éthe*, p.46-8.

5 Hauptstaatsarchiv Stuttgart M91 Bü 38 KTB IR 120; Bü 42 KTB I/IR 120. Simon, *Das Infanterie-Regiment „Kaiser Wilhelm, König von Preußen"* (2. Württemb.) *Nr. 120 im Weltkrieg 1914-1918* (Stuttgart, 1922) p.3.

6 Schwab/Schrener, *IR 127*, p.8.

The Battle of the Frontiers

7 Hermann Pantlen, *Das Württembergische Feldartillerie-Regiment König Karl (1. Württ.) Nr. 13 im Weltkrieg 1914-1918* (Stuttgart, 1928) pp.12-17.
8 Paris, 26 N 114, JMO 5 CA. Bircher, Éthe, p.199. *Armées Françaises*, I, I, pp.375-6.
9 Paris, 26 N 636, JMO 46 RI.
10 Herzog Wilhelm von Urach Graf von Württemberg, *Die 26. Infanterie-Division im Weltkrieg 1914-18 Teil I 1914-15* (Stuttgart, 1927) pp.1-17. Hauptstaatsarchiv Stuttgart, M 38 Bü 39, KTB 26 ID. Oertel, *Württemberger*, pp.33-36. Gerok, *Das 2. württ. Feldartillerie-Reg Nr. 29 „Prinzregent Luitpold von Bayern" im Weltkrieg 1914-1918* (Stuttgart, 1921) p.5.
11 Gemmingen-Guttenberg-Fürfeld, *IR* 119, pp.3-20. Hauptstaatsarchiv Stuttgart M 90 Bü 130 KTB I/ R 119; Bü 131 *Gefechtsberichte* I/119; Bü 132 KTB II/119; Bü 133 KTB III/119; Bü135 *Gefechtsberichte* MGK 119.
12 Stümhke, *IR* 125 pp.9-16.
13 Hauptstaatsarchiv Stuttgart M33/2 KTB XIII AK.
14 Moser, *Württemberger*, pp.206-7. Bircher, Éthe, pp.203-6. Brandenstein, *IR* 121, pp.4-5. Hellmut Gnamm, *Das Fusilier-Regiment Kaiser Franz Joseph von Oesterreich, König von Hungarn (4. württ.) Nr. 122 im Weltkrieg 1914-1918* (Stuttgart, 1921) pp.6-12. Oertel, *Württemberger*, pp.28-32.
15 Paris, 26 N 114, JMO 5 CA.
16 Hauptstaatsarchiv Stuttgart M33/2 KTB XIII AK.
17 Lossberg, *Meine Tätigkeit*, pp.17-18. Deutelmoser, 27 *ID*, pp.11-12.
18 Schwab/Schrener, *IR* 127, p.10.
19 Moser, *Württemberger*, p.21.

Chapter 11: The Battle South of Longwy

1 Reichsarchiv, *Weltkrieg* I, p.307.
2 *Armées Françaises*,I, I, pp.376-7, Annexes p.821.
3 Fernand Engerand, *La Bataille de la Frontière (août 1914) Briey* (Paris, 1920) pp.91-108.
4 Conrad von Goßler, *Erinnerungen an den Großen Krieg, dem VI Reservekorps gewidmet* (Breslau, 1919) pp.1-16. Goßler had seen action as a Lieutenant in the 2nd Guard Grenedier *Landwehr* Regiment at the siege of Strasbourg in 1870 and won the Iron Cross 2nd Class. He had been the VI AK Chief of Staff and Commander of the 11 RD. He had retired in 1910 and was recalled to active duty in August 1914 to lead VI RK and held that command until February 1917. Reichsarchiv, *Weltkrieg* I, pp.320-1.
5 Paul Nausch, *Geschichte des Reserve-Infanterie-Regiments Nr. 10 im Weltkriege* (Berlin, 1926) pp.16-18.
6 Konrad Scheidt, *Das Reserve-Infanterie-Regiment Nr. 51 im Weltkrieg 1914-1918* (Zeulenroda, 1936) p.4-5, 8.
7 Paris, 26 N 118 JMO 6 CA. Micheler, 'Le 6e Corps d'Armee', in : *Revue d'histoire de la guerre mondiale, octobre 1934, pp.*346-7. *Armées Françaises*, I, I, pp.377-8, Annexes pp.823-5.
8 Reichsarchiv, *Weltkrieg* I, p.321.
9 Gebhard, *Graf von der Schulenberg, Das Infanterie-Regiment Keith (1. Oberschlesisches) Nr. 22 im Kriege 1914-1918* (Berlin, 1932) pp.30-4.
10 Leder, *IR* 156, pp.28-39.
11 Otto Domisch, *Das Reserve-Feldartillerie-Regiment Nr. 11* (Zeulenroda, 1939) pp.5-6.
12 Nausch, *RIR* 10, pp.19-24.
13 No regimental history was written for RIR 11.
14 Scheidt, *RIR* 51, pp.19-25.
15 Hasselbach, von Skrodzki. *Das Reserve-Infanterie-Regiment Nr. 38* (Zeulenroda, 1938) pp.8-19.
16 Anon., *Reserve-Feldartillerie-Regiment Nr. 12* (Oldenburg i. O./ Berlin, 1928) pp.14-21.

Endnotes

17 Hans Altmann, *Das Fusilier-Regiment v. Steinmetz [Westpreußisches] Nr. 37 im Weltkriege 1914-1918* (Berlin-Charlottenberg, 1931) p.30. Altmann said that the regimental and battalion war diaries comprised 70 volumes.

18 Altmann, *IR* 37, pp.30-44.

19 Arens, *IR* 155, pp.57-63.

20 Oscar-Jesco von Puttkamer, *Das Königlich Preußische Reserve-Infanterie-Regiment Nr. 46 im Weltkriege* (Zeulenroda, 1938) pp.9-11.

21 Meißner, *RIR* 37, p.12.

22 Kessler, *RFAR* 9, pp.27-31.

23 RFAR 9 lost 3 OFF and 19 EM WIA, three horses dead and 12 wounded.

24 Max von Stockhausen, *Geschichte des Reserve-Infanterie-Regiments Nr. 7 (Zeulenroda in Th., 1941)* pp.8-11.

25 Reichsarchiv, *Weltkrieg* I, p.307, 322-3.

26 Eduard Simon, *4. Magdeb. Infanterie-Regiment Nr. 67. Band I* (Oldenburg i. O., 1926) pp.10-20.

27 Marx, *FAR* 69, pp.17-22. Marx, *Die glückhafte Batterie*, pp.63-86.

28 F. Isenburg, *Das Königs-Infanterie-Regiment (6. Lothring.) Nr. 5 145 im Großen Kriege 1914-1918 Band I* (Berlin, 1922) pp.25-32.

29 Fritz Richard Urbich, *Das 9. Lothringische Infanterie-Regiment Nr. 173 im Krieg und Frieden 1897-1918* (Oldenburg i. O./ Berlin, 1925) p . 39-42.

30 Ernst Schmidt, *Die Geschichte des Infanterie-Regiments Graf Werder (4. Rhein.) Nr. 30 im Weltkriege 1914-1918 1. Band: Das Jahr 1914* (Oldenburg i. O./ Berlin, 1922) p.15-25.

31 Anon., *FAR* 70, pp.21-23.

32 Marx, *FAR* 69, pp.17-22.

33 Dopheide, *IR* 135, pp.31-36.

34 Hess/ Breitenbach *FAR* 33, pp.59-60.

35 Micheler, 'Le 6e Corps d'Armee', pp.347-51. Paris, 26 N 118, JMO 6 CA.

36 Goßler, *Erinnerungen*, pp.13-15.

37 Micheler, 'Le 6e Corps d'Armee', pp.346-52. Paris, 26 N 118, JMO 6 CA.

38 Goßler, *Erinnerungen*, p.15

39 Marx, *Die glückliche Batterie*, pp.86-7, 93.

40 Micheler, 'Le 6e Corps d'Armee', p.351. Paris, 26 N 118, JMO 6 CA.

Conclusions

1 Wilhelm, *Erinnerungen*, pp.34-5. Reichsarchiv, *Weltkrieg* I, pp.325-6.

2 Engerand, *Bataille de la Frontière*, pp.135-8. *Armées Françaises* I, I, Annexes, p.844.

3 Reichsarchiv, *Weltkrieg* I, p.327-8

4 Valarché 'Frontières' pp.328-31. *Armées Françaises* I, I, Annexe, pp.717-8, 723-4, 871-3.

5 Engerand, *Bataille de la Frontière*, pp.144-6.

6 *Armées Françaises* I, Annexes, pp.841-2.

7 *Armées Françaises* I, Annexes, pp.839-40.

8 *Armées Françaises* I, Annexes, pp.859, 862, 865-7, 907-9. Engerand, *Bataille de la Frontière*, p.152. Valarché 'Frontières', p.327.

9 *Armées Françaises* I, Annexes, pp.843, 875, 877-8, 926, 935-6, 988. Valarché 'Frontières' pp.328-31.

10 Engerand, *Bataille de la Frontière*, pp.154-5.

11 Wilhelm, *Erinnerungen*, pp.35-9. Reichsarchiv, *Weltkrieg* I, pp.340-1.

12 Reichsarchiv, *Weltkrieg* I, pp.335-9.

13 Engerand, *Bataille de la Frontière*, pp.133-157.

14 Langle de Cary, *Souveniers*, pp.14-16, 136-8.

15 Bastin, *Un samedi sanglante*, pp.132, 145, 154, 196.

The Battle of the Frontiers

16 T. N. Dupuy, *A Genius for War. The German Army and General Staff* 1807-1945 (Englewood Cliffs NJ, 1977).
17 Moser, *Württemberger*, p.21.
18 Anon., *FAR 25*, p.420.
19 Goßler, *Erinnerungen*, pp.12-13.
20 Marx, *FAR 69*, pp.20-1.
21 Wilhelm, *Erinnerungen*, p.28.
22 Liebmann, 'Gefechtsvorschriften von 1914', pp.462- 87. Some of Liebmann's conclusions are based on experiences after the Battle of the Frontiers. Some seem based on his own experiences and are not supported by other evidence, as when he says that the German infantry threw away their entrenching tools (p.466). Yet other conclusions are flat wrong, as when he says that German artillery firing from open positions was always immediately destroyed (p.468), or that the German cavalry trained for mass charges. One would have to conclude that Liebmann was an infantryman who knew little of the other combat arms.
23 Thomasson, *Le revers de 1914*, pp.177-8.
24 Palat, 'Avant la bataille des Ardennes', pp.44-5. In typical French micro-managing style, the rest of the instructions went into details such as feeding the troops and unsaddling horses.
25 *Armées Françaises* I, I, Annexes, p.865.
26 Trentinian, *Éthe*, pp.7, 73-4.
27 Percin, *Erreurs*, pp.129-31.
28 Greiner, 'German Intelligence Estimate in the West 1885-1914' in: Zuber, *German War Planning*, p.35.
29 Ernest R. May argues in *Strange Victory* (New York, 2000), as does Julian Jackson in *The Fall of France* (Oxford, 2003) that the German victory in 1940 was an accident due mainly to French bad luck. They contend that the French army was as good as the German, and that had the French only known where the Germans were going to make their main attack, then the French could have massed there and defeated it. Luck had nothing to do with the French defeat, which was a direct result of superior German doctrine and training. The French were not strong enough to hold a continual defensive position, and once that position was broken, the French would have to engage the Germans in a mobile battle. The French were no more capable of doing so in 1940 than they had been in 1914.

Appendix

1 Kundt, *IR* 19, p.52.
2 Bastin, *Un samedi sanglante*, pp.242-8.
3 Bastin, *Un samedi sanglante,* pp.147.

Acknowledgments

I wrote this book to satisfy my curiosity as a professional soldier: I could find nothing that adequately described the tactical conduct of the first battles of the First World War on the Western Front. My work therefore emphasises military doctrine, training, tactics and operations, which places it far outside both the academic mainstream as well as the realm of popular military literature. It is only due to the fact that Professor Hew Strachan, the Chichele Professor of the History of War at All Souls College, Oxford, promotes new perspectives and fosters scholarly debate in military history that this book ever saw the light of day. In no ways should this be construed that Prof. Strachan is necessarily a partisan of my views.

For over two years I deluged the inter-library loan section at the University of Würzburg with stacks of requests for obscure 75 year-old books and periodicals. The librarians always responded with the professionalism for which German civil servants are justly famous. I owe a great debt to these librarians, Frau Kerstin Rhinow in particular.

Research at the Hauptstaatsarchiv Stuttgart and the Generallandesarchiv Karlsruhe was always a pleasure. These two archives are real gems. They are full of invaluable documents for the historians of the German army. In addition, they are superbly managed: no minute is wasted there, and document reproduction is quick and thorough. Just down the street from the Hauptstaatsarchiv Stuttgart is the Württembergische Landesbibliothek, which houses the Bibliothek für Zeitgeschichte, the former Weltkriegsbibliothek (Great War library), with an excellent collection of German books from the 1920s and 1930s and a helpful staff. My thanks also to the archivists of the Service historique de l'armee de terre in Vincennes (Paris), who went above the call of duty to be of assistance to me.

Dr. Dieter Storz, archivist at the Bavarian Army Museum in Ingolstadt, was kind enough to read the first chapter and rescue me from committing several errors.

The depth of talent to be found in a small Ohio valley town, such as New Martinsville, West Virginia, is quite remarkable. Heather Wetzel, the owner of the local bookstore and an accomplished artist, provided the maps and figures and put them in the proper electronic formants: her skill and dedication were indispensable. At West Virginia Northern Community College, librarian Janet Corbitt provided inter-library loans, while Shawna Christner and David Hanes lent me their computer expertise.

I would also like to thank the venerable military publishing house of Bernard and Graefe (Mönch Verlagsgesellschaft) for granting me the permission to use the pencil drawings which illustrate German units in combat in the first weeks of the war.

Jonathan Reeve, the editor at Tempus, and my copy-editors, Pascal Barry and Robin Harries, produced this book quickly, sensibly and efficiently, which is saying a great deal.

Whenever I conduct research in history, I am made aware of my debt to my Doktorvater, Prof. Wolfgang Altgeld, and the faculty of the University of Würzburg, especially Prof. Rainer Schmidt.

New Martinsville, WV
June 2007